Praise for

Philip & Elizabeth

'*Philip & Elizabeth* boldly goes where other royal biographers have previously feared to tread . . . The book is exceptionally hard to put down.'   —Humphrey Carpenter, *Sunday Times*

'Wonderfully entertaining . . . impressive . . . compelling.'
                    —John-Paul Flintiff, *Financial Times*

'Thoroughly entertaining . . . Filled with insights . . . He has had enviable access and he has used it well.'
                    —Penny Junor, *Daily Telegraph*

'Cheeky, gossipy, often highly amusing . . . A most engagingly intimate volume.'   —Peter Mackay, *Evening Standard*

'A joy . . . thoughtful . . . outrageous . . . sympathetic, wholly original, often hilarious, occasionally profound and unfailingly interesting . . . I came away with the strong feeling that I had glimpsed the Queen and Prince Philip for their first time as they really are.'
                    —Craig Brown, *Mail on Sunday*

'*Philip & Elizabeth* is a unique biography. It is a powerful and revealing portrait of a remarkable partnership, told with authority and insight, and illustrated with photographs from the couple's collections.'
                    —Ingrid Seward, *Majesty*

Also by Gyles Brandreth

Biography
Dan Leno: The Funniest Man on Earth
John Gielgud: An Actor's Life
Brief Encounters: Meetings with Remarkable People

Autobiography
Under the Jumper
Breaking the Code: Westminster Diaries

Novels
Who is Nick Saint?
Venice Midnight

Selected Non-fiction
Created in Captivity
Ice Cream for Ice Cream: Pearls from the Pantomime
Yaroo! The World of Frank Richards
The Joy of Lex and More Joy of Lex

Children's fiction
The Ghost at Number Thirteen and sequels
The Slippers That Talked and sequels
Nattie & Nuffin
Max: The Boy Who Made a Million
Maisie: The Girl Who Lost Her Head

Theatre
Lewis Carroll Through the Looking-Glass
Dear Ladies (with Hinge & Bracket)
Now We Are Sixty (with Julian Slade)
Zipp!

PHILIP & ELIZABETH

PORTRAIT OF A ROYAL MARRIAGE

Gyles Brandreth

W. W. Norton & Company
New York   London

Manufacturing by R. R. Donnelley, Harrisonburg
Production manager: Amanda Morrison

Library of Congress Cataloging-in-Publication Data

Brandreth, Gyles Daubeney, 1948–
Philip and Elizabeth : portrait of a royal marriage / Gyles
Brandreth.—1st American ed.
p. cm.
Includes index.
Rev. ed. of: Philip & Elizabeth : portrait of a marriage. 2004.
ISBN 0-393-06113-2
1. Elizabeth II, Queen of Great Britain, 1926– —Marriage.
2. Philip, Prince, consort of Elizabeth II, Queen of Great Britain, 1921–.
3. Marriages of royalty and nobility—Great Britain—History—20th century.
4. Princes—Great Britain—Biography.
5. Queens—Great Britain—Biography.
I. Brandreth, Gyles Daubeney, 1948–. Philip & Elizabeth.
II. Title. II. Title: Philip & Elizabeth.
DA590.B697 2005
941.085'092'2—dc22
[B]
2005023331

W. W. Norton & Company, Inc.
500 Fifth Avenue, New York, N.Y. 10110
www.wwnorton.com

W. W. Norton & Company Ltd.
Castle House, 75/76 Wells Street, London W1T 3QT

1 2 3 4 5 6 7 8 9 0

Contents

Introduction   1

PHILIP
Chapter One   9
Chapter Two   23

LILIBET
Chapter Three   47
Chapter Four   62

PHILIP & LILIBET
Chapter Five   83
Chapter Six   99

ELIZABETH & PHILIP
Chapter Seven   129
Chapter Eight   158

THE DUKE & THE QUEEN
Chapter Nine   185
Chapter Ten   215

MA & PA
Chapter Eleven   243
Chapter Twelve   288

PHILIP & ELIZABETH
Conclusion   335

Appendices
State & Commonwealth Visits   353
Prince Philip's Achievements   369

Family Trees
The British Royal Family   378
The Greek Royal Family   382
The Battenbergs & Mountbattens   384

Sources & Acknowledgements   386
Picture Credits   393
Index   395

Harold: You agree that a successful marriage is the greatest of human benefits?

Vita: Yes.

Harold: And that it must be based on love guided by intelligence?

Vita: Yes.

Harold: That an essential condition is a common sense of values?

Vita: Yes.

Harold: That the only things that will stave off marital nerves are modesty, good humour and, above all, occupation?

Vita: Yes.

Harold: And give and take?

Vita: And give and take.

Harold: And mutual esteem. I do not believe in the permanence of any love which is based on pity, or the protective or maternal instincts. It must be based on respect.

Vita: Yes, I agree. The caveman plus sweet-little-thing theory is long past. It was a theory insulting to the best qualities of both.

Harold Nicolson and Vita Sackville-West discussing marriage on
BBC radio in 1929, quoted in *Portrait of a Marriage* by their son,
Nigel Nicolson, 1973

Introduction

'People who write books ought to be shut up,' said King George V. 'This is Gyles Brandreth,' said the Duke of Edinburgh, introducing me to Queen Elizabeth II. As Her Majesty proffered me a tightly-gloved hand and, with a slightly nervous smile, murmured an almost inaudible, 'How do you do?', her consort continued: 'Apparently, he's writing about you.' The Duke paused and leant towards his wife's ear: 'Be warned. He's going to cut you into pieces.'

I have known the Duke of Edinburgh for a number of years. I am accustomed to his sense of humour. I like it. I like him. I admire him. This book has come about, in part, because I think he deserves to be better understood. Indeed, my first thought was simply to write a book about Prince Philip. In 2002, as part of the official celebration at the Royal Albert Hall in honour of his eightieth birthday, with his approval and involvement, I wrote a short account of his life. Researching it, and talking with him, I was particularly fascinated by his family history, his unusual childhood, and his impressive wartime career in the Royal Navy, but, looking at his story overall, I had to accept that, since 1947, he has only led the life he has because he married who he married. In our world, even today, very few men's lives are defined by their wives' roles. Prince Philip is interesting because he is interesting. He is doubly interesting because he is the Queen's consort.

As I explain in the Prologue, over a number of years in a number of roles – as chairman of a national charity of which the Queen is patron and the Duke of Edinburgh is president, as a member of parliament and government whip, and as a journalist and broadcaster – I have been able to observe the Queen and the Duke at close range. Watching the pair of them – two sharply contrasting characters, with wholly different natures, who are nonetheless, and undeniably, partners, allies, friends – I decided, possibly rashly (certainly presumptuously), to attempt a portrait of their marriage.

The phrase 'portrait of a marriage' has been used most famously, of course, by Nigel Nicolson as the title for his moving and revelatory account of his own parents' relationship – and relationships. Vita Sackville-West and Harold Nicolson led unusual and, to some extent, exotic lives. The Queen and Prince Philip have also led lives that are, by any standard, out of the ordinary.

Different marriages work (or fail) in different ways, and different people (and generations and classes) will have different expectations of what marriage has to offer. To begin to understand this particular royal marriage, we need – obviously – to understand the natures of the couple in question: what they are like as individuals, and why they are as they are, and how the way they are makes them relate to one another. Much of this book concentrates on the background and childhood of the Queen and Prince Philip because where they have come from tells us so much about where they are now. As Angela Carter has it: 'The destination of all journeys is their beginning.'

Some will regard aspects of this book as impertinent, unnecessary and intrusive. Prince Philip has complained to me more than once, 'The media have turned us into a soap opera.' It was ever thus. As Shakespeare puts it at the beginning of *Twelfth Night* (first performed before Elizabeth I four hundred years ago), 'What great ones do, the less will prattle of.' In 1947, the member of parliament and diarist, Henry 'Chips' Channon witnessed the royal unveiling of a statue of George V. 'The ceremony itself was over in twenty minutes,' he noted, 'but then followed that interminable pause whilst the Royalties greeted each other, interkissed and chatted. It is only in England that a crowd of several thousands can stand happily in the rain and watch one family gossip.' We are especially fascinated by this one family, not only because its story has all the essential romantic and melodramatic ingredients of a family saga in the tradition of Trollope or Galsworthy (and, at times, of an Angela Carter novel, too), but also, and principally, because the central characters are what used to be called 'Royalties'.

The hold of royalty on the public imagination is possibly less strong than once it was, but it is still there. Several million cheering people filled the streets – in three continents – to salute Elizabeth II on the occasion of her golden jubilee. Our Queen is the latest in a line of sovereigns that links her directly with King Edgar, Richard III, Henry VIII, George IV, and Queen Victoria. She is the embodiment of our history. Her presence links us to our past.

She is living history – and more than that. The Queen and Prince

Philip have something that even the greatest celebrities of the age do not have. They are the stuff of fairy-tale.

Marilyn Monroe, Elvis and David Beckham may have fame, fortune and talent, may even, eventually, join the ranks of the great immortals (they are heroic figures: the image of Marilyn could outlive the name of Helen of Troy – who knows?), but they are not royal. Elizabeth was born a princess. Philip was born a prince. It is wholly absurd, of course, but that makes them different. And, somehow, extra special.

I am a royalist, to the extent that I believe that the institution of the monarchy has served the United Kingdom well and can continue to do so. I believe, too, that the Queen, over more than five decades, has fulfilled her destiny with considerable skill and matchless dedication. And I reckon that the Duke of Edinburgh has played the bizarre hand that life has dealt him pretty flawlessly. This is a sympathetic portrait. It is also, I trust, an accurate one. I have met all the central characters in the story – including several who are no longer alive – and I quote no anonymous sources.

Before I embarked on the project I met separately with both Sir Robin Janvrin and Sir Miles Hunt-Davis, private secretaries to the Queen and Prince Philip, and outlined to them what I had in mind. I have had unfettered access to anyone I wished to speak to. This book is not 'authorised', but I hope it has authority. I admire Philip and Elizabeth. I hope I've got them right.

'The plan of jumping at once into the middle has been often tried, and sometimes seductively enough for a chapter or two; but the writer still has to hark back, and to begin again from the beginning . . .'
Anthony Trollope (1815–82), *Is He Popenjoy?*

PHILIP

Chapter One

'Uneasy lies the head that wears a crown.'

William Shakespeare, *Henry IV Part II*

In 1953, Coronation year, a book called *Manifest Destiny* was published. It was a handsome volume designed as a comprehensive celebration of the unique genius of the Mountbatten family. When invited by an equerry to sign a copy of the book, the Duke of Edinburgh obliged, adding, above his signature on the title page, two words: 'Manifest Bunkum!'

Prince Philip is wary of biographers, particularly those who come bearing purple prose and vivid imaginations. If his story is to be told he would prefer it to be done without exaggeration or speculation. If we could stick to the facts, and present them simply, chronologically and accurately, he would be obliged.

I shall do my best. It will not be easy. In talking about his early life, Prince Philip does not give a lot away. And, perversely, with a shrug of his shoulders, and a quizzical raised eyebrow, he likes to dismiss what, to us, seems a quite extraordinary start in life – lurid, disturbing, amazing: a grandfather assassinated, a father imprisoned, a peripatetic childhood with, from the age of nine, both parents absent, one in an asylum, the other with his mistress at Monte Carlo – as, somehow, almost normal, certainly unremarkable.

Royals are different from us: they have more relations. Prince Philip can claim kinship with the whole compass of European royalty: kings, emperors, kaisers, tsars. Include his sisters and his cousins and his aunts (princesses, admirals, grand duchesses) and it is the cast of a comic opera. (They even have the costumes.) Look at the story of the extended family over a century and a half and you have the plot of a comic opera as well: unlikely and confusing.

To know Prince Philip you need to know his family. To keep things simple, and as a reminder that almost all the people who feature in the pages that follow are related one to another, let us begin with Queen Victoria. We know where we are with her.

Queen Victoria had nine children. Her third child, and second daughter, was Princess Alice who, in 1862, at Osborne House on the Isle of Wight, married Prince Louis of Hesse-Darmstadt, later Grand Duke Louis IV of Hesse and by Rhine, one of the pocket principalities that made up much of Germany before unification. (We really are in comic opera country.[13]) Alice and Louis had seven children, including a future Princess of Prussia, who lived to see the Coronation of Elizabeth II in 1953, and the last Tsarina of Russia, who was less fortunate. They named their eldest Victoria and she became a favourite grandchild of the great Queen-Empress.

In April 1884, as she turned twenty-one, in Darmstadt, in the presence of Queen Victoria, Victoria of Hesse married her cousin, Louis of Battenberg, son of Prince Alexander of Hesse and grandson of Grand Duke Louis II of Hesse – or, possibly, in fact, grandson of the grand duchess's charismatic chamberlain, Baron Augustus Senarclens von Grancy. There were rumours . . . (There always are.)

Louis was rising thirty and, though thoroughly German (Queen Victoria called him Ludwig), a rising star in the British Royal Navy. He had connections, but he was also able and intelligent: conscientious yet outgoing, ambitious yet popular. There were rumours about him, too. In his bachelor days he had a self-confessed eye for the girls,[14] and he

---

[13] The Grand Ducal family lived in some two dozen assorted *Schlösser* in and around Darmstadt, a small town with a population, in the 1860s, of only a few thousand. In 1935, Germany's first *Reichsautobahn* was opened between Frankfurt and Darmstadt, a distance of twenty-five kilometres. In 1944, heavy Allied bombing of Darmstadt destroyed most of the inner city, killed 12,300 people and left 70,000 homeless. Today Darmstadt is thriving, with a population of around 150,000.

[14] As a protégé of the then Prince of Wales, Louis was introduced to the Prince's occasional mistress, the actress and noted beauty Lillie Langtry. Louis believed himself to be the father of the daughter born to Mrs Langtry in the spring of 1881. His legitimate younger son, Louis Mountbatten, believed it too, but it now seems not to have been the case. Given the scope of Mrs Langtry's conquests it is difficult to be sure, but the latest evidence lays the paternity suit at the feet of one Arthur Jones, one of Lord Ranelagh's litter of bastards. (He had at least seven.) Film producers in search of a subject offering royalty, lust and adventure in equal measure could do worse than make their way to the Hartley Library at the University of Southampton and dip into the early pages of Prince Louis of Battenberg's memoirs, kept with the Mountbatten

was noted for his virility, energy, charm and fondness for uniforms. Like his younger son, Louis Mountbatten, and, to a degree, his younger grandson, Prince Philip, Louis of Battenberg enjoyed dressing up. He had a variety of uniforms and an array of medals and, in public and in private, he relished parading in both. He also had an extravagant tattoo of a rampant dragon emblazoned across his chest and trailing down his legs. He lived life to the full.

Queen Victoria liked Louis and she loved her granddaughter and, consequently, she insisted that their first child be born not in one of their homes (they had two in Germany, another just outside Chichester in Sussex) but in one of hers. Princess Victoria of Hesse gave birth to the first of her four children in the Tapestry Room at Windsor Castle on 25 February 1885. The Queen recorded the event in her diary:

> Woke before 7. Hearing that Victoria had a bad night, I got up & went over to see her. She was very suffering. I had some breakfast, & then went back remaining with dear Victoria on & off, till at length, at 20m to 5 in the afternoon, the child, a little girl, was born. The relief was great for poor Victoria had had such a long hard time, which always makes me anxious. How strange and indeed affecting, it was, to see her lying in the same room, & in the same bed, in which she herself was born. Good Ludwig was most helpful & attentive, hardly leaving Victoria for a moment. The Baby is very small, thin & dark. I held it for a few moments in my arms.

Princess Victoria's mother, Princess Alice, had died of diphtheria, aged only thirty-five, in 1878. The new baby was named after her. This Princess Alice was to become Princess Andrew of Greece, mother of Prince Philip, and a most unusual woman: striking, strange, and, in her own way, heroic.

Princess Victoria was a pretty child and a handsome woman: reserved but direct, straightforward, unspoilt, and, by several accounts, somewhat masculine in her manner. Her daughter Alice was simply

papers there. Here can be found amazing tales of youthful conquests across several continents. The cast includes bold English princes, blushing American heiresses, willing Indian princesses, and memorable encounters with, among others, 'a young native girl in transparent white garments' and Cakobau, the cannibal king of Fiji, who 'could not deny that he had occasional yearnings for babies' legs, which he said were the best dish in the world'.

beautiful: a gorgeous baby, a lovely girl, a fine woman. The Prince of Wales is said to have declared: 'No throne in Europe is too good for her.'

She did, however, have one defect. She was hard of hearing. When she was four, her mother reported to Queen Victoria:

> The child has grown very much since you last saw her, is very lively & quick with her fingers, but decidedly backward of speech, using all sorts of self-invented words & pronouncing others very indistinctly, so that strangers find it difficult to understand her.

Alice was taken to ear specialists in Darmstadt and London: there was nothing to be done[15] and, for better or worse, her family decided to make no special concessions to her problem. Although, over time, she became a skilful lip-reader (in several languages) and, it seems, the degree of hearing loss varied at different stages in her life, the disability took its toll, making her more isolated than she might otherwise have been and making others, who did not know her well, regard her as, somehow, a bit odd.

In late May 1999, her son, Prince Philip, was accused, in newspaper reports, of openly mocking some deaf children at a pop concert in Wales. He was alleged to have jeered at them, 'Deaf? No wonder you are deaf listening to this row.' A few days later, on 4 June, he wrote to me from Buckingham Palace:

> You may have noticed that the tabloids were quick to suggest that I had made another 'gaffe' and 'insulted' some deaf children at Cardiff recently. Needless to say, the story is largely invention. It so happens that my mother was quite seriously deaf and I have been Patron of the Royal National Institute for the Deaf for ages, so it's hardly likely that I would do any such thing. Quite apart from that, I have no recollection of meeting a group of deaf children at the event for the Prince's Trust in the grounds of Cardiff Castle. There were young people milling all over the place and there may well have been a group of deaf children amongst them. What I do remember is that

---

[15] At least, not in the 1880s. Some members of the family maintained that Alice's hearing had been impaired because of an accident caused at sea during a rough crossing of the English Channel. The official diagnosis was that she suffered from a thickness of the Eustachian tubes. Today, according to my GP, the condition could be treated relatively simply.

the noise from various stages and bands was quite deafening and I may well have said at some point something to the effect that if anyone were to sit too close to the loud speakers they would certainly be in danger of going deaf.[16]

There would be echoes of his mother's childhood in Prince Philip's own. Her parents loved her dearly, but they left her, frequently for weeks at a time, sometimes for months, in the care of nannies and governesses and assorted family members. Today, Prince Philip shrugs his shoulders: 'It was the way it was.' Little Alice spent her peripatetic childhood in Darmstadt, at Sennicotts (the house the Battenbergs rented in West Sussex), in Malta (where the Mediterranean Fleet was stationed), in London (at different times, in Pimlico, Victoria and Knightsbridge), at Walton-on-Thames, at Sandgate, near Folkestone, and in the various residences of her great-grandmother: at Windsor, at Balmoral, at Osborne House on the Isle of Wight, in the Royal Yacht *Victoria and Albert*, and on the French Riviera where the Queen-Empress would take her spring holiday.

Despite her deafness, Alice was a bright child, likeable and liked, and mature for her age, in manner and appearance. 'She is eleven,' one of her great-aunts commented in 1896, 'but as big as a girl of fourteen.' By 1900 the Battenberg family was complete. Alice had one younger sister, Louise (1889–1965), who would one day become Queen of Sweden,[17]

[16] More recently, in May 2003, because it had made me smile, I told Prince Philip Roy Hattersley's story about his new hearing aid: 'It's the one Bill Clinton has. It's marvellous, so small you hardly notice it. You don't hear any better with it, of course, but it makes you irresistible to nineteen-year-olds.' Prince Philip laughed, and then sighed: 'God, can you imagine what would happen if I tried to tell a joke like that?' Once he encountered a blind lady with a guide dog and provoked 'outrage' in the popular press by saying to her, 'Do you know they have eating-dogs for the anorexic now.'

[17] She was sixty-one when, eventually, in October 1950, her husband succeeded his father as Gustaf VI Adolf, King of Sweden. She and her husband were happily married, but she did not find it easy adjusting to her ultimate role. She was ungrand and a little uncertain. In the 1950s, when out in London shopping on her own, in case she was knocked down by a bus and nobody would know who she was, she kept a small card in her handbag which read: 'I am the Queen of Sweden.' Recently, in December 2002, Queen Margrethe II of Denmark told me: 'European royalty like coming to England because no one knows who we are. We can be anonymous. And then when people discover who we are, they are always very helpful, so we get the best of both worlds. Our bread is definitely buttered on both sides. That is an advantage to being a queen. People always behave very nicely towards me.'

and two younger brothers, destined to follow their father into the British navy: Georgie (1892–1938) and Louis (1900–1979), known as Dick or Dickie almost from birth. He was the last great-grandson born in Queen Victoria's lifetime.

The Queen-Empress died on 22 January 1901. Her funeral took place at Windsor on 2 February. Alice and her parents were there. Sixteen months later, on 26 June 1902, Edward VII was due to be crowned. Alice and her mother were both expected and invited to stay at Buckingham Palace, where the distinguished guest list included an array of European royalty,[18] including Crown Prince Constantine of Greece and two of his younger brothers, George and Andrew. Prince Andrew (known in the family as Andrea) was twenty, a young officer in the Greek army, tall, blond and handsome. 'Interesting', too: he was short-sighted and wore spectacles. Princess Alice was seventeen-and-a-half: beautiful, intelligent, and hard of hearing. The young people fell in love.

There was time for romance. Three days before the day set for his Coronation, Edward VII was taken suddenly ill and operated on for peritonitis. The Coronation was postponed, but the royal house party went on. The German princess and the Greek prince lingered at Buckingham Palace for a fortnight more. Love blossomed.

Andrea was a Greek prince, living in Greece, the fourth son of King George I of Greece, but he was not really Greek at all. (This is, in part, a comic opera, remember.) He was German, Danish, Dutch and Russian.

In the late 1820s, when modern Greece managed to shake itself free from Turkish domination, the newly independent kingdom was in want of a monarch. Having nothing home-bred to hand, the Greeks shopped around (literally) for a royal figure of sufficient international standing and authority and shipped in Prince Otto of Bavaria as their first king.[19] He stayed the course for thirty years, but, following an unpleasant insurrection in 1862 (not the first), made his excuses and left. The

---

[18] 'You think of us as "European royalty",' the Queen of Denmark said to me, 'We think of ourselves as "family". We are all cousins. That's why we are easy together.'

[19] Perhaps my tone should be less condescending. Following the London Protocol of 1830, Otto of Bavaria was promoted as an appropriate head of state for newly independent Greece by Great Britain, France and Germany. As I write this, in May 2003, in the aftermath of the overthrow of Saddam Hussein, I read in the newspapers that the Americans and British are 'shopping around' for a potential head of state for newly liberated Iraq.

search for a king resumed and, this time round, the lot fell to one Prince William, younger son of King Christian IX of Denmark. He was only seventeen. He changed his name, his nationality and his destiny. He served as King George I of Greece for fifty years, from 1863 until he was murdered by a lunatic while out for a stroll in the streets of Salonika in the spring of 1913.

George I of Greece had an older brother (who became King Frederick VIII of Denmark in 1906) and two younger sisters: Alexandra, married to England's Edward VII, and Marie, married to Russia's Tsar Alexander III. George I also married a member of the Russian royal family: the Grand Duchess Olga, a granddaughter of Tsar Nicholas I. Over a period of twenty years the couple had eight children, the youngest-but-one of whom was Andrea: intelligent, humorous, conscientious, committed to Greece (he could speak English, German, Danish, Russian, French, but he spoke in Greek to his parents) and committed to a career in the army. In her preface to his volume of military memoirs – the aptly titled *Towards Disaster*, published in 1930 – Princess Alice wrote: 'He took his duties very seriously as he loved his profession, and he wished to earn his promotion like any other officer.'

The Coronation of Edward VII was rescheduled for 9 August 1902. The courts of Europe reassembled in London. Alice and Andrea met once more. Indeed, their families seemed happy to encourage the match: Alice and her mother travelled to Westminster Abbey in the same carriage as Andrea and his brother, George.

Fourteen months later (mostly months when they were apart: Andrea's military duties kept him away), in Darmstadt, on 6 and 7 October 1903, they were married. It was a fairy-tale wedding, complete with carriages and kings, three ceremonies (one civil, two religious), feasting, dancing, laughter and happy tears. She was eighteen, a beautiful princess, with orange blossom in her hair; he was twenty-one, a handsome prince, decked out in the glorious uniform of a Red Dragoon. They did not live happily ever after.

It all began well enough. They had a quietly domestic honeymoon in Darmstadt and, early in the new year, set off for Greece. Having spent several winters in Malta as a child, Alice was at least accustomed to a Mediterranean climate, and her new in-laws evidently did everything they could to give the young bride – still a teenager, partially deaf, in a strange country where she did not yet speak the language – a warm welcome and a sense of security. George I appears to have been a wise man: unstuffy, courteous, considerate, capable, honest, and keenly aware of his position as an 'imported' monarch. He would advise his sons: 'Never forget that you are foreigners among the Greeks, and never let them remember it.'

George I rode the roller-coaster of Greek politics for half a century. He survived censure, insurrections, intrigues and at least one assassination attempt before the one that killed him. He accepted his destiny, and did what he sensed was his duty, but he made it clear, repeatedly, in public and in private, that he was ever-ready to step down from the throne if his services were no longer required.

I believe his grandson, Prince Philip, feels much the same way. It infuriates Philip if he is portrayed in the press as someone who revels in the life of a prince, who clings to the trappings of monarchy, who believes in the survival of the Crown above all else. He doesn't. If a monarchy serves a purpose, and if, on the whole, most people are mostly comfortable with it, so be it. If not, fine, let's stop buggering about and have done with it. The Queen would be deeply saddened no longer to be Queen of Canada or Australia (we know how the Queen feels about the Commonwealth, old and new), but Prince Philip is ready to say, in terms, as he did, in Canada in 1969: 'It is a complete misconception to imagine that the monarchy exists in the interests of the monarch. It doesn't. It exists in the interests of the people. If at any time any nation decides that the system is unacceptable, then it is up to them to change it.'

George I of Greece was a family man, by all accounts a good man, decent, God-fearing and happily married. That said, according to the memoirs of the well-connected Prince von Bülow (gossipy, gripping, but generally considered reasonably reliable), George I did allow himself 'an occasional relaxation' at Aix-les-Bains, on his annual French holiday away from his queen. When his eldest son, Constantine, followed his father's example, the crown prince's dismayed wife, Sophie (another of Queen Victoria's grandchildren), turned to her father-in-law for guidance. 'You must consult your dear mother-in-law,' he is supposed to have told her, 'she will be able to give you the best advice on this point.'

Over ten years, Alice and Andrea had four daughters: Margarita (1905–81), born in the none-too-comfortable Royal Palace in Athens, and Theodora (1906–69), Cécile (1911–37), and Sophie (1914–2001), all born at Tatoï, the royal family's cherished country estate nearby. Life at home was fairly placid: Alice rode, sewed, read, played with her children, corresponded with her family. In the streets, it was a little livelier. This was a turbulent decade in Greek politics (yet another one), the ups and downs including a *coup d'état* and the resignation of all the royal princes from the Greek army in 1909, followed by their reinstatement at the outset of the first of the Balkan wars in 1912. (An incidental side effect of the princes' period outside the army was that they did not venture out socially as much as previously: accustomed to appearing in public in uniform, they felt underdressed – emasculated, even – in civilian clothes.)

During much of this period Alice and her daughters were abroad, visiting her parents and other members of the extended family in Germany, England, Malta and Russia, joining house parties, attending weddings, christenings, funerals. In May 1910, Alice and Andrea were in London when Edward VII died. They attended his funeral. Alice's father had been a friend of the King's (they had shared Mrs Langtry, after all); Queen Alexandra was Andrea's aunt.

In March 1913 George I of Greece was murdered outside a café in Salonika, shot in the back by a single bullet from a lone assassin. A motive was never established. The murderer, a Greek, apparently deranged, threw himself to his death from an upstairs window on the way to his cross-examination. In his will, the old king left some words of counsel for his son and successor, now King Constantine I:

> Be calm and never forget that you are reigning over a southern people who are easily roused and may in a moment do and say many things which they will probably forget a few hours after. For this reason never fall into a passion and never forget that it is preferable that the King should suffer rather than his people.

In his will, the old king also left Andrea and Alice a useful annuity and gave them his house, Mon Repos, on the pretty island of Corfu. (The British had given Greece the Ionian Islands at the time of George I's accession.) Alice mourned the loss of her father-in-law. He had been a good friend to her, had taken her seriously and admired and encouraged her good works.

The tradition of royal princesses, born to privilege, with time on their hands and status at their disposal, both setting an example and at the same time achieving a degree of self-fulfilment, by giving practical service to the community, is a relatively young one. Prince Albert, Queen Victoria's Prince Consort, very much encouraged it. In Darmstadt, Victoria and Albert's daughter, Alice, had established a sisterhood of young women, known as 'Alice's nurses', committed to giving service to the community as trained district nurses. In Russia, this Alice's daughter (young Alice's aunt), Ella (married to Grand Duke Serge), established a convent of nursing sisters and built a church for her community. In Greece, George I's wife, Queen Olga (another Russian grand duchess by birth), founded four separate hospitals, as well as building a prison for women and a reformatory school for boys.

These women were models for Alice. She was inspired by their example, both by the practical hands-on alleviation of suffering that the nurses could achieve, and, especially in Aunt Ella's case, by the spiritual zeal that fuelled it. In due course, foreshadowing Alice's own spiritual crisis,[20] Ella would renounce the grand-ducal life completely and declare to her nursing sisters, with pride: 'I am about to leave the brilliant world in which it fell to me to occupy a brilliant position, but together with you all I am about to enter a much greater world – that of the poor and the afflicted.'

When she arrived in Athens in 1904, still a teenager, the first community work Alice undertook was assisting at the Greek School for Embroidery, where young girls were taught a specific skill that would help them support their families. Eight years later, in 1912, at the onset of the Balkan wars, Alice would galvanise the young embroiderers and set them to the task of making and mending warm and durable clothes (jackets, scarves, hoods) both for the troops and for refugees.

The first Balkan war – in which Greece, alongside Bulgaria, Montenegro and Serbia, sought to reclaim territory from the Turkish European empire and secure Crete for Greece – saw Andrea back in uniform, as a lieutenant colonel with the 3rd Regiment of Cavalry, posted to Larissa, an established garrison town on the old Turkish border. Alice accompanied her husband, but she went with a mission of her own: to establish her own first-aid field hospitals at the front. She sent her mother written reports:

> I went to the Military Hospital and saw the arrival of some 15 to 20 wounded soldiers from a skirmish at Elassona who had taken 14 hours coming here over utterly impossible roads, over a fearful

---

[20] Is there a strain of religious mania in this family? Prince Philip is deeply interested in the spiritual – as is his son, Prince Charles. Philip's library contains 634 volumes on religious and spiritual matters. When once I asked him to talk on the record about his interest in religion, he declined: 'If I start talking about religion, the press will say I'm barking. *You'll* say I'm barking.' For many years, many said his mother *was* barking.

mountain pass – Melouna – at the frontier, where huge boulders and rocks stuck out of the road, and on hearing of their agony and the impossibility of bringing severely wounded at all to Larissa, and news which reached us of the army's tremendously rapid advance, I instantly decided to move my hospital to Elassona.

Over the next three months – first at Elassona, then in Serbia, then in Macedonia, and finally at Epirus – Alice displayed the most extraordinary courage, compassion, determination, energy and organisational skill. She set up hospitals, she marshalled nurses, she bullied doctors, she commandeered vehicles, houses, a school. She would not be denied: 'I sent my surgeon to the battlefield with a motor of the General Staff, which I took upon myself to sign an order for.' She attended the sick, she tended the dying, she assisted at an amputation. For days she barely ate or slept and did not change her clothes. She witnessed the full horror of war. 'But, God!' she told her mother, 'what things we saw! Shattered arms, and legs and heads, such awful sights – and then to have to bandage those dreadful things for three days and three nights. The corridor full of blood, and cast-off bandages knee-high.'

Reading her letters to her mother,[21] you can see she was appalled by what she saw, and exhausted by the experience, but she was exhilarated too. There is manic energy here: touches of Joan of Arc as well as Florence Nightingale. Her forcefulness rubbed some people up the wrong way; it left others worrying about the effect on her health when she came down from her 'high'. What no one doubted was her courage and commitment. In November 1913, George V decorated her with the Royal Red Cross, 'in recognition of her services in nursing the sick and wounded among the Greek soldiers during the recent war'.

The Balkan wars, of course, were merely the curtain-raiser for the Big Show, the 1914–18 conflict. Constantine I was resolved that Greece should remain neutral. Britain and the Allies were where Greece's traditional allegiance lay, but Germany under the Kaiser looked formidable and might not prove magnanimous in victory. It was a difficult call. He hedged his bets. Besides, his family had close kith and kin on both sides of the argument.

---

[21] They are powerful and moving letters, reproduced in Hugo Vickers' authorised biography, *Alice, Princess Andrew of Greece*, 2000. Chapter X alone would make an amazing feature film.

In London, in October 1914, Alice's father, Louis of Battenberg, First Sea Lord since 1912, resigned. He was married to a granddaughter of Queen Victoria, he had served with great distinction in the Royal Navy for forty-six years, but he was German. There was no denying it. He had a home in Germany, he spoke German, he kept German staff. The *Daily Mail* did not look kindly on any of that. And Winston Churchill, now First Lord of the Admiralty, wanted him replaced in any event. The Battenberg family was devastated. His younger son, Dickie, a fourteen-year-old naval cadet, vowed to avenge the slight.[22]

Louis of Battenberg's wife, Victoria, railed against the stupidity of those responsible. 'The King is a nobody,' she declared. In fact, the King was somebody of some substance and, though several parts German himself, determined, for reasons of patriotism and self-interest, to assert the Britishness of the British Crown. In 1917, George V disowned the Kraut connection. The House of Saxe-Coburg, also known as Wettin, also known as Wipper, would henceforward be known as the House of Windsor. (The Kaiser, on hearing the news, was reported to have quipped that he was 'off to the theatre to see *The Merry Wives of Saxe-Coburg Gotha*'.) The Queen's brothers, from the proud House of Teck, would become the Marquess of Cambridge and the Earl of Athlone, and the Battenbergs would be transliterated into the Mountbattens. Queen Victoria's 'dear Ludwig' was given a peerage and a title with a comforting British ring to every syllable: Marquess of Milford Haven.[23]

Louis was forcibly retired, but his sons, with their new names, continued to serve in the British navy. Victoria professed herself resigned to whatever fate might have in store for them. 'I can't be grateful enough that I was given the nature of a fatalist,' she wrote to a friend. 'All my life I have felt that all of us have our appointed time on earth & that nothing will alter it. Perhaps the way my mother & little

---

[22] He did. Forty-one years later, in 1955, as Winston Churchill stepped down as prime minister for the final time, Admiral of the Fleet Lord Mountbatten of Burma was appointed First Sea Lord.

[23] Do I sense this still rankles within the family? Look up the entry for Louis's great-grandson in the 2003 edition of *Debrett's People of Today* and you will see that the 4th marquess describes the first as, 'HSH Prince Louis of Battenberg, who relinquished, at the King's request, the style and title of Serene Highness and Prince of Battenberg, instead assuming the surname of Mountbatten by Royal Licence 1917'. Louis of Battenberg was staying at his elder son's house in Scotland at the time his new title was officially approved. He wrote in his son's visitors' book: 'June 9th arrived Prince Hyde; June 19th departed Lord Jekyll.'

sister were swept away by that vile diphtheria has helped me to strengthen the feeling . . . I feel too that if it is Georgie's time to go, he will go & my Dickie too, but not otherwise, & so I hope I shall not worry more than is inevitable when Dickie goes to sea.'

In the event, Georgie died in April 1938, of bone marrow cancer, aged forty-five, three days after his mother's seventy-fifth birthday. Dickie died, full of years (and honours), aged seventy-nine, murdered by the IRA in August 1979. At the time, the *Chicago Tribune* calculated that no single family in recorded history, including the Borgias and the Cosa Nostra families of Sicily, Chicago and New York, was more susceptible to violent death among its members than the family of Queen Victoria and her descendants.

In 1917, in the aftermath of the Bolshevik revolution, George V was unwilling to send a British warship to rescue his first cousin, the overthrown Tsar Nicholas II. In July 1918, the Tsar and Tsarina (Alix, Alice's aunt) and their children were executed and Alix's sister, the Grand Duchess Ella – Alice's aunt and inspiration – and other members of the Russian royal family were thrown alive down a mine shaft, where they were heard singing psalms before Bolshevik soldiers killed them by throwing a grenade into the mine shaft after them. Eighty years on, in July 1998, Ella, now recognised as a saint by the Russian Orthodox Church, was one of ten twentieth-century martyrs whose carved effigies above the Great West Door of Westminster Abbey were dedicated in the presence of Prince Philip and the Queen.

Alice and her four daughters spent much of the First World War in Athens. Andrea was stationed in Salonika until 1916 when his brother sent him on diplomatic missions to London and Paris to assure the Allies of Greece's commitment to neutrality. Constantine I did not play his hand well. He was mistrusted by the Allies, wholly at odds with the Greek prime minister, Eleutherios Venizelos, no longer in step with the Greek people. In June 1917, he was overthrown, driven into exile in Switzerland and replaced, not by the Crown Prince, George (who, it was thought, might be sympathetic to the German cause), but by his second son, Alexander. Andrea, Alice and the girls joined the exodus to Switzerland. The hotel accommodation was reasonably priced and the weather quite congenial. The skiing and the skating were both excellent. There are worse spots to endure the humiliation of exile than the shores of Lake Lucerne.

Greek politics being what it is, by 1920 they were all back. King Alexander, aged twenty-seven, died of blood poisoning, having been bitten by a monkey. In a plebiscite, King Constantine I was restored to the Greek throne by a vote of 1,010,788 to 10,887, and Prince Andrea, now sporting a monocle, climbed back into uniform, promoted to the rank of major general. He was thirty-eight, Alice was thirty-five. Seven years after the birth of their fourth daughter, they were due to have another child. On 10 June 1921, on the dining-room table at Mon Repos, Prince Philip was born.

Chapter Two

'If one is not caressed . . . one develops thorns.'

Beryl Bainbridge (1934–), *According to Queeney*

The sun was high, the day was hot, the scent of orange and lemon, of cypress and magnolia, filled the air. Mon Repos, built by the British in 1824, is a handsome villa by the sea, a family mansion (not a palace), spacious, and comfortable, and its setting (at least, in 1921, before Corfu became a major-league holiday destination) near-idyllic. The house, surprisingly cool in summer, was surrounded by olive groves, wisteria and wild flowers growing in the long grass. Prince Philip was only born on the dining-room table because the doctor felt that it would be more convenient than Princess Alice's bed.

'He is a splendid, healthy child, thank God,' his mother reported to one of the family back in Darmstadt. 'I am very well too. It was an uncomplicated delivery & I am enjoying the fresh air on the terrace.' Though the years of wars and revolution – the years of her marriage, in fact – had taken their toll on Alice – on her health, on her spirits, on her looks – her life was not without its consolations. She was a princess and she was treated like one. She had a lady-in-waiting. She had domestic staff. She had a French governess for her daughters and an English nanny, Mrs Nicholas, for her son.

The standing of European royalty might not be what once it was – for a start, the crowned heads of Germany, Austria and Russia were no more – and the position of the monarchy in Greece had always been precarious, but, nonetheless, Alice and her family – though they faced high drama in their lives, and pain, and personal tragedy – were mostly spared the mundane drudgery that is – and, especially, was then – the lot of most working people. Alice and Andrea were not rich – by the standards of the Windsors, say, or the Dukes of Westminster – and there were to be times when their financial worries would be considerable – but they were not truly poor, ever, and all their lives, if there were not always servants hovering, still there was deference in the air.

This is true of Prince Philip, even today. He is unspoilt, unstuffy, good-humoured, easy to talk to, occasionally scratchy, but always a prince and always treated like one. Cars come, guards salute, breakfast is served, valets press your suits, the fairies clean your shoes. I have watched Prince Philip padding alone along the long narrow corridors of Buckingham Palace, barely noticing as nodding footmen step aside, pages bow and private secretaries back discreetly into doorways. If you are due to meet him in his study, whether for the first time or the thirty-first, his equerry will invite you to stand in the room, at a specific angle in a particular spot, and remind you to bow as His Royal Highness enters and call him 'Sir'. I don't have a problem with any of this: I am in favour of due respect, I like old-fashioned courtesy, I even still try to stand up when a lady enters the room: I mention it here and now only because if this is the way you have lived your life – as Prince Philip has and his parents did – it will affect you, like it or not, believe it or not.

Prince Philip must have been a beautiful baby: the early photographs show a cherubic child, bonny, smiling, a little chubby. He had the blondest hair and the bluest eyes and was the darling of a household crowded with women. From London, Alice's mother, Victoria, now Marchioness of Milford Haven, wrote to one of her friends: 'I knew you would rejoice with us at Alice having a boy. Poor Andrea had the bad luck of leaving the day before the event & so has not seen his son.' Andrea had just been given command of the Greek army's 12th Division in Asia Minor and, on 9 June 1921, embarked on the campaign that would prove his undoing. It would be several months before he set eyes on his baby son.

Victoria, in fact, got to see Philip before Andrea did. In September, Louis Milford Haven died, aged sixty-seven, and Alice came to London to console her mother, bringing Philip with her. Alice showed off her son to her assorted English relations, including, of course, her own youngest brother, Dickie Mountbatten, now nearly twenty-two and already smitten with the young Edwina Ashley.

Just a month before he died, George V had honoured Louis Milford Haven – and thrilled him to the core – by appointing him Admiral of the Fleet. Louis might have had a German accent, but he had done the state some service. And the King now offered Louis's widow a home: an apartment at Kensington Palace, where she lived for the rest of her long life.

Philip's grandfather was a naval officer of real distinction. Coming to a sure assessment of the merits of Prince Philip's father as a military commander is not so easy. Andrea enjoyed life as a soldier – his life *was* soldiering. He was committed, conscientious, capable, but, ultimately, his career ended in failure.

The trigger for his downfall was, as I say, the conduct of the campaign launched in the month of Prince Philip's birth. The Greeks and Turks were at war over the possession of Anatolia, once Turkish territory, but awarded to Greece after the 1914–18 war. There may not have been a great deal to choose between the military capacity of the two sides, but there is little doubt that the Greek forces were seriously overextended, poorly equipped, inadequately led and simply unable to sustain a successful campaign in the Anatolian desert, so far away from base.

From the outset, Andrea had been convinced that the Asia Minor campaign was doomed. His own division was manned by new recruits, inexperienced and ill-equipped, and he had no faith in the campaign's overall commander, one General Papoulas, a soldier, according to Andrea, notable for his 'ignorance of the science of war'.

On 9 September 1921, Papoulas sent an order to Andrea in the desert to make an 'immediate violent attack' on the enemy to the north. Andrea considered the proposal absurd – 'a cry of ill-concealed panic' he called it – and replied to his commander-in-chief: 'Attack by 2nd Corps in the direction indicated impossible.' He had an alternative plan, involving different troop movements and no attack. He acted on his plan and sent word to Papoulas that he had done so. Under the circumstances, Papoulas's reaction does not seem surprising: 'Astonished at plan of abandoning positions. I order corps to remain in its position. Only person competent to judge and decide is myself as Commander-in-Chief. Cancel all orders of transfer movements.'

This order Andrea obeyed, but the following day, outraged to dis-cover that overnight the Commander-in-Chief had relieved him of his Chief of Staff, volunteered his own resignation. He sent word to Papoulas: 'It is absolutely impossible for me to continue in command of corps. Please order my immediate relief.'

Papoulas felt unable to oblige: 'I desire, and the situation demands, you should remain in your place.' Andrea did as he was told. The Turks attacked. The Greeks responded. The battle was neither lost nor won, but the drive towards Ankara was halted and then abandoned. Andrea and his men were in retreat.

If, today, you read *Towards Disaster*, Andrea's own account of what took place, you are left feeling (or, at least, I am left feeling) that the prince protests too much. When ordered to attack, he did not do so. Further, he informed his commander-in-chief of his alternative plan of action as he was undertaking it. In his apologia, he concedes that the message he sent Papoulas 'was not in accordance with ordinary practice', but asserts, 'beyond that, it does not constitute an infraction of orders, nor does it show any lack of fighting spirit'. This much – but no more – he is ready to accept: 'There is, however, a breach of formality, and this lies in the fact that in the message the correct phrase "subject to approval" was omitted, but the omission of this phrase cannot possibly form the basis of an accusation for disobedience and abandoning one's position.'

Prince Philip is like his father. He now looks like him, though Andrea had more protuberant ears, a moustache and a monocle. By several accounts, they shared a joshing sense of humour. And from my reading of *Towards Disaster* and my observation of Prince Philip in action, I reckon they have in common, too, a stubborn streak, a wilful contrariness, a need to have the last word, and a slightly exasperated (occasionally despairing) sense that they are right and the other chap doesn't know what he's talking about.[24]

Andrea and Papoulas remained at odds and, at the end of September 1921, the prince was granted three months' leave and returned to Corfu to meet his baby son for the first time. Within eight weeks, however, he was called back to active service, first as a member of the Supreme

---

[24] I happen to be writing this on a day – in May 2003 – when I have just had lunch with Prince Philip at the Landmark Hotel in west London, by Marylebone Station. As I escorted HRH to his car – a specially converted electric London taxicab – he said, 'I've been to this place before.' I said, 'It used to be the headquarters of the British Railways Board.' 'No,' said Prince Philip, 'that was at Euston.' 'I'm sure it was here, Sir,' I said. 'No, no,' he insisted, 'I opened the building. It wasn't British Rail. That was Euston.' I persisted, 'This was the headquarters of British Rail.' 'No,' he said firmly, 'that was Euston, this was something else.' I turned to one of the hotel executives hovering by the door. 'Yes,' murmured the man, 'this was the headquarters of BR.' HRH sighed, shook his head in disbelief and clambered, still muttering, into his car. I half expect a letter in the morning: 'The building may at some point have housed the British Railways Board, but British Rail also had headquarters at Euston, and I expect that I visited the building at Marylebone after it had ceased to be used by the Railways Board and before it became an hotel.'

Army Council, then as commander of the 5th Army Corps. General Papoulas was replaced by one General Hadjianestis (for whom Andrea had rather greater regard), but the fighting went no better. Within the year, the Turks had triumphed and the Greeks were in full retreat, forced back, literally, into the sea. Asia Minor was lost, the collapse was complete, the casualties horrendous. There were more than a million Greek refugees.

In the aftermath of the catastrophe, there was a military coup: a colonels' revolt. King Constantine I was overthrown and sent once more into exile. General Hadjianestis and five others were put on trial and swiftly executed. Andrea was arrested, charged with disobeying orders and abandoning his post in the face of the enemy, and tried in Athens, in the Chamber of Deputies, by a jury of junior officers. He was found guilty and expected to be sentenced to death. 'I think you might add,' says Prince Philip, 'that my father was charged by the new republican government as a scapegoat.'

There is a telling photograph that was taken of Andrea during his trial. He is impeccably dressed in an elegant lounge suit, with a white handkerchief in his breast pocket, folded exactly as Prince Philip folds his today. In the picture he sits staring into the middle distance, his attaché case unopened on the table in front of him. He looks gaunt and anxious, but unbowed.

At Mon Repos, Alice, under police surveillance, and denied access to her husband, was sending desperate messages in every direction, pleading for help from all quarters. Internationally, there was little desire to get involved in Greek politics, but, in London, Alice's brother Dickie saw the King and lobbied the prime minister, and Lord Curzon, the Foreign Secretary, arranged for a British agent – Gerald Talbot, previously naval attaché in Athens, and a man with useful contacts among the high command of the new regime – to slip discreetly into Greece 'to see what might be done'. The upshot was a secret deal, negotiated by Talbot, whereby Andrea was spared his life, but condemned to 'perpetual banishment'.[25]

For many years, in the British press and elsewhere, Prince Philip was nicknamed 'Phil the Greek'. Briefly, he had been sixth in line to the throne of Greece, but he has no Greek blood in him and no particular

---

[25] There is potential here for another exciting movie. I refer producers to *Towards Disaster*, to chapter sixteen of Hugo Vickers' biography of Princess Andrew, and to *Ionian Vision* by Michael Llewellyn Smith, 1973.

fondness for Greece or the Greeks. As he has said to me, more than once, 'A grandfather assassinated and a father condemned to death does not endear me to the perpetrators.' Talking to him today (at lunch at the Landmark Hotel) about divided Cyprus, he seemed to me to be as sympathetic to the Turks as to the Greeks. Talking to him anytime about the traumatic events of 1922 is less rewarding. 'I was barely a year old when the family went into exile,' he says, reasonably enough. 'What do you expect me to remember?'

His sister Sophie, who was eight at the time, did remember and did talk about the experience before she died. 'It was a terrible business,' she recalled, 'absolute chaos.' The British had sent a ship, a cruiser, HMS *Calypso*, to carry the family into exile. When Andrea was released from gaol, he was driven straight from his prison to the quayside. On Corfu, Alice, her lady-in-waiting, the governess, the nanny, the four girls and baby Philip, were bundled into cars, loaded with all the possessions they could muster in the hours before their escape, and taken in a small boat from the island harbour to *Calypso* waiting offshore. Sophie's abiding memory of the flight from Mon Repos was of the smell of smoke from the grates in every fireplace. Alice had instructed her daughters to burn everything: letters, papers, documents, to leave nothing behind.

The sea – not having much respect for royalty – was rough. The ship's officers were more gracious, giving up their cabins for the royal refugees and providing an on-board concert to distract and entertain the children and their parents. The exiles were taken across the Adriatic to Brindisi, on the heel of Italy, 'a ghastly place', according to Sophie, 'the worst town I've ever been in'. From there, as dawn broke, they took a train to Rome. On the train, Philip made himself filthy, crawling everywhere. 'He was very active,' said Sophie. He even licked the windowpanes. His mother reprimanded him. 'Leave him alone,' said Nanny.[26]

Their hope and expectation had been to travel on to London, but George V, while ready to help save his cousin's neck, was not so eager to offer him sanctuary. Buckingham Palace took the view, endorsed by

[26] Princess Sophie told her story in 1990 to Tim Heald, Prince Philip's biographer. Heald told me: 'I liked her very much. She could not have been more friendly. I stood with her at Buckingham Palace watching the Guards rehearse for Trooping the Colour. She spoke with a marked German accent and occasionally had to search for the *mot juste*, but if not quite bilingual she was certainly completely fluent. I sensed her relationship with Prince Philip was still very much big sister/kid brother.'

the Foreign Office, that it would be politically more comfortable if the exiled Greek prince could settle somewhere quietly on the Continent, out of controversy's way. What about Palermo in Sicily, where the overthrown King Constantine had taken refuge?

In the event, the exiles and their entourage (a family of seven, plus a total of six servants) went on from Rome to Paris, then – after several days of awkward diplomatic wrangling – briefly to London and then, finally, and permanently, back once more to the French capital. Paris dictated itself as the city in which to settle because Andrea's older brother, Prince George, now aged fifty-three, was already living there and had a home to spare that was large enough to accommodate the royal refugees.

In 1907 Prince George (known in the family as 'Big George') had married Marie Bonaparte, great-granddaughter of the Emperor Napoleon's brother Lucien, and, rather more usefully, granddaughter of the celebrated Monsieur Blanc, founder of the casino at Monte Carlo. Marie was an interesting woman: an heiress, an antiquarian, a dog-lover, a psychoanalyst of some distinction, and a friend and patroness of Sigmund Freud. George and Marie and their two children (Peter and Eugénie, aged fourteen and twelve in 1922) lived in a substantial mansion at St Cloud, on the outskirts of Paris. In the garden they had a lodge and this became Andrea's and Alice's family home for the rest of the 1920s.

When the exiles had arrived in Rome they were penniless (the British ambassador had to lend them money to pay for the train tickets to Paris), but, once they were able to make contact with their bankers, they were not without some means. They were not poor, they did not go hungry, but they were impoverished, and now, to an extent, dependent on the kindness of others. As well as Big George and his wealthy wife Marie Bonaparte, their principal benefactors were Andrea's younger brother, Christo, and his wealthy wife, Nancy Leeds, and Alice's younger brother, Dickie, and his wealthy wife, Edwina Ashley.[27] Edwina was especially generous, in all sorts of ways. When he was just a toddler, she took out an insurance policy for Philip. When she had her dresses made, she asked the dressmaker to include extra in the seams so that, in due course, the dresses could be let out and passed on to Alice and her girls.

[27] 'But I knaw'd a Quaäker feller as often 'as towd me this: "Doänt thou marry for munny, but goäwheer munny is!"' *Northern Farmer, New Style* by Alfred, Lord Tennyson (1809-92).

Prince Philip insists that what memories he has of life in Paris in the 1920s are good ones. By all accounts, he was a cheerful, active, inquisitive, friendly little boy. He did not lack companionship. He had doting sisters. Big George had children. Another of the brothers, Prince Nicholas, lived in St Cloud, with his young daughters. There were other cousins in the neighbourhood and family lunches in Big George's big house every Sunday. 'It was a normal family life, as far as I was concerned,' says Prince Philip.

For his parents, however, life was now very different from anything they had previously known. They dined with family and friends. They travelled quite extensively: to America and the South of France, on holiday, to Italy and England and Germany, to visit assorted royal relations. They kept themselves occupied, but they had no occupation. In Paris, Alice gave some of her time to a small Greek shop called Hellas in the Faubourg St Honoré, raising money to help Greek expatriates, and Andrea, who had for so long lived the life of a professional soldier, now spent the heart of most days sitting about in clubs and restaurants, meeting with other Greek exiles, talking politics, regretting the fate that had befallen Greece. He was, by all accounts, enormously charming and, under the circumstances, surprisingly cheerful. He had enthusiasms: he loved animals, he enjoyed painting, he read, he wrote. In his enforced retirement (he was just forty in 1922), his apologia, *Towards Disaster*, published in London in 1930, was his most significant undertaking, written by him in Greek and translated into English for him by Princess Alice. Alice admired her husband, as a soldier and as a man. She hoped and, sometimes, believed the family might return to Greece one day. Briefly, energetically, but to little effect, she worked on a plan to install Andrea as president of a reformed Hellenic republic.

But her principal preoccupation was not politics. It was religion. As a young woman, Alice had been inspired by the example of her Russian aunt, Ella. Alice thought a great deal about Ella, and the sisterhood she had founded, and the martyrdom she suffered. Alice read widely and deeply about comparative religion. She took a particular interest in Christian Science. Encouraged by her young brother-in-law, Christo, she dabbled in the occult. This was a period when interest in spiritualism was widespread. In Britain, Sir Arthur Conan Doyle was attending séances. In America, Harry Houdini was denouncing false mediums. In Paris, Princess Alice was turning over cards and receiving messages from the spirit world. Increasingly, those who met her found her a little strange.

Hugo Vickers, in his biography of Alice, suggests that an unfulfilled love affair may have tipped her over the edge. In 1925, the year she turned forty, when her oldest daughter was twenty and Prince Philip just three, she met a married man, an unidentified Englishman, and fell overwhelmingly in love with him. Nothing 'happened'. According to Hugo Vickers, 'Everything in Alice's background was strictly conventional. She herself had high moral principles and nothing in her character was flighty or flippant. She was no Edwina Mountbatten or Nada Milford Haven.[28] The fact of falling in love and resisting temptation almost certainly needed an outlet of some kind. Without even knowing why, Alice turned to religion as a safe outlet for these repressed feelings.'

I am not so sure. My instinct is that the hopeless passion – intense yet impossible, feverishly pursued but ultimately abandoned – and the religious fervour – complete with visions, voices and the acquisition of the gift of healing – had the same root cause: mania, the kind of mania associated with what we now call bipolar disorder or manic depression. I think the evidence is there.

Alice's behaviour at this time displays the classic symptoms of bipolar disorder: inappropriate elation, impulsiveness, extreme motor activity. When she embarked on her mission to secure for Andrea the presidency of Greece, she did so with manic energy. She pursued politicians and diplomats, she organised a clandestine meeting with representatives of the League of Nations, she dashed to London to lobby George V face-to-face at Buckingham Palace. Those she met, listened courteously and then let her down gently. 'Ladies get carried away,' said George V benignly to his private secretary, adding: 'I think it would be most unwise for Prince A. to go near Greece.'

When, in 1928, she decided to convert to the Greek Orthodox faith (not unreasonably: this was the Church into which her husband and her children had been baptised), the English, Anglican, members of her family took her decision comfortably in their stride. When she took to lying on the floor in order to enhance her mystic powers, when she

---

[28] In 1916, Dickie's older brother, Georgie, married Countess Nadejda (Nada) Torby, a daughter of Grand Duke Michael of Russia. Georgie was reputed to have a large and adventurous collection of pornography, and Nada was a noted lesbian, whose lovers included Gloria Vanderbilt Sr. When I put it to Nada's niece, Gina Wernher (now Lady Kennard), that Nada was 'a bit of a goer', she smiled and said, 'Yes, she had many sides to her, and she was a real rebel. There was no stopping her – in all sorts of ways.'

became convinced that her hands contained the gift of healing, when she announced that she was a saint and the bride of Christ, it was a different matter. The medical experts were called in. Alice was clearly not well. Sometimes she seemed quite happy, seraphically so: she would talk incessantly, laugh immoderately, declare herself to be in a state of ecstasy. At other times, she would be listless, seemingly exhausted, unable to do anything, unwilling to eat. She lost weight, she had headaches, she recognised that something was amiss.

Her gynaecologist, brought to Paris from Athens, concluded that her condition was not menopausal. Her sister-in-law, Marie Bonaparte, suggested she seek help from a fellow Freudian, Dr Ernst Simmel, at his clinic at Tegel, on the outskirts of Berlin. Simmel diagnosed Alice as 'schizophrenic paranoid'. He concluded that she was suffering from a 'neurotic-pre-psychotic libidinous condition'. Reading between the lines and stripping away the euphemism, it seems the psychoanalyst's view of her situation was that she was a woman who was hungry for sex and no longer getting it. This was disturbing the balance of her mind. Freud himself was consulted and proposed, as a palliative treatment, to help subdue her sexual appetite and so calm her nerves, 'an exposure of the gonads to X-rays, in order to accelerate the menopause'.

Alice was given the prescribed treatment. Whether or not she knew exactly what was being done to her is unclear, but, gradually, she began to put on weight and, for a while, to feel better in herself. She returned home, but, in truth, she was no better. She was preoccupied with sex and religion. She was obsessed by her relationship with Christ. Andrea could not cope.

In May 1930, with Andrea's agreement, Alice's mother, Victoria, took the decision that Alice should be interned in an asylum. Against her will, and under sedation, Alice was taken to the Bellevue Clinic at Kreuzlingen in Switzerland, the psychiatric sanatorium of Dr Ludwig Binswanger.

To all intents and purposes, Alice's marriage, and her family life, were now over. Things had not been comfortable for some while. There is a formal photograph taken of the family at St Cloud in 1928, at the time of Andrea and Alice's silver wedding anniversary. Everybody in the picture looks miserable. Andrea, seated, arms and legs folded, cigarette holder in hand, is gazing remotely into the middle distance. The two older daughters look almost haunted, the two younger ones, positively sullen. Oddly, Alice, and young Philip, age seven, in his sailor suit, holding his mother's hand, both staring solemnly at the camera, appear the most composed, the least ill-at-ease.

In 1928 Philip was still a pupil at his first school in Paris, The Elms, a pre-preparatory establishment run by an American couple, the MacJannets, and catering largely for the children of wealthy American businessmen and the multi-national offspring of the diplomatic corps.[29] Philip already spoke English, German and Greek. Now he perfected his French. (Typically, Prince Philip is wholly dismissive of this attainment: 'I could hardly fail to learn French during nearly ten years' residence in Paris,' he says.) If his parents' marriage was under strain and his home circumstances unusual, the effect on Philip appears to have been minimal. Every account of him at this time contributes to a picture of a perfectly straightforward little boy: lively, boisterous, adventurous, not especially academic (but by no means a dunce), self-confident, self-reliant, noticeably charming.

In 1929, when he was eight, he was sent to boarding school in England, to Cheam, in Surrey, England's oldest preparatory school, where his mother's younger brother, Georgie (the 2nd Marquess of Milford Haven), had once been a pupil, and where Georgie's eldest son, David, was a near-contemporary, and, though two years his senior, would become Philip's closest school friend and, eighteen years later, his best man. Cheam, founded at the turn of the seventeenth century, was a typical, traditional, English prep school of the period, complete with cold showers, wet runs, corporal punishment, compulsory chapel, compulsory games, compulsory Latin and compulsory Classical Greek. Philip appears to have thrived in this environment.

His arrival at Cheam, of course, coincided with a range of dramatic changes in his immediate family's situation. His mother virtually disappeared from his life for the rest of his childhood. For several years he received no word from her of any kind, not even a birthday card. His four sisters were all married within the space of eight months, between December 1930 and August 1931. His father gave up the house at St Cloud and moved, on his own, to live in a small flat in Monte Carlo. Prince Philip makes no complaint about any of this. 'It's simply what happened,' he says. 'The family broke up. My mother was ill, my sisters

---

[29] When I included this sentence in the account of Prince Philip's life prepared for his eightieth birthday, he wrote from Windsor Castle: 'The Elms catered largely for children of the Diplomatic Corps. I am sorry to upset your obsession with wealth!!' (Double exclamation marks are very much a feature of the Prince's writing style.)

were married, my father was in the South of France. I just had to get on with it. You do. One does.'

Alice was incarcerated in the Bellevue Clinic at Kreuzlingen for two and a half years. Her condition did not improve. There were times when she was 'high' – drafting loopy articles and working on a book of spiritual revelations – but, mostly, she was depressed, and, occasionally, she was suicidal. Philip visited her once, accompanying his grandmother. Andrea visited once, too. The environment at Kreuzlingen was not uncongenial (I get the impression of a country house hotel set in well-tended parkland) and the clinic's staff appear to have been kindly and intelligent people. There was no electric shock treatment, no automatic recourse to drugs, and straitjackets would be used rarely and only to restrain the most violent patients. Alice was offered care, kindness and attention. The hope seems to have been that rest would lead to recuperation. It didn't, and the princess felt imprisoned. She resented being detained against her will. In July 1932, jumping through a window, she managed to escape. Her freedom was short-lived. Within a matter of hours, she was apprehended at the local railway station and forcibly returned to the clinic.

Alice did not want to live with her own family (she was clear about that), but she did want to leave Kreuzlingen, and, eventually, later in 1932, she persuaded her mother that the time had come when she should be allowed 'freedom under surveillance'. For the next five years, Alice led a somewhat nomadic existence, travelling between Italy, Switzerland and Germany, living quietly in small hotels and in rented rooms. She sent Philip and her daughters the occasional message or birthday card. She did not see any of her children for five years. She lived among strangers. Gradually, she recovered her equilibrium.

Andrea, meanwhile, was living on the French Riviera.

In 2001, in the account of Prince Philip's life published to mark his eightieth birthday, I wrote that Andrea had left Paris in 1930 'and floated down to Monte Carlo'. Prince Philip wrote to me from Windsor Castle: 'I am not sure what you mean by "floated" down to Monte Carlo. He was in exile with no home and very little money. It was a lot cheaper than living in Paris. He had a very small flat there and spent a lot of time visiting his daughters.'

Prince Philip's loyalty to the memory of both his parents is impressive. He is not a gossip and, as a rule, especially for somebody with a reputation for irascibility, he is remarkably positive in his judgements of people. Occasionally, I have heard him make withering comments about members of his own family, but about his parents – who, in effect, left him without a settled home and family from the age of ten – I have only heard him speak with sympathy, respect and affection. Fine portraits of them both hang in his study. To this day he wears his father's signet ring.

I had used the word 'floated' because it seemed appropriate in the case of a tall, elegant, monocled prince-in-exile, who smoked and drank more than was good for him and had a reputation as something of a boulevardier. Andrea lived, variously, in a small flat, in hotel rooms and on board the smart yacht of a wealthy friend moored in Cannes harbour. From around 1930 up until the time of his death he had a lady-friend, the Comtesse Andrée de La Bigne, granddaughter of a mistress of Napoleon III. He was undoubtedly charming and enjoyed the company of women, but there is no evidence to suggest that he was a serial philanderer. He died at the Hotel Metropole in Monte Carlo on 3 December 1944. He was sixty-two.

Young Philip, in the school holidays, travelled, without complaint, between the homes of assorted relations: his grandmother at Kensington Palace, his English Uncle Georgie (Milford Haven) in Berkshire, his sisters and their new husbands in Germany.[30] He did see his parents together just once more, in late November 1937, as a consequence of a family tragedy. A Hesse-Darmstadt cousin was getting married in London and Alice's and Andrea's middle child, Cécile, and her husband and their two boys (aged six and four), were all killed on their way to the wedding, when the aeroplane taking them from Darmstadt to England crashed in heavy fog outside Ostend. Alice travelled to Darmstadt from Berlin for the family funeral. Andrea brought Philip from London.[31] The death of their daughter and two of their grandchildren was a shocking event: Alice and Andrea were

---

[30] Prince Philip writes from Windsor Castle: 'Why "without complaint"? What did I have to complain about? Why "assorted" relations? They were my sisters and their in-laws.' Margarita married Prince Gottfried of Hohenlohe-Langenburg; Theodora married Berthold, Margrave of Baden; Cécile married George Donatus, Hereditary Grand Duke of Hesse; and Sophie married, first, Prince Christoph of Hesse, and, later, Prince George of Hanover.

[31] At the funeral, Alice's brother Dickie (whom she had not seen since 1929) represented George VI and Queen Elizabeth. Both Kaiser Wilhelm (Queen Victoria's grandson, who lived until 1941) and the Third Reich were represented. Hermann Goering came in person.

united in grief. Alice, in better health than she had been for several years, was ready to consider the possibility of sharing a life with her husband again, but for Andrea it was too late: he had moved on.

From Prince Philip's early childhood, I have three reliable anecdotes to offer, each illustrating a different aspect of his character: his generosity, his get-up-and-go, his pig-headedness. The first illustrates his instinctive kindness – one of his most attractive and least recognised characteristics. The story dates from the mid-1920s, when Philip was five or six, and on a family holiday, playing on the beach at Berck Plage, the seaside resort in the Pas-de-Calais. A well-meaning visitor arrives on the beach one day with toys which he gives out to each of the children in the party – except for one little girl, who is disabled and whose disability, the visitor assumes, will prevent her from being able to play. Immediately, Philip goes into the house and collects his assorted toys and treasures and presents them to the little girl.

The second story – again set at Berck Plage – illustrates his initiative. Inspired by the nomadic salesmen – usually from North Africa – who plied their exotic wares along the beach, Philip collected a couple of oriental rugs from the house and set himself up on the beach in direct competition.

The third story demonstrates his stubborn streak. It was told to me by Patricia Mountbatten, his first cousin, Dickie Mountbatten's elder daughter, and dates from a few years later. 'I suppose Philip was about twelve and I was about nine,' she remembers. 'Our mutual grandmother took a great interest in Philip. She played an enormous part in his upbringing. But they were both strong-willed individuals and sometimes they argued – and sometimes Philip was really quite rude. I remember vividly the time when they had an argument about something and our grandmother said, "Philip, go up to your room." And he wouldn't. He just hung about in the hall. He would *not* go up to his room. Eventually, our grandmother came out into the hall and actually had to chase him up the stairs.'

When in England as a boy, and not staying either with his grandmother, Victoria Milford Haven, or her son, Georgie, Philip spent part of his holidays with the Wernher family, either at Thorpe Lubenham, near Market Harborough, or at their splendid Bedfordshire mansion, Luton Hoo. In 1916, Georgie married Countess Nadejda (Nada) Torby, daughter of Grand Duke Michael of Russia and his wife, Countess Torby (an heiress from the Caucasus), and great-granddaughter of Tsar Nicholas I. In 1917, Nada's older sister

Anastasia, known as Zia, married Harold Wernher,[32] for a while considered the richest catch in England. The Wernhers had three children and their daughter Gina, born in 1919, still has vivid memories of Prince Philip as a little boy. 'I suppose I was about eight and he was about six when I first met him,' she told me. 'He was a very obstreperous, rough little boy. Very strong, very active. He had a great sense of humour. We had a lot of fun. There were four of us who played together all the time: Philip, Philip's cousin, David Milford Haven (he was my cousin, too, of course), me (I was known as 'George') and my younger brother, Alex, who was exactly Philip's age and who was killed in the war, in 1942, aged twenty-one. We called ourselves "The Four Musketeers".'

I asked Gina Wernher – now Lady Kennard[33] – whether she thought Prince Philip was happy as a boy. 'As a little boy, he was very happy,' she said. 'Very jolly, very lively. As he grew older, he became more thoughtful, more introspective. He never saw his parents, you know. Never. And he minded that. He told me so. He was perfectly happy at boarding school, but he said to me – I remember this clearly – "Everybody has a family to go back to. I don't." He loved his sisters very much and when Cécile was killed in that air crash, in 1937, it affected him deeply. He was very quiet. He didn't talk about it much, but he showed me a little bit of wood from the aeroplane. It was just a small piece, but it meant a lot to him.'

In 1933, aged twelve, Prince Philip first came under the influence of the German educationist Kurt Hahn. Hahn had been secretary and

---

[32] Wernher, who inherited a mining fortune in South Africa (as well as Luton Hoo), was an industrialist of distinction, chairman of Plessey, chairman of British Telephones, chairman of Associated Theatre Properties (London), and, notably, chairman of Electrolux (1926–63). He inherited the baronetcy bestowed on his father and acquired numerous distinctions in his own right: KCVO, GCVO, TD, DL, as well as foreign honours, including the Legion of Merit degree of Officer in the US army and knighthoods in the Swedish Order of the Vasa (1930) and the Swedish Order of the Pole Star (1959).

[33] Georgina Wernher (born 1919) was married first, in 1944, to Lt Col. Harold 'Bunnie' Phillips (1909–80), sometime lover, I believe, of Edwina Mountbatten, and, much later, as his fourth wife, to Sir George 'Loopy' Kennard, who commanded the 4th Queen's Own Hussars and whose autobiography, *Loopy*, published 1990, is the most original and entertaining military memoir I know. I would like to persuade Lady Kennard to write her own book. She has known some extraordinary people. Two of her daughters are now the Duchess of Abercorn and the Duchess of Westminster. Her son, Nicholas Phillips, committed suicide at Luton Hoo on 28 February 1991.

friend to Prince Max of Baden, former Chancellor of the German Empire, whose son Berthold had married Philip's sister, Theodora, in 1931. A decade or so before that, Hahn and Max of Baden had founded a pioneering school together, based at the Baden family home, Schloss Salem, on the shores of Lake Constance, and designed as much to build the characters of its students as to educate them. Prince Max said of the school: 'I am proud of the fact that there is nothing original here. We have cribbed from everywhere, from the public schools, from Goethe, from Plato, from the Boy Scouts.'

Philip left Cheam and came to Salem. Prince Philip explained to me, 'The suggestion came from my sister and brother-in-law who owned the school: it had the great advantage of saving school fees.' Philip remained at the school for two terms. He might have stayed longer had it not been for Hitler's rise to power (he became Chancellor that year) and the growing and malevolent influence of the Nazi Party. Under the circumstances, Philip's family felt he should return to school in Britain. 'It was certainly a great relief to me,' he says. At Salem, Philip could not take the 'Heil Hitler' salute at all seriously: at Cheam, exactly the same arm gesture was used to indicate to a master that a boy wanted permission to go to the lavatory. (Prince Philip asks: 'Do you really want to keep the last sentence?' 'Yes' is the answer, because it illustrates the Prince's contempt for the Nazi Party even at an early age. When a Jewish fellow pupil had his head shaved by anti-Semites, Philip gave the boy his Cheam school cap to hide the indignity. He has nothing but scorn for the Nazis, yet, to this day, there are those who persist in portraying him as a racist. I have come across two websites that label him, uncompromisingly, as a crypto-Nazi.)

Kurt Hahn himself – not only Jewish, but also an outspoken critic of Hitler – was arrested by the Nazis in March 1933. He was later released and fled to Britain, ending up in Scotland, in Morayshire, where he founded another school, at Gordonstoun House, in a location close to the sea and mountains, where the wind and weather were appropriate to his challenging educational philosophy. Hahn believed that young people were 'surrounded by a sick civilisation . . . in danger of being affected by a fivefold decay: the decay of fitness, the decay of initiative and enterprise, the decay of care and skill, the decay of self-discipline, the decay of compassion'.

At Gordonstoun – where Prince Philip arrived in the autumn of 1934 – the regime was designed to tackle this decay and, years later, of course, Hahn's radical philosophy and methods would play their part in shaping two of the national and international ventures with which Prince Philip has been most closely involved: the Outward Bound Trust and the Duke of Edinburgh's Award Scheme. How would Philip describe Hahn? 'Eccentric perhaps, innovator certainly, great beyond doubt.'

Hahn's chief eccentricity lay in his appearance. As a young man, he had brain surgery which involved a silver plate being implanted in his skull. As a result of the operation, he had an aversion to light, wore a huge black cape, a broad-rimmed black hat and, when travelling by car, covered his face with a dark cloth. According to Philip, 'There was an air about Hahn which commanded instant wariness and respect. Apart from that, his famous mannerisms – the stooping gait, the ball handkerchief in the mouth, the large-brimmed hat and the flashing quizzical eye – all helped to signal the presence of an exceptional being.'

Hahn was an intellectual. He had read Greats at Oxford. He had studied at the universities of Berlin, Heidelberg, Freiburg and Göttingen. He believed in books. He also believed in the power of 'the great outdoors'. He said, 'My best schoolmaster is the Moray Firth.' As a teenager, Philip learnt to sail in the chilly, challenging waters of the Moray Firth. He says: 'I was wet, cold, miserable, probably sick, and often scared stiff, but I would not have missed the experience for any-thing. In any case the discomfort was far outweighed by the moments of intense happiness and excitement. Poets and authors down the centuries have tried to describe those moments but their descriptions, however brilliant, will never compare with one's own experience.'

Prince Philip's experience of Gordonstoun would inform the rest of his life. In 1938, when he left the school – as 'Guardian', or head boy – Hahn gave him a glowing final report: 'Prince Philip is universally trusted, liked and respected. He has the greatest sense of service of all the boys in the school.' Hahn recognised his 'intelligence and spirit', a touch of 'recklessness' and a 'determination not to exert himself more than was necessary to avoid trouble'. He was 'often naughty, never nasty'.

Philip was not especially academic and, at Gordonstoun, while he played Donalbain in the school production of *Macbeth*, his enthusiasms were, on the whole, more sporting than artistic. (At this point, he says to me, very reasonably, 'I don't see the connection between not being academic and taking part in a school play. I was just a very bad actor. I did at least pass the Civil Service Exams to enter the Navy!!')

Having passed the necessary exams, on 1 May 1939, six weeks short of his eighteenth birthday, Prince Philip of Greece joined the Royal Naval College at Dartmouth and set himself on course for a career in the Royal Navy. He says today that, left entirely to his own devices, 'I'd have gone into the Air Force without a doubt.' Flying has been one of the great unremarked-on passions of his life. He made his first flight, from White Waltham in Berkshire, in a Chipmunk, on 12 November 1952; his last, in a BAe 146, flying from Carlisle to Islay, on 11 August 1997. Over forty-five years, Prince Philip clocked up a total of 5,986 hours of flying in fifty-nine types of aircraft, including nine helicopters. (An RAF pilot might only clock up 8,000 hours in a full career.)

That Philip was persuaded to opt for the Navy rather than the Air Force in 1938 is hardly surprising. As he points out, there was some-thing of a family tradition: 'I was following my grandfather [Louis of Battenberg] and two uncles [Georgie Milford Haven and Dickie Mountbatten]. My Danish grandfather had been in the Danish Navy and my uncle George (of Greece) served in the Greek Navy.'

Who were the key influences on the young Prince Philip? Kurt Hahn was one, certainly. As were Philip's uncle, Georgie Milford Haven, and the industrialist Harold Wernher, with whose families Philip spent part of several of his holidays. He also spent holidays with his sisters and their husbands. He says, 'I saw more of my third sister's husband (George Donatus of Hesse) as I usually spent most of my holidays with them in Darmstadt or at Wolfsgarten' – their idyllic country house: an old hunting lodge built around a courtyard in a woodland setting, apparently remote, but, in fact, not far from Frankfurt. Working out exactly where Philip should go for his holidays was often a challenge – not because he was not welcome wherever he went, but because his father, although largely absent, liked to be involved in the plans relating to his son. For example, in late July 1934, Victoria was with Philip at Wolfsgarten, but, as she explained in a letter to her son, Georgie, in England, she was not quite sure what to do with her grandson next:

Philip may go there (Hemmelmark) with us & back to England with me via Hamburg & Southampton but we can settle nothing about his movements until having discussed them with Andrea, who after a delay of 4 weeks turns up this evening, we suppose en route for a cure in Marienbad. I hope it is not too inconvenient to leave you without definite news of Philip's movements, but it has been unavoidable.

Andrea was interested in his son, and proud of his son, but not very hands-on – or reliable – when it came to the care of his son.

If Wordsworth is right and the child is father of the man, what is the effect Prince Philip's extraordinary childhood is likely to have had on him? The man himself is not one for this kind of speculation. But I am. Or, at least, I would be intrigued to know what a practising psychoanalyst like his aunt Marie Bonaparte – his uncle Big George's wife – could tell us about the impact of Philip's upbringing on his behaviour.

Marie Bonaparte (1882–1962) is a fascinating figure. Born at St Cloud, a Catholic, brought up in Paris, she married Prince George of Greece in 1907. Their relationship was not conventional.[34] She was wealthy, glamorous, passionate, intelligent, restless. Her lovers included Aristide Briand, famously depicted by Toulouse-Lautrec and ten times prime minister of France. Her enthusiasms included sex, her pet chow-chows and Dr Sigmund Freud. In 1925 she entered analysis with Freud in Vienna and trained as a psychoanalyst. She went on to become a pivotal figure in the French Psychoanalytical Society and the international psychoanalytical community. She was fascinated by criminal psychopathology and published a gripping account of a woman who had murdered her pregnant daughter-in-law, *Le Cas de Madame Lefebvre*, as well as an acclaimed study of Edgar Allen Poe, whom she termed 'one of the darkest minds there has ever been', and the first full study of female sexuality, *La Sexualité Feminine*. She experimented with early forms of genital surgery and twice underwent an unusual procedure to alter the position of her clitoris to bring it closer to the point of penile contact. She was sympathetic to the view of Freud's mentor, Jean-Martin Charcot, that when looking for the root cause of nervous disorders, '*c'est toujours la chose génitale, toujours, toujours*'. It was to her that Freud posed his celebrated question, 'What does a woman want?'

Marie Bonaparte became one of Freud's closest friends. She lavished gifts on him. In the aftermath of the Nazi *Anschluss*, she used her connections and her considerable financial resources to help secure his – and his family's – safe passage from Vienna to London in 1938. According to Freud's son Martin, 'She had most of father's chief characteristics – his courage, his sincerity, his essential goodness and

---

[34] They had two children, Peter and Eugénie, born in 1908 and 1910, but when Prince George died in 1957, a few months before their golden wedding anniversary, Marie said: 'I bent over his cold forehead and kissed it. Not his lips, which he had always refused me.'

kindliness and his inflexible devotion to scientific truth.' She became a close friend, too, of Freud's daughter, Anna Freud, the pioneer of child psychoanalysis, and maintained a lifelong affectionate interest in her husband's nephew, Prince Philip. What would Marie Bonaparte and the classic Freudians have made of Philip's childhood?

In search of an authoritative answer I travelled to 20 Maresfield Gardens in Hampstead – the Freud family's London home, now the home of the Freud Museum – to meet Brett Kahr, noted Freudian psychologist, Winnicott Clinic Senior Research Fellow in Psycho-therapy, and a student of the life and work of Marie Bonaparte. He said at once, 'I am not allowed to talk about a person I have never met, but if you want to know what Princess Marie Bonaparte might have made of Prince Philip's childhood history I am happy to speculate.' Where to begin? 'I think Marie would have begun right at the beginning – with Philip's mother and his birth. Prince Philip was born into a household of women. There was his mother, and his nanny, and probably a wet nurse, and certainly a lady-in-waiting, and, most significantly, four older sisters. His father was away at the wars. Philip was the only boy, literally a beautiful blue-eyed boy, born into a household of devoted, doting women. And he is the fifth child, the longed-for son. After four girls – whose ages range from sixteen to seven when Philip is born – here is a boy, and what do boys have that girls do not have? A penis. Into this household of women and girls comes this perfect boy. It is very exciting. There is within the household – in the phrase of Phyllis Greenacre, a Freudian from the 1950s – "penis awe". It is unspoken, but it is there. And the admiration and devotion of these women, especially the four older sisters, will have given Philip, as he grew up, what might be termed a certain "phallic swagger", a sense of self-assurance and self-confidence, a certain cockiness.'

Will there have been disadvantages to all this feminine attention? 'Possibly,' says Brett Kahr – still, of course in the guise of Marie Bonaparte. 'Children with multiple carers sometimes struggle with depression. And being given lots of different affection from different people – nannies, nurses, sisters, aunts, grandmothers – can leave a child confused as to who is his primary attachment figure. Children with multiple carers, however loving, become sexually promiscuous because they don't have a model of falling in love with just one person.

'In Prince Philip's case there is nothing to suggest that Princess Alice was not devoted to her son, but she was a princess who would have expected to share the child-rearing with nannies and, from about the time Philip was nine or ten, she virtually disappeared from his life. No child is immune from a mother disappearing. And, in Philip's case, his father virtually disappeared, too. A history of broken parental attachments is one of the keys to depression.

'There is some evidence that Prince Andrea was depressed after his departure from Greece. It would hardly be surprising. He was forced into exile and had to give up a career he loved. Unemployment and enforced idleness can lead to depression. The family moves to Paris. The father is depressed and leaves home. The mother suffers a nervous breakdown and is sent to a sanatorium. How does the child Philip feel about this? Children are self-referential. Children are grandiose and think the world revolves around them. A child can have omnipotent infantile fantasies. Prince Philip was just a year old when his family were forced into exile. The military debacle that triggered Prince Andrea's downfall coincided precisely with Philip's birth. One wonders whether, subconsciously, Philip saw himself as responsible for the fate that befell his parents?'

I point out to Brett Kahr that Philip himself has never complained about any aspect of his childhood. 'It's simply what happened' is what Prince Philip says today, in his characteristic matter-of-fact way. 'The family broke up. My mother was ill, my sisters were married, my father was in the South of France. I just had to get on with it. You do. One does.' Brett Kahr nods. 'Yes, his mother was ill and in a clinic in Switzerland; his father was depressed and on a boat in the south of France; his sisters were married and living in Germany; and Philip was away at school in England and Scotland. From the age of ten he saw his parents only rarely. He saw his sisters in the school holidays, but seeing them and their husbands became increasingly difficult with the rise of Nazi Germany through the 1930s. And in 1937, his sister Cécile and her husband – who, apparently, is his favourite brother-in-law – they are the sister and brother-in-law he sees most during his holidays – these two key figures in his world, and their children, are all killed in an aeroplane accident. And in 1938, what happens? Georgie Milford Haven, his favourite English uncle and his guardian, dies of cancer of the bone marrow. Philip is not yet seventeen. By any standards, Philip has known a lot of loss in his young life and one way people deal with loss is with stoicism. To take on board the full throttle of what has happened to you is too painful, so you use your defence mechanisms well. You rationalise your experience. You don't dwell on it. You don't discuss it. Stoically, you soldier on.'

People who knew Prince Andrea in the 1930s have described him alternately as 'melancholy' and 'as funny as all-get-out'. 'There is a touch of manic depression in most of us,' says Brett Kahr. I think there is little doubt that Princess Alice, in the late 1920s and early 1930s, suffered from quite severe bipolar disorder. Princess Marie Bonaparte took a personal and practical interest in Alice's condition. She kept in touch with Prince Philip through the years as well. Philip can be urbane and engaging one day and sullen and crabby the next. How does Brett Kahr believe that Marie would have characterised the mature Prince Philip's occasional mood swings? 'She would have believed that everything springs from our childhood experience. Philip was born into a household of adoring women – that's indisputable. Prince Philip suffered from the trauma of parental loss – that's indisputable, too. Marie Bonaparte would not have been surprised, therefore, to find in the adult Philip a man who could, by turns, be charming and swaggering, and then dour, sour-faced, proto-serious.'

Before leaving Brett Kahr and the spirit of Marie Bonaparte (and the actual ashes of Sigmund Freud, now resting at Maresfield Gardens in an ancient urn given to Freud by the princess), I thought I would risk one final question: 'Is a man with phallic swagger prone to promiscuity?'

Brett Kahr's answer surprised me. 'Not necessarily. He will be confident with women because he is confident in himself. Phallic swagger might help if you were planning to woo and wed the next Queen of England – the most sought-after, least attainable girl in the world – but it would not of itself make you a serial philanderer. I know nothing of Prince Philip's private life, but I've heard the stories. He likes the company of attractive, younger women, of his own class and kind. That much we know. I wonder if these women are his attempt to replicate the family of sisters who adored him so? Could he simply be looking for playful friendships? That is possible. Or could he be looking for something more? That is also possible. Prince Andrea spent much of the 1930s in the South of France with his mistress. If Prince Philip had knowledge of his father's marital infidelity during his own teenage psycho-sexual development, that might have been a model for him and had an effect on his own behaviour later in life. Or not. Who knows? Perhaps you do?'

LILIBET

Chapter Three

'All things bright and beautiful, / All creatures great and small,
All things wise and wonderful, / The Lord God made them all.
. . . The rich man in his castle, / The poor man at his gate,
God made them high or lowly, / And ordered their estate.'

Mrs C. F. Alexander (1818–95)

Queen Victoria's father was Edward, Duke of Kent, fourth of the six sons of George III, 'Mad King George'. Edward was the baldest member of the family. The playwright Richard Brinsley Sheridan, liked to say this was because grass does not grow upon deserts. Edward responded to the sally rather well. 'If Sheridan means that I haven't genius,' he said, 'I can tell him that such a gift would have been of small value to a Prince, whose business it is to keep quiet. I am luckier in having, like my country, a sound constitution.'

In fact, Edward had a poor constitution and succumbed to a fever in the cruel winter of 1819, and died on 23 January 1820, when his baby daughter, Victoria, his only child, was barely eight months old. Before the madness took hold of him, George III led a calm and continent domestic life, married to Queen Charlotte, one-time Princess Sophia Charlotte of Mecklenburg-Strelitz. George's sons did not follow their father's example. Extravagance, self-indulgence, promiscuity and adultery characterised their personal lives.

Edward had abandoned his French mistress to marry a German princess in the hope of producing an heir. As a young widow with two small children, Princess Victoria of Saxe-Coburg[35] was, recognisably, a

[35] Her first husband was the Prince of Leiningen, by whom she had two children, Charles and Feodore. Her brothers included Prince Leopold, later King of the Belgians, and Prince Ernst, Duke of Saxe-Coburg, father of Prince Albert, destined to become her daughter Victoria's beloved Prince Consort.

sound breeder. When she married Edward and became Duchess of Kent, she spoke not a word of English, but she produced a vigorous child for him in baby Victoria.

Little Victoria – she never reached five feet in height – was blessed with both a sound constitution and a certain genius. She lived more than eighty-one years, from 24 May 1819 to 22 January 1901. She came to the throne aged eighteen and reigned longer than any other English monarch. She gave her name to a century, and its achievements and constraints, its values and aspirations, and was Britain's first and only Queen-Empress. She was small and round (at nineteen, she weighed 125 pounds), but she cast a long shadow. Whenever Queen Elizabeth II and Prince Philip appear on the balcony of Buckingham Palace they look out over the Victoria Memorial. The Queen has much in common with her great-great-grandmother, not least her longevity, sense of duty, acceptance of destiny, and sometimes complicated relationship with her eldest son. Prince Philip, while an admirer of the Prince Consort, does not like to take the comparison very far. 'Queen Victoria was an executive monarch,' he said to me, somewhat brusquely, when I raised the subject. 'Prince Albert was the Queen's secretary. He could do things. It's very different now.'

Victoria adored her husband and it is clear from her journal that, at least when she was young, her approach to the physical aspects of love was anything but 'Victorian':

> I NEVER NEVER spent such an evening!!![36] My DEAREST DEAREST DEAR Albert sat on a footstool by my side, & his excessive love & affection gave me feelings of heavenly love & happiness, I never could have *hoped* to have felt before! He clasped me in his arms, and we kissed each other again and again! His beauty, his sweetness and gentleness – really how can I ever be thankful enough to have such a *Husband*!

Despite the discomforts and indignities of childbirth ('I think . . . of our being like a cow or a dog at such moments,' she said), she bore nine children. The first was born on 21 November 1840, nine months and eleven days after her wedding. 'Oh, Madam,' said her physician, Dr Locock[37], 'it is a Princess.' 'Never mind,' answered the Queen feebly,

---

[36] A fondness for multiple exclamation marks appears to be a family characteristic!

[37] Twenty-five years ago, a young woman named Victoria Locock came to my house to give my wife a piano lesson. I said to her, 'It's amazing: you look exactly like Princess

'the next will be a Prince.' It was. Eleven and a half months after the birth of Princess Victoria, known first as Pussy, then as Vicky, on 9 November 1841, Bertie, the Prince of Wales, the future King Edward VII, was born.

Victoria's reign was long and, overall, hugely successful. When Albert died, on 14 December 1861, the Queen was only forty-two. Utterly bereft, she closeted herself at Windsor Castle, and her sustained seclusion – at Windsor, at Balmoral, at Osborne House – did not endear her to the press or public. She was temperamental, emotional, volatile: there were times when her family, and her ministers, feared for her sanity. She was also able, intelligent and perceptive, though susceptible to flattery – 'Gladstone treats the Queen like a public department,' said Benjamin Disraeli, 'I treat her like a woman'; of course, the Queen preferred Disraeli – and wilful to the point of obstinacy. She would not give up her devoted, drunken, highland servant, John Brown, however much her family wanted her to do so. She would not abandon her Indian secretary, Abdul Karim, 'the Munshi', however anxious the Indian Office and others were at his constant presence by her side. Victoria, especially as she grew older, was instinctively conservative, but neither a snob nor, in any way, racially prejudiced.

As Queen, she had dignity, determination and unique dynastic skills. She came to be known as 'the grandmother of Europe' with good reason. Vicky married a future German emperor. Bertie married the Danish princess Alexandra, whose brother became King of Greece and whose sister was Empress of Russia. It was Queen Victoria's third child, Alice, who married the Grand Duke of Hesse and launched the line that produced, among others, the last Tsarina and Prince Philip. Her fourth child, Alfred, also married into the Russian royal family and, in

Anne.' She said, 'I know.' The piano teacher turned out to be a descendant of Henry Locock, born in December 1867 and brought up as the son of Sir Charles Locock, gynaecologist or 'First Physician Accoucher' to Queen Victoria, but long rumoured within the family to be the illegitimate son of Queen Victoria's sixth child, Princess Louise (1848–1949). In 1870, Louise, said to be something of a 'goer', married the Marquess of Lorne (heir to the dukedom of Argyll), often said to be a promiscuous homosexual – although Elizabeth Longford (Princess Louise's biographer) claimed there was 'no evidence whatever' for this 'in Lorne's family archives or traditions'. From 1880, Louise and her husband lived separate lives and Louise was the only one of Queen Victoria's children who apparently had no issue. The Locock family is now hoping to exhume the body of Henry Locock (who died in Canada in 1907, after falling from a train) for DNA testing.

time, his daughter became Queen of Romania. After Helena and Louise came two more sons: Arthur, Duke of Connaught, whose daughter became Crown Princess of Sweden, and Leopold, Duke of Albany. Her youngest, Beatrice, married Henry of Battenberg, and became the mother of the Queen of Spain.

As a mother, grandmother and great-grandmother, Victoria was interested and involved, concerned and conscientious. There is a lovely photograph of her, taken in April 1886, with her daughter Princess Beatrice, her granddaughter Princess Victoria of Battenberg, and her great-granddaughter, Princess Alice (Prince Philip's mother), aged one. They all look contented. The Queen is smiling happily.

When Victoria was not amused[38] it was all too often because of Bertie. Victoria and Albert viewed the young Prince of Wales as a problem child. He was not academic; he was not athletic; he did not inherit his father's appetite for work. Instead, he seemed to have inherited his assorted, dissolute, great-uncles' appetites for good food, fine wines, gaming and loose women. In 1861, when he was still nineteen and a young officer stationed with his regiment in Ireland, a compliant young actress, Nellie Clifton, was slipped between his sheets. Prince Albert heard all about it and was appalled. What if the liaison were to result in a child? In his anguish, the Prince Consort wrote to the Prince of Wales:

> If you were to try and deny it, she can drag you into a Court of Law to force you to own it & there with you in the witness box, she will be able to give before a greedy Multitude disgusting details of your profligacy for the sake of convincing the Jury, yourself crossexamined by a railing indecent attorney and hooted and yelled at by a Lawless Mob!! Horrible prospect, which this person has in her power, any day to realise! And to break your poor parents' hearts!

Albert died only a few weeks later, possibly of typhoid, possibly of

---

[38] There is no record of Queen Victoria ever saying 'We are not amused.' On the contrary, her journals frequently include the phrase, 'I was very much amused.' Elizabeth Longford, one of Victoria's best biographers, told me there are 'many recorded instances' of the Queen laughing out loud, and heartily, often at stories or incidents that other Victorians might have considered quite *risqué*. Like Elizabeth II, Victoria enjoyed the absurd. She regularly repeated the story of the time her mother, the Duchess of Kent, had emerged from the dining room carrying a fork, mistaking it for her fan.

cancer. In the extremis of her grief, Victoria attributed her husband's death to the distress he had been caused by their son. 'Oh! that boy,' she said, despairingly, 'much as I pity him I never can or shall look at him without a shudder . . .'

At five foot seven inches, Bertie was a little taller than his mother, and rounder. At his heaviest he weighed more than sixteen stone – 224 pounds. His nickname was 'Tum-Tum'. He enjoyed five substantial meals a day – breakfast, luncheon, afternoon tea, dinner, supper – and smoked as many as twenty cigarettes and a dozen fat cigars between daybreak and sunset. He coughed and he wheezed, but he safeguarded his own health by requiring others not to smoke while he was doing so. Despite his weight and his wheezing, throughout his adult life he enjoyed a series of mistresses: occasionally actresses, like the young Nellie Clifton and the celebrated Lillie Langtry, more often the willing wives of his complaisant aristocratic and racing friends.

On 10 March 1863, Bertie, aged twenty-one, married Princess Alexandra of Denmark. She was just nineteen, beautiful, tall, sweet-tempered, good-natured, a little vacant, chronically unpunctual, wonderfully tolerant. She endured her husband's selfishness, self-indulgence and promiscuity for almost half a century. When he was dying in the late spring of 1910, she allowed Alice Keppel, his last and most enduring mistress, to come to his bedside. Queen and mistress shook hands and Alix, with extraordinary generosity, said to Alice, 'I am sure you always had a good influence over him.'

She probably did. In many ways, Bertie was a spoilt child and Mrs Keppel ('My little Mrs George'[39] as he called her) could coax and tease him out of his sulks and ill-humour. The present Prince of Wales (Bertie's great-great-grandson) is also reported to have occasional sulking moments and bouts of ill-humour, and his mistress-turned wife, Mrs Camilla Parker Bowles (the great-granddaughter of Mrs Keppel, as chance would have it) is said to have a similarly useful influence over him.

Prince Charles's first wife, Diana Spencer, was, to an extent,

[39] George Keppel is an intriguing figure, tall, elegant, mustachioed, with more than a touch of the music hall dandy about him. Encouraging his wife to consort with the King enabled him to enjoy a lifestyle he might not otherwise have been able to afford – and pleasuring royalty was, and is, a Keppel family tradition. William III – William of Orange – was bisexual and brought sixteen-year-old Arnold Joost van Keppel with him from Holland to England as his catamite in 1688. In due course he made him Earl of Albemarle.

consoled by the affection in which she was held by the public at large and by her strong and loving relationship with her own children. The same was true of Princess Alexandra. She was strikingly beautiful, much admired, and genuinely loved by the people. She did good works. With the Alexandra Rose Day, she introduced a new form of charitable fundraising to Britain. Despite increasing deafness[40] and a slight limp, triggered by rheumatic fever when she was twenty-two, she was easy with strangers and especially comfortable with children.

Her own children were a special joy to her. She had six, the youngest of whom, a boy, died when only a few hours old. Her daughters called her 'darling Motherdear' and were so devoted that Bertie feared they might never leave the nest. In the event, the eldest, Princess Louise, the Princess Royal, married the Duke of Fife, and the youngest, Princess Maud, married Prince Charles of Denmark, later to become King Haakon VII of Norway. Only the middle girl, another Princess Victoria, remained a spinster all her life.

As seems to be the custom with the British Royal Family, it was the eldest son who proved to be the problem child. Prince Albert Victor, the Duke of Clarence, known in the family as Eddy, was born prematurely at the start of 1864 and died prematurely in the spring of 1892. He was neither bright nor ambitious and devoted most of his short life to the pleasures of the boudoir and the polo field. When the police raided a male brothel in Cleveland Street in central London they discovered a clutch of the Prince of Wales' friends and associates among the regular clientele and learnt that Bertie's eldest boy, the young Duke of Clarence, had not long before visited the establishment in the (forlorn) hope of seeing a display of naked women. Eddy was notorious and his dissolute behaviour fuelled the rumours that he was 'Jack the Ripper', the man who murdered and mutilated a number of prostitutes in the Aldgate and Whitechapel districts of London in 1888.

Just as Albert and Victoria had hoped that marriage would magically transform their eldest son ('marry or burn' was the phrase they used), so Bertie and Alix hoped that matrimony would make a man of the wretched Eddy. Finding a bride for this particular prince was not easy.

---

[40] She may have exploited her deafness on occasion. When her sister-in-law Vicky's son, Wilhelm, the German Kaiser, held forth at length, she responded: 'Willy dear . . . I am afraid I have not heard a single word you were saying.' And, a hundred years on, in royal circles, they still tell the story of the equerry who asked her, 'Did you know, Ma'am, that His Majesty has a new car?' to which she replied, 'A new cow?' 'No, Ma'am, a new *car.*' 'Yes, yes, I hear you. I understand the old one has calved.'

First, he rejected an anyway reluctant Princess Margaret of Germany; next, he was turned down by Alix of Hesse (the one who went on to become the luckless last Tsarina of Russia); then, he fell passionately in love with Princess Hélène d'Orléans, who was a Catholic as well as French, and consequently (despite her readiness to become a Protestant) wholly *hors de concours*.

In due course, he was persuaded to propose to Princess Victoria Mary of Teck, known to all as May, who was three years his junior and not nearly so 'royal', but was willing, able, available and sound. Queen Victoria invited her to Balmoral and gave a grandmotherly seal of approval, judging May to be 'a superior girl – quiet and reserved *till* you know her well – . . . & so sensible and unfrivolous'.[41]

Princess May agreed to marry Prince Eddy, but she was spared what would certainly have been an ordeal. In the run-up to the wedding, while shooting at Sandringham in the winter of 1891, Eddy was taken ill. He died of pneumonia on 14 January 1892. In his final fever, as May and his mother took turns to keep watch, repeatedly he called out, 'Hélène, Hélène.' His fiancée was understandably disconcerted. His mother was understandably bereft. For years, in her bedroom, Alix kept the hat her hapless son had been wearing on his final shoot, and she preserved his quarters as they had been on the day he died: his tooth-paste tube as he had left it, a fresh cake of soap ready by the washbasin. Her second son, George, wrote to her: 'Gladly would I have given my life for his, as I put no value on mine . . . Such a tragedy has never before occurred in the annals of our family.'

In truth, tragedy (or, at least, melodrama tinged with bathetic comedy) was probably averted by Eddy's death. He was not good-husband or good-monarch material. Prince George turned out to be both. Princess May, having received the old Queen's seal of approval, was too good a catch to let slip, and, within eighteen months, May, having been engaged to one heir apparent, had married the next. It was

---

[41] This was not how anybody would have described May's parents. Her mother, Princess Mary Adelaide, who was a granddaughter of George III, was garrulous, extravagant and greedy: she was reckoned to be at least the weight of Bertie, Prince of Wales. Her father, Franz, Duke of Teck, came from a family that had married beneath itself but resolutely refused to recognise the fact. Franz was argumentative, temperamental and sensitive about his status. The parents, as vulgar spendthrifts, embarrassed their daughter, who was a decent, discreet, dignified sort, fair-haired, blue-eyed, clear-skinned, handsome rather than beautiful, with a look we would now recognise in her great-granddaughter, Princess Anne.

a fortunate match. George later wrote to his wife: 'People only said I married you out of pity and sympathy; that shows how little the world knows what it is talking about.'

Queen Victoria and Edward VII were the last two monarchs whose names alone would conjure up the flavour of the eras in which they reigned. Since 1952, we have not been living in a new Elizabethan age. Elizabeth II is an impressive woman, with special gifts that have been much to the benefit of Crown and country, but she has not set the tone or temper (or tempo) of the time in which she has lived. Far from it. At moments during her long reign she has struggled to keep pace with the swirling changes taking place around her. In part, this is a reflection of the gradually diminishing power and position of the monarchy, but it also has something to do with the personalities – and the perception of the personalities – involved. A statue of Queen Victoria immediately evokes the Victorian age. A photograph of Edward VII – especially one taken at the races, or at a country house party – at once triggers a wider picture of Edwardian England. There is no image of Elizabeth II that conveys the spirit of Britain in the second half of the twentieth century.

Bertie was in his sixtieth year when Victoria died and he succeeded her as the first king to be called Edward since the middle of the sixteenth century. He had been waiting in the wings a long time. 'I don't mind praying to the eternal Father,' he once said, 'but I must be the only man in the country afflicted with an eternal mother.' Despite the lengthy and chequered apprenticeship, to the surprise of many he managed the transition from playboy Prince of Wales to king-of-some-substance without difficulty. As King, he eased up a touch on the womanising (well, we all get older), but his other appetites remained undiminished and his generous girth was seen as evidence of his humanity and endeared him to his subjects. 'Good old Teddy,' they said, and they meant it. You could argue that the last time Great Britain could be described as 'a nation at ease with itself' was in the Edwardian era, when toffs were toffs, the middle classes were comfortable, and the workers – rather like the King – accepted their lot in life and took their pleasures where they could.

Edward VII took his role seriously. He had the presence of a leader and the skills of a diplomat. His achievement in encouraging a loosening of the national bias towards Germany and the signing of the 1904 *Entente Cordiale* with France was real. He also took himself seriously. When Bertie was a guest at the Comédie Française and a stranger enquired what His Royal Highness thought of the play, the

Prince rebuked him: 'I don't think I spoke to you.' He would tease his friends and indulge in his fondness for practical jokes at their expense,[42] but his intimates were not permitted to respond in kind. If you overstepped the mark, if you answered back, if, in your cups, momentarily, you forgot who you were, and, more to the point, forgot who he was, your bags would be packed and your carriage summoned. The word lese-majesty comes from the French *lèse-majesté*, which comes from the Latin *laesa majestas*, which means 'hurting' or 'injuring' majesty.

In his memoirs, *A King's Story*, the Duke of Windsor, briefly Edward VIII, grandson of Edward VII, recalled a conversation he had had, when, as Prince of Wales, he had asked a senior courtier, Sir Frederick 'Fritz' Ponsonby, to give him a candid opinion of how he was faring in his role:

'If I may say so, Sir, I think there is a risk in making yourself too accessible,' he answered unhesitatingly.

'What do you mean?' I asked.

'The Monarchy must always retain an element of mystery. A Prince should not show himself too much. The Monarchy must remain on a pedestal.'

I maintained otherwise, arguing that because of the social changes brought about by the [1914–18] war, one of the most important tasks of the Prince of Wales was to help bring the institution nearer the people.

'If you bring it down to the people,' Fritz Ponsonby said coldly, 'it will lose its mystery and influence.'

'I do not agree,' I said. 'Times are changing.'

He replied severely, 'I am older than you are, Sir; I have been with your father, your grandfather, and your great-grandmother. They all understood. You are quite mistaken.'

[42] 'According to Mrs Hwfa Williams, sister-in-law of the Prince's friend, Colonel Owen Williams, he would place the hand of the blind Duke of Mecklenburg on the arm of the enormously fat Helen Henneker, observing, "Now, don't you think Helen has a lovely little waist?" And he would be delighted by the subsequent roar of laughter – "in which no one joined more heartily than Helen". Similarly, he would pour a glass of brandy over Christopher Sykes's head or down his neck or, while smoking a cigar, he would tell Sykes to gaze into his eyes to see the smoke coming out of them and then stab Sykes's hand with the burning end. Shouts of laughter would also greet this often-repeated trick as the grave and snobbish Sykes responded in his complaisantly lugubrious, inimitably long-suffering way, "As your Royal Highness pleases."' Christopher Hibbert, *Edward VII*, 1976.

Victoria, Edward VII and George V understood the requirements of monarchy and, in their different ways, delivered in full measure. Edward VIII did not.

One Saturday morning in May 1910 the future Edward VIII and his younger brother, the future George VI, aged sixteen and fifteen respectively, learnt of the death of their grandfather, Edward VII, when they woke up and looked out of the window of Marlborough House and saw the Royal Standard flying over Buckingham Palace at half-mast. Moments later they were called downstairs. 'My father's face was grey with fatigue,' the Duke of Windsor later recalled, 'and he cried as he told us that Grandpapa was dead. I answered sadly that we had already seen the Royal Standard at half-mast. My father seemed not to hear as he went on to describe in exact detail the scene around the deathbed. Then he asked sharply, "What did you say about the Standard?" "It is flying at half-mast over the Palace," I answered. My father frowned and muttered, "But that's all wrong," and repeating as if to himself the old but pregnant saying, "The King is dead. Long live the King!" he sent for his equerry and in a peremptory naval manner ordered that a mast be rigged at once on the roof of Marlborough House.'[43]

George V, as he had become at a little before midnight on the night before, was noted for his peremptory naval manner. As a boy, he had been a naval cadet. He spent twenty years in the service and, according to his eldest son, throughout his life 'retained a gruff, blue-water approach to all situations, a loud voice, and also that affliction common to Navy men, a damaged ear-drum'. Apparently, 'Damn fool!' was his favourite expression. He had an explosive temper, a simple sailor's sense of humour, and a horror of change for change's sake. He liked things to be 'ship-shape'; he appreciated order; his chief delight was his stamp collection. He was a creature of habit: carefully, he checked the barometer, every morning and every night. When his wife, Queen Mary

---

[43] This is an interesting story and makes an important point about the Royal Standard. When Diana, Princess of Wales, died in 1997, there was an outcry in the press about the Royal Standard at Balmoral not being flown at half-mast. The Queen was both hurt and angered by the criticism. She felt it betrayed a lack of understanding of history and tradition. The Royal Standard *never* flies at half-mast. The flagpole at Buckingham Palace was bare because flags are only flown over a royal residence when the sovereign is in residence. The Queen could see no reason – no reason at all – to break with precedence. After several days, against her better judgement, she was persuaded to change her mind and allow a compromise: the Union flag – not the Royal Standard – was flown over Buckingham Palace at half-mast once the Queen had left the Palace to go to Westminster Abbey.

(as Princess May was known after the accession), attempted to shorten her skirts in line with the fashion of the day, the King would have none of it. As their eldest son recalled, 'He disapproved of Soviet Russia, painted finger-nails, women who smoked in public, cocktails, frivolous hats, American jazz and the growing habit of going away for weekends.'

George was in awe of his father and adored his mother. He treated Edward VII with respect, tinged with fear, and Queen Alexandra with an almost puppy-like devotion. Even when he was King, he was Alix's 'darling Georgie boy'. On paper, in correspondence (especially with his 'Motherdear'), he could be sentimental to the point of soppiness. In person, it sometimes seemed that he had an easier, more comfortable, relationship with his beloved pet parrot, Charlotte, than he did with either his wife or children. 'I was frightened of my father,' he once said, 'and I'm damn well going to see that my children are frightened of me.'

Georgie and May had six children.[44] The family was brought up in the main at York Cottage, a comparatively cramped and – by every account – cluttered and uncomfortable house in the grounds of the Sandringham estate. As parents, Georgie and May saw their children twice a day: once, briefly, in the morning, and then, for an hour, at teatime. The eldest, David, the future Edward VIII, had a particular loathing of the family nanny:

> Before carrying me into the drawing-room, this dreadful 'Nanny' would pinch and twist my arm – why, no one knew, unless it was to demonstrate, according to some perverse reasoning, that her power over me was greater than that of my parents. The sobbing and bawling this treatment invariably evoked understandably puzzled, worried, and finally annoyed them. It would result in my being peremptorily removed from the room before further embarrassment was inflicted upon them and the other witnesses of this pathetic scene. Eventually, my mother realised what was wrong, and the nurse was dismissed.

---

[44] The future Edward VIII (always known in the family as David), 1894–1972; the future George VI (known as Bertie), 1895–1952; Mary, later the Princess Royal (and mother of the present Earl of Harewood), 1897–1965; Henry, Duke of Gloucester (father of the current Duke), 1900–1974; George, Duke of Kent (father of the current crop of Kents: the present Duke of Kent, Princess Alexandra and Prince Michael), 1902–42; and John, 1905–19, who was born brain-damaged, suffered epileptic fits and died young, and whose strange, sad story was brought fully into the open in Stephen Poliakoff's 2002 television film, *The Lost Prince*.

Queen Mary was no 'Motherdear'. She was a concerned parent, but not a cosy or a cuddly one. To her children (as to the public at large) she seemed somewhat removed, forbidding and formidable. She was a devoted and dutiful wife: she accepted her place and her husband's character. She knew that his gruff exterior concealed a kindly nature. He suffered from dyspepsia, smoked excessively and had a rough tongue. Their son David said his father had 'a most horrible temper':

> He was foully rude to my mother. Why, I've seen her leave the table because he was so rude to her, and we children would all follow her out; not when the staff were present, of course, but when we were alone.

Queen Mary did not have the confidence of being a full-blooded royal, she was naturally diffident, she accepted (as much of the world did in her day) that women were the weaker vessels, and, of course, she respected her husband as both master and monarch. She expected her children to do the same. 'I always remember,' she said, solemnly, 'that as well as being their father he is also their King.' She was a serious-minded traditionalist, conversationally limited, emotionally cautious. She and King George brought up their one daughter, Princess Mary, to be the same. Mary's son, George Harewood, remembers a family where emotional inhibition was the order of the day. 'We did not talk of love and affection and what we meant to each other,' he says, 'but rather of duty and behaviour and what we ought to do.'[45]

Mary was the King's favourite and, to a limited extent, indulged. He was much tougher on his sons, especially the elder two. He picked on them, mocked them, made sarcastic remarks about them, and generally found ways of finding fault with them at every turn. According to Bertie, 'It was very difficult for David. My father was so inclined to go for him. I always thought it was a pity that he found fault with him

---

[45] Queen Mary wore long Edwardian dresses long after they went out of fashion. She was rarely seen in public without her trade-mark toque. The diarist Henry 'Chips' Channon said meeting her was 'like talking to St Paul's Cathedral'. At Lord Harewood's wedding, the novelist E. M. Forster, his eyesight failing, bowed to the multi-tiered cake, mistaking it for Her Majesty. (That reminds me: Fritz Ponsonby used to tell the story of how fond George V was of a certain silver statuette of Lady Godiva. The reason? Once upon a time, as she peered at it, the myopic Queen Olga – mother of Prince Andrew of Greece and grandmother of Prince Philip – had been heard to murmur appreciatively, 'Ah, dear Queen Victoria.')

over unimportant things – like what he wore. This only put David's back up.'

Bertie was not spared. He was a left-handed child but, as was the custom of the time, was forced to become right-handed. He was also knock-kneed and, during his pre-adolescence, for several hours every day, and throughout the night, he was made to wear corrective wooden splints. He developed a pitiful stammer, which dogged him all his days and infuriated his father. When Bertie was struggling to speak a word, his impatient papa would bark at him, 'Get it out, boy, get it out!'

David, as he grew older, and especially once he had become Prince of Wales, deliberately defied his father, doing his own thing in his own way, and seemingly taking perverse pleasure in irritating – even shocking – his unbending parent. Bertie was more compliant. He gave way to occasional outbursts of frustrated rage – known in the family as his 'gnashes' – but, on the whole, he kept out of trouble's way. Bertie was second-in-line, so, in any event, his public profile was lower, but his stammer also meant that he had less to say. He was shy, awkward, hesitant, in a way David was not. Famously, as a little boy, at lunch with his grandfather, Edward VII, David had dared interrupt the King in full flow. He was immediately reminded that children are to be seen, not heard, and to speak only when they are spoken to. Eventually, he was given permission to say whatever it was he had wanted to say. 'It's too late now, Grandpapa,' he chirruped. 'It was a caterpillar on your lettuce, but you've eaten it.'

King George's chaffing of his sons amounted to bullying. Queen Mary chose not to intervene but others were bolder. Margot Asquith, second wife of Herbert Asquith, Liberal Prime Minister at the start of George's reign, told the King that his treatment of his sons would drive them to drink. During the First World War, to set an example, the King imposed a drinking ban on the entire royal household, but after the war, once they were adults, each of the four surviving royal princes drank much more than was good for him. The fourth son, Prince George, eight years' David's junior, even dabbled with morphine and cocaine.

Henry (created Duke of Gloucester, at twenty-eight, in 1928) was the family dullard, a cavalry officer and a country gentleman, who drank too much whisky, but meant well and did no harm. George (created Duke of Kent, at thirty-two, in 1934) was his mother's favourite and the most socially adept and easy of her boys. He had an artistic temperament, a fondness for high society and low living, and a loathing for the naval career into which he felt he had been forced by his father. He was a notorious ladies' man who was, apparently, equally at home among the homosexual set. He was once arrested, briefly, in a gay nightclub known as the Nut House. In 1934, he married the beautiful Princess Marina of Greece (granddaughter of George I of Greece, niece of Prince Andrea, cousin of Prince Philip), which may have tempered his behaviour, but didn't halt the rumour-mongering. It is often said that Noël Coward, playwright, performer and theatrical darling of the era, was one of his lovers, but when I put the suggestion to Graham Payn, Coward's companion for thirty years, his denial was emphatic: 'Oh, no. That story about Noël and the Duke of Kent, it wasn't true. We can put the record straight on that. I asked Noël about it and he was quite clear. "We did not get over-friendly."'[46]

George was tall and handsome. David and Bertie were shorter, slighter, slimmer, more athletic, more reticent and wholly heterosexual. They were good-looking (well, they were young, well-dressed, well-heeled, well-mannered) and they were princes (it counts for a lot) and they could pull as they pleased. It seems they did. The Prince of Wales had a series of infatuations and affairs before his obsession with Wallis Simpson cost him the crown and changed the course of royal history. His first heavy-duty love affair was with Freda Dudley Ward, the liberal wife of a Liberal MP, and it is from their correspondence that we learn that, in the pre-marital love stakes, stammering Bertie was not as tongue-tied as earlier biographies have suggested. He lost his virginity, it seems, in Paris towards the end of the 1914–18 war. According to David, that's where 'the deed was done'. Back in London Bertie enjoyed the company of several chorus girls and, on at least one occasion, in 1919, entertained Jack Buchanan's leading lady, Phyllis Monkman, star of the happily titled hit *Tails Up*, to a late supper in a private room in Half Moon Street.

David embarked on his affair with Freda Dudley Ward in March

---

[46] Graham Payn also told me Coward 'always preferred the Yorks, long before there was any thought they might be King and Queen. He used to visit them quite often, much to the irritation of Queen Mary who felt her eldest was being upstaged. Let's face it, the Windsors [as Edward VIII and his wife, Wallis Simpson, became] were not exactly joy unconfined. The Duke, to be honest, was an extremely dull man. Noël said he even danced a boring Charleston, which is no mean feat. One evening Wallis said to Noël, "You know I don't understand why the British dislike me so much." There was a terrible pause before Noël replied, "Well, because you stole their Prince Charming." She rather liked that. On social occasions, the Duke rarely spoke, not because his mind was preoccupied, but simply because he had nothing to say. Noël used to say, "He had the charm of the world with nothing to back it up."'

1918 and evidently encouraged his younger brother to find himself a married mistress of his own. Sheila Chisholm was young, lively, Australian and game. She was married to Lord Loughborough and she had a baby son (Anthony, born in May 1917), but, nevertheless, she was up for some fun. David and Freda, Bertie and Sheila, called themselves 'The Four Do's', and certainly did. 'What marvellous fun we 4 do have, don't we, Angel?' wrote the Prince of Wales to Mrs Dudley-Ward, '& f— the rest of the world.' In 1926, Sheila and Lord Loughborough were divorced, but in 1919 the unfortunate cuckold appears to have been unaware of what his young wife and the two kings-to-be were up to. 'After tea,' David reported gleefully, 'I managed to lure Loughie away on the pretext of wanting to play a few more holes of golf . . . so as to give Sheilie a chance of being alone with Bertie . . . I'm sure Loughie doesn't suspect Bertie at all!'

That was in June 1919. A year later, on 2 June 1920, Bertie, now twenty-five, and created Duke of York by his father, George V, only the week before, accompanied his mother, Queen Mary, to a Derby Night ball in Grosvenor Square. At around eleven o'clock, the young duke saw a smiling girl across a crowded room. She was chatting to his equerry. The duke asked to be introduced. Lady Elizabeth Angela Marguerite Bowes-Lyon, ninth child and fourth daughter of the 14th Earl of Strathmore and Kinghorne, was nineteen and pretty as a picture. Bertie later claimed it was love at first sight.

Chapter Four

'. . . Never take a second mouthful before you have finished the first. Do not finish the last crumb or spoonful, or scrape your plate. When finished do not clutch your knees. *General remarks.* Do not read too much. Do not eat too much butter or jam. Say your prayers. Keep your hair in order.'

Rules drawn up by her sisters for Margaret Gladstone, 1882

'It was always love at first sight. No one could resist her. No one. Everybody who met her fell under her spell. Always.'

It is Monday 30 June 2003 and I am spending the morning in the Garden House at Windsor Great Park with the Hon. Margaret Rhodes, seventy-eight, cousin, childhood playmate and life-long friend of Elizabeth II, niece and sometime lady-in-waiting to Queen Elizabeth the Queen Mother. Mrs Rhodes's mother was Lady Mary Bowes-Lyon, one of Lady Elizabeth's three sisters.

Mrs Rhodes is trim and bird-like. She has a smoker's voice and the beady eye of one who has seen the world and, on the whole, been gently amused. Her elegant, slightly faded, drawing room is littered with signed photographs of assorted royals. Her small kitchen table is cluttered with old newspapers, correspondence, invitations, bills. In the downstairs lavatory, beneath the formal picture of the Queen and the Duke of Edinburgh on their wedding day, there is a well-thumbed copy of *The Prince Philip Throneside Book.* Mrs Rhodes is devoted to the memory of her aunt. 'Everybody adored her,' she says, 'Everybody.'

Certainly, I have not met anybody who didn't. Lord David Cecil, who was a childhood friend, told me that 'even as a girl, she had a certain twinkle as well as extraordinary sweetness. She made you feel part of a delightful conspiracy.' Woodrow Wyatt said to me, 'She is the most truly charming person in the world.' Sir John Mills told me, 'No one is more captivating. I have been lucky enough to meet some of the most glamorous women of our time. She outshines them all.' I asked one of her sons-in-law, Lord Snowdon, to sum her up in a single word and, without hesitation, he said, 'Fun'.

In 1920, according to Mabell, Countess of Airlie, who knew her then, Lady Elizabeth's 'radiant vitality', combined with 'a blending of kindness and sincerity' made her 'irresistible to men'. She was pretty, not spectacularly beautiful. She was small (five foot four inches), but not petite. She had flawless skin, bright blue eyes, but shortish, rather dull, dark hair, cut in a noticeably unsexy fringe. She was anything but 'modern'. According to Lady Airlie, 'she was very unlike the cocktail-drinking, chain-smoking girls who came to be regarded as typical of the 1920s.' She came from one of Scotland's oldest, grandest, families. Her forebears included Robert the Bruce. The family properties included Glamis Castle in Scotland; another, lesser, castle, Streatlam, in County Durham; a fine, eighteenth-century country house, St Paul's, Walden Bury, in Hertfordshire; and a handsome town house in London, in St James's Square, between Piccadilly and Pall Mall.

Her father, Lord Strathmore, was a Scottish nobleman of the old school. He was God-fearing, courteous, kindly, conscientious, conservative and only mildly eccentric. At breakfast he made his own cocoa and, at lunch, he ate plum pudding every day. Mrs Rhodes recalls the huge dining hall at Glamis and her grandfather at the head of the table: 'I can picture the food being sort of thrown onto the plates and him catching it. I remember, too, he had a wonderful droopy moustache and he smoked endless cigarettes. This was before the age of tipped cigarettes and we children kept watch as his cigarette burnt slowly down to see if it would set fire to his moustache. It never did.' Lord Strathmore took his duties seriously (as a landowner and Lord-Lieutenant of Angus) and his recreations were exactly those you would expect: fishing, shooting and cricket. He was an authority on forestry. According to Mrs Rhodes, 'He really loved his trees. Queen Elizabeth used to tell the story of people telephoning Walden Bury and enquiring, "Is his Lordship down from Glamis yet?" "No," the butler would say, "his Lordship only comes when the sap rises."'

Lady Strathmore, born Nina-Cecilia Cavendish-Bentinck, also came from good aristocratic stock. Her father, a clergyman, was heir to the 5th Duke of Portland. She, too, took her religion seriously: the chapel at Glamis was in regular use. She was also outgoing, unpretentious, warm, practical and creative: she was an enthusiastic gardener and an accomplished pianist. Mrs Rhodes told me: 'She died when I was thirteen, but I can see her clearly – a lovely, voluminous figure, in a long black dress with a lace collar. She was a heavenly, smiling granny.' She seems to have been pretty perfect as a mother as well. According to Mrs Rhodes: 'Queen Elizabeth always spoke of her mother with enormous warmth and affection.' In a letter to Osbert Sitwell, she once wrote: 'I have nothing but wonderfully happy memories of childhood days at home.' She was ever grateful to her parents for providing 'Fun, kindness, & a marvellous sense of security.'

In July 1920, in the run-up to her twentieth birthday on 4 August, Lady Elizabeth Bowes-Lyon was, arguably, London's most eligible debutante. She had it all: breeding, looks, intelligence, vivacity, charm. She also had a certain maturity. She had seen something of life. During the 1914–18 war, one of her brothers was killed in action, at the Battle of Loos, and another was severely wounded and captured by the Germans. As part of the war effort, Glamis Castle was turned into a convalescent hospital for wounded soldiers and Elizabeth helped her mother care for the men. If Prince Albert fell for her instantly, as he later claimed, he was not alone. Other suitors also made the pilgrimage to Glamis. One of them was Ronald Barnes, 3rd Baron Gorell, who later claimed, 'I was madly in love with her. Everything at Glamis was beautiful, perfect. Being there was like living in a van Dyck picture. Time, and the gossiping, junketing world, stood still. Nothing happened . . . but the magic gripped us all. I fell *madly* in love.'[47] Gorell listed Lady Elizabeth's principal qualities: 'Her charm was indescribable . . . She was also very kind and compassionate. And she could be very funny – which was rare in those circles. She was a wag.'[48]

The list of eligible young men who took a shine to the waggish, wide-eyed, heart-faced enchantress of Glamis was a long one. It included, among others, Prince Paul of Serbia, a good friend of one of her brothers, who did most of his wooing, it seems, by paying court to Lady Strathmore (not a bad stratagem); Henry Gage, the 6th Viscount, who owned Firle Place in Sussex, plus, he liked to say, 'about 10,000 acres';

[47] In 1920 Ronald Gorell became President of the National Council for Combating Venereal Diseases. He was a remarkable character: a poet, a publisher, a pilot, a doer of good works of all kinds. He was sixteen years older than Elizabeth Bowes-Lyon and never a serious suitor for her hand. In 1922, he married Elizabeth Radcliffe, daughter of a lawyer and one of England's most respected collie-fanciers.
[48] Famously, as a little girl in want of pocket money, she sent a telegram to her father: 'S.O.S. L.S.D. R.S.V.P. ELIZABETH'.

the 10th Earl of Airlie's younger son, Brucie, who courted Elizabeth's attention by dancing on the dining-room table while playing the ukelele; Christopher Tennant, the 2nd Baron Glenconner, who was a millionaire and a charmer (and whose first wife, Pamela, would produce Colin Tennant, the future owner of Mustique and friend of Princess Margaret); and James Stuart, the third son of the 17th Earl of Moray, who, at the age of nineteen, had won one Military Cross at the Battle of the Somme and a second at the Battle of Arras. James Stuart was more than a hero: he was reckoned – by many – to be the handsomest man in the kingdom. He was also the new Duke of York's equerry and the man who first introduced Bertie to Lady Elizabeth at the Derby Night ball in Grosvenor Square.

Of her many suitors, none was better connected than HRH The Prince Albert, Duke of York, but most were more obviously attractive: more outgoing, more articulate, less inhibited, less shy. How, then, did Bertie secure his bride? In the old way, it seems: simply, by persistence.[49] James Stuart was delightful: dashing, debonair, dangerous. He was a serial flirt. He was not reliable. Bertie was different. Bertie was dogged. Single-mindedly, he pursued Elizabeth for nearly three years. And he was not unattractive: he was slim, fit, well-dressed, well-mannered, a good shot, a brilliant dancer (this was an age in which that counted for something), a decent cove – kindly and courteous (in any age that counts for a lot) – with sound instincts and an impeccable pedigree. He was, after all, a royal duke, the second son of the King.

Bertie proposed to Elizabeth three times. Twice she refused him. He would not go away. He did not give up. Eventually, he secured his prize. On a Sunday walk in the woods at St Paul's, Walden Bury, in January 1923, she said 'yes', and did so whole-heartedly. She belonged to a class and generation where every woman's destiny was to be a wife and a mother – and nothing more. To secure the ideal husband was everything. Elizabeth sensed that in Bertie she had found a good man and that theirs would be a happy match. She was right.

The Strathmores were not besotted with royalty. 'As far as I can see,' Lady Strathmore is said once to have remarked, 'some people have to be fed royalty like sea lions fish.' She was not one of them, but nonetheless to be the mother of the first 'commoner' to marry legitimately

---

[49] 'In time refractory oxen come to plough, in time horses are taught to bear pliant reins, an iron ring is worn by constant use . . . Only persevere, you will overcome Penelope herself.' Ovid, c. 1 BC.

into the royal family was undoubtedly 'something'. Bertie's mother, Queen Mary, was equally delighted. 'Elizabeth is charming,' she wrote in her diary, 'so pretty & engaging and natural. Bertie is supremely happy.'

The Duke of York and Lady Elizabeth Bowes-Lyon were married in Westminster Abbey on 26 April 1923. The political situation was uncertain and the economy fragile. The King declared that 'the arrangements should be of as simple a character as possible and that no unnecessary expense shall be incurred.' The wedding was grand, but not ostentatious. The bride wore a dress of machine-made Nottingham lace, designed in medieval style by Queen Mary's dressmaker, with a veil of Flanders lace lent by the Queen. The groom wore the uniform of a group captain of the recently created Royal Air Force. The ceremony was filmed – in long-shot – for the cinema newsreels, but not broadcast on the fledgling BBC wireless. The Archbishop of Canterbury was concerned that 'disrespectful people might hear the service, perhaps some of them sitting in public houses with their hats on'.

In the run-up to the wedding, Elizabeth made what seems to have been the only unforced error of her public life. An enterprising reporter from the *Star* newspaper turned up at her parents' Mayfair front door and asked Lady Elizabeth for a brief interview. He was granted one. The King was not amused. 'Those filthy rags of newspapers' was how His Majesty regarded the press. Elizabeth never spoke on the record to a journalist again – and the coverage she received over the next eight decades was extraordinary and, almost always, adulatory. She had an instinct for doing what was right and doing it in a way that would be well-received. On her wedding day, as she entered Westminster Abbey, apparently spontaneously, she placed her bouquet of white heather and York roses on the tomb of the Unknown Soldier.

The guests at the wedding included a raft of royals, the cream of the aristocracy, a smattering of the great and the good, and thirty boys chosen by the Industrial Welfare Society to represent the ordinary youth of Britain. The Duke of York was President of the IWS and genuinely interested in giving sporting, recreational and training opportunities to young people. He founded – and attended – an annual summer camp where two hundred working-class lads and two hundred young chaps from public schools came together for an integrated adventure holiday. He pioneered 'social inclusion' seventy years before it became government policy. He undertook good works both because he believed in them and because that was what was expected of a king's second son in the aftermath of the Great War. He and his young duchess did their duty as required – he shyly, she gaily – but, once the excitement of the wedding was over, they neither sought, nor received, undue press or public attention. He was not the king and not ever expected to be. The Prince of Wales was not yet thirty. He was the glamorous one who was in the front line and in the spotlight. His younger brother could – and did – lead a relatively private life.

The Yorks honeymooned at Polesden Lacey in Surrey[50] and at Glamis. The weather in Scotland was atrocious and the new duchess contracted whooping cough, 'not,' she conceded, 'a very romantic disease'. This dampener behind them, the young couple settled in to the life of near-unparalleled privilege – and occasional duty – that was to be their lot. Everybody was utterly enchanted by the duchess. Most found the duke a touch awkward. His equerry, James Stuart, who had also been, of course, his rival in love, said of the young duke: 'He was not an easy man to know or to handle.' The prince was capable of sudden, unpleasant, bursts of anger, his notorious 'gnashes'. Margaret Rhodes remembers him 'for his totally schoolboy sense of humour'. She told me: 'He laughed like a drain at ridiculous things, but he had an explosive temper. I saw him once grouse-shooting in a butt. He hadn't shot very well. In fact, he'd shot badly. He threw his guns into the heather in his rage and frustration.'

Elizabeth did her best to tease him out of his ill humour by taking his pulse and quietly counting: 'Tick, tick, tick, one, two, three.' She also did all she could to help him conquer the speech impediment that was the blight of his life. She went with him on his regular visits to Harley Street to see his speech therapist, Lionel Logue. She lay beside him on the floor as he practised his breathing and relaxation exercises. She repeated after him the assorted tongue-twisters designed to help him

---

[50] The house was put at their disposal by Mrs Ronald Greville, described by Cecil Beaton (Elizabeth's favourite photographer) as 'a galumphing, greedy, snobbish old toad who watered at her chops at the sight of royalty'. Another of my favourite diarists, Harold Nicolson, described her as 'a fat slug filled with venom'. Elizabeth was more charitable. When Maggie Greville died in 1942, the Queen wrote to Osbert Sitwell: 'She was so shrewd, so kind and so amusingly *un*kind, so sharp, such fun, so naughty.' Mrs Greville, daughter of the brewing magnate William McEwan, left all her jewellery – including Marie Antoinette's diamond necklace – to the Queen, 'with my loving thoughts', and a bequest of £20,000 to Princess Margaret.

jump the hurdles of especially challenging consonants. ('Let's go gathering heathy heather with the gay brigade of grand dragoons' was a particular favourite, apparently.) She checked the drafts of speeches he was due to deliver to eliminate the worst stumbling blocks – and, when he came to deliver those speeches, she was on hand, with an encouraging smile, willing him to succeed. He never wholly conquered his impediment, but, over time, he managed to contain it. Lionel Logue said, 'He was the pluckiest and most determined patient I ever had.'

Elizabeth was good for Bertie. On that, everyone agreed. She was altogether, as Sellar and Yeatman (two of her favourite historians) would have it, A Good Thing.[51] Naturally, she was not without flaws. Her time-keeping was terrible. More than once, her husband was seen, impatiently pacing the hallway, checking the clock, muttering to himself, 'Where is that damned woman?' But such was her charm, and her lightness of touch, that, it seems, everyone forgave her everything. Even the King – perhaps especially the King – would indulge her. When, once, famously, she arrived late for dinner with His Majesty, she, of course, apologised. 'Not at all,' said the King, to everybody else's amazement. 'You are not late, my dear. I think we must have sat down early.'

Elizabeth was not overawed by her father-in-law. 'Unlike his own children,' she said, after his death, 'I was never afraid of him.' George V and Queen Mary enjoyed Elizabeth's company. She was easy with them in a way that very few others were. Beady-eyed Virginia Woolf – for me one of the shrewdest and sharpest observers of the period – was at the theatre one evening (at a performance of an Edgar Wallace thriller) and saw the royal party on display:

There was a cheer, and behold a great golden Queen bowing in a very small bow windowed box. Also, when the lights went up, the King, red, grumpy, fidgeting with his hands; well-groomed, bluff; heavy-looking, with one white flower in his buttonhole, resenting the need, perhaps, of sitting to be looked at between one of the acts – his duty to be done. Once the Duchess of York sat with the Queen; a simple, chattering, sweethearted little roundfaced young woman in

---

[51] W. C. Sellar and R. J. Yeatman, a schoolmaster and an advertising copywriter respectively, published *1066 and All That*, their spoof history of England, in 1930. As they explained in the preface, 'History is not what you thought. *It is what you can remember*. All other history defeats itself.'

pink; but her wrists twinkling with diamonds, her dress held on the shoulder with diamonds. An odd feeling came to me of the shop window decorated for the public: these our exhibits, our show pieces. Not very impressive – no romance or mystery – the very best goods.[52]

The young Duchess of York delivered in full measure. In due course, at 2.40 a.m. on Wednesday 21 April 1926, after a difficult labour, and by Caesarean section, she gave birth to her first child, a baby girl, 'a little darling', according to Queen Mary's diary, 'with a lovely complexion and pretty fair hair'. The new princess was named Elizabeth Alexandra Mary, after her mother (at Bertie's insistence: there was no thought of Elizabeth I), her grandmother (Queen Mary) and her great-grandmother (Queen Alexandra, who had died of a heart attack, aged eighty, the previous November). She was born in Mayfair, at 17 Bruton Street, the tall, handsome eighteenth-century town house that had recently become the Strathmores' London home. She was christened five weeks later, on 29 May, in the chapel at Buckingham Palace. Her godparents included the King and Queen; her other grandmother, Lady Strathmore; her royal aunt, Mary, later to become the Princess Royal; a non-royal aunt, Lady Elphinstone (mother of Margaret Rhodes); and Arthur, Duke of Connaught (1850–1942), Queen Victoria's last surviving son.

Princess Elizabeth was born as the General Strike was reaching its climax. 1926 was a year of political, social and industrial unrest. It was also the year in which A. A. Milne wrote and published *Winnie-the-Pooh*. The tone of Elizabeth's childhood reflected the latter rather than the former. She was brought up in a golden cocoon: her nursery world, like Christopher Robin's, was cosy, Christian, safe, certain, utterly secure. There were differences, of course. Christopher Robin was a middle-class boy. Elizabeth was a princess and third in line to the throne.

The Yorks never liked the house assigned to them on their marriage.

---

[52] 15 December 1929. The actress Dame Eileen Atkins introduced me to *A Moment's Liberty: The Shorter Diary of Virginia Woolf*, when she, Dame Eileen, was playing the part of Queen Mary in a television film about Bertie and Elizabeth. She said to me, 'The joy of the diary is that there's a gem on every page,' and proved her point by opening the book at random and putting her finger on the entry for 18 May 1930: 'The thing is now to live with energy and mastery, desperately. To despatch each day high handedly. So not to dawdle and dwindle, contemplating this and that. No more regrets and indecisions. That is the right way to deal with life now that I am forty-eight and to make it more and more important and vivid as one grows old.'

White Lodge in Richmond Park (now the home of the Royal Ballet School) was huge and unappealing, unwieldy and uncomfortable. Soon after Elizabeth's first birthday, the family moved to 145 Piccadilly, overlooking Green Park, an impressive town house, running to five floors (with electric lift) and featuring assorted reception rooms, a fine dining room, a proper ballroom, a good library, twenty-five bedrooms (including several fit for a king) and an impeccably appointed nursery floor. The indoor staff included a housekeeper, a cook, three kitchen maids, a butler, an under-butler, two footmen, a valet for the duke, a dresser for the duchess, an orderly, a handyman, a night watchman and a couple of lads: one to wait on the senior servants, one to operate the in-house telephone exchange. Up on the nursery floor, the little princess had her own retinue. In command was Clara Cooper Knight, known as 'Alah' (to rhyme with Clara), a traditional English nanny, originally from Hertfordshire, who had looked after Lady Elizabeth when she was a baby. Alah, now in her late forties (but looking older in the photographs), was assisted by a young Scots nurserymaid, aged twenty-two, the daughter of a railway worker from Inverness, Margaret MacDonald, known as 'Bobo'. Quite soon, little Elizabeth would come to be known by her own diminutive: Lilibet – King George's pet name for his favourite grandchild.

The King gave Lilibet the time, attention and affection he had denied his own children. He played with her – properly, down on all fours. He indulged her, sitting her at his side at breakfast and tea and feeding her titbits from his own plate. He took her with him on holiday, to Sandringham and Balmoral – even to Bognor, in 1929, where he was recuperating from a near-fatal illness.[53] Most significantly, perhaps, he shared with her his love of dogs and horses. He had a passion for racing and racehorses and loved nothing better than to take little Lilibet around the stud at Sandringham. For her fourth birthday, in April 1930, he gave her her first pony, a Shetland called Peggy.

[53] When George V died, in 1936, the story quickly circulated that his final words were 'Bugger Bognor!', apparently muttered in response to one of his doctors who had tried to lift his spirits by suggesting that he would soon be well enough to convalesce at his favourite seaside resort. I prefer the version of the story set in 1929. The King is recovering well and about to leave Bognor. A deputation from the town council comes to call on His Majesty, both to pay its respects and to ask that the town might in future be known as Bognor Regis. The request is conveyed to His Majesty by his private secretary, Lord Stamfordham. 'Bugger Bognor!' says the King. The private secretary returns to the delegation: 'His Majesty is touched by your request and graciously pleased to accede to it.'

Margaret Rhodes – then Margaret Elphinstone – was ten months older than her cousin, and, when Lilibet was staying in Scotland, at Glamis or Balmoral, a natural playmate. 'What did we play? We endlessly played at horses. That was her idea. We galloped round and round the field. We were horses of every kind. Carthorses, racehorses, circus horses. We spent a lot of time as circus horses.'

Mrs Rhodes laughs and lights another cigarette and gazes into the middle distance. 'We played "Catching happy days". Do you know it? It's a game you play in the autumn. You just run around trying to catch the leaves as they fall from the trees before they hit the ground. It's a wonderful game.

'I remember, too, we invented a play. We put it on in Scotland and then again at St George's Hall at Windsor Castle. It was the story of one family through the ages. I remember carrying the Queen across the threshold. I was the young man in the play. Anyway, I dropped her. Of course, in those days, there wasn't the faintest idea she might be Queen.'

In fact, by the end of 1930, the possibility that Princess Elizabeth might indeed one day be Queen was being openly discussed. In August, the Yorks had produced a second child, but it was a girl. Rumour was rife: as adolescent naval cadets both Bertie and David had contracted mumps, which might have affected their fertility. The Prince of Wales was thirty-six and still unmarried. Even if he found a wife in the foreseeable future, would he be able to father an heir? Producing Lilibet and her sister – Princess Margaret Rose – had taken the Yorks all of seven years. Were they now likely to have a third child, and, if they did, would it be a boy?

The public, the press, even her parents, were speculating as to little Lilibet's destiny. Queen Victoria had succeeded her uncle. Would Princess Elizabeth succeed hers? Did she, even as a toddler, have the makings of a monarch? Osbert Sitwell recalled the Duke of York telling him: 'From the first moment of talking she showed so much character that it was impossible not to wonder that history would not repeat itself.' In September 1928, Winston Churchill – who would, one day, be Elizabeth II's first prime minister – stayed at Balmoral as a guest of King George and Queen Mary. He wrote to his wife: 'There is no one here at all, except the family, the household and Princess Elizabeth – aged two. The latter is a character. She has an air of authority and reflectiveness astonishing in an infant.'

Margaret Rhodes remembers her as 'a jolly little girl, but

fundamentally sensible and well-behaved. Princess Margaret was the naughty one. She was always more larky. She used to tease the servants. There was a wonderful old page and, as he carried the plates around the dining room, Margaret used to stare at him, trying to make him laugh. But she never got herself reprimanded. She got away with everything. She made her father laugh.'

When she was a little girl, Lilibet's closest friend outside the family was Sonia Graham-Hodgson, now Sonia Berry, aged seventy-eight. Sonia was the daughter of Sir Harold Graham-Hodgson, radiographer to the Royal Family, and a Mayfair neighbour of the Yorks. Sonia and Lilibet met in 1931, playing in Hamilton Gardens, behind Piccadilly. 'I was five and she was four,' Sonia recalls. 'I had no idea who she was, but I can see her now in a pink or red dress. She says I was wearing a blue coat, but we always argue over what we were wearing. I was the bossy one then – I rather rubbed in that I was eight months older. I was tall and she was rather small.'

Sonia and Lilibet played together in the gardens in Mayfair, in the nursery at 145 Piccadilly, in the thatched Wendy House at Royal Lodge, Windsor. Sonia has evocative photographs of the pair of them (uniformed nannies in attendance) walking hand in hand in the park. Another picture shows them out cycling together: Lilibet, on her tricycle, looking very determined. 'We quarrelled like normal children,' says Sonia, 'but she was a thoughtful and sensitive child, and naturally well-behaved. She never seemed aware of her position and paid no attention to the people who stood by the railings to watch her play.' And the Yorks as parents, by the standards of their time and class, were noticeably hands-on. 'The Duchess, having had a very happy childhood herself, was all the more determined that, because the children were royal, they should have an ordinary childhood. The Duke never seemed shy, he didn't stutter and he played games, like Sardines. I remember my starchy nanny saying that she found it very undignified having to hide in a bush with him.'

The Yorks were a happy family. They had reason to be. These were the years of the Wall Street Crash and the Great Depression, but – though the King ordered a general tightening of the royal belt – his family was mostly cushioned from the harshness of reality. The Yorks led comfortable, ordered lives. They already had a fine house in London and, in September 1931, the King gave them, in addition, a handsome weekend retreat in the mock-Gothic shape of the Royal Lodge in Windsor Great Park. They spent Easter at Windsor Castle; Christmas and the New Year at Sandringham; August and September in Scotland. There was nothing rackety about their lives. The Prince of Wales might desport himself on the Continent with one or other of his mistresses, but the Yorks only ever went abroad on duty. They took their duties seriously. They took their role as parents seriously as well.

Yes, they would travel to foreign parts when they had to (in January 1927, when Lilibet was only nine months old, they went without her on an official visit to Australia and New Zealand that kept them away for six months), but when they were at home – and they were mostly at home – they were much more intimately involved in the care and upbringing of their children than many aristocratic parents of their generation. The Yorks gave time and attention to their daughters: they played with them, they bathed them, they read to them, they gathered round the piano after tea and sang songs together. Prince Philip barely saw his parents throughout his adolescence. Lilibet saw hers every day.

'Of course,' says Mrs Rhodes, lighting another cigarette and putting her head to one side, 'we were educated at home. The Queen and I were really the last generation of gels who didn't go to school. We thought school would be ghastly. You'd have to play hockey. We didn't want to play hockey. I had a French governess. The Queen and Princess Margaret had Crawfie.' Mrs Rhodes smoothes out her skirt with an anxious hand. 'I knew Crawfie. She was very nice really, but then she wrote the book. I haven't read it.'

A silence falls. 'It's rather good,' I say.

'It probably is,' says Mrs Rhodes, stubbing out her cigarette and laughing. 'I still haven't read it. I don't think I shall.'

'Crawfie' was Marion Crawford, the young Scots woman who joined the York household as Lilibet's governess in the spring of 1932. 'The book' is *The Little Princesses*, Crawfie's account of the childhoods of Lilibet and Margaret Rose based on her sixteen years of royal service and published – to the dismay and astonishment of the House of Windsor – in 1950. Crawfie was tall, trim, intelligent, ambitious. She had trained as a teacher at Moray House in Edinburgh, working with young children from difficult backgrounds. She had plans to go on to train as a child psychologist. She was introduced to the Yorks by another of the duchess's older sisters, not Lady Elphinstone (Margaret Rhodes's mother), but Lady Rose Leveson-Gower, whose daughter Mary had been taking lessons with her. Crawfie was an excellent governess and a good friend to Lilibet and Margaret Rose, until, by publishing her book, she betrayed their trust – and became, overnight, a 'non-person'.

There is nothing shocking in *The Little Princesses*. Far from it. The tone is altogether deferential, the literary style overly sweet and sentimental (Crawfie's prose had been 'improved' by her American publishers), but the observation is often shrewd and the details revealing. Here is Crawfie's account of her entry into the nursery world of Royal Lodge and her first encounter with Alah Knight, the formidable nanny, 'a tall, noble-looking woman', and little Princess Elizabeth, the heroine of her story, and ours:

Alah awaited me with that mixture of reserve and apprehension felt by all nannies when the governess is introduced. I like to remember that in all my years at 145 Piccadilly, London, and later at Buckingham Palace, Alah and I remained good friends; and if on her side the neutrality was sometimes armed to the teeth, I was always very careful not to tread on her toes.

Alah had entire charge in those days of the children's out-of-school lives – their health, their baths, their clothes – while I had them from nine to six. She had to help her an under-nurse and a nursemaid. These two girls are there still – Margaret MacDonald and Ruby MacDonald, two sisters, who have become the personal maids and friends of two sisters.

The night nursery was decorated in pink and fawn, the Duchess's favourite colour scheme. A small figure with a mop of curls sat up on the bed. She wore a nightie with a design of small pink roses on it. She had tied the cords of her dressing gown to the knobs of the old-fashioned bed, and was busy driving her team.

That was my first glimpse of Princess Elizabeth.

'This is Miss Crawford,' said Alah, in her stern way.

The little girl said, 'How do you do.' She then gave me a long, comprehensive look I had seen once before, and went on, 'Why have you no hair?'

I pulled off my hat to show her. 'I have enough to go on with,' I said. 'It's an Eton crop.'

She picked up her reins again.

'Do you usually drive in bed?' I asked.

'I mostly go once or twice round the park before I go to sleep, you know,' she said. 'It exercises my horses.' She navigated a dangerous and difficult corner, and went on, 'Are you going to stay with us?'

'For a little while, anyway,' I replied.

The account has the feel of a novella, but also the ring of truth. We are introduced immediately both to Lilibet's discriminating, observant eye and to her passion for horses. We can picture the child, the nanny and the governess quite clearly. While friends of the Queen who have read the book tell me that much of it is fanciful and not to be relied upon, I reckon that, overall, Crawfie's portrait of the little princesses is both accurate and telling. Lilibet comes across as an intelligent child, a dutiful daughter and a responsible older sister. Her love of dogs and horses – practical as well as passionate – is essential to her happiness. 'Lilibet's first love of all was undoubtedly Owen the groom, who taught her to ride.' She was not yet six. 'What Owen did or said was right in her sight for many years.' In 1933, when Lilibet was seven, her father gave her her first corgi.

Because Crawfie had reservations about some of Alah's methods – Alah was a wholly traditional nanny: she believed in order, discipline, routine, calmness at all times, the virtues of emotional constraint – Crawfie, in her book, may have exaggerated the degree of Lilibet's obsession with orderliness. Alah believed in the regimented life and, from the earliest age, Lilibet was a stickler for domestic order. Crawfie tells us how carefully Lilibet lined up her toy horses, how neatly she folded her clothes, how – night after night – she took care to position her shoes exactly parallel underneath her chair. After a family lunch one day, when their parents allowed the little princesses a spoonful each of sugar crystals, Margaret Rose ate all hers at once: before eating them, Lilibet arranged hers meticulously, one by one, in a straight line according to size.

Crawfie comes back, time and again, to her charges' contrasting personalities:

> Of the two children, Lilibet was the one with the temper, but it was under control. Margaret was often naughty, but she had a gay bouncing way with her which was hard to deal with. She would often defy me with a sidelong look, make a scene and kiss and be friends and all forgiven and forgotten. Lilibet took longer to recover, but she had always the more dignity of the two.
>
> The Duke was immensely proud of her. He had a way of looking at her that was touching. But Margaret brought delight into his life. She was a plaything. She was warm and demonstrative, made to be cuddled and played with. At one time he would be almost embarrassed, yet at the same time touched and pleased, when she

wound her arms round his neck, nestled against him and cuddled and caressed him. He was not a demonstrative man.

Lilibet took after him. She, too, was reserved and quiet about her feelings. If you once gained her love and affection you had it for ever, but she never gave it easily.

In January 1936, aged seventy-one, George V died. His favourite grandchild was not quite ten.

Lilibet in her sensitive fashion felt it all deeply. It was very touching to see how hard she tried to do what she felt was expected of her. I remember her pausing doubtfully as she groomed one of her toy horses and looking up at me for a moment.

'Oh, Crawfie . . . ought we to play?'

The old King was much mourned. His face was red, his manner was gruff, his voice was loud, but he had done his duty with dignity and some skill. His reign encompassed the Great War, the Russian Revolution, civil war in Ireland, the Great Depression, the advent of Britain's first Labour government. He had risen to the challenges. He had dropped few catches. He had survived. He would be missed. 'The people of America are mourning, as if for their own King,' Virginia Woolf noted in her diary, 'and the Japanese are in tears.' The BBC suspended normal service and simply broadcast the sound of the ticking of a clock. The Prime Minister, Stanley Baldwin, addressed the nation and Virginia Woolf reckoned Baldwin hit the right note:

He gave out the impression that he was a tired country gentleman; the King another; both enjoyed Christmas at home; and the Queen is very lonely; one left the other taken, as must happen to married couples; and the King had seemed to him tired lately, but very kind, and quiet as if ready for a long journey; and had woken once or twice on the last day and had said something Kind ('Kind' was the adjective always) and had said to his Secretary 'How is the Empire?' – an odd expression. 'The Empire, Sir, is well'; whereupon he fell asleep . . . The shops are all black. Mourning is to outlast the London season. A black Ascot.

'Kind' was not necessarily the word his elder sons would have used to encapsulate the essence of their father. His relationship with each of them – which became very different – was never easy. He was much more comfortable with the women in his family. Perhaps they had the measure of him. The Duchess of York teased him. Playing horse and groom, little Lilibet led him around the drawing room by his beard. Until her death (a few weeks before his own) the old King and his unmarried younger sister Victoria chatted, daily, on the telephone. Once – Elizabeth Longford told me this story and assured me she had it on good authority – Princess Victoria telephoned the King at Buckingham Palace and said, 'Is that you, you old fool?' The operator interrupted: 'Beg pardon, your Royal Highness, His Majesty is not yet on the line.'[54]

The reign of George V lasted more than a quarter of a century. The reign of Edward VIII came to an abrupt end after eleven months and twenty-one days. As Prince of Wales, David had been popular with public and press alike. He was good-looking, charming, socially adept; he appeared articulate, energetic and able; he came over as unstuffy and contemporary, both human and humane. Those who saw him at closer quarters got a different picture. Beatrice Webb, socialist pioneer and co-founder of the *New Statesman*, met him at dinner in the summer of 1930 and recorded in her diary: 'He is neurotic and takes too much alcohol for health of body or mind. If I were his mother or grandmother I should be very nervous about his future . . . his expression was unhappy – there was a horrid dissipated look as if he had no settled home either for his intellect or his emotions . . . He must be a problem to the conventional courtiers who surround him.' He was.

In January 1931, at Melton Mowbray in Leicestershire, at the country house of one mistress, Thelma Furness (the second wife of the 1st Viscount Furness), David met his next mistress, his last, the non-negotiable love of his life: Wallis Simpson. Mrs Simpson was thirty-five, American, chic rather than beautiful, the Baltimore-born second wife of a New York businessman, Ernest Simpson (who had an English-born father), and who had come to London to run the British end of the family firm. David's interest in Wallis developed gradually. It began as a flirtatious friendship. The affair blossomed in the spring of 1934. By

---

[54] Possibly less reliable, but equally charming, are the two George V stories recounted by George Lyttelton in his correspondence with Rupert Hart-Davis: 'Much may be forgiven him for (a) when asked what film he would like to see when convalescing, announcing "Anything except that damned Mouse" and (b) when the footman, bringing in the early morning royal tea, tripped and fell with his load and heard from the pillow, "That's right; break up the whole bloody place."'

1935 the Prince was wholly infatuated. Within court circles the affair was an open secret, but it was not a matter that was discussed within the Windsor family. As one of David's nephews, George Harewood, the Princess Royal's son, points out: it was a different world, a world in which 'anything awkward' was best avoided. 'People kept much more private and much more quiet about things like that and were much more able to bottle up their feelings. I think the whole of my mother's family tended to bottle up their feelings very much.'

The crisis reached its climax in the autumn of 1936. In August, the new King – not yet crowned: his Coronation was set for the following May – holidayed at Balmoral, with his mistress installed in the rooms that, a year before, had been occupied by Queen Mary. In September, he asked the Yorks to take his place at the official opening of a hospital in Aberdeen so that he could meet Mrs Simpson, secretly, at the railway station. In October, Mrs Simpson secured her second divorce and became free to marry for a third time. In November, the King – Supreme Governor of the Church of England which did not then recognise divorce – told his mother, his brother and the prime minister that he had decided to marry his American divorcée and, if necessary, to give up his throne in order to be able to do so. 'Oh,' stammered Bertie, 'that's a dreadful thing to hear. None of us wants that, I least of all.'

Of all this, until the beginning of December, the majority of the British public knew nothing. Around the world, especially in the United States, reports of the King's relationship with Mrs Simpson had been widespread. In the United Kingdom, a deferential press had breathed not a word of scandal. Up on the nursery floor at 145 Piccadilly, Crawfie and Alah and the little princesses sensed something ominous in the air, but no one told them anything. Evidently something was about to happen, but what was it? 'It was impossible not to notice the change in Uncle David,' said Crawfie, in retrospect. 'He had been so youthful and gay. Now he looked distraught, and seemed not to be listening to what was said to him. He made plans with the children, and then forgot them.'

On Thursday 3 December, Crawfie went out and bought an evening paper. Standing on the doorstep, 'I remember I read the headline while I waited for the front door to open . . . THE KING AND HIS MINISTERS. GREAT CONSTITUTIONAL CRISIS . . . I do not know what we would have done at that time without the swimming lessons. They were a great diversion and took our minds off other matters.'

As the drama of the Abdication unfolded at Buckingham Palace and in Downing Street, down at the Bath Club, Lilibet and Margaret Rose, aged ten and six, were learning to swim. ('I remember the Bath Club well,' says Gina Kennard. 'Princess Elizabeth was always so nicely behaved. I remember she used to have a bag of sweets and, after swimming, would take the bag round, offering everybody a sweet.') The King could not marry Mrs Simpson and make her his Queen. A morganatic marriage, allowing her the position of wife but not the status of Queen, might be possible, but would require legislation. The government advised against it. The King agonised. The press fulminated. The Church pontificated. Mrs Simpson left the country to escape the furore. Queen Mary shook her head in sorrow and in anger. Bertie wept on his mother's shoulder, overwhelmed by the prospect of what was to come. Elizabeth retreated to her bed with a bout of influenza. At the poolside, Crawfie and Alah wrapped Lilibet and Margaret Rose in huge bath towels and, as each was awarded her Life Saving Certificate, rewarded the girls with hugs and a small box of chocolates.

The King was ready to sign the Instrument of Abdication. Edward VIII was about to become Prince Edward, Duke of Windsor. Prince Albert, Duke of York, was about to become King George VI.[55] At 145 Piccadilly, Crawfie was standing in an alcove on the landing outside the Duchess of York's bedroom. The door opened. 'Queen Mary came out of the Duchess's room. She who was always so upright, so alert, looked suddenly old and tired. The Duchess was lying in bed, propped up among pillows. She held out her hand to me. "I'm afraid there are going to be great changes in our lives, Crawfie," she said . . . When I broke the news to Margaret and Lilibet that they were going to live in Buckingham Palace they looked at me in horror. "What!" Lilibet said. "You mean for ever?" . . .' Crawfie went on:

> I had to explain to them that when Papa came home to lunch at one o'clock he would be King of England, and they would have to curtsy to him. The Royal children from their earliest years had always curtsied to their grandparents.
>
> 'And now you mean we must do it to Papa and Mummie?' Lilibet asked. 'Margaret too?'

---

[55] A new monarch can choose any name he pleases. Bertie chose 'George' to emphasise the natural succession to his father.

'Margaret also,' I told her, 'and try not to topple over.'

When the King returned, both little girls swept him a beautiful curtsy. I think perhaps nothing that had occurred had brought the change in his condition to him as clearly as this did. He stood for a moment touched and taken aback. Then he stooped and kissed both warmly. After this we had a hilarious lunch.

PHILIP & LILIBET

Chapter Five

'Behind the complicated details of the world stand the simplicities:
God is good, the grown-up man or woman knows the answer to
every question, there is such a thing as truth, and justice is as
measured and faultless as a clock. Our heroes are simple: they are
brave, they tell the truth, they are good swordsmen and they are
never in the long run really defeated. That is why no later books
satisfy us like those which were read to us in childhood – for those
promised a world of great simplicity of which we knew the rules,
but the later books are complicated and contradictory with experience; they are formed out of our own disappointing memories.'

Graham Greene (1904–91), *The Ministry of Fear*

'Dickie, this is absolutely terrible.' As Edward VIII prepared to sign the
Instrument of Abdication, his younger brother Bertie turned to their
cousin Louis Mountbatten – now thirty-six and a rising star in the
Admirality, where, of course, his own father, Louis of Battenberg, had
once been First Sea Lord – and shared his sense of desperation,
bordering on panic. 'I never wanted this to happen,' he bleated. 'I'm
quite unprepared for it. David has been trained for this all his life. I've
never even seen a State paper. I'm only a Naval Officer. It's the only
thing I know about.'

Mountbatten, a staunch ally of the King's until the moment of
Abdication,[56] offered David's reluctant successor an anecdote by way

---

[56] And, in fairness, beyond. David, as Prince of Wales, had been best man at
Mountbatten's wedding to Edwina Ashley in 1922. Following the Abdication,
Mountbatten offered his services as best man to David – or, at least, claimed to have
done so. The Duke of Windsor, as he had become, had hoped his brothers, the new
King and the Duke of Kent, might be his supporters at his wedding to Mrs Simpson.
In the event, there was no royal representation at the wedding at Candé on

of consolation and encouragement. 'This is a very curious coincidence,' he said. 'My father once told me that, when the Duke of Clarence died, your father came to him and said almost the same things that you have said to me now, and my father answered: "George, you're wrong. There is no more fitting preparation for a king, than to have been trained in the Navy."'

George V, the second son of Edward VII, was almost forty-five when he became King in 1910, four years before the outbreak of the First World War. George VI, the second son of George V, was almost forty-one when he became King in 1936, three years before the outbreak of the Second World War. Wars that are won can do much to enhance the reputation of the reigning monarch. Bertie, as Duke of York, was unexceptional, unexciting, a good family man, a decent chap, not overstretched, but conscientious when duty called. Bertie, as King, was stretched to the limit and not found wanting. René Massigli, the French ambassador to London at the time of Bertie's death just over fifteen years later, wrote in a report to the French foreign minister: 'If the "greatness" of a king can be measured by the extent to which his qualities corresponded to the needs of a nation at a given moment in history, then George VI was a great king, and perhaps a very great king.'

George VI – decent, dignified, determined – was the right man in the right place at the right time. He might lack his older brother's obvious glamour and panache, but you could see – and hear – from the way he wrestled with his speech impediment that he had courage. He might not be blessed with great imagination or any very obvious intellectual gifts, but he had palpable integrity. He looked to be what he was: a softly spoken, well-intentioned, quietly uncomplicated, honest English gentleman. And one blessed with a matchless Scottish wife.

Famously, in his Abdication broadcast (which he scripted himself, though he showed the draft to Winston Churchill who may have added the odd rhetorical flourish), David had said, 'You must believe me when I tell you that I have found it impossible to carry the heavy burden of responsibility and to discharge my duties as king as I would wish to

3 June 1937. Mountbatten had been loyal to David when he was King and would be loyal, too, to Bertie. On 11 December 1936 he wrote to the new King: 'My dear Bertie, Heartbroken as I am at David's departure and all the terrible trouble he has brought on us all I feel I must tell you how deeply I feel for Elizabeth and you having to shoulder his responsibilities in such trying circumstances. Luckily both you and your children have precisely those qualities needed to pull this country through this ghastly crisis.'

without the help and support of the woman I love.' Might the same not have been true of Bertie? Could he have coped as King without Elizabeth Bowes-Lyon as Queen? Certainly, he could not have coped as well. And, equally certainly, he found the burden to be a cruelly heavy one. When, later, someone commented on how well the exiled Duke of Windsor was looking, Queen Elizabeth responded, 'Yes. And who has got the lines now?' Sir Alexander Hardinge, who served as assistant and then principal private secretary to George V, Edward VIII and George VI, said of Bertie: 'As a result of the stress he was under the King used to stay up too late and smoked too many cigarettes – he literally died for England.'

There was no love lost between Queen Elizabeth and the Duke and Duchess of Windsor, but her niece, Margaret Rhodes, who was also, later, her lady-in-waiting, and spent many hours with her, is anxious to tell me – and you – that 'Not once in all the years I was with her – not once – did I ever hear her say anything remotely unpleasant about the Windsors. I know she liked David and, I promise you, I never heard her say anything uncharitable about the Duchess. Becoming Queen was not what Queen Elizabeth wanted or expected, but, when it happened, she accepted it.' And grew into the role and, I suspect, over time, rather relished it.

Sensibly, Queen Elizabeth kept her feelings about Wallis Simpson – and much besides – to herself. The females of the family (Queen Mary, Queen Elizabeth, Queen Elizabeth II, Princess Anne) are good at that. Mrs Simpson was less circumspect. 'Really David,' she wrote to the Duke of Windsor, having seen photographs and newsreel of the new Queen going about her duties, 'the pleased expression on the Duchess of York's face is funny to see. How she is loving it all.'

In March 1937, only three months into the new King's reign, Harold Nicolson, diarist and recently elected member of parliament, found himself (in knee breeches and silk stockings – court dress – it was a different world) attending the grandest of dinners at Buckingham Palace: 'The dining-table is one mass of gold candelabra and scarlet tulips.' The meal was disappointing, but the wine 'excellent and the port superb'. After dinner, in the drawing room, Nicolson observed the new Queen going the rounds: 'She wears upon her face a faint smile indicative of how much she would have liked her dinner-party were it not for the fact that she was Queen of England. Nothing could exceed the charm or dignity which she displays, and I cannot help feeling what a mess poor Mrs Simpson would have made of such an occasion. It demonstrated to us more than anything else how wholly impossible that marriage would have been.'

The evening over, Nicolson went home with friends and sat, over beer, late into the night, discussing 'the legend of monarchy'. At dinner, George VI had sat with Stanley Baldwin and David Lloyd George discussing affairs of state. In truth, he would have little impact upon them. The King was still Head of State, the figurehead, the font of honour, but he was no longer a force to be reckoned with. Queen Victoria had been (in Prince Philip's phrase) 'an executive monarch' who could 'do things'. As a diplomat, as an operator on the European stage, Edward VII had been able to make a difference. Even George V had had opinions – and taken action – that, to an extent, affected the course of history. But by the time Edward VIII's reign had ended, exactly a century after Queen Victoria's had begun, the *power* of the monarch had all but disappeared. Edward VIII was forced to abdicate because the government and parliament of the day – in the Dominions as much as in Britain – would not let him do as he pleased. George VI was the first of a new kind of monarch: a symbol, not a player.

'Until the King became King,' Margaret Rhodes said to me, 'he was always "Uncle Bertie". Then, overnight, he became "Sir".' The simple fact of being King gave the hesitant Duke of York a new authority. The machinery of the monarchy – well-oiled and with its own momentum – swept him, relatively effortlessly, through the first few months of his reign. Privately, he felt the strain, but, so far as the public was concerned, it was a matter of 'business as usual'. Bertie and Elizabeth might, silently, be brooding about David and Wallis across the water,[57] but, at home, the court, the press and the people were ready to move on. 'Least said, soonest mended' was the unstated national policy. 'The King is dead! (well, moved to France which comes to the same thing . . .) Long live the King!' The coronation, on 12 May 1937, was not Edward VIII's Coronation *manqué*: it was wholly George VI's, and the day when the new King – according to several observers – seemed, for the first time, wholly to accept his destiny.

Lilibet, now eleven and Heiress Presumptive, seems always to have

---

[57] They were not altogether silent. Bertie made it clear there was no prospect of Wallis ever being granted the title Royal Highness, nor of David returning to any kind of public life in the United Kingdom. Encouraged by Queen Mary – who had been quite horrified by her oldest son's behaviour – Bertie and Elizabeth ostracised David's closest and most ardent supporters, notably the celebrated hostess and shipping-line widow, Emerald, Lady Cunard.

accepted hers. Her life was to be different from here on in and there was nothing she could do about it. In public, even her closest chum, Sonia Graham-Hodgson, now had to curtsy to her and could no longer call her Lilibet. The family moved to Buckingham Palace. According to Sonia, Princess Elizabeth's parents, who, previously, had simply been 'downstairs' were now 'miles away' and very much busier. 'She grew up very fast.' According to Margaret Rhodes, 'I believe, briefly, she hoped that she might have a brother and be let off the hook, but I think she knew that wasn't very likely. She knew she would be Queen one day, but she thought it would be a long way off. She didn't talk about it much. In fact, I don't think she talked about it at all.'

What she did talk about, and take the keenest interest in, according to Crawfie, was her father's Coronation. Crawfie read to her Queen Victoria's account of her own Coronation in 1837. In 1937, as a present for her parents, in a neat hand, written in light pencil on lined paper, the little princess produced her own record of their great day:

> To Mummy and Papa
> In Memory of Their Coronation
> From Lilibet
> By Herself
> An Account of the Coronation

It's vivid stuff. The day begins with Lilibet, wrapped in an eiderdown by her faithful nursemaid Bobo, gazing out of her nursery window 'onto a cold misty morning'. Once they were breakfasted and dressed, the young princesses showed off their Coronation outfits 'to the visitors and housemaids':

> . . . I shall try and give you a description of our dresses. They were white silk with old cream lace and had little gold bows all the way down the middle. They had puffed sleeves with one little bow in the centre. Then there were the robes of purple velvet with gold on the edge.
>
> We went along to Mummy's bedroom and we found her putting on her dress. Papa was dressed in a white shirt, breeches and stockings, and over this he wore a crimson satin coat. Then a page came and said it was time to go down, so we kissed Mummy, and wished her good luck and went down.

Lilibet and Margaret Rose in their Coronation finery travelled in procession to Westminster Abbey in a glass coach: 'At first it was very jolty but we soon got used to it.' She watched the three-hour-long ceremony sitting alongside her grandmother, Queen Mary, in a specially created royal box:

> I thought it all *very, very* wonderful and I expect the Abbey did, too. The arches and beams at the top were covered with a sort of haze of wonder as Papa was crowned, at least I thought so.
>
> When Mummy was crowned and all the peeresses put on their coronets it looked wonderful to see arms and coronets hovering in the air and then the arms disappear as if by magic. Also the music was lovely and the band, the orchestra and the new organ all played beautifully.
>
> What struck me as rather odd was that Grannie did not remember much of her own Coronation. I should have thought that it would have stayed in her mind for ever.
>
> At the end the service got rather boring as it was all prayers. Grannie and I were looking to see how many more pages to the end, and we turned one more and then I pointed to the word at the bottom of the page and it said 'Finis'. We both smiled at each other and turned back to the service.

The service over, the princesses were escorted to 'our dressing room' and offered 'sandwiches, stuffed rolls, orangeade and lemonade' before taking the 'long drive' home.

> Then we all went on to the Balcony where *millions* of people were waiting below. After that we all went to be photographed in front of those awful lights.
>
> When we sat down to tea it was nearly six o'clock! When I got into bed my legs ached terribly!

The unique souvenir she presented to her parents (carefully tied together with pink ribbon) tells us much about the essential Lilibet. She is observant. She has a nice sense of humour. She lives in a world of nursemaids and housemaids and pages and accepts it completely. She goes out on to the balcony and '*millions* of people' are waiting below. The only thing she doesn't enjoy is being photographed. At the end of a long day her legs ache terribly. It's all a taste of things to come – and there's a telling phrase there, too, that, in many ways, sums up the phlegmatic approach to life that will stay with her – and sustain her – through the years: 'At first it was very jolty but we soon got used to it.'

Lilibet's composition – well-structured, with sound punctuation and impeccable spelling – tells us something about Crawfie, too. She was a good teacher. In February 1937, Crawfie, along with Alah and Bobo and their young charges, moved from 145 Piccadilly across Green Park to Buckingham Palace. 145 had been a home, albeit a grand one staffed by eighteen servants. Buckingham Palace was the headquarters of an empire, with a staff in excess of four hundred. 'I still recall with a shudder that first night spent in the Palace,' said Crawfie. 'The wind moaned in the chimneys like a thousand ghosts.' Crawfie was disconcerted by the sheer scale of the place and not impressed by the (in every sense) Victorian quality of much of the accommodation. The rooms were dark and musty. The light switch for Crawfie's bedroom was outside the door, two yards down the corridor. To reach the bathroom and lavatory you had to cross the passageway in your slippers and dressing gown, and risk bumping into the Palace postman on his early morning round. Crawfie did not like it. She was homesick.

Lilibet was less troubled. To her, it was a home – this was where her grandparents had lived – and the corridors, while endless ('People here need bicycles' she said), were more fun than forbidding. 'There was very little restraint placed on the children,' Crawfie reported. 'The Prime Minister, coming to see the King on affairs of State . . . might easily find himself tangled up with two excited little girls racing down the corridors. Or one stoutish little girl panting, "Wait for me, Lilibet. Wait for me!" Perhaps Dookie, the Queen's devoted corgi, might take a nip at a passing leg. Dookie adored the taste of strange trousers.'[58]

Gradually, the governess came to terms with her new surroundings. Improvements were made, walls were repapered, facilities were enhanced. The new Queen added her special touch. 'Elizabeth can make a home wherever she is,' said Bertie, proudly. 'Mice continued to be a menace,' said Crawfie, tartly. However, even she had to acknowledge that the gardens at the back of the Palace were a bonus, and there were still the weekends, 'now the best part of all our lives'

---

[58] And not just of trousers. Crawfie regarded Dookie as generally 'very sour-natured': 'He bit me once quite severely, and on another occasion took a piece out of Lord Lothian's hand. With great fortitude his lordship averred it was nothing! It did not hurt him at all. "All the same, he bled all over the floor," Lilibet pointed out.'

when 'we escaped from the Palace' and went down to Royal Lodge, Windsor. 'At Royal Lodge, court etiquette was forgotten, and ceremony left behind. We were just a family again.' In fact, nothing was to be quite the same again.

The Yorks were now King and Queen; Lilibet and Margaret Rose were first and second in line to the throne. Queen Mary, who, since her own Coronation, twenty-six years before, had always been the personification of majesty, and had long shown an interest in her grand-daughter's upbringing, now insisted that touches of regality be introduced to the children's routine. Meals on the nursery floor were served by liveried footmen. The food was English, but the menus were in French. Crawfie continued to be in charge of the princesses' education, but Crawfie's staple fare – Bible, History, Grammar, Arithmetic, Geography, Literature, Poetry, Writing and Composition, with Music, Drawing or Dancing after lunch – was now supplemented by lessons in constitutional history (for Lilibet) and, later, for both girls, by special classes in French, provided by a Mrs Montaudon-Smith (soon known as 'Monty'), and, later still, French Literature and European history, provided by a Belgian aristocrat, the Vicomtesse de Bellaigue (known as 'Toinon': her Christian name was Antoinette).

Lilibet's personal tutor in constitutional history was Henry Marten, co-author of a much-respected standard *History of England* and Vice-Provost of Eton College, the celebrated boys' school conveniently situated not far from Royal Lodge. Marten described his royal pupil as 'a somewhat shy girl of thirteen who when asked a question would look for confidence and support to her beloved governess, Miss Crawford'. The teacher, a bachelor, then in his sixties, who had been a master at Eton since 1896, does not seem to have been wholly at ease himself, never managing to look his first-ever female student directly in the eye, frequently addressing her as 'Gentlemen', and, alternately, biting his handkerchief and nervously crunching lumps of sugar produced at regular intervals from his jacket pocket.

Marten's syllabus covered more than a thousand years of royal heritage, starting with the reign of King Egbert, the king of the West Saxons (802–39), 'the first to unite all Anglo-Saxons', and culminating with the two most significant events of modern times: the advent of broadcasting and the 1931 Statute of Westminster. According to Marten, the Statute, which recognised the independence of the Dominions within the Commonwealth, gave a new significance to the Crown as the one remaining link between the United Kingdom and the Dominions, and the arrival of broadcasting enabled the wearer of the crown to sustain that link, in a personal way, by speaking directly to people around the world.

Princess Elizabeth was gradually being groomed for her destiny. Crawfie, meanwhile, was determined to keep the royal feet firmly on the ground: 'I suggested one day that it would be a very good idea for the children to start a Girl Guide Company at the Palace. Besides keeping them in touch with what children of their own ages were doing, I knew it would bring them into contact with others of their own ages and of all kinds and conditions.' So, in 1937, the Buckingham Palace Guide Company was formed, divided into three patrols, with a small Brownie pack tacked on for the benefit of Princess Margaret, who was still only seven. The girls – about three dozen in all – included royal cousins, royal friends, the children of courtiers and, according to Crawfie, 'those of Palace employees'. The Company met on Wednesday afternoons: in summer, in the Palace gardens; in winter, in one of the Palace's many echoing reception rooms. 'Just at first,' noted Crawfie, 'some of the children who joined started coming in party frocks, with white gloves, accompanied by fleets of nannies and governesses. We soon put a stop to all that.'

Princess Elizabeth was in the Kingfisher patrol and second-in-command to Patricia Mountbatten, Louis Mounbatten's elder daughter, who was two years her cousin's senior. 'Princess Elizabeth was a first-class Guide,' Countess Mountbatten told me, 'really efficient and completely level-headed. You could really rely on her. She'd never let you down. She quickly became a leader in her own right.'

The girls enjoyed their guiding. 'The Company was formed so that Elizabeth and Margaret Rose could meet and mix with ordinary children,' Countess Mountbatten told me, with a charming little chuckle. 'Well, there's ordinary and ordinary, of course. I think the children were quite carefully vetted. I think they had to be "suitable". But we did do ordinary guiding things. The long corridors at Buckingham Palace were ideal for practising signals and we went on wonderful expeditions in the Windsor forest, trekking and bird-watching and cooking sausages over the camp fire. The King's Piper came and played for us and we did Highland dancing. That was fun.'

What was Lilibet like at thirteen? Henry Marten said she was shy and looked to Crawfie to give her confidence. Crawfie said that, at thirteen, 'when so many are gawky', Lilibet 'was an enchanting child with the loveliest hair and skin and a long, slim figure'. She was growing up. She was no longer biting her nails. She was almost as tall as her mother. Soon her wardrobe of 'very simple afternoon frocks' – 'usually of tussore silk, often hand-smocked, quite short with knickers to match' – would give way to something more sophisticated: a hemline below the knees, silk stockings in place of white cotton ankle socks, a beret instead of a winter bonnet or a summer straw hat. Lilibet and Margaret Rose who, according to Crawfie, 'were never in the least interested in what they were going to wear and just put on what they were told', no longer appeared, automatically, in matching outfits. The child was giving way to the young adult.

Was she a moody adolescent? 'No,' says Patricia Mountbatten. 'Far from it,' says Margaret Rhodes, 'she was always very controlled – or, should I say, in control?'

Countess Mountbatten says, 'The Queen told me recently that she had been quite nervous of me when we were in the Guides together and she was my second-in-command. That surprised me, but, of course, she has always been guarded about her feelings. Even as a girl, she was careful how she appeared in front of others. For example, if she fell and hurt herself she knew she mustn't be seen to cry.' 'Only once,' according to Crawfie, 'did she walk right into my arms, thinking of nothing but that for the moment she had to have a little comforting . . . "Oh, Crawfie, Grandfather Strathmore is dead," she said, and burst into tears.'

Like her father and, to an even greater extent her royal grand-parents, King George and Queen Mary, Princess Elizabeth was not given to public displays of emotion. She was, from an early age, self-controlled, self-contained, self-sufficient. Was that healthy? We might not think so, living, as we do, in the let-it-all-hang-out twenty-first century, but things were very different seventy years ago. Rudyard Kipling was still alive.[59] The 'stiff upper lip' wasn't a joke: it was a much-vaunted national characteristic. Lilibet was a Girl Guide[60] and the daughter of a king – and of a king of England, too.

---

[59] He was born in 1865 and died in 1936. Interestingly, his poem *If*, which encapsulates the traditional values of his time, was recently voted 'Britain's most popular poem'. And, coincidentally, the 1946 film *Brief Encounter*, a love story that turns on self-denial and repressed emotion, was voted 'most popular romantic movie of all time'.

[60] The Boy Scouts and Girl Guides movement was founded by Robert Baden-Powell (1857–1941). On 4 July 1911, in a letter to a friend, he wrote: 'I know my weak points and am only thankful that I have managed to get along in spite of them! I think that's the policy for this world: Be glad of what you have got, and not miserable about what you would like to have had, and not over-anxious about what the future will bring.'

Besides, as Margaret Rhodes pointed out to me, she had an outlet for her emotions. She might stand, as, by her own account, she did, for hours, gazing out of the window of Buckingham Palace, 'watching the people and the cars there in the Mall', saying little, but wondering 'what they were doing and where they were all going, and what they thought about outside the Palace'. But, then, she could scamper off and play with the corgis and the labradors – with Dookie and Spark, Flash and Mimsey, Scruffy and Stiffy – or go for a ride on Peggy or Comet. Margaret Rhodes stubs out yet another cigarette and ponders, 'Perhaps she didn't repress her feelings. Perhaps she channelled them through her animals. Dogs are faithful. And they don't tell tales. I don't know. All I do know is that the real love of her life, then, as now, was dogs followed by horses.'

Christopher Robin, introduced to the world in the same year as Princess Elizabeth, blamed his troubled adolescence on his parents and on the global fame attached to his name as a consequence of his father's four best-selling children's books. He later accused A. A. Milne of 'building his reputation by standing on a small boy's shoulders'. Princess Elizabeth, like Christopher Robin, received sackfuls of post from unknown admirers. Like Christopher Robin, she was photographed, written about and featured in newspapers and magazines around the world. He appeared, with Pooh, in the window of Selfridges department store in Oxford Street. She appeared, with her pony, as a waxwork at Madame Tussaud's exhibition in Marylebone Road. Unlike Christopher Robin, however, Elizabeth did not grumble: she accepted her lot.

And it was a bizarre lot to have to accept. Aged eleven, when she was taken to a children's matinée at the Holborn Empire, as she entered the auditorium, fifteen hundred children got to their feet and sang a specially written children's verse of the national anthem. Aged twelve, she was attending the Buckingham Palace Garden Parties, walking dutifully behind her parents through a throng of three thousand excited subjects, who bowed and curtsied as she passed. Aged thirteen, she accepted her first official post: as President of the Children's League of the Princess Elizabeth of York Hospital, which had been named after her. From birth, she had been a public figure: now, she had increasingly to become accustomed to public life, to exposure to public gaze, to being – literally – the centre of attention.

Princess Elizabeth was blessed with parents who were loving – and united. Prince Philip's parents were loving, too, after their fashion, but they lived apart from one another and Philip did not live with them. In November 1937, Philip, aged sixteen, saw Andrea and Alice together for the first time in six years – and for the last time ever. That was when the family gathered in Darmstadt for the heartbreaking business of the funeral of Philip's sister Cécile and her husband and two of their three children. Andrea was devastated by the deaths: Cécile had been his favourite daughter. Alice coped the better of the two. Her sister Louise (now married to the Crown Prince of Sweden) said Alice was 'so balanced & so splendid about her sorrow'. She appeared to have regained some of her old equilibrium. She was even ready to consider the possibility of living with her husband once more. That was not a prospect Andrea was willing to entertain. He returned to the South of France and the singular life of a displaced prince. He moved between Monte Carlo and Nice, between hotel rooms and the yachts of friends. He drank, he charmed, he reminisced. At a distance, he followed the complexities of Greek politics. When he could, he visited relations. At the beginning of 1938, he asked Philip to join him on an expedition to Athens to attend the wedding of Crown Prince Paul of Greece and Princess Frederika of Hanover.

Cécile's youngest child, her baby daughter Johanna, had been too small to take on the fatal flight in November 1937. She died, nonetheless, aged barely two, of a fever, in June 1939. Alice, who was at her little granddaughter's deathbed, wrote to Philip: '. . . we had such a sweet picture before our eyes of a lovely sleeping child with golden curls, looking for me so very like Cécile at that age that it was like losing my child a second time and I was thankful that Papa was away travelling and did not see that, for Papa adored Cécile when she was small and could never bear to be parted from her.' This was the month in which Philip turned eighteen. His mother, having disappeared from his life throughout his adolescence, was in touch with her boy once more. A week later she wrote to him again: 'I am quite exhausted by the strain and the sadness of it all.'

The Yorks, undoubtedly, were more conventional parents. Inevitably, as King and Queen, however, they saw less of their daughters than they would have liked. In the summer of 1938, with the clouds of war gathering across Europe, Lilibet and Margaret Rose were left at home as papa and mama undertook their first foreign assignment: a state visit to France intended to reinforce the *Entente Cordiale*. In May 1939, with war now imminent (despite Chamberlain's determination to secure peace), the King and Queen were despatched on a longer and more ambitious expedition: to Canada and the United States. The American President, Franklin Roosevelt, invited the little princesses along for the ride. 'I shall try to have one or two Roosevelts of approximately the same age to play with them!' he promised.

In the event, the girls were left at home, perhaps wisely. The tour proved arduous and the transatlantic crossing, on board the *Empress of Australia*, potentially perilous. Off the coast of Newfoundland, the fog was treacherous. The Queen reported by letter to her mother-in-law, Queen Mary: 'For three & a half days we only moved a few miles. The fog was so thick, that it was like a white cloud round the ship, and the foghorn blew incessantly. . . . We were nearly hit by a berg the day before yesterday, and the poor Captain was nearly demented because some kind cheerful people kept on reminding him that it was about here that the Titanic was struck, & *just* about the same date.'

George VI and Queen Elizabeth were the first reigning British monarchs to visit North America and their tour was a triumph. Even in Quebec, the cry went up: '*Vive le Roi! Vive la Reine!*' The Governor-General of Canada was Lord Tweedsmuir (better remembered as the novelist John Buchan) who chaperoned the King and Queen for much of the Canadian leg of the tour and drafted the text of the King's principal speeches. For Tweedsmuir, the most telling moment came at the unveiling of a war memorial in Ottawa:

> The King spoke admirably and clearly, as he has done each time since he landed. After the ceremony the Queen said to me that she wanted to go down among the veterans, and I thought, knowing what excellent fellows they are, that it would be worth chancing it. A most extraordinary scene followed. The King and Queen, and my wife and myself, were absorbed in a crowd of six or seven thousand ex-soldiers, who kept the most perfect order among themselves, and opened up lanes for Their Majesties to pass through. There was no need of the police, and indeed the police would have had no chance. It was a wonderful example of what a people's king means . . . One old man shouted to me, 'Ay, man, if Hitler could see this!' It was extraordinarily moving because some of these old fellows were weeping . . . The capacity of Their Majesties for getting in touch with the people amounts to genius.

Tweedsmuir was smitten. The King was a 'wonderful mixture' of 'shrewdness, kindliness and humour': 'He is simply one of the best people in the world. I never thought that I should feel the romantic affection for my sovereign that I felt for him.' The Queen 'has a kind of gentle, steady radiance which is very wonderful' and 'a perfect genius for the right kind of publicity, the unrehearsed episodes here were marvellous.' When he had dried his eyes and cleared his throat, the Governor-General reported to the British prime minister: 'The Statute of Westminster is now much more than a mere piece of paper, for we have been given a visual revelation of its meaning.' Henry Marten, Lilibet's tutor, would have been gratified.

The King and Queen were as rapturously received in the United States. They took to the President. 'He is so easy to get to know,' wrote the King, '& never makes one feel shy.' Roosevelt was equally charmed, and impressed – and possibly a little surprised – to find his British guests quite knowledgeable 'not only about foreign affairs in general but also about social legislation'. 'The British sovereigns have conquered Washington,' said the *New York Times*. Crowds turned out to cheer and an initially sniffy press was quickly won over. The misty-eyed Lord Tweedsmuir murmured to His Majesty: 'It is a pleasant saying in the United States at the moment that you have taken the "g" out of kingship.' The King himself, whose confidence grew as the tour proceeded, learnt from the experience. 'There must be no more high-hat business,' he reflected during the tour, 'the sort of thing that my father and those of his day regarded as essential as the correct attitude – the feeling that certain things could not be done.'

The King and Queen returned to England on 22 June 1939. The imminence of war, combined with glowing coverage of the tour in the British press, ensured a properly patriotic and heart-tuggingly warm welcome home for the royal travellers. Lilibet and Margaret Rose had not seen their parents for seven weeks.[61] The girls, accompanied by Alah and Crawfie, travelled by train to Southampton. There they were taken, by destroyer, to meet their parents' ship mid-Channel. While Crawfie and the princesses ate cherries with the captain on deck, Alah retreated to a cabin ('I think she was not feeling very well,' Crawfie

---

[61] The matter of these royal separations bravely borne needs to be kept in perspective. At the time, it was not unusual for middle- and upper-class girls and boys of this age (nine and thirteen) to be away at boarding school for twelve-week terms. There was a half-term 'exeat', but the children of diplomats, serving soldiers and the like, often did not see their parents for months at a time – and survived. In my dormitory at my prep school, in the 1960s, I recall that Bowden (aged seven) cried himself to sleep in a quite pitiful manner – but only for the first few nights of term.

reported, lips pursed). At last, 'The *Empress of Britain* came in sight and we went below to tidy. The Captain's cabin amused us, with its, to us almost primitive amenities.' Back on deck, they saw *Empress* 'heaving to' and the King and Queen amidships. 'The little girls could hardly walk up the ladder quickly enough,' recalled Crawfie, 'but when they reached the top they rushed to Mummie and Papa. They kissed them and hugged them again and again . . . The Queen kissed me and said how much the children had grown and how well they looked, and all the time the King could hardly take his eyes off Lilibet.'

In the ship's dining room happiness reigned. There was much merriment, and balloons and bunting, too. The King pushed some of the balloons through a porthole. Lord Airlie popped some of them with his cigarette. Champagne cocktails were served and Crawfie got a little squiffy. We can imagine what Alah thought. We are told the Queen said, 'Poor Crawfie, I ought to have warned you. They make them rather strong aboard.'

There was rejoicing in the streets as well. From Southampton to Waterloo, all along the railway route, Their Majesties' subjects turned out to cheer. From Waterloo to Buckingham Palace, the King and Queen travelled home in state. According to police estimates, some fifty thousand people crowded in to the Mall to salute them, the men raising their caps and bowler hats (and furled umbrellas) in greeting, the women and children waving flags and handkerchiefs. As the Royal Carriage passed through Parliament Square, MPs of every party came out of the House of Commons to watch the parade. 'Such fun,' Harold Nicolson reported to his wife, Vita Sackville-West: '. . . The bells of St Margaret's began to swing into welcome and the procession started creeping round the corner. They went very slowly, and there were the King and Queen and the two princesses. We lost all our dignity and yelled and yelled. The King wore a happy schoolboy grin. The Queen was superb. She really does manage to convey to each individual in the crowd that he or she have had a personal greeting. It is due, I think, to the brilliance of her eyes.[62] But she is in truth one of the most amazing Queens since Cleopatra. We returned to the House with lumps in our throats.'

---

[62] And, I think, to the way she let them rest, however momentarily, upon you. She didn't appear to be scanning the crowd. The way she nodded her head, as well as her wave, added to the effect that she was looking directly at you. It was, of course, an illusion, but, as Houdini pointed out, 'That's the nature of magic.'

The King and Queen were riding high. To date, this was their finest hour. Perhaps it needed to be: it was the prelude, after all, to Britain's darkest hour. War was looming. There was a whiff of romance in the air as well. On 22 July, exactly a month after their triumphal return from America, and five weeks and a day before the declaration of war on 3 September, the King and his family and their entourage – Crawfie and Alah and all – set off for a brief excursion on the Royal Yacht *Victoria and Albert*. Their first port of call – part duty, part pleasure – was along the Devon coast, at the mouth of the estuary of the River Dart, at Dartmouth, at the Royal Naval College, where the King – a cadet at the College in the years before the Great War – was to carry out an inspection, and Princess Elizabeth, age thirteen, was to meet Prince Philip of Greece, age eighteen. Lilibet later claimed it was love at first sight.

Chapter Six

'He had never kissed me, and I wondered whether he would.'
Vita Sackville-West (1892–1962), *Portrait of a Marriage*

'How do you do?'

He was standing over her, looking gently amused. He was tall and slim, blond and blue-eyed, and his dark blue naval uniform suited him. He was eighteen and achingly handsome.

'I'm quite well,' she said. 'Thank you.' She was sitting on the floor, her knees tucked under her, leaning over the track of a toy railway set, trying to make an engine stand steady on the rails.

'You haven't had mumps then?' he asked. He seemed to be half laughing as he spoke. She sensed he was teasing her, but she did not mind.

'No,' she said, 'but Papa – the King – he had the mumps when he was a cadet here. He said we should be careful. He says it's really horrid.'

Philip nodded, slowly. 'Yes, beastly. I know one of the chaps who's got it now. He's having a rotten time.' Her brow furrowed. She was trying to look sympathetic. He thought she was anxious. He smiled. It was a kindly smile. 'Don't worry,' he said, 'I'm not contagious.' He crouched down beside her and took the engine out of her hand. 'Let me.'

'Thank you,' she said, again.

'To be honest,' he said, when they had watched the small train rattle around the track four times more, 'I don't see you as a clockwork railway sort of girl. Do you fancy a game of tennis?'

She looked uncertain. 'I haven't got –'

He interrupted: 'Of course not.' He got to his feet. 'But we could jump the nets or something. Or we could play croquet. Do you play croquet? It's a filthy game. Vicious. Shall we play croquet?'

'Yes,' she said, smiling. 'I'd like that.'

He took her right hand in his and pulled her to her feet. 'Come on,' he said, 'Let's go.'

Well, dear reader, it might have been like that. Who knows? He says he can't remember much about it, and she's not saying, and all the other witnesses are long since dead.

What we do know is this. Prince Philip of Greece, fresh out of Gordonstoun, just turned eighteen, apparently very engaging (there is evidence), certainly very handsome (there are photographs), was undoubtedly at the Royal Naval College, Dartmouth, on the weekend of 22/23 July 1939. He was coming to the end of his three months' initial officers' training course. He was not a traditional Dartmouth cadet. They came to the College at thirteen and stayed for five years. Philip was a Special Entry recruit. These were public school boys, who joined up at eighteen, and would normally begin their naval careers on a training cruiser. However, in anticipation of war, HMS *Frobisher*, the cruiser in which Philip would have expected to train, was being refitted and rearmed, hence the presence of Philip – and the other 'Specials' – at Dartmouth.

We know, too, that on Saturday 22 July, the day *Victoria and Albert* arrived at Dartmouth, Philip was invited to join the royal party. It is hardly surprising, really, since he was a cousin of the King's, and his uncle, Louis Mountbatten, was in attendance on board the Royal Yacht. On 22 July, Mountbatten noted in his diary: 'Philip accompanied us and dined on board.' On 23 July, Mountbatten reported: 'Philip came back aboard V and A for tea and was a great success with the children.'

It seems he entertained them ashore as well. According to the ever-present Crawfie, 'On the Sunday morning we were going to the College because there was to be a special service. . . . I remember it was a lovely day, though it became a bit cloudy around eleven. Just about the time the service was scheduled to start and the boys had been paraded before the King and Queen, the Dartmouth College doctor said, "I am very, very sorry, but two of the boys have developed mumps." There was a long conversation as to whether the children ought to go into the chapel . . .'

Eventually, it was decided – 'better safe than sorry' – that Crawfie should take the girls across to the Captain's House and that Prince Philip would be detailed to entertain them. Lilibet and Margaret Rose were busy playing with the captain's children's train set when Philip appeared. 'A fair-haired boy, rather like a Viking, with a sharp face and piercing blue eyes' is how Crawfie remembered him. 'He was good-looking, though rather off-hand in his manner. He said, "How do you do," to Lilibet, and for a while they knelt side by side playing with the trains. He soon got bored with that. We had ginger crackers and lemonade, in which he joined, and then he said, "Let's go to the tennis courts and have some real fun jumping the nets." '

Off they went, chaperoned by Crawfie. 'I thought he showed off a good deal,' she recalled, eleven years after the event, 'but the little girls were much impressed. Lilibet said, "How good he is, Crawfie. How high he can jump." She never took her eyes off him the whole time. He was quite polite to her, but did not pay her any special attention. He spent a lot of time teasing plump little Margaret.'

How much of this happened in fact and how much in Crawfie's imagination, it is impossible to say. There are, however, in existence two photographs taken that weekend, each featuring Philip and Elizabeth, and each telling its own story. The first is a snapshot of the two of them alone playing croquet in the garden of the Captain's House. The focus of the picture seems to be ships moored in the Dart estuary, but in the foreground, glimpsed behind a parapet, are the two teenagers. The eighteen-year-old boy appears to be concentrating on his next stroke. The thirteen-year-old girl, standing by a hoop, in her neat double-breasted summer coat, small hands clasped together in front of her, is gazing at him intently. She does look happy.

The other photograph shows the entire royal party watching the cadets on parade. Sitting in the front row, staring somewhat vacantly into the middle distance, is Lilibet. She is wearing a solemn expression and what looks like a beret to match her coat. She seems very young. Three places along, seated next to a tiny Princess Margaret (who doesn't look plump at all), is the Queen, wearing a fabulous hat and chatting graciously to the captain. Standing immediately behind them, side by side, are Louis Mountbatten and Prince Philip. Mountbatten is looking amused and avuncular. Philip is leaning forward, grinning, gesticulating with his right hand: he is, without doubt, in the middle of telling a funny story. He has the unmistakable look of a charming young man who is often in the middle of telling a funny story.

That weekend the boy certainly made his mark. When the time came for *Victoria and Albert* to set sail, permission was given to the cadets to commandeer what vessels they could – rowing boats, motorboats, dinghies – and take to the estuary to give the royal visitors a memorable send-off. As the Royal Yacht made her stately progress out of the harbour she was escorted by a veritable flotilla of small craft manned by enthusiastic young men. 'They followed the *Victoria and Albert* quite a long way,' according to Crawfie, who was on deck with the royal party. 'Then the King got very alarmed and said to Sir Dudley North [the Commander of the Royal Yacht], "It's ridiculous, and most unsafe. You must signal them to go back." Most of the boys did go back immediately, and all the others followed shortly except this one solitary figure whom we saw rowing away as hard as he could, who was, of course, Philip. Lilibet took the glasses and had a long look at him. In the end the King said, "The young fool. He must go back, otherwise we will have to heave to and send him back." At last Philip seemed to realise they did want him to go back – they were shouting at him through the megaphone – and he turned back while we gazed at him until he became just a very small speck in the distance.'

Today, Prince Philip says that the story, as told by Crawfie, is somewhat exaggerated – the small boats only followed the Royal Yacht for a few hundred yards, then turned round and went home – but he does not deny the essence of it. And today, the Queen does not deny the essence of it either: that was the weekend she fell for Philip.

And why not? He was enviably good-looking. He was fit.[63] He was fun. He was funny. At this stage in the story, Louis Mountbatten – Uncle Dickie – did not know Philip that well. Through his teens, because he sometimes stayed with him during the school holidays, Philip had been much more under the wing of his other Mountbatten uncle, Dickie's older brother, Georgie, the 2nd Marquess of Milford Haven, the father of David, Philip's best friend at school and later, at his wedding, his best man.

Georgie had died of cancer of the bone marrow on 8 April 1938, aged only forty-five, mourned by all who knew him. Dickie wrote in his diary that day: 'The sweetest natured, most charming, most able, most brilliant, entirely lovable brother anyone ever had is lost. Heartbroken.' Gina Kennard, who was nineteen at the time, and whose mother's sister was married to Georgie, told me: 'You couldn't not love Georgie.

[63] In 2001, at the Royal Variety Performance, I told Prince Philip that a beautiful young pop singer called Mylene Klass (a member of the fleetingly-famous band Hear'Say) had told me that she regarded him as 'right fit' – meaning physically attractive. He was intrigued by the phrase and pleased with the news. He watches his figure: he cares about his appearance.

Everybody adored him. I remember as a girl sitting under the dining room table, hidden under the table cloth, thinking how lovely he was. Princess Elizabeth told me she loved him, too. His death was another blow for Philip, especially coming, as it did, only a matter of months after his sister Cécile and her family were killed in that awful air crash. It was a difficult time.'

On Georgie's death, Dickie, aged thirty-eight, with only daughters himself, assumed the role of Philip's informal guardian. The month before, in March 1938, Dickie had already had him to stay at Adsdean, the Mountbattens' country house just outside Portsmouth. 'Philip was here all last week doing his entrance exams for the Navy,' Dickie reported to his wife. 'He had his meals with us and he really is killingly funny. I like him very much.'

Prince Philip will deny it today, but I get the impression of a young man who felt some obligation to sing for his supper. He was handsome, engaging, well-mannered. He was also homeless. And, by royal standards, virtually penniless. 'Rubbish,' he snorts. When he wasn't at boarding school, he stayed with his grandmother (Princess Victoria of Hesse, widow of Louis of Battenberg, 1st Marquess of Milford Haven) in her grace-and-favour apartment at Kensington, or with one of his English uncles, or, until the prospect of war made it impossible, one of his sisters and their German husbands. He accepts that his parents were not well heeled. His father, Prince Andrea, had managed to get some funds out of Greece and Russia and gave Philip a small allowance when he joined the navy. His mother, Princess Alice, now received nothing from Andrea, and depended on an allowance from the ever-generous banking heiress, Edwina Mountbatten.[64] 'We weren't well-off,' says Prince Philip, 'but I don't remember wanting for anything.'

He cannot be cajoled or tempted into complaining about any aspect of his upbringing. Nor is he interested, it seems, in analysing the effect

---

[64] She was the daughter of Wilfrid Ashley MP (a grandson of the great Earl of Shaftesbury) and Maud Cassel, the only daughter of Sir Ernest Cassel, the banker known as 'Windsor Cassel' because of his role as financial adviser to Edward VII when he was Prince of Wales. Cassel's wife died in 1880. Maud died in 1911. Edwina came to live with her grandfather at Brook House in Mayfair when she was just seventeen. When he died, Edwina inherited some £2.3 million. When Cassel's sister died, Edwina inherited Brook House and yet more money. When her father died, she also inherited Broadlands, near Romsey in Hampshire, where she and Dickie started their honeymoon in 1922 and Philip and Elizabeth theirs in 1947. Edwina was amazing: brilliant, bedazzling, promiscuous, generous, wild.

it might have had on him. 'My father was in the south of France and my mother was just ill. I had to get on with it.' From the age of eleven, really until he married Princess Elizabeth when he was twenty-six, he did not have one fixed address. 'Whither the storm carries me, I go –' he wrote in a visitors' book at the beginning of 1946, '– a willing guest.'

And a welcome one. He had the glamour and energy of youth. He was funny. He had an engaging and memorable laugh. He was articulate and he was no fool. When he took the entrance examination to get into Dartmouth he came sixteenth out of thirty-four. At the College, his written work was no more than average, but in the oral exam, he scored 380 out of a potential 400 marks. At Gordonstoun he had become 'Guardian' or head boy. At Dartmouth he was awarded the King's Dirk as the best all-round cadet of his entry. He had leadership qualities and ambition. He strove to live up to the ideal of manhood set out in Kipling's famous poem. Certainly, he 'walked with kings' without losing 'the common touch'. In the run-up to taking the Dartmouth entrance exam, he stayed, as a paying guest, with a Mr and Mrs Mercer in Cheltenham. By day, Mr Mercer prepared young men for their naval examinations. By night, according to Philip's cousin and exact contemporary, Alexandra of Yugoslavia,[65] Mr Mercer's teenage daughter entertained the student prince to 'radio or record sessions' in the family sitting room. Alexandra also recalled Philip enjoying a holiday dalliance in Venice at about the same time. 'He was very amusing, gay, full of life and energy and he was a tease,' she said. 'Blondes, brunettes and redhead charmers, Philip gallantly and I think quite impartially squired them all.'

It is frequently asserted that Saturday 22 July 1939 was the day on which Philip and Elizabeth first set eyes on one another. Not so. They had met before. They were cousins, after all. In Queen Victoria and Prince Albert they had the same great-great-grandparents. In Queen Alexandra (the proper one: the wife of Edward VII) they had the same great-aunt. As a small child, Philip was taken to tea at Buckingham Palace with Queen Mary who considered him 'a nice little boy with very blue eyes'. His mother was born at Windsor Castle. His grandmother lived at Kensington Palace. His grandfather had been an

[65] Princess Alexandra of Greece (1921–93), granddaughter of Andrea's eldest brother, King Constantine I, married King Peter of Yugoslavia in 1944. In 1959, she published *Prince Philip: A Family Portrait*, regarded, at Buckingham Palace, as 'a somewhat unreliable memoir'.

ADC[66] to Queen Victoria, Edward VII and King George V. At his prep school, Philip had a photograph of the King-Emperor, signed 'From Uncle George'. (He did not flaunt it: it was spotted by a dorm-mate hidden in his trunk.) Prince Philip believes that he and Princess Elizabeth probably first met – aged thirteen and eight – at Westminster Abbey on 29 November 1934, when his cousin, Princess Marina of Greece and Denmark, married Lilibet's uncle George, Duke of Kent. They certainly met again at the Coronation of George VI in 1937. What distinguishes their meeting in July 1939, of course, is not Philip's attitude to Elizabeth – he was interested in girls, girls of his own age, not thirteen year olds – but hers to him. In *The Power and the Glory*, Graham Greene says, 'There is always one moment in childhood when the door opens and lets the future in.'

Through her field glasses on the deck of *Victoria and Albert* Lilibet may have gazed at Philip in his rowing boat until he disappeared from view, but romance was some way off.[67] There was a war to contend with first. At the beginning of August, the Prime Minister, Neville Chamberlain, convinced that war was not, in fact, imminent, set off for a spot of salmon-fishing.[68] On 6 August, the King, who liked and trusted Chamberlain, set off for Balmoral for his customary family holiday. The grouse were expected to be particularly good that year. On 9 August, duty called, and the King came down briefly from Scotland to inspect the Reserve Fleet at Weymouth and, after the event, reported to his mother, Queen Mary: 'I feel sure it will be a deterrent factor in Hitler's mind to start a war.' On 22 August news came that Germany and Russia had signed the Nazi-Soviet Pact. On 24 August parliament was recalled and the King returned to London. The grouse had been magnificent. On 29 August he told a British ambassador who called at Buckingham Palace that he had never seen so many grouse, that he had bagged 1,600 brace in six days, that it was 'utterly damnable that the villain Hitler had upset everything'. Happily, now that Britain had signed a formal treaty of alliance with Poland, he was convinced there would be peace and that 'this time Hitler's bluff had been called'. Unhappily, His Majesty was mistaken.

[66] The role of aide-de-camp in this context was more honorary than onerous.

[67] In the movie, a rainbow will be permissible in this shot. Apparently, there really was both rain and sunshine that afternoon.

[68] Salmon-fishing was always his priority. Declining the office of Chancellor in May 1923, he wrote: 'What a day! Two salmon this morning and the offer of the Exchequer this afternoon.'

On 1 September German troops crossed the Polish border. On 2 September Britain and France issued an ultimatum to Germany: withdraw or face war. A deadline was set for eleven o'clock on Sunday 3 September. Germany failed to respond with the undertakings demanded. The Second World War was under way.

'Who *is* this Hitler, spoiling everything?' demanded Princess Margaret. 'I remember trying to give the Princess a painstaking and unbiased character sketch,' said Crawfie, 'but it wasn't very easy.' The King and Queen were now based at Buckingham Palace, staying at Windsor Castle overnight and at weekends. Margaret and Lilibet remained in Scotland, at Birkhall on the Balmoral estate, with Alah and Bobo and Crawfie. 'Why had Mummie and Papa to go back, Crawfie?' asked Margaret, 'Do you think the Germans will come and get them?' Crawfie was predictably reassuring and Lilibet, apparently, 'was very calm and helpful, as usual, and at once ranged herself on the side of law and order.' 'I don't think people should talk about battles and things in front of Margaret,' she said. 'We don't want to upset her.'

The princesses' parents telephoned their daughters every night at six o'clock. 'Stick to the usual programme as far as you can, Crawfie' was the Queen's instruction. 'Up there among the moors and heather it was easy to do this,' said Crawfie. 'The River Muick rippled merrily through the gardens just as usual in those lovely autumn days, while Poland was being over-run and "lights were going out all over Europe".'

Now and then the horrors of war managed to penetrate the peace of the Highlands. The children listened to the wireless. They heard the anti-British propaganda broadcasts made by William Joyce, the notorious 'Lord Haw-Haw', and threw books and cushions at the wireless set in protest. On 14 October they heard the news of the sinking of *Royal Oak* at Scapa Flow with the loss of more than eight hundred lives. 'Lilibet jumped horrified from her chair,' according to Crawfie, 'her eyes blazing with anger . . . "Crawfie, it can't be! All those nice sailors."'

On 18 December, to their surprise and delight, they were summoned to Norfolk to join their parents for the traditional Royal Family Christmas at Sandringham. They did not know what the future would hold. No one did. They listened to their father as he made his Christmas Day broadcast, live, seated in front of two large microphones, dressed in the uniform of an Admiral of the Fleet. The hesitancy with which he spoke – at one point having to start a passage again from the beginning – made what he had to say all the more moving:

A new year is at hand. We cannot tell what it will bring. If it brings peace, how thankful we shall be. If it brings continued struggle we shall remain undaunted. In the meantime I feel that we may all find a message of encouragement in the lines which, in my closing words, I should like to say to you:

'I said to the man who stood at the Gate of the Year, "Give me a light that I may tread safely into the unknown." And he replied, "Go out into the darkness, and put your hand into the Hand of God. That shall be better than light, and safer than a known way." '

May that Almighty Hand guide and uphold us all.

The King's children were moved by what they heard. So were the British people. George VI had a good war. At first, he was frustrated. 'I wish I had a definite job like you,' he wrote to Louis Mountbatten, now captain of HMS *Kelly* and commander of the 5th Destroyer Flotilla. 'Mine is such an awful mixture, trying to keep people cheered up in all ways, and having to find fault as well as praising them.' He was a constitutional monarch: his lot was to advise, counsel and warn the government of the day. He was Head of State and Commander-in-Chief of the Armed Forces: his role was to look the part, to lead by example, to *be* rather than to *do*. He delivered in full measure. He wore his uniform throughout the war. He paraded, he saluted, he inspected, he handed out medals whenever and wherever was required. When rationing was introduced, he made it clear that he and his family expected – wanted – to share the privations of the people.

And when, in September 1940, Buckingham Palace was bombed, it was akin to a blessing in disguise. 'The King & I saw two of the bombs drop quite close to us in the quadrangle,' the Queen wrote to Osbert Sitwell. 'They screamed past the window and exploded with a tremendous boom and crash about fifteen yards away. We both thought we were dead, & nipped quickly into the passage, where we found our two pages crouching on the floor. They rose at once & we then descended to the basement, pretending really that it was nothing.' It was quite something: the King and Queen were in the firing line and seen to be. As the Queen remarked, famously, after the bombing: 'Now I feel I can look the East End in the face.' 'Thank God for a good King,' someone shouted in the street as the sovereign inspected the damage done by yet another enemy air raid. 'Thank God for a good people,' the King replied.

George VI and his family knew, liked and trusted Neville

Chamberlain. When, in May 1940, he resigned as prime minister they were much distressed. After his farewell broadcast, the Queen wrote to him: 'My eldest daughter told me, that she and Margaret Rose had listened to it with real emotion – In fact she said "I *cried*, Mummy." ' Later, the King wrote to Chamberlain, now dying from cancer: 'You were my Prime Minister in the earliest years of my reign, & I shall ever be grateful to you for your help & guidance during what was in many ways a difficult period.' The Queen was unequivocal: 'How deeply I regretted your ceasing to be our Prime Minister.' The King was more circumspect: 'I have sympathised with you very much in seeing your hopes shattered by the lust & violence of a single man.' He was not referring to Winston Churchill – although the King shared Chamberlain's reservations about the arch-opponent of appeasement. Churchill, after all, wasn't just a maverick: he had also been one of Edward VIII's staunchest allies at the time of the Abdication. The King – whose constitutional duty it was to invite the parliamentarian best placed to form an administration to do so – would have liked to see Lord Halifax, the Foreign Secretary, as Chamberlain's successor, but he bowed to the inevitable. 'There was only one person whom I could send for who had the confidence of the country,' he noted in his diary, '& that was Winston.'

At first, their relationship was uneasy: at best, joshing; at worst, strained. In time, as they got to know one another better and to recognise each other's strengths, they became close comrades. When, five years later, on VE Day, 8 May 1945, they stood together on the balcony at Buckingham Palace, they did so as firm friends, conscious that each, in his own way, had played his part in the victory. Churchill's task, no doubt, had been infinitely more complex, challenging and significant, but the King's contribution – as a sounding board, as a figurehead, as a focus for national unity – was also key.

It was George VI who first described the House of Windsor as 'the family firm'. It helped that – while, yes, they lived in castles and palaces and were surrounded by flummery and flunkies – there were only four of them, and they seemed – well, almost ordinary. The King's shyness, diffidence and stammer served to underline his decency. The Queen's charm was simply irresistible. She wasn't slim and chic and brittle (as 'Queen Wallis' would have been): she was soft and round, regal yet real, classy but comfortable and comforting. And the two girls – moving slowly through adolescence but still, mostly, seen dressed in matching outfits – looked to be model daughters: quite unspoilt and thoroughly wholesome.

Lilibet and Margaret Rose lived through the war years at Windsor Castle. They arrived at the beginning of May 1940, as the Germans began their assault on Belgium and the Netherlands, and France prepared to fall, thinking they were to be there for a few days. They remained for five years. Where they were was an official secret. Press and public were simply informed that the royal children had been evacuated to 'a house in the country'. Some in government – fearful that they might be captured by the Nazis and used as hostages – wanted them evacuated to Canada. Churchill was opposed to the idea. So was the King.

Crawfie painted a lurid picture of the princesses' arrival at the ancient castle 'in the gathering twilight of that May evening': 'We were tired, and it was very gloomy. Pictures had been removed, and all the beautiful glass chandeliers had been taken down. The State Apartments were muffled in dust-sheets, the glass-fronted cupboards turned to the walls. About the stone passages the shadowy figures of servants and foremen loomed, attending to the black-out. I remember one old man remarking to me dryly: "By the time we've blacked out all the windows here, it's morning again, miss." The two little girls clung to me apprehensively. Alah, as always when she was bothered or anxious, was cross.'

The Queen's recollection of her war years at Windsor is rather different from Crawfie's. 'Windsor Castle was a fortress,' said Crawfie, 'not a home.' To the Queen it was a home, and still is, and a favourite home, too. It is frustrating to Her Majesty that, simply because Crawfie wrote a book, every account of her childhood is seen, in large part, from her governess's perspective. Emotionally, Lilibet was closer to Alah and to Bobo than to Crawfie. And, perhaps, closer still to Jane and Crackers and Carol and Susan and Ching – some of the dogs – and Jock and Hans, two of the ponies. If, today, you talk to the Queen about the war, she won't mention Crawfie, but she will talk, happily, about her animals.

From 1938 she was taking formal riding lessons from the royal instructor, Horace Smith. She learnt to ride side-saddle. She was introduced to carriage driving. In 1943 and 1944, driving her own pony and cart, she won first prize in the Royal Windsor Horse Show. In 1942, the King took her up on to the Wiltshire Downs, to the Beckhampton Stables, to watch the royal racehorses being trained. She visited the Royal Stud at Hampton Court. She went to Newmarket to see more royal racehorses in training. In 1943, aged seventeen, she first rode to hounds. She still spent several hours each day closeted with Crawfie, conscientiously learning her lessons – and, twice a week, taking instruction on English history and the British constitution from Sir Henry Marten who came up to the Castle in his dogcart – but, undoubtedly, during these years, she was most alive, most at ease, most happy, with her dogs and her horses, the sustaining passions of her life.

These adolescent years were also the ones during which another, quite different, sustaining force took a lifelong hold on the young Princess. On 1 March 1942, when she was not quite sixteen, Lilibet was confirmed and took her first communion. Her father was Head of the Church of England, but not just in name. In his most celebrated broadcast, at the beginning of the war, he had said, 'I believe from my heart that the cause which binds together my peoples and our gallant and faithful Allies is the cause of Christian civilisation.' His daughter believed it, too. At his Coronation – and hers – at the heart of the service, the sovereign is given a copy of the Holy Bible, with the words: 'We present you with this Book, the most valuable thing that this world affords. Here is wisdom; this is the royal Law; these are the lively Oracles of God.' The Queen, not as a matter of form, but as a matter of faith, says 'Amen' to that.

So, Lilibet was a teenage girl who played with her dogs, groomed her ponies, said her prayers and lived in a castle. She had friends: cousins and the children of courtiers. She had dancing lessons on Saturday mornings with Miss Vacani, dancing-mistress to the gentry.[69] She continued with the Girl Guides and became leader of her patrol. For four consecutive Christmases, she and Margaret Rose appeared in quite elaborate Christmas pantomimes, produced by a master from the local Church of England school and featuring neighbourhood children and young evacuees as well as the two princesses. There was a war going on, and a golden childhood, too.

[69] Betty Vacani died on 21 August, 2003, aged ninety-five. Princess Elizabeth greatly valued all she learnt from her, and, in due course, invited her to give a weekly class at Buckingham Palace for Prince Charles, Princess Anne and several children of the royal household. Miss Vacani was a passionate teacher and a particular favourite with the Royal Family because, unlike Crawfie, she was wonderfully discreet. She did reveal that Prince Charles was a particular favourite with her because of his seriousness and his commitment to the Highland Fling, but when asked about the abilities of Lady Diana Spencer – who, on leaving school herself, taught briefly at the Vacani School in Brompton Road (a few doors down from Harrods) – she would only say that Lady Di 'had a rather full social life, which distracted her from teaching dancing as a career'.

Margaret Rhodes is a year older than her cousin Lilibet. 'I was at Windsor during the war,' she explained to me, 'because I was doing a shorthand and typing course at Queen's College which had moved out to Egham. I lived at Windsor and went in to Egham on the bus. And, later, I worked at MI6 and lived at Buckingham Palace. Queen Elizabeth's great achievement during the war was that she kept family life going, kept it as normal as possible. When we were about sixteen or seventeen, she had little parties with the young Grenadier officers, so we could have a dance. And when the bombs were falling, she was always so calm. I remember there was a wonderful butler who would come in, bow and say solemnly, "Purple warning, Your Majesty," which meant that the Germans were closer than they ought to be. We had to go to the air-raid shelter, along miles of corridor. Queen Elizabeth would not be hurried. If people tried to hurry her, she simply slowed down.'

At Windsor, Lilibet and Margaret Rose believed they shared the privations of the people. Their food may have been served to them by the nursery footman, but they were told it was subject to the rationing restrictions that applied to the public at large. There were lone light bulbs hanging from the ceiling in their chilly, draughty bedrooms. Fires were limited, hot water was restricted, a black line was painted around the royal bathtubs as a reminder that the water should not be more than five inches deep. The children were also expected to contribute to the war effort.

In October 1940, when Lilibet was fourteen and a half, she made her first broadcast, introducing a series of 'Children in Wartime' programmes for the BBC. 'She was so good about the endless rehearsals we had to have to get the breathing and phrasing right,' said Crawfie. Her voice was high-pitched, her accent high-falutin', but her performance was flawless. John 'Jock' Colville, then twenty-five and assistant private secretary to the prime minister, and, much later, private secretary to Princess Elizabeth herself, listened and was 'embarrassed by the sloppy sentiment' of the broadcast, but, by every other account, the people – in Britain, in the Dominions, in America – loved it. The message was straightforward: 'Thousands of you in this country have had to leave your homes and be separated from your father and mother. My sister Margaret Rose and I feel so much for you, as we know from experience what it means to be away from those we love most of all.' According to Crawfie, 'Lilibet herself put in several phrases that were quite her, and everyone who heard this particular speech will remember the most spontaneous and amusing end. Lilibet, always anxious to bring her small sister forward, said, "Come on, Margaret, say good night," and a small, clear voice piped in rather pompously, "Good night, children."'

In fact, the end was not spontaneous. It was fully scripted and Margaret's farewell line actually read: 'Good night and good luck to you all.' Nor did Lilibet need to do much to bring her small sister forward. Margaret was naturally precocious. She was always the livelier and naughtier of the pair. She appears to have been encouraged in this by Crawfie who claimed, 'Margaret and I were very given to practical jokes and we each egged the other on.' The Heiress Presumptive did not approve. 'Lilibet was always too serious-minded,' said Crawfie. On one occasion, Margaret and Crawfie wanted to ring the alarm bell on the Castle terrace to see if it would bring out the guard from all over the Castle. On another, they took one of the elderly gardener's brooms from his wheelbarrow and hid it in the bushes. 'Lilibet was always ashamed of us on these occasions,' reported Crawfie, without any apparent sense of remorse, 'and walked away from us rather pink in the face.'

Sarah Bradford, in her biography of George VI, quotes an unnamed courtier as saying of Margaret Rose: 'She was a wicked little girl, there were moments when I'd have given anything to have given her the hell of a slap.' These were moments that the general public were not privy to. 'They spoiled her,' said the courtier of Margaret's parents. 'They adored her; the King used to look at her as if he couldn't believe anybody could be so much fun. But I think he fully realized that much as he admired Princess Margaret – he said something once that made it quite clear – that he realized the Queen was the best of the two.'

Their cousin Margaret Rhodes said to me: 'The Queen and Princess Margaret were such different people. Occasionally, she was driven mad by her, but they were sisters.' From an early age, Margaret was spoilt, outspoken, playful and flirtatious. Lilibet was not. During the war years at Windsor, young Grenadier Guards officers would sometimes join the girls and their governesses for lunch or tea. Margaret would chatter away gaily. Lilibet was more restrained, more formal, more dignified. Cosmo Lang, the Archbishop of Canterbury, who conducted her confirmation, spent some time alone with her and concluded that 'though naturally not very communicative, she showed real intelligence and understanding'. Eleanor Roosevelt, wife of the American President, came to tea and reported that the princess was 'quite serious and with a great deal of character and personality. She asked me a number of questions about life in the United States and they were serious questions.'

Lilibet was a serious young woman. She listened to the BBC news bulletins with care. She charted the progress of the war with her own large wall map with little flags that were moved from place to place. Under the instruction of Sir Henry Marten, she was taken through the niceties of *The English Constitution* by Walter Bagehot (1826–77), required reading for monarchs-in-the-making. She was being prepared – and preparing herself – to fulfil her destiny.

To mark her sixteenth birthday, in 1942, she was made Colonel of the Grenadier Guards, in place of her great-great-uncle and godfather, the Duke of Connaught, who had died recently, aged ninety-one. 'It was a bit frightening inspecting a regiment for the first time,' she reported to a friend, 'but it was not as bad as I expected it to be.' She had her father at her side, and, in truth, all that was required of her was to stand stock still while the troops marched to and fro. More of an ordeal for her will have been the small-talk she had to make afterwards, mingling with the officers and men, and the photographers she had to face. Ten press cameramen were admitted to the event and the unofficial court photographer, Cecil Beaton, was invited to take a special birthday portrait. It is a fabulous shot, both sexy and innocent: the sixteen-year-old princess, looking straight into the camera, is not quite smiling. She is in uniform, but her jacket is unbuttoned and her hat is at an angle that is almost provocative. The picture was reproduced around the world. A life of being photographed had begun.

Today, the Queen and Prince Philip do not warm to the idea of image-makers. They would disdain the notion of being involved in what we now call 'spin'. In fact, whether consciously or not, sixty years ago George VI and his private secretary, Alexander Hardinge, allowed carefully wrought images of the young princess to be used as visual propaganda for both the war effort and the House of Windsor. Different kinds of image were required to tell different aspects of the story. Cecil Beaton – whose brilliantly lit and composed pictures (often with painted backdrops) had helped transform the bosomy, somewhat cosy and domestic Duchess of York into a fully-fledged Queen – was used to give the world a romantic Princess Elizabeth. (His eighteenth-birthday portrait has her set against an idealised skating scene, eyes wistfully cast down.) Lisa Sheridan was brought on board to produce more of a home-and-hearth series of pictures of Lilibet and Margaret Rose: nice girls, in sensible clothes, with perfect manners and adorable pets, the princesses-in-the-castle-next-door. When, in February 1945, Lilibet joined the Auxiliary Territorial Service as No. 230973 Second Subaltern Elizabeth Alexandra Mary Windsor 'aged 18, eyes blue, hair brown, height 5ft 3in'), she was photographed, on her knees, spanner in hand, on the ATS car mechanics course at Aldershot, learning how to change a wheel.

Nearly sixty years later, in October 2003, at the opening of an exhibition at the Imperial War Museum, the Queen was reunited with six of her wartime ATS colleagues. Betty Royle, aged eighty-two, said: 'I think she has never quite forgotten us, because those were the days when she had a kind of freedom.' Pat Blake, eighty-two, who had been an ATS sergeant, said: 'You've got to remember that in those days people knew little about royalty. There was no telly. Once in a while you saw them on a newsreel in a local cinema. She really did seem a remote person to us all . . . She and her sister seemed like fairytale people. The fact that we were going to work alongside her doing night driving, learning first aid, military law and theory and practice of mechanics was quite spellbinding . . . She seemed very, very young – but she was very easy and just very unaffected and pleasant.'

In theory, on the course young Princess Elizabeth was 'to be treated in exactly the same way as any other officer learning at the driving training centre'. Well, she was – and she wasn't. She was taught along-side the others (who were instructed to call her 'Your Royal Highness' and then 'Ma'am to rhyme with jam'), and barked at when they were barked at, but, in class, she sat in the centre of the front row, and, at night, when the rest of the girls kipped down in the dormitory she was driven back to Windsor Castle. Her 'normal' life was anything but normal. For her wardrobe she was dependent on clothing coupons like everybody else, but, somehow, the royal household was issued with *more* coupons than everybody else. The world was told she received just five shillings a week in pocket money and more than half of that the kind princess donated to good causes. It was true, and it was good of her, but, of course, to her, money had no real meaning. She wanted for nothing. Her life was never – would never be, could never be – 'real'. But the war was real enough.

In August 1942, it claimed the life of her uncle, the Duke of Kent, killed on board an RAF Sunderland flying boat bound for Iceland where he was due to inspect RAF installations. In atrocious weather the craft flew into the side of a Scottish hill. The King was devastated. It was a family tragedy: the Duchess of Kent was a widow at thirty-five, with three small children, the youngest of whom, Prince Michael of Kent, was only seven weeks old. The duke's nieces shared in the family sadness. 'It was the second uncle they had lost completely,' Crawfie observed, 'for though the first, Uncle David, was not dead, they did not see him any more. The Royal conspiracy of silence had closed about him as it did about so many other uncomfortable things. In the Palace and the Castle his name was never mentioned.'

Lilibet's adolescence coincided with the Second World War. She was a child of thirteen at the outset in September 1939, a woman of nineteen when victory came in the summer of 1945. In the intervening six years, she grew up: she was confirmed; she made her first broadcast; she shot her first stag; she inspected her first regiment; she launched her first ship; she learnt to drive; in her ATS training she tested herself, for the first time (perhaps for the only time), against contemporaries from ordinary backgrounds; indeed she mixed, after a fashion, with ordinary people for the first time; she rode her horses; she loved her dogs; she learnt to dance; she became a Counsellor of State and, in her father's absence, visiting the Eighth Army in Italy in 1944, she performed her first constitutional functions, signifying the Royal Assent to Acts of Parliament. 'There was always a strong sense of duty mixed with *joie de vivre* in her character', according to her French tutor, the Vicomtesse de Bellaigue. Princess Elizabeth had a good war, and she remembers it as, essentially, a happy time in her life.

She is not alone, of course. A number of her contemporaries, and those just a little older than her, still speak of the war as the happiest time of their life. In a conversation about what brings happiness to people's lives – of which more later – I asked the eminent Irish psychiatrist Professor Anthony Clare why that might be. He told me:

Among those who fought in the Second World War there was a comradeship. People who might otherwise have found it difficult to socialise were thrown in together. They had no choice. And there was a shared philosophy, a common purpose. The basic fighting man felt he was doing something worthwhile. That was why the 1939–45 war was so different from Vietnam, or even the Gulf wars. And those engaged in the war were testing themselves. That seems to be rather important. Happy people are rarely sitting around. They are usually involved in some ongoing interchange with life. Of course, we're talking about people who survived the war, not those who were wounded or killed. And I'm not sure how many back home felt that way, other than those in the blitzed cities where, again, there was this comradeship.

Prince Philip of Greece had a good war, too. His mother, Princess Alice, who had returned to live in Athens in November 1938, had hopes that her son might choose to serve in the Greek navy. From Philip's point of view, it was not an inviting prospect. The Greek navy was tiny. Philip's knowledge of the Greek language and people was sketchy. He was a prince of Greece, but he had spent most of his life in England, France and Germany. Where did his loyalty lie? He could see there was a dilemma and he was torn – but not for long. King George II of Greece (the son of King Constantine I, Prince Andrea's eldest brother) let him off the hook. Philip had started his naval training in Britain. The King decided it was only sensible he should continue it there.

Philip has no regrets about the decision. He is not greatly given to 'regrets', in any event. 'What's the point?' he asks. Nor is he given (despite the presence of C. S. Forester's Hornblower novels on his shelves) to recounting tales of his wartime adventure on the high seas. He was 'mentioned in despatches', but he would not want – for a moment – to exaggerate his contribution or achievement. In 1948, when, as the Duke of Edinburgh, he was presented with the Freedom of the City of London, he looked back on his war service and said, 'In every kind of human activity there are those who lead and those who follow . . . I would like to accept the Freedom of this City, not only for myself, but for all those millions who followed during the Second World War. Our only distinction is that we did what we were told to do, to the very best of our ability, and kept on doing it.'

His first appointment, as an eighteen-year-old midshipman, in January 1940, was to an old battleship, HMS *Ramillies*, then in Colombo, Ceylon, and working as an escort to convoys that were part of the Australian Expeditionary Force moving from Australia to the Middle East. The ship, a veteran of the Great War, was uncomfortable; the appointment – at least in the eyes of a young man eager for action – somewhat unexciting. He was, of course, Prince Philip of Greece, and Greece was not yet at war. That was an issue. For the time being, the powers that be felt it necessary to keep him out of the main line of fire. Did he find that frustrating, I asked him. He shrugged his shoulders. 'Inevitable,' he said. 'And it was useful experience. I was quite young.'

It turns out that Louis Mountbatten had proposed to George VI that Philip be sent to a ship on the China Station. Today, Prince Philip bridles somewhat at the suggestion that Mountbatten was the orchestrator of his career. Uncle Dickie took an avuncular interest, certainly; he put in a good word where he could, for sure; but Prince Philip hopes he achieved whatever he achieved in the navy through his own best endeavours. He is not entirely sure that being a prince, and nephew to a noted 'operator' like Mountbatten, may not have been positively to his disadvantage. In September 1943, when Mountbatten, aged only forty-three, was appointed Supreme Allied Commander to South-East Asia, and promoted to the rank of Acting Admiral, Philip, still only twenty-two, wrote teasingly to him:

What are they going to make you? Acting Admiral of the Fleet or something? You had better be careful . . . before you know what you will have the prospect of 40 years without promotion in front of you. What a thought! As a string-puller, of course, you've practically lost all value, you're so big now that it might smell of nepotism (just to make sure I had the right word, I looked it up in the dictionary, and this is what it says: undue favour from holder of patronage to relatives, originally from Pope to illegitimate sons called nephews).

In 1940, after four months in *Ramillies*, Philip served briefly in HMS *Kent*, in a shore station in Ceylon, and in HMS *Shropshire*. 'Action' continued to prove elusive. 'We have something to look forward to,' he noted, optimistically, in his logbook at one point in his time in *Kent*: 'there is an enemy raider in the Indian Ocean and there is just a chance our tracks will cross'. They didn't. The only 'fun' to be had was thanks to the swirl of the ocean: 'On one occasion a particularly heavy sea completely smothered the bridge and platform, and even the crow's nest felt the spray from it. Steaming with the sea on the beam and at twenty-one knots the rolling was greatly emphasised, and a lot of innocent fun was had in the mess, watching the Goanese stewards diligently laying the table, and then the plates, knives, forks, spoons, butter dishes, toast racks and marmalade landing in a heap on the deck.'

The catering arrangements were clearly taken seriously on board HMS *Kent*. When the ship was off Bombay, the 1st lieutenant noted in his log: 'It rained most of the Morning Watch. Luckily had

Prince Philip as the snotty[70] and he makes the best cup of cocoa of the lot.'

In 1999, in a tribute to Terry Lewin, his friend and fellow snotty (who became First Sea Lord in 1977 and was Chief of the Defence Staff at the time of the Falklands conflict in 1982), Prince Philip recalled what happened next: 'I remained in the East Indies Station until June 1940, when the Italians invaded Greece and I became a combatant. I was appointed to HMS *Valiant* in the Mediterranean Fleet, where I found Terry as Senior Midshipman of the Gunroom. I remember it as a very happy Gunroom, which was a reflection of his good humour and powers of leadership. The fact that he had a typical rugby player's build and an all-round athletic ability helped to establish his authority. *Valiant* saw quite a lot of action during the latter part of 1940, including Malta convoys, the bombardment of Bardia, and the night action off Cape Matapan in March 1941, and the evacuation of Crete in May.' It was for his contribution to the success of the Battle of Matapan, manning the searchlight on board his battleship, that Prince Philip, not yet twenty, received his 'mention in despatches'.

On the night of 28 March 1941, as darkness fell off the coast of Cape Matapan, at the southernmost point of the Peloponnese, Admiral Sir Andrew Cunningham, Commander of the British Mediterranean Fleet, in his flagship, HMS *Warspite*, was leading his battleships – including HMS *Valiant* and HMS *Barham* – towards three Italian cruisers. 'My orders,' Prince Philip noted in his log, 'were that if any ship illuminated a target I was to switch on and illuminate it for the rest of the fleet, so when this ship was lit up by a rather dim light from what I thought was the flagship I switched on our midship light which picked out the enemy cruiser and lit her up as if it were broad daylight.' Then the fun started:

> She was only seen complete in the light for a few seconds as the flagship had already opened fire, and as her first broadside landed and hit she was blotted out from just abaft the bridge to right astern. We fired our first broadside about seven seconds after the flagship with very much the same effect . . . By now all the secondary armament of both ships had opened fire and the noise was considerable. The Captain and the Gunnery Officer now began shouting

[70] Slang for 'midshipman'; etymology unknown; first recorded use, 1903; used by Kipling, 1904.

Prince Philip of Greece

Princess Elizabeth of York

Philip's father,
Prince Andrea, centre,
during the Asia Minor
campaign, 1921

Andrea, facing trial in
Athens, December 1922

Elizabeth's parents, Lady Elizabeth Bowes-Lyon and Prince Albert, Duke of York, on their
wedding day, 26 April 1923, with, left, the bride's parents, the Earl and Countess of Strathmore
and, right, the groom's parents, Queen Mary and King George V

Philip's mother with her family in 1917, the year the Battenbergs became Mountbattens. R-l, Alice, her parents, Louis, 1st Marquess of Milford Haven, and Victoria, with their younger son, Dickie, and second daughter, Louise (later Queen of Sweden)

Philip's parents and all five of their children, photographed in Paris for their silver wedding anniversary in 1928 – the only known photograph of the family together

Philip and his mother,
Princess Alice, October 1928

Elizabeth and her nanny,
'Alah' Knight, December 1929

Philip at
St Cloud in 1929

Elizabeth, photographed by her father, in 1930

Philip at school: The Elms, 1928;
Cheam, 1932; Salem, 1933

Philip at Gordonstoun, 1935

Lilibet at home, in the garden
at 145 Piccadilly, protecting
Jane and Dookie, July 1936

Philip at Gordonstoun, 1938

Elizabeth and Margaret
with 'Crawfie', 1939

The first photographs: Philip, aged eighteen, and Elizabeth, thirteen, at the Royal Naval College, Dartmouth, July 1939

Queen Elizabeth and George VI, seated centre, with Elizabeth, far left, and Philip, in uniform, standing next to Dickie Mountbatten

Elizabeth's favourite wartime
photograph of Philip

Elizabeth in her ATS uniform, 1945

The Windsor Castle pantomime,
December 1944: Elizabeth and Margaret
in *Old Mother Red Riding Boots*

Elizabeth playing tag on board HMS *Vanguard* on the voyage to South Africa, February 1947

...lip instructing the school for ...y officers, HMS *Royal Arthur*, ...rsham, Autumn 1947

The first look: the tell-tale photograph of Philip and Elizabeth arriving at the wedding of Patricia Mountbatten and John Brabourne, October 1946

The first dance: Lt Philip Mountbatten and his fiancée dance together publicly for the first time, Edinburgh, July 1947

The engagement picture: Elizabeth, photographed with her engagement ring and on Philip's arm for the first time, [Bu]ckingham Palace, 10 July 1947

The best man: David Milford Haven with his girl-friend, Robin Dalton, on holiday in France, 1946

Philip, with Mike Parker and Dickie Mountbatten, at Philip's Stag Night at the Dorchester Hotel, 19 November 1947

Wedding Day: Thursday 20 November 1947

The wedding group photographed by Baron in the Throne Room at Buckingham Palace.
David, 3rd Marquess of Milford Haven, is standing on Elizabeth's right; Princess Margaret is
on Philip's left; the page boys are Prince William of Gloucester and Prince Michael of Kent.
In the front row, left to right, are: Elizabeth's grandmother, Queen Mary; Philip's mother, Alice,
Princess Andrew of Greece; Elizabeth's parents, King George VI and Queen Elizabeth; and Philip's
(and David Milford Haven's) grandmother, Victoria, Dowager Marchioness of Milford Haven.
Among the bridesmaids, on the far left of the picture, is The Hon Margaret Elphinstone,
now Margaret Rhodes. (*Below*) The marriage licence.

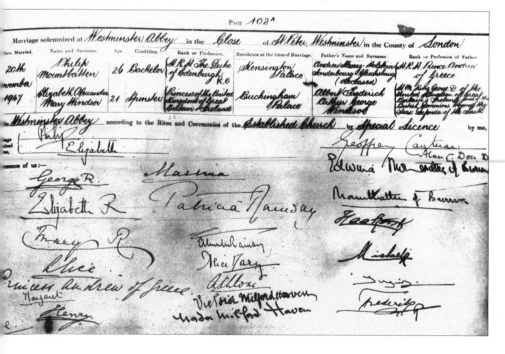

Into the woods: the honeymoon at Broadlands, Susan in attendance, 23 November 1947

from the bridge for the searchlights to train left. The idea that there might have been another ship, with the one we were firing at, never entered my head, so it was some few moments before I was persuaded to relinquish the blazing target and search for another one I had no reason to believe was there. However, training to the left, the light picked up another cruiser, ahead of the first one by some 3 or 4 cables. As the enemy was so close the light did not illuminate the whole ship but only about ¾ of it, so I trained left over the whole ship until the bridge structure was in the centre of the beam . . . she was illuminated in an undamaged condition for the period of about 5 seconds when our second broadside left the ship, and almost at once she was completely blotted out from stem to stern.'

Through the noise and the pounding – 'the glasses were rammed into my eyes . . . flash almost blinding me' – Philip kept his searchlight on target. 'More than 70% of the shells must have hit,' he recorded, with justifiable satisfaction. 'When the enemy had completely vanished in clouds of smoke and steam we ceased firing and switched the light off.'

The Battle of Matapan was, for the time being, the last British victory in the Eastern Mediterranean. It was made possible, not only by Prince Philip's steady hand on the searchlight – the action which brought his 'mention in despatches' – but, also, by British supremacy in the air. The Italians had no aircraft at Matapan. British aircraft – from Cunningham's aircraft carrier *Formidable* – had been deployed during the afternoon of 28 March and had done serious damage to a number of the Italian ships. When it came to the Battle of Crete, seven weeks later, it was a different story. Here, the Germans had command of the air. On 22 May, within fifteen miles of Crete, Philip recorded in his log: 'We were bombed from a high level by a large number of small bombs dropped in sticks of 12 or more. One Dornier came straight for us from the port beam and dropped 12 bombs when he was almost overhead. We turned to port and ceased firing, when suddenly the bombs came whistling down, landing very close all down the port side.'

Within forty-eight hours, three cruisers and six destroyers were lost, among them HMS *Kelly*, under the command of Louis Mountbatten. At 0800 hours on the morning of 23 May, twenty-four Junkers dive bombers appeared in the sky above his ship. 'Christ, look at that lot,' Mountbatten is said to have said, quite calmly. Within thirty seconds of being hit, with guns firing and the captain standing firm on the bridge, *Kelly* was capsizing. 'I felt I ought to be last to leave the ship,'

Mountbatten wrote to his daughter, Patricia, soon after, 'and I left it a bit late because the bridge turned over on top of me and I was trapped in the boiling, seething cauldron underneath. I luckily had my tin hat on, which helped to make me heavy enough to push my way down past the bridge screen, but it was unpleasant having to force oneself deeper under water to get clear.' He managed it. He 'suddenly shot out of the water like a cork released' and, with his 1st lieutenant, set about swimming desperately through the oily water around the wreckage rescuing wounded men and dragging them to the safety of a raft. As the ship finally went down, he called for three cheers for the *Kelly* and, bobbing up and down in the treacherous water, led his surviving crew in an extraordinary chorus of 'Roll out the Barrel!' It was the heroic stuff of which movies are made.[71]

Mountbatten and his surviving crew were picked up by HMS *Kipling* and taken to Alexandria, where Uncle Dickie, to his surprise, was met by 'the cheery grinning face' of his nephew, Philip. 'He roared with laughter on seeing me,' Mountbatten reported to his wife, 'and when I asked him what was up he said, "You have no idea how funny you look. You look like a nigger minstrel!" I had forgotten how completely we all were smothered in oil fuel.'

Separately, Uncle Dickie and his nephew now returned to England: Mountbatten, to brief Churchill (unbidden) on the need for greater air support in the Mediterranean and to take command of the aircraft carrier *Illustrious*; Philip, to take his sub-lieutenant's courses and exams at Portsmouth. He worked hard and he played hard. In the exams – covering seamanship, signals, navigation, gunnery and torpedoes – he secured the top grade in four sections out of five. In March 1942, staying in London with the Mountbattens, he went out on the razzle with his cousin, Dickie's other nephew, David Milford Haven, who was also in the navy. The young men borrowed the Mountbatten Vauxhall to help transport themselves around the more fashionable West End

---

[71] In July 1941, back in England, Mountbatten went to the pictures with Noël Coward. 'Dickie told whole story of the sinking of *Kelly*,' Coward noted in his diary. 'Absolutely heart-breaking and so magnificent.' In 1942, Coward turned the story into a fine propaganda film, *In Which We Serve*, and Mountbatten – who was involved at every stage, although officially the film was based 'on no Royal Navy destroyer in particular' – took the King and Queen and their daughters along to Elstree Studios to watch some of the filming. Coward admired Mountbatten inordinately ('I would do anything in the world for him') and Mountbatten was suitably appreciative of Coward's cinematic skills. He saw the film at least fifteen times.

and Mayfair nightspots and, at 4.30 a.m., collided with a traffic island, wrote off the car, and returned to their uncle's residence, bloodied if unbowed. 'So,' reflected Mountbatten, 'after facing death many times over at sea, they got their first wounds in a London blackout.'

In June 1942 Philip was appointed to the destroyer HMS *Wallace* and, that October, when *Wallace's* 1st lieutenant was appointed elsewhere, the Commanding Officer asked that Prince Philip take his place. At just twenty-one, Philip became one of the youngest 1st lieutenants in the Royal Navy. More than forty years later, his friend Lord Lewin said to me that if Prince Philip had stayed in the navy, 'he'd have gone right to the top'. When I put the possibility to Prince Philip, he shook his head. 'No,' he said, emphatically. 'Given the way of the British press, I wouldn't have got very far. Every promotion would have been seen as me being treated as a special case.'

HMS *Wallace* was one of the destroyers on convoy duty on the British east coast, constantly moving up and down 'E-Boat Alley', as it was known, from Sheerness to Rosyth and back. It wasn't glamorous, but it was necessary, arduous, and, given the effectiveness of the German E-boats' torpedoes, not without its hairy moments.

At the beginning of July 1943, *Wallace* joined the armada of ships (and 150,000 men) massed off the coast of Sicily ready to invade the island. According to Harry Hargreaves, a yeoman aboard *Wallace*, 8 July was the night Prince Philip of Greece saved the day. 'The stars were bright and the sea was black,' recalls Hargreaves. 'There was only one problem: the water shone and sparkled, and our progress created a long, glowing trail which made it extremely easy for enemy aircraft to spot us.' At midnight the first plane struck. 'We were sitting ducks. It was inevitable that one of the bombs would hit us. We had little chance of survival and all 163 of us on board thought we were facing death.'

After the first attack – which hit the side of the ship – the enemy aircraft disappeared. 'We knew it would return in minutes – with other aircraft.' At this point, according to Hargreaves, Philip came up with 'a brilliant plan that was destined to save our lives'. He got a group of men to lash together large planks of wood to make a raft, attaching smoke floats at each end. They launched the raft into the sea and activated the smoke floats. 'Billowing clouds of smoke and small bursts of flame made it look like the flaming debris of our ship floating in the water.' *Wallace* then steamed away from the raft for 'a good five minutes' before the captain ordered the engines stopped. When, shortly afterwards, the enemy aircraft returned, 'I heard the scream of bombs falling,'

Hargreaves recalls, 'but they were aimed at the raft, not at us. The 1st lieutenant's ruse had worked.'

Hargreaves has only good memories of Philip, who, on the day they first met, when *Wallace* was docked at Tilbury, rustled up a meal of sausages and powdered egg for them both, despite the fact that Philip was an officer and Hargreaves 'merely a yeoman': 'He was a down-to-earth, ordinary man. He had no airs or graces, and when the captain told me he was a prince, I said, "He doesn't look like that to me."'

In 1944, as the war in Europe moved decisively the Allies' way, Philip was appointed to a brand-new destroyer, HMS *Whelp*, still building in Newcastle when he joined her, and, subsequently, set off with her for more exotic climes: the Far East and the climax of the war against Japan in the Pacific. En route, *Whelp* called at Colombo and Philip spent a memorable Christmas Eve with Uncle Dickie, now Supreme Allied Commander, South-East Asia, and Mountbatten's new chief of staff, Lieutenant General Frederick 'Boy' Browning. According to Philip Ziegler, Mountbatten's official biographer, the night went gloriously awry because 'the Singhalese cook, overawed by the occasion, took refuge in drink and served dinner cold, late, and back to front: Christmas pudding at midnight, turkey at 1 a.m. Nobody minded – least of all Mountbatten.'

Dickie was increasingly a father figure for Philip. Earlier in December he had had to break the news to his nephew that his actual father, Prince Andrea, was dead. Andrea, aged sixty-two, unreachable in Vichy France, had died of a heart attack in his bedroom at the Hotel Metropole in Monte Carlo in the early hours of 3 December. His lady friend, the Comtesse Andrée de la Bigne, was with him. His widow, Princess Alice, living reclusively in Athens, received the news two days later. Somehow she got word to Dickie, who sent a naval message to Philip on board HMS *Whelp*. The message was deciphered precisely as follows: 'So shocked and grieved to hear of the death of your (?) father and send you all my heartfelt sympathy. Following has been received from your mother: "Embrace you tenderly in our joint sorrow. Your loving mama."'[72]

---

[72] The family seems rarely not to have been in mourning. In February 1938, Andrea's brother, Prince Nicholas, had died. Nicholas's daughter, Marina, was married to the British Prince George, Duke of Kent, who was killed in a flying boat accident over Scotland in August 1942. In April 1938, Alice's brother, Georgie, 2nd Marquess of Milford Haven, had died. In January 1940, another of Andrea's brothers, the youngest, Prince Christo, died, aged sixty-one, followed, later in the same year, by his closest

In November 1938, Princess Alice had returned to live in Greece. From Athens, on 5 December 1938, she had written to Philip: 'I have taken a small flat just for you and me. Two bedrooms, *each* with a bathroom and two sitting rooms, a little kitchen & pantry. I found some furniture stored away in various places from our rooms in the Old Palace, which I had not seen again since 1917, a most agreeable surprise & the family here are giving me things to complete it.' Philip was happy to visit his mother in Greece, but he had been educated in Britain, he was joining the Royal Navy: Athens was to him a port of call, not his home. Just before the outbreak of war, in August 1938, he stayed with his mother in her small flat in Athens. In January 1941, on leave from HMS *Valiant* in Alexandria, he visited her again. George II, still King of Greece (if only just), wrote to Alice's mother, Victoria, at Kensington Palace: 'With Alice we talk and think of you often. She is very busy looking after the needy families of soldiers and we only get to see her on Sundays. A few days ago Philip arrived here on leave, which naturally is a great source of joy for her. He is looking very well and happy.'

Philip had returned to his ship in the middle of February 1941. By the end of March that year he had become one of the heroes of the Battle of Matapan. On 6 April 1941, the Germans had come to the rescue of the defeated Italians and invaded Yugoslavia. By 17 April, German forces were advancing through Greece. On 23 April, King George II and his immediate family were on their way into exile: first to Crete, then to Egypt, then to London. On 26 April 1941, German troops marched into Athens and the Nazi flag was raised above the Acropolis. Alice stayed put. Her mother wrote to Dickie: 'I rely on her pluck & common sense to carry her through these times, which must be very painful to her.'

Alice lived in Athens throughout the German occupation, and beyond. As her biographer, Hugo Vickers, says: 'Alice was no threat to the Germans, politically or personally, and she moved about relatively unnoticed. She did her best to alleviate the suffering of the Greeks, but more as a nurse than as a princess.' She shared in the privations of the Greek people. Food was in scant supply. During the first bitter winter of the occupation she lost twenty-six kilos in weight. She was sometimes

sister, Princess Marie, aged sixty-four. At least some of those who died in these years had lived long lives: Queen Victoria's last surviving daughters (Alice's great-aunts), Princess Louise and Princess Beatrice, died in 1939 and 1944, aged ninety-one and eighty-seven respectively. Prince Arthur, Duke of Connaught, died in 1942, aged ninety-one.

lonely, often hungry, frequently cold, but she had spirit – and hope. She imagined herself and her son – a prince of Greece – living together in Athens after the war. In December 1941, she had written to Philip: 'Even in these anxious times I am full of hope and when I go for walks I look at all the houses to see if there is not a suitable one for us later on, as I am tired of flats and prefer a whole house. . . . I am still busy with my charities . . . Don't worry about me. I am really and truly in good heart.'

She was of good heart, too. She worked in one of the largest soup kitchens in Athens; she worked in a refuge for orphans; she organised a group of district nurses to provide care in the poorest areas of the city. She was in no way ostentatious about her good works. She was quietly determined, dogged, devoted and ready to take risks. When the Nazi threat to the Jews of Athens was at its height, Alice offered refuge to a family of Cohens. When neighbours enquired, she said that Mrs Cohen was a former Swiss governess to her children. When the Gestapo questioned her, she simply exaggerated her deafness and looked uncomprehending.

She never talked about hiding the Cohens. When, recently, I tried to talk to Prince Philip about his mother, he was reluctant to be drawn. When I told him how moving I had found Hugo Vickers' account of her life, Philip said, in a very matter-of-fact way, 'Yes, he did a lot of research.' When I said Princess Alice seemed to me to be an extraordinary woman, he said, 'Mm', and asked if I had yet read the new book that tells the story of the Royal Yacht *Britannia*. Philip shares a number of his mother's characteristics. He guards his privacy. He does not wear his heart on his sleeve. He hides his light under a bushel. He finds it quite uncomfortable to talk about himself. His manner is deceptive. He is a kindly person and a caring one. He is more sensitive than he would like us to think or know. He can be prickly. He can be perverse. He can be visionary. He can be stubborn. He is wilful. His spiritual life is important to him. He is undoubtedly proud of his mother.

In the late 1980s, some years after her death in 1969, surviving members of the Cohen family sought to honour the memory of Princess Alice. They secured for her a 'Certificate of Honour' as one 'Righteous among the Nations': she 'risked her life to save persecuted Jews'. In October 1994, Prince Philip and his surviving sister, Sophie, went to Jerusalem, to the Holocaust Memorial at Yad Vashem, to accept the posthumous award on their mother's behalf. In his speech on the day,

Prince Philip said of his mother: 'As far as we know she had never mentioned to anyone that she had given refuge to the Cohen family at the time when Jews throughout Greece were in danger of being arrested and transported to the death camps. I suspect that she never thought of it as something special. She was a person with deep religious faith and she would have considered it to be a totally natural human action to fellow human beings in distress.'

I would have been intrigued to know the range of thoughts passing through Sophie's mind as, with her brother, in her mother's memory, she laid a wreath in the Holocaust Museum in 1994. Sixty years earlier, her beloved husband, Prince Christoph of Hesse, had joined the Nazi Party and become a member of the SS – the *Schutzstaffel*, 'Hitler's bodyguard'. As time went by, Prince Christoph grew less enamoured of the Führer, but in 1935 he was thirty-four, patriotic and ready to serve the greater German cause. He joined the Luftwaffe. In October 1943, he was killed in a flying accident in the hills outside Rome. Alice, in German-occupied Athens, was given permission to travel to Germany to visit her widowed daughter.

Alice's daughters suffered from the dilemma that faced several of Queen Victoria's grandchildren and great-grandchildren during the two world wars of the twentieth century: divided loyalties. Their grandmother lived in Kensington Palace, under the protection of the British King. Their grandfather had become a British marquess. Their brother, Philip, and their uncle, Dickie, were officers in the British navy. They were married to Germans. Whose side were they on?

Hermann Goering had attended the funeral of Cécile and her husband in 1937. Sophie's husband had been a member of the Nazi Party.[73] Theodora's husband, Berthold, was a German, but not a Nazi. He was severely wounded in the leg in France at the outset of the war and was invalided out of active service. The oldest sister, Margarita, had the oldest husband, Gottfried (known as Friedel), who was already in his forties when war was declared. Relatively speaking, through the hostilities, they managed to keep a low profile and out of harm's way.

While Athens was occupied by the Germans, Alice was able to get permission to visit her sister in Sweden and her daughters in Germany and Switzerland. In October 1944, when, three and a half years after being driven out, British troops returned to Greece, Alice's daughters

---

[73] But she had regrets. In 1945, Sophie told her grandmother: 'Since 2 years my eyes have been open & you can imagine what feelings one has now about those criminals.'

were, once again, behind enemy lines. Throughout the war years, Philip was unable to make contact with his sisters. While Greece was in German hands, he was unable to see his mother. He was twenty-three, and in a ship bound for Colombo, when his father – whom he hadn't seen for five years – died in his hotel bedroom in the South of France.

'You're a poor bloody orphan just like me,' thought Mike Parker when he met Philip at the time, 'a poor bloody orphan'.

ELIZABETH & PHILIP

Chapter Seven

'Don't praise my charm too much . . .
Don't take my arm too much,
Don't keep your hand in mine . . .
People will say we're in love!'

                    Oscar Hammerstein II (1895–1960), *Oklahoma!*

Mike Parker was an Australian, from Melbourne. Born in June 1920, he
was one year older than Prince Philip. They met in 1942, as fellow 1st
lieutenants – Philip in HMS *Wallace*, Parker in HMS *Lauderdale* – on
convoy duty on 'E-boat Alley'. They became life-long friends. Parker's
father was a captain in the Royal Australian Navy. Parker came to
Britain to join the British Royal Navy to prove his independence. 'I was
an orphan,' Parker liked to say, 'because I came from Australia. Philip
was an orphan because he came from nowhere. His parents weren't
anywhere to be seen.'

The two men had much in common. They were young, they were
ambitious ('We were highly competitive,' said Parker, 'we both wanted
to show that we had *the* most efficient, cleanest and best ship and ship's
company in the Navy'), and they shared a sense of humour. For a
prince, Philip was remarkably unstuffy. As an Australian, Parker did
not stand on ceremony. In an unlikely way, each felt he was the other's
equal. The traditional middle-class British naval officer was relatively
well-heeled. Not so Philip of Greece and Parker of Melbourne. 'He was
better off than I was,' said Parker, 'but compared with many people he
didn't have a brass razoo!'

Prince Philip dates the beginning of their close friendship to 1944,
when, by coincidence, they found themselves in sister ships – Philip in
HMS *Whelp*, Parker in HMS *Wessex* – on their way to the Pacific as part
of the 27th Destroyer Flotilla under Admiral Sir James Somerville.

They were looking forward to some action against the Japanese; they arrived just in time for the Japanese surrender in September 1945. In Tokyo Bay, *Whelp*'s final wartime assignment was to ferry newly released prisoners of war to light fleet carriers which then brought them back to Britain.

En route for the Far East and after the Japanese surrender, Philip and Mike Parker took shore leave together, both in North Africa and in Australia. In 1990, interviewed by Tim Heald for his biography of Prince Philip, Parker recalled: 'Of course we had fun in North Africa, but never anything outrageous. We'd drink together and then we'd go and have a bloody good meal. People are always asking, "Did you go to the local estaminets and screw everything in sight?" And the answer is, "No! It never came into the picture. There was so much else to do."' He did admit, however: 'There were always armfuls of girls.'

What exactly did he mean by that? When I asked him, Mike Parker simply exploded: 'Nothing, for Christ's sake.' Commander Parker (as he became: and MVO, then CVO and Order of Australia, too) died at the very end of 2001, aged eighty-one, a plain-speaking Australian to the last.[74] 'Jesus, I wish I'd never used that phrase,' he said to me. 'Yeah, there were always "armfuls of girls", showers of them, but nothing happened – nothing serious. What I meant was this: we were young, we had fun, we had a few drinks, we might have gone dancing, but that was it. In Australia, Philip came to meet my family, my sisters and their friends. There were girls galore, but there was no one special. Believe me. I guarantee it.'

In 1945 Philip was twenty-four, a bearded Adonis. According to his cousin, Alexandra of Yugoslavia, who wasn't there, 'Philip, with a golden beard, hit feminine hearts, first in Melbourne and then in Sydney, with terrific impact.' According to Mike Parker, who was, 'Philip was actually quite reserved, quite restrained really. He was always good company, but he was self-disciplined, too. And self-contained. And careful. He didn't encourage gossip. He certainly didn't wear his heart on his sleeve. He didn't give away a lot. There have been books and articles galore saying he played the field. I don't believe it. People say we were screwing around like nobody's business. Well, we

---

[74] He was, among other things, chairman of Australian Dredging and General Services, a director of Spacelift Australia and chairman of the Australian Plain English Foundation.

weren't. You didn't. We didn't. That's the truth of it.' Besides, in 1943, Mike Parker got married. 'In those days, if you slept with a girl, you married her.'

Robin Dalton – now a distinguished film producer[75] based in London and Biarritz; in 1945 a twenty-four year old Australian girl working as secretary to the commanding officer of the ordnance department of the Southwest Pacific Area – remembers it a little differently. In her *Memoir* she writes: 'What would seem like shocking promiscuity – not only physical but emotional – in peacetime, was felt as a beneficence of the heart. The fact that it was also rarely that one was caught out in one's perfidious spread of affection blinded one to the dangers. The pleasures were freshly minted each week, as the turnover in admirers was brisk. If possible, our affections were limited to one per squadron, or PT boat, or Marine battalion, and the chief dread was that their leaves would overlap. They seldom did. We did not consider ourselves promiscuous. We were in love.' Robin was in love with Philip's cousin, David Milford Haven. They met in 1944, in Sydney, at a cocktail party on one of the warships. He was a signals officer working for Admiral Vian. Their affair lasted five years. 'I met Philip through David,' she told me, 'They were like brothers, you know.' She recalls that Philip had two special girlfriends in Australia at the end of the war: 'A society girl called Sue Other-Gee, and then Sandra Jacques – that was a terrific love affair.'

Perhaps there was a licence to be more uninhibited in Australia? Sitting in the elegant drawing room of her third-floor flat off Sloane Square in October 2003 (in the week she turned eighty-four), Prince Philip's childhood friend Gina Kennard looked back on life in England sixty years before and said to me, emphatically: 'It was a different world. Unmarried girls didn't sleep with their boyfriends. It really wasn't done. You went for dinner, you went dancing, you went shooting, you had fun, but you knew where to draw the line. Of course, some girls stepped over the boundary, but that was the exception, not the rule.' Gina and her sister and their friends were brought up in an age when the Church of England's traditional teaching on sexual morality went virtually unquestioned and mostly unchallenged. Married women (like

---

[75] Her films include *Country Life*, *Madame Sousatska* and *Oscar and Lucinda*. She is an extraordinary bundle of energy, intelligence and charm, and should really be making a film of her own life. I recommend her two very different, but equally fascinating, volumes of memoirs: *Aunts Up at the Cross*, 1963, and *An Incidental Memoir*, 1998.

Dickie's wife, Edwina) might have affairs, and, because there was a war on, some unmarried sweethearts might indulge their boys on the way to the front, but, on the whole, most nice girls expected to be married as virgin brides. And there were practical considerations as well as moral ones: contraception was uncertain, illegitimacy a stigma, abortion illegal.

I asked Gina Kennard if Prince Philip had been her boyfriend. She laughed. 'Everybody said he was in love with me. My mother used to say that his mother – who was a saintly person, deaf but lovely – would have been very happy for Philip to marry me, but it never came up. I said to him recently, "Are you still in love with me?" and he said, "Yes, of course I am." The truth is, he was wonderfully attractive – he still is – and we were friends, best friends, and we went out together and had just the best time, but nothing really serious happened. It wasn't like that. He was young and handsome and, of course, I loved him. At that age, you fall in love all the time, don't you? Philip knew lots of girls. There was Osla Benning, wasn't there? We were just young people having fun.' In 1944, both Gina and Osla (a striking Canadian debutante) became engaged to other men.

Through the war years, Prince Philip kept in touch with his cousin, Princess Elizabeth. He wrote to her, 'from here and there'. He saw her, 'now and again'. Sixty years on, he says he really doesn't remember much about it. In 1970, talking to his official biographer, Basil Boothroyd (whom he liked and trusted), he said, with the diffidence and touch of defensiveness that are the hallmarks of any conversation about his personal life: 'During the war, if I was here [in Britain] I'd call in and have a meal. I once or twice spent Christmas at Windsor, because I'd nowhere particular to go. I thought not all that much about it, I think. We used to correspond occasionally. You see it's difficult to visualise. I suppose if I'd just been a casual acquaintance it would all have been frightfully significant. But if you're related – I mean I knew half the people here, they were all relations – it isn't so extraordinary to be on kind of family relationship terms. You don't necessarily have to think about marriage.'

Prince Philip is adamant. He did not think about marriage in any serious sense until more than a year after the war, when he went to stay at Balmoral in 1946. 'I suppose one thing led to another,' he says. 'It was sort of fixed up. That's really what happened.'

By 'fixed up', he does not mean arranged by others. He means that was when he and Lilibet came to a mutual understanding that met with the approval of their families. If he had thoughts of marriage much before 1946, he kept them to himself. He certainly did not share them with Mike Parker, his contemporary and closest wartime friend. 'He was the same, then as now,' Parker told me, 'good at keeping his feelings to himself. He didn't tell me anything and I didn't ask. I might have had my suspicions, but until around 1946, when an engagement was in the air, I didn't know a thing.'

Others had their suspicions as far back as 1941. Henry 'Chips' Channon was one such. A wealthy American from Chicago, Channon came to Britain aged twenty-one in 1918, married Lady Honor Guinness, and became an English MP. He liked to feel he knew everybody and everything. He was a waspish chronicler of the social scene and took a special interest in royalty. In January 1941 he found himself staying at the British Legation in Athens and noted in his journal: 'The Royal set-up at Athens is complicated: there is the isolated King who sees no-one; there are the Crown Prince and Princess (Frederika) who, madly in love, remain aloof from the world with their babies and their passion. She is a touch unpopular, being German (I met her first dining with General Goering in 1936); there is Princess Andrew who is eccentric to say the least and lives in semi-retirement: there is Prince Andrew, who philanders on the Riviera whilst his son, Prince Philip, is serving in our Navy . . .' This was the January when Philip, on leave from HMS *Valiant*, was staying in Athens with his mother. On the 21st Channon was taken to 'an enjoyable Greek cocktail party': 'Philip of Greece was there. He is extraordinarily handsome, and I recalled my afternoon's conversation with Princess Nicholas [Ellen, Philip's aunt, widow of Andrea's brother Nicholas]. He is to be our Prince Consort, and that is why he is serving in our Navy. He is charming, but I deplore such a marriage; he and Princess Elizabeth are too inter-related.'

Prince Philip deplores the kind of tittle-tattle in which Chips Channon revelled. In January 1941, Philip was nineteen, Elizabeth was fourteen, and, whatever his match-making aunt or her gossip-mongering teatime companions might care to invent, as far as Philip was concerned – is concerned – marriage was not on the agenda – not even remotely. Channon, however, retained his watching brief. On 16 February 1944, he noted in his diary: 'My parents-in-law, the Iveaghs, called to see me, after having had tea with the King and Queen at Buckingham Palace . . . I do believe that a marriage may well be arranged one day between Princess Elizabeth and Prince Philip of Greece.' In October the same year, Channon's nose went into an overdrive of twitching when he found himself a guest of Princess Marina, Duchess of Kent, at Coppins, her country house in Buckinghamshire. 'As I signed the visitors' book,' he reported to his journal, with a note of triumph worthy of Sherlock Holmes, 'I noticed "Philip" written constantly. It is at Coppins that he sees Princess Elizabeth. I think she will marry him.'

Prince Philip has no time for *Chips: The Diaries of Sir Henry Channon*. He and Princess Elizabeth were cousins; they became friends; they got to know one another better; they became closer; in due course, they became engaged. That's about it, really. What Philip felt exactly, and when he felt it, is (a) frankly, none of our business, and (b) honestly, quite difficult to recollect at this distance in time. Getting an insight into his feelings about his relationship with Elizabeth is not easy. Getting an insight into her feelings about him is much more straightforward. The Queen is happy for you to know that, in her heart and in her way, she has been committed to Prince Philip from the age of thirteen.

Horace Smith, her riding instructor when she was both a child and a young woman, had the measure of her. He saw that she was single-minded, not one to take up interests 'lightly, only to drop them just as easily a short time later. If and when her interest is aroused, she goes into whatever subject it is with thoroughness and application, nor does her interest wane with the passing of time or the claim of other new matters upon her attention.'

As it was with her horses – and her dogs, and her faith, and her duty – so it was with Philip. Her first cousin, near-contemporary and friend, Margaret Rhodes, said to me: 'Princess Elizabeth was enamoured from an early age. I've got letters from her saying, "It's so exciting. Mummy says 'Philip can come and stay'." She never looked at anyone else. She was smitten from the start.' 'Yes,' agreed Lilibet's grandmother, Queen Mary, 'it does happen sometimes and Elizabeth seems to be that kind of girl. She would always know her own mind. There's something very steadfast and determined in her – like her father.'

At Christmas 1943, when the Windsor Castle pantomime was *Aladdin*, and Lilibet, aged seventeen, in fetching tights and tunic, was 'principal boy', and Margaret Rose, thirteen, played the heroine, 'Princess Roxana', Philip, now twenty-two, attended the third and final performance and sat in the very front row. Crawfie was impressed: 'He looked more than ever, I thought, like a Viking, weather-beaten and strained, and his manners left nothing to be desired.' Lilibet was positively pink with excitement. 'I have never known Lilibet more animated,' said her governess. 'There was a sparkle about her none of us had ever seen before.' According to Crawfie, 'From then on, the two young people began to correspond.'

But what did Crawfie know? The two young people had, in fact, been corresponding for some time. Writing to a friend in January 1944, Queen Mary insisted that the two young people had actually 'been in love for the past eighteen months. In fact longer, I think . . . But the King and Queen feel that she is too young to be engaged yet. They want her to see more of the world before committing herself, and to meet more men.'

'Poor darlings,' the King wrote of his daughters in his diary as the war rumbled to a close, 'they have never had any fun yet.' His Majesty need not really have worried. Princess Margaret was to have plenty of 'fun' in the years to come and Princess Elizabeth never complained that her life lacked excitement or romance. She was not a natural gaiety girl: she never felt she was missing out on what her mother's friend Noël Coward called 'cocktails and laughter – and what comes after . . .'. As Margaret Rhodes puts it: 'She was not a flibberty-gibbet, by any stretch of the imagination.'

And she did have fun, in her own way. At Windsor, as the war was ending, she was allowed her own space, beyond the nursery and the schoolroom. Crawfie described it: 'There was a little boudoir done in pink tapestry between the schoolroom and her bedroom . . . This she could use as her private apartment. Lilibet was enchanted . . .' At Buckingham Palace, as the war ended, she was given her own suite: a bedroom (in pink and beige, her mother's favourite colours), a bathroom, a sitting room, all of her own, along the corridor from Margaret's rooms, and Crawfie's and Bobo MacDonald's. Alah, the nanny, was no longer part of the nursery family: she died of meningitis, at Sandringham, at Christmas 1945. Lilibet was growing up – and having fun, albeit pretty innocent fun by today's standards. When Philip came to call, reported Crawfie, 'The three of them [Philip, Elizabeth and Margaret Rose] had dinner together in Lilibet's sitting-room, and later romped in the corridor.' Elizabeth was nineteen, Philip was twenty-four. According to Crawfie (who appears to have been as taken with the golden prince as her young charge), 'There was nothing of the polished courtier about him. He came into the Palace like a refreshing sea breeze . . . Presently he began to come up as a matter of course, and have dinner informally, in the old comfortable nursery fashion, in the old nursery, which Margaret now used as her sitting-room. The food was of the simplest. Fish, some sort of sweet, and orangeade. Philip does not smoke and drinks very little.'

After dinner, apparently, along the palace corridors, there would be what Crawfie liked to describe as 'high jinks': 'Philip removed from the door the old card with "Nursery" on it, and substituted another marked "Maggie's Playroom". They would play ball (a good many electric-light bulbs suffered) and race about like a bunch of high-spirited children. It was always a threesome, unless I took a hand and did something about it by removing Margaret on some pretext or other. I felt the constant presence of the little sister, who was far from undemanding, and liked to have a good bit of attention herself, was not helping on the romance much.'

Needless to say, Prince Philip today has little recollection of any of this. The Queen today is not inclined to talk about Crawfie, nor, I imagine, to think about her much. Crawfie had a vivid imagination and, if she did indeed ease love's path in the way she describes, there is no evidence that the young lovers were appreciative of her efforts. What the Queen does not deny, however, is that she and Prince Philip went to the Rodgers and Hammerstein musical *Oklahoma!* when it opened in London in 1947 and that, consequently, 'People Will Say We're in Love' became a favourite number.[76]

Princess Elizabeth did meet other men, of course. Her parents encouraged her to do so. Her mother organised small dances, to which young courtiers, Guards officers and aristocrats were invited. Crawfie, apparently, tried to encourage her 'to give little cocktail parties of her own, in her own sitting room, to return the hospitality of her many friends. I could never get her to do this. She was too accustomed to leaving it all to Mummie. Mummie always had done all the entertaining, and the habit was hard to break.'

Princess Elizabeth's paternal grandfather, great-grandfather and great-great-grandmother had been royalty who had married royalty.

---

[76] The Queen has a good recall of songs of the 1940s. Deborah Bean, for many years senior correspondence secretary at Buckingham Palace, told me, shortly before she retired in 2003, that when the George Formby Society wrote asking if the Queen remembered their hero, Her Majesty told her, 'I still remember all his songs and sing them!' When the movie of her life comes to be made and there is a sequence of Her Majesty walking steadily down a red-carpeted Palace corridor quietly trilling 'When I'm Cleaning Winders', you'd better believe it.

Her father (only second in line to the throne) had merely married aristocracy ('a different gether altothing', as Princess Margaret liked to quip), but his marriage was universally accepted as a triumph, and, consequently, it was generally accepted that it would be equally acceptable for Elizabeth, although Heiress Presumptive, to settle for an aristocrat (top-of-the-range, of course), as Papa did when he married Mummie.

Heading the list of potential candidates were two young Grenadier Guardsmen, both born in 1919, who were the heirs to the dukedoms of Rutland and Grafton. Each became a good friend of the princess, but neither caught her fancy and both married other girls during the course of 1946. The Duke of Rutland's marriage lasted just ten years. The Duke of Grafton[77] was more fortunate. His marriage survived (and thrived), and his wife, Fortune Smith (daughter of Captain Eric Smith MC), became one of Elizabeth's closest companions: Lady of the Bedchamber to the Queen from 1953 to 1966, Mistress of the Robes since 1967. When I was travelling with the Queen's party on one of her regional tours in 2001, someone in the crowd was heard asking if the Duchess of Grafton, seated next to the Queen in the royal limousine, was the Queen's sister. This really delighted the duchess. 'I do feel like her sister,' she said to me.

The other young Guards officer of that generation who became one of Elizabeth's closest friends was Henry, Lord Porchester (known as 'Porchey'), born in 1924, grandson of the 5th Earl of Carnarvon, who had been a distinguished racehorse breeder (and co-discoverer of the tomb of Tutankhamun in 1922), and son of the 6th Earl who, following the family tradition, bred the 1930 Derby winner, Blenheim. Shortly before he died – on 11 September 2001, the day of the al-Qaeda attacks on the United States – I asked Lord Carnarvon (who became 7th Earl

---

[77] He was the Earl of Euston at the time. He succeeded as 11th Duke of Grafton on his father's death in 1970. The best aristocratic families will have acquired a series of titles over time – the Duke of Grafton, for example, is also Viscount Ipswich as well as Earl of Euston – and the custom is to give the eldest son, as a courtesy title, the second most senior title in the series. It is known as a courtesy title because it is there merely for courtesy's sake, conferring no privileges – specifically, no seat in the House of Lords. In descending order the ranks of the British aristocracy are as follows: Royal Duke, Duke, Marquess (also spelt Marquis), Earl, Viscount, Baron. A few years ago, when I presented a weekly radio show in London, I set myself the task of having a different titled guest over successive weeks, presenting them in the correct order of precedence. My guests were: the Duke of Edinburgh, the Duke of Devonshire, the Marquess of Bath, the Earl of Snowdon, Viscount Norwich and Lord Montagu of Beaulieu.

on his father's death in 1987) how he first came to meet Princess Elizabeth. 'My father knew the King and I think the King thought I might be the right kind of chap to accompany the princess to the races. I'm glad he did. We hit it off at once.' And ever after. From October 1945 – when he accompanied her to Newmarket – until the end of his life, Elizabeth and Porchey were regular racing companions, and special friends.

Horse-breeding has long been an interest of the British Royal Family. A royal stud was established at Hampton Court back in the sixteenth century. In the late nineteenth century, Elizabeth's great-grandfather, Edward VII, as Prince of Wales, established a royal stud at Sandringham. In 1962, Elizabeth II, encouraged by Porchey, took on the Polhampton Lodge Stud in Hampshire to breed royal racehorses. In 1969, Porchey was officially appointed Her Majesty's racing manager. Porchey and Elizabeth shared a passion for horses, for racing, for breeding. 'We've learnt a lot together,' he told me, 'and from one another. And we've had a great deal of fun.'

I asked Porchey's son, Geordie, now 8th Earl of Carnarvon (who was born in 1956 and is also one of the Queen's godchildren), what he felt the Queen gained from her relationship with his father. 'The Queen is completely at ease in the world of horses,' he said. 'It's a world she knows and loves. It's quite separate from the rest of the universe she inhabits. When she's in it, she is wholly absorbed by it. And I suppose my father was the centre of that part of her life. The Queen has a long and successful history as an owner and breeder. She knows the background of the stallions, she knows all the good bloodlines. My father had a photographic memory – he could remember the names of all the descendants of the great horses with no difficulty at all. The Queen and he could talk about horses for hours. They had a shared interest that was all-consuming – and a shared sense of humour. When my father and the Queen were together, there were always a lot of laughs. The Queen is more comfortable around men, anyway. She is easy with them, more chatty. And I think their relationship was special because they knew each other so well. They were happy together. You could tell. When he died, quite unexpectedly, the Queen came to his funeral. She very rarely goes to funerals, as you know.'

Princess Anne once said that Porchey was the one person in the world who could telephone the Queen and always be put through at once. In seven months, between 11 September 2001 and 30 March 2002, the Queen lost three key figures in her life: Porchey, her sister and her mother.[78] With Porchey and Queen Elizabeth, she shared a passion – and, according to the psychiatrist Anthony Clare, having a passion is one of the secrets of achieving happiness. Prince Philip is a serious equestrian with a passion for carriage-driving, but he has never shared his wife's commitment to the turf or her passion for horse-breeding. He left that to Porchey.

On 8 May, 1945, VE Day, Prince Philip was on board HMS *Whelp* in the Far East and Princess Elizabeth was at Buckingham Palace with her parents. Dressed in her ATS uniform, she joined the King, the Queen, Princess Margaret and the Prime Minister, Winston Churchill, on the Palace balcony, and waved to the cheering multitude below.

Later in the day, the King and Queen, a little reluctantly, allowed their daughters to go down into the streets and join the throng. According to the Comtesse de Bellaigue, who, with Crawfie and a Guards' major, were the princesses' chaperones for the expedition, 'The King drew the line about Piccadilly Circus, which was to be avoided.' According to Porchey, who was part of the party too, 'We went down Birdcage Walk, up Whitehall, up Piccadilly, into the Ritz Hotel and back to Hyde Park Corner down to the Palace. Everyone was very jolly, linking arms in the streets, and singing "Run Rabbit Run", "Hang Out the Washing on the Siegfried Line", "Roll out the Barrel!", that sort of thing . . .' The Comtesse de Bellaigue said, 'I shall never forget running wildly down St James's Street, with a puffing Major of the Grenadiers,

[78] The Queen's telephone conversations with her mother and her racing manager were a regular, and very happy, feature of her adult life. They would discuss every aspect of the horsey world, including the form of the day's runners – but not with a view to placing bets. In the week of Queen Elizabeth's death, when I interviewed her niece and lady-in-waiting, Margaret Rhodes, she was anxious to dispel the myth that Her Majesty was a betting woman. 'What was the other thing I read in the paper this week?' she said to me. 'Queen Elizabeth had rung up her turf accountant from Concorde? Well, I don't think she knew what a turf accountant was, apart from anything else. And I should think she never had a bet in her entire life. In fact, I'm perfectly sure she'd never had a bet in her entire life.' Mrs Rhodes was eager to scotch quite a few myths that day. With a laugh, and while offering me a glass of sherry, she said: 'Her drinking. I read in one of the papers somebody saying Queen Elizabeth had hollow legs and that she'd start drinking gin and Dubonnet after breakfast. That is total fallacy. She would have a glass of gin and Dubonnet before lunch and a Martini before dinner and that was it. She enjoyed it. She'd have red wine with dinner. She drank normally, like we would – but absolutely not to excess.' 'And what about her famous high teas?' I asked. Mrs Rhodes exploded: 'High tea? She *never* had high tea. She had ordinary tea at a quarter to five. If she was at Birkhall and people had been out shooting or stalking or fishing, then there'd be scones and jam and cake and biscuits – but high tea? Never.'

to keep pace with the Princesses. When we reached the Palace they shouted like the other people, "We want the King", "We want the Queen". On the whole we were not recognised. However, a Dutch serviceman, who attached himself to the end of our file of arm-in-arm people (the Princesses being in the centre of the file) realised who the Princesses were. He withdrew discreetly and just said, "It was a great honour. I shall never forget this evening." All our group got back to the Palace through a garden gate. The Queen was anxiously waiting for us. Her Majesty provided us with sandwiches she made herself.'

By the time the princesses took to the streets again, thirteen weeks later, for a similar expedition on VJ Day, 15 August 1945, Churchill was no longer Prime Minister. With victory in Europe achieved, the Labour Party, under Clement Attlee, reckoned the time had come to end the wartime coalition. Churchill had no choice but to dissolve parliament and call a general election. Polling began on 5 July, with the voting and counting period specially extended to allow the troops overseas to vote. When the result was announced on 26 July, it was a landslide victory for Labour. Churchill's Conservatives lost 160 seats. Attlee's Labour Party gained 230. The age of nationalisation was upon us: the Welfare State was about to be born: King George VI was a monarch with misgivings.

The King was instinctively conservative, wary of change and apprehensive about the pace and degree of his new government's socialist agenda. He appears to have done rather well at keeping his personal feelings under wraps. Herbert Morrison, chief architect of Labour's election victory, and second-in-command in the new administration, said the King 'accepted calmly and willingly the changes of political outlook and of personality in the kind of minister he had known throughout his reign'. Morrison found the monarch 'fair in his observations' and 'meticulously observant in his constitutional position'. Princess Elizabeth learnt much from her father's example.

Privately, the King said (to his brother, the Duke of Gloucester) that he found the new government 'difficult to talk to' and his new prime minister 'positively mute'.[79] Churchill, of course, was positively verbose (and elaborately solicitous when it came to his dealings with any

---

[79] His colleague Aneurin Bevan said of Attlee: 'He brings to the fierce struggle of politics the tepid enthusiasm of a lazy summer afternoon at a cricket match.' Attlee was aware of how others viewed him, and, in retirement, composed a wry limerick about himself: 'Few thought he was even a starter / There were many who thought themselves smarter / But he ended PM / CH and OM / An earl and a Knight of the Garter.'

monarch), but the King had been wary of him, too, back in 1940. In due course – in fact, quite quickly – George VI and Clement Attlee came to understand, respect and even value one another. Michael Foot, who became an MP in 1945 and, later, leader of the Labour Party, knew Attlee well. He told me: 'Clem was not an emotional man. He was not given to public shows of feeling. The only time – ever – that I saw tears in his eyes and sensed a crack in his voice was when he spoke of the death of George VI.'

The King made it his business to work harmoniously with his prime minister. The relationship prospered. In November 1951, he honoured Attlee with the Order of Merit. In July 1945, however, he was simply appalled by Attlee's triumph and Churchill's defeat. 'I was shocked at the result,' he told Churchill, '& thought it most ungrateful to you personally after all your hard work for the people.' With a heart 'too full', he wrote at length (and by hand) to say 'how very sad I am that you are no longer my Prime Minister', concluding:

> For myself personally, I regret what has happened more than perhaps anyone else. I shall miss your counsel to me more than I can say. But please remember that as a friend I hope we shall be able to meet at intervals.
> Believe me,
> I am,
> Your very sincerely and gratefully,
> GRI[80]

The King's world was changing.

Philip and Lilibet were in love. There was no doubt about it. Walking in the park at Windsor, they were glimpsed holding hands. (The moment they realised that they had been spotted, they sprang apart.) Attending the wedding of Philip's first cousin, Patricia Mountbatten, to John Knatchbull, 7th Baron Brabourne, they were photographed gazing, longingly, into one another's eyes. When Elizabeth went to visit a factory, on one of the solo official outings that she was now beginning to undertake, someone in the crowd called out, 'Where's Philip?'

With the war with Japan at an end, Philip and HMS *Whelp* came home. In January 1946, in Portsmouth, as the destroyer's 1st lieutenant, Philip's immediate post-war duty was to preside over her

---

[80] *Georgius Rex Imperator* – George King-Emperor.

decommissioning. His next postings – to Pwllheli in North Wales and Corsham, near Bath, in Wiltshire – were land-based and less romantic, but, he insists (naturally!), no less rewarding. He talks today with particular pride of his time at the Corsham naval training establishment, HMS *Royal Arthur*. It was a school for petty officers and, by all accounts, Philip was an innovative, imaginative and effective instructor. 'We had some new ideas,' he says. 'It was satisfying work.'

Away from his naval base, he still had no home to call his own. When, recently, I went to meet Countess Mountbatten and Lord Brabourne, they showed me their first visitors' book – from 1946, the year they were married – and there, marking his visit over the weekend of 20–22 December, was Philip's signature and, next to it, in the address column, he had written: 'No fixed abode!' He had a base with his grandmother at Kensington Palace; he stayed with his cousin, Princess Marina, and her family, at Coppins; regularly, at weekends, when the Mountbattens were away at Broadlands, he cadged a bed for the night at 16 Chester Street, their London house. According to the Mountbattens' butler, John Dean, the Mountbatten household servants all adored him: 'He was so considerate, so anxious to avoid giving trouble to people who, after all, were paid to look after the family, that we all thought the world of him and looked forward to his visits.'

Dean later went to work for Prince Philip as his valet and, eventually, 'did a Crawfie', publishing a memoir of his happy years as the prince's trouser-presser. From start to finish, the prince remained a hero to his valet. Dean noticed how, immediately after the war, Philip seemed to have very few clothes and what he had wasn't in the best nick. Philip would come up to town, in his black MG, with just his razor in his pocket. Overnight, Dean would wash and iron the young prince's only shirt and darn his threadbare socks for him. 'He was very easy to look after, and never asked for things like that to be done for him, but I liked him so much that I did it anyway.'

Philip worked hard. He played hard. He drove hard. In April 1946, he managed to borrow an army vehicle to drive across war-torn Europe, to Salem, to attend his youngest sister Sophie's second wedding. 'Tiny', as she was known, left with five young children when her husband, Prince Christoph of Hesse, was killed in Italy in 1943, was marrying Prince George Wilhelm of Hanover, now headmaster of Salem, the school founded by Prince Max of Baden and Kurt Hahn, where Philip had briefly been a pupil before moving to Hahn's Scottish outpost, Gordonstoun, in 1934. After years of separation, Philip was reunited with his sisters. He was reunited with his mother, too. Alice travelled to London to stay with her own mother at Kensington Palace and to see her son again: it was the first time they had been together for five years. 'She is full of energy & good sense,' Alice's mother reported of her daughter, '& she and Philip get on well together.'

Philip also made a post-war pilgrimage, in 1946, to Monte Carlo – accompanied by Mike Parker – to meet up with his late father's lady friend, the Comtesse de la Bigne, and collect a few of Prince Andrea's personal effects: some books, some pictures, some clothes, a pair of hairbrushes, his ivory-handled shaving brush, his signet ring. Andrea left his son very little because he had very little to leave.[81] The young men arranged to meet the comtesse at the Café de Paris. Mike Parker told me: 'We got there first, ordered cocktails and waited. Then she arrived. It was like a scene from a film. We realised it must be her at once. She made a proper entrance. She was elegant. She wore blue glasses, I remember. Very striking. She seemed totally at home. She and Philip hit it off at once.'

When he died, Andrea had been laid to rest in the Russian Orthodox church in Nice. In 1946, his body was taken by Greek cruiser to Athens and buried in the gardens of the royal palace at Tatoï.

Andrea had been the son of King George I of Greece. In September, 1946, following a plebiscite, George I's grandson, Andrea's nephew, George II, was restored to the Greek throne. His renewed reign was short-lived. In April 1947, he suffered a sudden stroke and died, unexpectedly, aged fifty-six. His younger brother, Paul (husband of the formidable Princess Frederika of Hanover), succeeded him.

King Paul was Prince Philip's first cousin. Prince Philip was a great-great-grandson of Queen Victoria. If Princess Elizabeth was to follow the custom, long-established, of British monarchs-in-waiting marrying into European royalty, there was a certain inevitability about her match with Prince Philip. That is certainly how his immediate family all felt – in Greece, in Germany, in England. He acknowledges the fact himself. 'After all,' he says, 'if you spend ten minutes thinking about it – and a lot of these people spent a great deal more thinking about it – how many obviously eligible young men, other than people living in this country, were available?'

---

[81] Other than debts. These were not finally resolved until 1947, and then only thanks to help from Dickie and Edwina Mountbatten, and Nada Milford Haven's brother-in-law, Sir Harold Wernher.

One of 'these people' thinking about it, long and hard, over several years, was undoubtedly Lord Louis Mountbatten. Thus far, I have tried to tell the story of the royal romance without too much reference to Uncle Dickie, simply because that is the way the Queen and the Duke of Edinburgh would prefer it. In every other published account of the run-up to their official engagement in July 1947, Mountbatten stands centre stage. If you must know – and they are not sure that you must: it is really a private matter, as far as they are concerned – but, given the prurience of the age, and to set the record straight – if you *must* know: the principals see it quite differently. The off-stage murmurings and machinations of others were neither here nor there. This affair was their affair and nobody else's – right from the start. Their families knew one another. They met. They fell in love – she, at once; he, over time. They thought about it; they talked about it; eventually, they decided to make their lives together, for better or worse. It is as simple as that.

That Dickie Mountbatten was anxious to encourage the union is not in question, but his eagerness to be involved may have been more of a hindrance than a help. On more than one occasion, Philip had to urge his uncle to moderate his enthusiasm. In September 1945 he wrote to him: 'Please, I beg you, not too much advice in an affair of the heart, or I shall be forced to do the wooing by proxy.' In January 1947, as the prospect of the engagement grew closer, Philip wrote to Dickie about the impact his uncle's attitude might have on Lilibet: 'I am not being rude, but it is apparent that you like the idea of being the General Manager of this little show and I am rather afraid that she might not take to the idea as docilely as I do. It is true that I know what is good for me, but don't forget that she has not had you as Uncle *loco parentis*, counsellor and friend as long as I have . . .'

Mountbatten was a well-intentioned control freak. He was also a loving uncle, rightly proud of his impressive young nephew, and understandably excited by the possibility of being in *loco parentis* to the next Prince Consort. Indeed, as the engagement appeared ever more likely, he began looking into the precedent and encouraged his sister Alice to help him with his research. Mountbatten revelled in royalty; he was ambitious for his kith and kin; he was fascinated by genealogy; he was an instinctive matchmaker. According to his biographer Philip Ziegler, some time in the early 1930s, he prepared for his cousin David, then Prince of Wales, a list of eighteen unmarried European princesses, ranging from the thirty-three-year-old Alexandra of Hohenlohe-

Langenburg to Princess Thyra of Mecklenburg-Schwerin, who was a mere fifteen. He knew his *Almanack de Gotha*. He knew there was no more glittering match for the son he never had than the Heiress Presumptive to the British throne.

Other members of the family were almost as excited by the prospect of the union as was Dickie. But Philip gave them no encouragement. In February 1944, Philip's grandmother, Victoria, having had Philip to stay on leave, reported to Mountbatten: 'As he has not touched on the subject you spoke about to me with reference to his future, I also refrain from doing so.' In March, having seen more of Philip, she wrote again to Dickie: 'I touched on the subject on which you gave him advice, but he was not inclined to confide in me, so I did not press him.' In June, Alice wrote to her son from Athens, hoping to tickle some titbits from him: 'I heard you stayed with Marina [at Coppins] at Easter and paid an interesting visit, as well as lunching with a certain young lady & her parents before you left . . .' Philip did not rise to the bait.

Philip was his own man, resistant to all outside interference. Yes, his cousin Marina was helpful in providing a discreet venue for the young couple to meet – where else could they meet, after all? He had no home of his own and they could hardly have romantic trysts in public places – but she was not party to any intriguing. In January 1945, she wrote to Dickie: 'Of course the less said about the question we have sometimes discussed the better – & as you say it must take its course.'

Lilibet did not hide her feelings from her mother or her sister or her closest friends. Margaret Rhodes told me: 'She'd say, "Philip's written again" or "Philip's coming to stay – isn't that exciting?" She was happy to be in love.' On the mantelpiece in her sitting room, she kept a framed photograph of Philip. 'Is that altogether wise?' asked Crawfie. 'A number of people come and go. You know what that will lead to. People will begin all sorts of gossip.' The teenage princess removed the offending portrait – and replaced it with another one, featuring her adored 1st lieutenant hidden behind a full naval beard. 'There you are Crawfie,' she said, 'I defy anyone to recognise who that is.'

Philip had a picture of Lilibet, too, a small one, kept – according to John Dean, who discovered it in the Prince's overnight travelling bag – in a scuffed leather frame. Philip did not discuss his love-life with his uncle's butler, nor even, if he could help it, with his uncle. He did not discuss it, either, with the women in his family or – until the engagement was imminent – with his two closest contemporary male friends: his first cousin, David Milford Haven, and his fellow 1st lieutenant, Mike Parker. I think he is a man (like many) who does have difficulty in openly expressing his feelings. He will deny it. He will simply say that he is not a man who likes to wear his heart upon his sleeve – for daws to peck at, and hacks to feed upon.

Where young Philip did cooperate with his uncle was in the matter of achieving British nationality. Philip was a prince of Greece, but he did not feel Greek and, as I say, had never (has never) professed any particular sympathy for the Greek people. In terms of blood, he is not Greek at all. He is Danish, German, Russian and English. He was born in Greece, but spent his early childhood in France and Germany. From his adolescence onwards, he was based in England. Once he had joined the Royal Navy, therefore, and started to make headway as a young officer, becoming a naturalised British subject seemed to be a wholly sensible move. Mountbatten took the initiative, and did so with the family's general approval. In September 1944, Victoria wrote to Dickie: 'I think it is the best thing for him & it will give a firm basis for his life, which without a fixed career or home country it was wanting in, poor boy.' Princess Marina concurred: 'I think it is a very good idea & apart from it being a help in his naval career it might also be an asset for other "matters".'

Turning Philip from Greek prince to British subject proved a more challenging undertaking than Mountbatten had envisaged. For a start, the blessing of both George II of Greece and George VI of Britain was an essential requirement, and, initially at least, neither monarch seemed in a hurry to give it. In George II's case, it may have been a matter of national pride, a reluctance to have Greece lose any prince to another country. In George VI's case, it may have been because the King suspected that Mountbatten's concern over Philip's nationality was as much to assist his nephew with the 'other matters' as with his naval career. In August 1944, when the King's private secretary, Sir Alan 'Tommy' Lascelles, called on the permanent secretary of the Home Office to discuss the matter, he noted in his diary: 'I suspect there may be a matrimonial nigger in the woodpile.'

This hesitation of the two kings, combined with sustained doubts in government circles about the wisdom of getting embroiled in any aspect of Balkan politics except when absolutely necessary, and simple bureaucratic delay (there was a war on and this was not a priority), meant that it took three years – and much toing and froing and huffing and puffing, lobbying and letter-writing by Mountbatten – to arrive at a satisfactory outcome. Eventually, in February 1947, the deed was done.[82] The news of Philip's naturalisation was officially posted in the *London Gazette*, alongside that of several hundred others, many of them Poles who had fought with the British through the war, many of them German Jewish refugees. Once, when I asked Prince Philip how he thought he was seen by most people in Britain, he said, after a moment's consideration, 'Refugee husband, I suppose.'

Along with a new nationality he needed a new name. The surnames on offer on his father's side of the family had little to commend them. Prince Andrea was the grandson of the King of Denmark and the family name of the Danish royal house was Schleswig-Holstein-Sonderburg-Glucksburg. Another, more manageable, paternal family name was Oldenburg and a bright spark at the College of Arms suggested that 'Oldcastle', as its English equivalent, might find favour. It didn't.[83] Instead (apparently at the suggestion of James Chuter Ede, Clement Attlee's Home Secretary), Philip agreed to take the already established Anglicised version of his mother's surname, Battenberg. Prince Philip of Greece became Lieutenant Philip Mountbatten, RN.

In time (in the mid-1980s), his mother-in-law, Queen Elizabeth, would describe Prince Philip as 'an English gentleman – completely'. In the mid-1940s, she was less certain. Her younger brother, David Bowes-Lyon, to whom she was very close (Elizabeth and David were the Benjamins of the family, respectively seventeen and nineteen years younger than their oldest sister), did not believe that Philip was an appropriate husband for the future Elizabeth II.

According to Gina Kennard, 'David Bowes-Lyon was a vicious little

---

[82] It transpired, subsequently, that it need not have been done at all. As the result of a case brought, in 1955, by Prince Ernst August of Hanover to establish his own British nationality, it became clear that, as a consequence of the Act of Settlement of 1701 – designed to assure the succession of Queen Anne should she die without issue – all direct descendants of the Electress Sophia of Hanover (granddaughter of James I and mother of George I) would, by Act of Parliament, be deemed British. As a direct descendant of the Electress Sophia, Prince Philip, like Prince Ernst August (and some four hundred others, mostly Germans), was, it appears, from birth, automatically a British subject.

[83] Fortunately perhaps. While Oldcastle is a good old English surname with an interesting pedigree, Sir John Oldcastle (c. 1375–1417) served in the Welsh campaigns of King Henry IV and was a friend of Prince Hal, before converting to the doctrines of John Wycliffe and leading a Lollard conspiracy to capture Henry V. Oldcastle ended his days hanged and burned at St Giles's Fields. In Shakespeare's *Henry IV* the character of Falstaff was originally named Oldcastle.

fellow. He had it in for Philip right from the start. He was completely against him.' He was not alone. Lord Salisbury (whose ancestor had been on hand to advise Elizabeth I, after all) had profound reservations. As did Lord Stanley and the Earl of Eldon. As did most of the senior men at court. Philip might now be eligible for a British passport, but he wasn't really British. He was German and you couldn't trust a Hun. Yes, he was royal (of sorts), but Greek royalty was a standing joke. The Greek throne was notoriously unstable and the Greek royals undeniably the bottom of the pack. All right, he was serving in the Royal Navy – and that 'mention in despatches' was to his credit – but where had he been to school? Gordonstoun? What was that all about? And where were his parents, for God's sake? And wasn't he a protégé of Dickie Mountbatten's? Need more be said?

Many at court, and much of the Establishment, were wary of Mountbatten. As his daughter Patricia put it to me, with a smile, 'My father was a progressive and the one thing the courtiers were not was progressive.' Never mind 'progressive': the courtiers considered Mountbatten dangerously left wing. And not quite as royal as he liked to think he was. Hadn't his grandfather, Prince Alexander of Hesse (whose own parentage was doubtful), run off with a lady-in-waiting – a Polish girl called Julie Hauke? She might have been elevated to the rank of Serene Highness eventually, but she was certainly a blot on the Battenberg escutcheon.[84] Mountbatten had a questionable pedigree and a rum set of louche and left-leaning friends – such as Tom Driberg.[85] He was also, in the eyes of those who did not take to him, inordinately full of himself, impossibly pushy and incurably inclined to interfere where he wasn't wanted. 'Yes,' chuckles Patricia Mountbatten, 'my father had colossal energy and drive. He was a dynamo. He made things happen. He got things done. And he didn't go through "the usual channels". He by-passed the officials. That really infuriated them. If he wanted to speak to the King, he just picked up the telephone. I'm sure they thought he'd be a very bad influence on Philip and that Philip might prove to be a chip off the old block.'

---

[84] 'I believe that the Battenbergs have always behaved somewhat peculiarly,' commented Heinrich Himmler after studying the Gestapo file on Mountbatten and his family.
[85] Tom Driberg (1905–76) was a journalist, Labour MP and notoriously promiscuous homosexual. It was Mountbatten's easy way with people like Driberg – and Noël Coward – that fuelled the rumours of his possible bisexuality. In his official biography Philip Ziegler explores these exhaustively and dismisses them.

Sir Alan Lascelles (*Educ.*: Marlborough; Oxford; *Address*: Sutton Waldron House, Blandford; *Clubs*: Travellers', Pratt's, MCC; *TA*: Fontmell-Magna), assistant private secretary to the Prince of Wales throughout the 1920s, assistant private secretary and private secretary to successive kings from 1935,[86] encapsulated some of the family's and most of the courtiers' initial estimation of Lt Philip Mountbatten: 'They felt he was rough, uneducated and would probably not be faithful.'

In time, the King's private secretary warmed to Philip, describing him (to Harold Nicolson in June 1948) as 'such a nice young man', and 'not a fool in any way', saluting his 'sense of duty' and acknowledging him to be 'so much in love poor boy'. The King himself warmed to the young prince from the start. In the spring of 1944 he told Queen Mary: 'I like Philip. He is intelligent, has a good sense of humour & thinks about things in the right way.' The King's only real reservation in the early days of the romance was his daughter's youth, but by the summer of 1946 Lilibet was twenty, so when Philip, now twenty-five, came to stay with the Royal Family at Balmoral – and proposed to her, and was accepted – there was little the doting father could do but bow to the inevitable – and play for a bit more time. The King agreed, in principle, to the union, but made two conditions: there could be no formal engagement until after the Princess's twenty-first birthday in April 1947 and, before that, there would be a period of reflection while the King and Queen took their two daughters with them on a twelve-week tour of southern Africa.

The tour was memorable on several counts. Princess Elizabeth was unhappy to be going away – Crawfie reports 'tears in her eyes' at the moment of departure – but ready, as ever, to do her duty, and excited by the prospect of her first trip outside the British Isles. The timing, however, was unfortunate. As the Royal Family set off from Portsmouth – 'us four', as the King called them – on 1 February 1947, on board HMS *Vanguard*, the Royal Navy's newest battleship, the weather in the

---

[86] In *Friends, Enemies and Sovereigns*, Sir John Wheeler-Bennett described Lascelles: 'Tall and aristocratic of bearing, with a long face and long thin hands and feet, his manner was at the outset austere.' He typified the courtier of his time: a 'jealous guardian of the royal prerogative; a man who had the reputation not only of not suffering fools gladly, but of rarely enduring their presence in the same room.' Apparently, those who knew him well appreciated his 'caustic wit' and 'the delightful and unusual workings of his mind'. Of course, appearances can be deceptive. You would have thought he was a Balliol man with a First. In fact, he was a Trinity man with a Second.

English Channel was appalling. The weather on the mainland was even worse. Britain was suffering its cruellest winter of the century.

By 12 February, when the royal travellers were basking in sub-equatorial sunshine, the news from home was dire: 'Heavy snowstorms and sub-zero temperatures are combining with a serious fuel shortage to bring Britain to its economic knees. More than four million workers have been made idle by power cuts, and with hundreds of coal trains unable to battle their way through 20–feet-high snow-drifts, thousands of homes are without heat or light for long periods of the day.' The Thames at Windsor had frozen over. Buckingham Palace was candle-lit. The King volunteered to return home. The Prime Minister, Clement Attlee, said 'Thank you, but no thank you': a dramatic return would simply exacerbate the crisis, advertising it worldwide: besides, the African trip was also designed, in part, to give the King – exhausted by the war and in failing health – a well-deserved opportunity for rest, recuperation and sunshine.

On board ship, when the calmer seas were reached, there was certainly some of that. The King and Queen relaxed. The princesses had fun. There are delightful photographs of Lilibet and Margaret Rose playing deck games with the younger officers. They look really happy. (There is a key to these people in those pictures: as a rule, the Windsors are most comfortable and carefree, not in conversation or con-templation, reading books or listening to music, but when they are playing games, playing sport, riding, shooting, having larks, enjoying practical jokes, taking part in Scottish country dancing.) Off-duty in *Vanguard*, picnicking in Southern Rhodesia, visiting the Orange Free State, Basutoland and Bechuanaland in a special 'White Train', almost as tourists, the trip had many highlights. The girls sent regular reports to Crawfie:

> The letters I got back were a great pleasure to me. They were also a wonderful picture of the different make-up of the two sisters. Margaret [now sixteen] wrote with her usual gaiety, all about the fun they were having, how beautiful the White Train was, how warm the sun, how wonderful the food.
>
> Lilibet wrote, immensely distressed by all that was going on in England in the bitter weather. It bothered her to feel she was far away having a good time, in a land so full of everything. She felt she ought to be at home.

The South African leg of the tour was the longest and most trying. The King was in sympathy with the ageing South African Prime Minister, Field Marshal Jan Christian Smuts,[87] who was striving valiantly against the odds to achieve Anglo-Afrikaner unity. The Boers – whose Nationalist Party would defeat Smuts and his United Party government in the election of 1948 and usher in the era of apartheid – were not in sympathy with the King, nor with the 'mingling' of Europeans and non-Europeans in the crowds that came to greet him. The atmosphere was tense. The King was tired and tetchy. At Benoni, a gold-mining town in the south of the Transvaal, there was an unfortunate incident when a man broke from the jostling crowd and rushed towards the open royal car. The King, unnerved, began shouting angrily at the driver to get a move on. The Queen, fearing an attack, hit at the man with her parasol. The man was immediately felled by one of the attendant policemen, and half beaten-up, before it became apparent that he was not a would-be assailant at all, but an ardent royalist who was trying to present Their Majesties with a ten-shilling note as a twenty-first birthday present for Princess Elizabeth. The King, distressed by the misunderstanding, sent to enquire after the unfortunate man, and later apologised for his own behaviour to his equerry, Group Captain Peter Townsend. 'I'm very sorry about today,' he said. 'I was very tired.'

The South African tour had a profound impact on Princess Elizabeth. It was her first first-hand experience of the reality of the British Commonwealth and Empire, of a divided country, of native people, of the tensions of African politics and the nastiness of white supremacists. The Nationalists – who sneered at the King's halting attempt to say a few words in Afrikaans at the opening of parliament – trumpeted the '*swart gevaar*' (the 'black danger') and campaigned to keep '*Die kaffer op sy plek*' ('the nigger in his place') and '*Die koelies uit die land*' ('the coolies – i.e. the Indians – out of the country'). Lilibet was not impressed.

The Princess, however, was taken with Africa and the African

[87] Jan Smuts (1870–1950) was twice prime minister: 1919–24 and 1939–48. He had enlisted South Africa on the side of the Allies during the Second World War, while the Nationalist Party refused to support Britain and expressed sympathy for Nazi Germany. Smuts described apartheid as 'a crazy concept, born of prejudice and fear'. Nelson Mandela saw Smuts' defeat as a defining moment in South African history: 'From the moment of the Nationalists' election, we knew that our land would henceforth be a place of tension and strife.'

people – and the feeling was reciprocated. According to Peter Townsend, the Africans really loved her. As she drove past, they shouted 'Leave the Princess behind!', 'Stay with us!' A popular song was composed in her honour:

> Princess, in our opinion,
> You'll find in our Dominion
> Greetings that surely take your breath,
> For you have a corner in every heart,
> Princess Elizabeth

The climax of the tour coincided with her twenty-first birthday. Field Marshal Smuts declared 21 April a national holiday. There was a birthday parade, a birthday ball and a civic reception at City Hall in Cape Town; Smuts presented the Princess with a gemstone necklace and a gold key to the city; the Princess reviewed hundreds of troops, shook scores of hands and delivered a short speech at a celebratory 'youth rally of all races'. She also made one of the key broadcasts of her life.

Her old tutor in constitutional history, Sir Henry Marten, had impressed on her the special significance to the modern monarchy of both the advent of broadcasting and the development of the Commonwealth. He must have been mighty proud of his diligent pupil's birthday broadcast to the Empire and Commonwealth. 'Although there is not one of my father's subjects, from the oldest to the youngest, whom I do not wish to greet,' she began, 'I am thinking especially today of all the young men and women who were born about the same time as myself and have grown up like me in the terrible and glorious years of the Second World War. Will you, the youth of the British family of nations, let me speak on my birthday as your representative?'

The essence of the message was unsurprising and comfortably generalised: in the dark days of the war, the British Empire had saved the world and 'has now to save itself'. With determination – faith, hope and endeavour – the future of the Commowealth might be yet more glorious, prosperous and happy than its past. Then came the peroration – much less predictable and much more personal – spoken, in a steady high-pitched voice, and heard, by many millions, around the world:

There is a motto which has been borne by many of my ancestors – a noble motto, 'I serve'. Those words were an inspiration to many bygone heirs to the throne when they made their knightly dedication as they came to manhood. I cannot do quite as they did, but through the inventions of science I can do what was not possible for any of them. I can make my solemn act of dedication with a whole Empire listening. I should like to make that dedication now. It is very simple.

I declare before you all that my whole life, whether it be long or short, shall be devoted to your service and the service of our great Imperial family to which we all belong, but I shall not have the strength to carry out this resolution alone unless you join in with me, as I now invite you to do. I know your support will be unfailingly given. God help me to make good my vow and God bless all of you who are willing to share in it.

She meant it, and you could tell. She did not write it, of course. The author was Dermot Morrah (1896–1974), historian, and leader-writer and correspondent for *The Times*. Morrah sent his draft of the speech to Sir Alan Lascelles, the King's private secretary, who was travelling with the royal party on board the White Train. At first, the draft went missing. According to Lascelles, who wrote to Morrah from the train on 10 March, 'The steward in the Protea diner had put it in the bar, among his bottles, little knowing that was itself of premier cru.' Lascelles saluted Morrah's achievement: 'I have been reading drafts for many years now, but I cannot recall one that has so completely satisfied me and left me feeling that no single word should be altered. Moreover, dusty cynic though I am, it moved me greatly. It has the trumpet-ring of the other Elizabeth's Tilbury speech, combined with the immortal simplicity of Victoria's "I will be good."' Lascelles told Morrah how much it had pleased Princess Elizabeth and her mother: 'The ladies concerned, you will be glad to hear, feel just as I do. The speaker herself told me that it had made her cry. Good, said I, for if it makes you cry now, it will make 200 million other people cry when they hear you deliver it, and that is what we want.' And so it proved. When the speech was broadcast, there was barely a dry eye on the planet.

On 24 April, as the royal party set off once more for home, Lascelles reported to his wife: 'From the inside, the most satisfactory feature of the whole business is the remarkable development of P'cess E.' He summed up her essential characteristics: 'A perfectly natural power of enjoying herself . . . Not a great sense of humour, but a healthy sense of fun. Moreover, when necessary, she can take on the old bores with much of her mother's skill, and never spares herself in that exhausting part of royal duty. For a child of her years, she has got an astonishing solicitude for other people's comfort; such unselfishness is not a normal characteristic of that family.'

Elizabeth was – and is – a conspicuously unselfish individual. But uniquely so? In 1936, Elizabeth's Uncle David selfishly abandoned his duty to pursue the love of his life – no question – yet, nineteen years later, in 1955, Elizabeth's sister Margaret – certainly spoilt and undoubtedly self-indulgent in many ways – sacrificed the love of her life when she agreed not to marry a divorcé in the becoming shape of her father's former equerry, Peter Townsend. Elizabeth's grandfather, George V, was not an easy parent, but he was a conscientious king, wilful but not notably selfish. His wife, Elizabeth's grandmother, Queen Mary, shared her husband's stern sense of duty, but liked to get her own way. Famously, when she came to call, if there was a *bibelot* in your drawing-room that took her fancy, she expected you to present it to her. Elizabeth's mother was justly celebrated for her courtesy, charm and commitment, and while, on the whole, she did as she pleased, and led a wonderfully pampered – and nonchalantly extravagant – life, enhanced by an enviable capacity for ignoring the unpleasant, she, like her daughter, was always solicitous for other people's comfort.

That said, when Crawfie – while her charges were in South Africa – came to see Queen Mary to tell her of her own plans to marry, the old Queen, now in her eightieth year, 'spearing for me a muffin on a small silver fork: Her Majesty never touches any food with her fingers', said at once, 'My dear child. You can't leave them!' Crawfie, now in her thirty-eighth year, pointed out that Margaret Rose, at seventeen, was nearly done with her schooling and that Princess Elizabeth was likely to get married before too long. The Queen was unmoved. 'I don't see how they could manage without you,' she said. 'I don't think they could spare you just now.' Queen Elizabeth, on her return from South Africa, was equally unbending. 'Does this mean you are going to leave us?' she asked the governess. 'You must see, Crawfie, that it would not be at all convenient just now. A change for Margaret is not at all desirable.' Crawfie hoped Her Majesty might say something about the family's plans for Lilibet's future, but, according to Crawfie, the Queen 'said nothing further, and I curtsied and withdrew'.[88]

[88] This family are masters of the art of saying nothing. Sometimes they do it to protect themselves. Sometimes they do it to indicate that the conversation is at an end. Often they do it to indicate disapproval. I happen to be writing this on 10 October 2003 and in today's newspaper there are reports of an employment tribunal that has turned down

Crawfie compromised: on 16 September 1947 she married her man (Major George Buthlay, a divorcé from Aberdeen, fifteen years her senior), but, after the honeymoon, returned to her duties at Buckingham Palace. She was not there much longer. By the end of 1948 Princess Margaret had turned nineteen and Princess Elizabeth had given birth to her first son. After sixteen years of loyal and effective service (she was a good teacher: intelligent, imaginative and quite adventurous by the standards of her time), Crawfie retired. The Queen wrote thanking her for her 'devotion and love' and she was awarded one of the honours in the sovereign's personal gift, becoming a Commander of the Royal Victorian Order. (She had been hoping to become a Dame, but she was a little too junior for that, both in years and in station. She had a good opinion of herself – and why not? – but, possibly, *des idées au dessus de sa gare*. She was just the governess, dammit.) Her happiest reward – besides, of course, her fond memories of her years with the little princesses – was the lifetime tenure of Nottingham Cottage at Kensington Palace, a dream home of 'seasoned red brick . . . with roses round the door . . . in the little square garden' – or £100 per annum in lieu. She did not enjoy the charms of Nottingham Cottage for very long.

In 1949, she wrote *The Little Princesses*, her account of her years in royal service. The book was originally published in the United States and serialised in the *Ladies' Home Journal*. Queen Elizabeth's friend Nancy, Lady Astor, happened to know the magazine's editors and was prevailed upon to send Her Majesty a copy of the manuscript. The Queen was appalled. The invasion of her family's privacy and the betrayal of their trust left Her Majesty 'shocked and distressed'. Her private secretary wrote to Lady Astor: 'Such a thing is utterly alien to the spirit and custom of Their Majesties' households and staff and great regret is felt by all those who care for the sanctity of their family life at this unhappy breach of decency and good taste.'

Crawfie was not to be silenced. She received $6,500 for the US serialisation and £30,000 when the book appeared in the UK, serialised in *Woman's Own*. The money was good, and she was pleased with her own writing, but, in her heart, she knew she had done wrong. John Gordon, editor of the *Sunday Express*, tried to persuade her to write for

a claim for unfair dismissal brought against Princess Anne, the Princess Royal, by one Caroline Brown who, for thirteen years, was housekeeper at Gatcombe Park, the Princess's home in Gloucestershire. Ms Brown told the tribunal what happened when she took an unexpected day off : 'That evening when HRH returned from London she was plainly not speaking to me. This is the royal way of showing disapproval.'

him. He reported to the *Express*'s proprietor, Lord Beaverbrook: 'Persuasion is difficult at the moment because she has been brought to the edge of a nervous breakdown by all the trouble, but she will bend in good time.' She didn't – at least, not for the *Express* – but for *Woman's Own* she continued to exploit her erstwhile royal connections with a weekly column that ultimately proved her undoing. In the summer of 1955 she gave her readers vivid and personal accounts of both the Sovereign's Birthday Parade and Royal Ascot. Unfortunately for Crawfie, these annual events did not take place that year: they were unexpectedly cancelled due to a national rail strike.

Crawfie abandoned Nottingham Cottage (which Queen Mary had helped furnish for her) in the autumn of 1950. The court's low opinion of her was made plain. Her neighbours, according to John Gordon, 'were afraid even to be seen speaking to her. So she decided to pack up and go.' Five years later, when her reputation as a reliable royal correspondent was finally exploded, she retired to Aberdeen, childless, largely friendless and living in a marriage that turned out to be a disappointment. She died on 11 February 1988. There were no flowers from Lilibet or Margaret Rose at her funeral. It had been very different forty years before. At her wedding in September 1947, Crawfie had been showered with royal gifts, including a complete dinner service from Queen Mary, a coffee set from Lilibet and three bedside lamps from Margaret Rose.

Crawfie had been determined to marry her man and Their Majesties had no choice but to accept her decision, however inconvenient. Lilibet, in her way, was just as determined. She had accompanied her parents to South Africa: she had done her duty: she had passed her twenty-first birthday and broadcast her solemn commitment to the world: now she was coming home to claim her prize. One of the ladies-in-waiting accompanying the royal party reported that, as *Vanguard* steamed into harbour, Lilibet 'danced a little jig of sheer delight at being home again'.

'At last things were moving,' wrote Crawfie of the summer of 1947.

Suddenly that look of strain we had all been conscious of disappeared from Lilibet's eyes. One day she poked her head into my room looking absolutely radiant . . . 'He's coming tonight,' she said, and then she kissed me and danced away. Next morning was Wednesday, July the ninth. Lilibet came to my room much earlier than usual. I have never seen her look lovelier than she did on that day, not even on her wedding morning. She wore a deep yellow frock, a shade that has always suited her very well. She closed the door behind her and held out her left hand. Her engagement ring sparkled there. It was a large square diamond with smaller diamonds either side. At the same time it was too large for her, and it had to go back to be made smaller. It was a ring they had chosen secretly, but of course she had been unable to go and try it on.

In fact, neither Lilibet nor Philip had been able to choose the ring personally. Philip's mother Alice, currently in London, undertook the task. She had managed to reclaim her own jewellery – deposited for safety's sake at an English bank in Paris in 1930 – and took a selection of her diamonds to a jeweller's in Old Bond Street, 'as Philip dared not show his face at jewellers,' she explained to her brother, Dickie, 'for fear of being recognised. I think the ring is a great success.'

On 10 July 1947, the engagement was formally announced from Buckingham Palace:

It is with the greatest pleasure that the King and Queen announce the betrothal of their dearly beloved daughter The Princess Elizabeth to Lieutenant Philip Mountbatten, RN, son of the late Prince Andrew of Greece and Princess Andrew (Princess Alice of Battenberg), to which union the King has gladly given his consent.

Chapter Eight

'To have and to hold from this day forward, for better for worse, for richer for poorer, in sickness and in health, to love and to cherish, till death us do part, according to God's holy ordinance.'

The Book of Common Prayer

How great was their pleasure? How glad was the King's consent? Was George VI really happy with the engagement? Yes, overall, I think he was. Naturally, he was loath to lose a daughter – he was a fond father and they were good companions to one another – but he saw Philip's merits. He liked the fact that Philip was royal – and therefore 'one of us'. He liked the fact that Philip was making a career in the Royal Navy, as he had done. He appreciated his future son-in-law's intelligence, energy and broad sense of humour. Above all, he saw that Lilibet was wholly in love and, now she was of age, could find no reason to deny her her heart's desire.

Queen Mary and Queen Elizabeth, however, still had their doubts. Fuelled by David Bowes-Lyon, and by the Queen's other close aristocratic friends, and by the senior courtiers led by Sir Alan Lascelles, they really were not sure. Was Philip right for Lilibet? Was he good enough? Was he, in truth, a suitable consort for a future Queen? To the senior courtiers, to the aristocrats in Queen Elizabeth's immediate circle, Philip did not feel like 'one of us'. He spoke perfect English, he had impeccable manners, but he was by no stretch of the imagination a classic English gentleman. He was neither an Etonian, nor a Guards officer, nor a huntsman.[89] And what little was known of his parents was

[89] Even today, fox-hunting is at the heart of country life for many in the Queen's immediate circle. Despite the controversy it attracts, Prince Charles continues to hunt. Prince Philip never has. He says, 'I don't think I've even seen a fox hunt.' He is opposed

not encouraging. The royal establishment did not welcome Philip with open arms. Far from it. According to John Brabourne, 'They were bloody to him. We were at Balmoral that summer' – the summer of the engagement – 'and they were absolutely bloody to him. They didn't like him, they didn't trust him, and it showed. Not at all nice.'

What was Philip's reaction to the hostility, I asked.

'I think it hurt,' said Brabourne. 'But he didn't let it show. He just got on with it.' It certainly rankled with Philip – and rankles still. He was snubbed by snobs. He was treated as an outsider, when he was anything but. His grandfather, after all, had been an ADC to Queen Victoria, Edward VII and George V. Prince Philip told me the story of the first time he visited Windsor Castle after his engagement, when a courtier, patronisingly, began to tell him about the history of the place. Philip interrupted and said, 'Yes, I know. My mother was born here.'

Alice was in England at the time of her son's engagement. She was staying with her own mother at Kensington Palace. She was happy to see Philip and, together, they spent time sorting through cases of Andrea's old possessions – his papers and books, clothes and bric-a-brac – sent up from the South of France following Philip's visit to the Comtesse de la Bigne. Alice now spoke of Andrea almost as if they had never parted. She had high hopes for her son's future happiness.

The betrothal was announced on 9 July, because a Buckingham Palace garden party was scheduled for the 10th and the young couple could make their first public appearance there. Alice sent a happy report to Dickie, now in India in his new role as Britain's last Viceroy: 'It amused me very much to be waiting with the rest of the family, for Philip to come down grandly with Bertie, Elizabeth & Lilibet. The young couple made their rounds of the garden alone, accompanied by the court people & received ovations from the guests. This morning the two came alone to visit Mama, who was delighted as she is very fond of Lilibet & likes her character very much.'

Lilibet was head-over-heels in love. No one was in any doubt about that. But what of Philip? How did he feel? In July 1947, had he been asked if he was in love – as his son Charles was to be asked at the time of his engagement in February 1981 – would Philip, like Charles, have said, 'Yes – whatever love means'? Different witnesses give different

to a ban on fox-hunting – 'I don't understand the prejudice against it,' he says – but, even after sixty years of rubbing shoulders with them, there is almost nothing of the huntin'-shootin'-fishin' English aristo in his manner or his attitudes.

assessments of the temperature of Philip's passion. Mike Parker told me, 'He was completely in love with her, absolutely.' John Brabourne agrees: 'It was a love-match, certainly.' Alice told Dickie: 'He was so excited he hardly knew what he was doing.' Gina Kennard told me: 'Philip used to speak to me about Princess Elizabeth before they were engaged. He was extremely fond of her, always. He said, "I think we could do a lot together."' Robin Dalton told me: 'Philip was always charming and fun, but I couldn't tell you what he really felt. All I know is that in 1945 David [Milford Haven] told me Philip was definitely planning to marry Elizabeth one day. He saw it as his destiny.'

The engagement announced, preparations for the wedding began at once. By royal standards, it was not to be an extravagant affair. Times were hard: the winter had been cruel, the economy was fragile, rationing was the order of the day. Tom Driberg, the Labour MP, wrote to his friend Dickie Mountbatten to warn him that the government's backbenchers would not look kindly on public funds being lavished either on his nephew's wedding or on his subsequent lifestyle. From India (where he had been transformed from Viceroy to Governor-General following India's independence) Mountbatten sent a swift response to Driberg: 'You can rest assured that he [Philip] thoroughly understands this problem and indeed he spoke to me about it when I was home in May. I am sure he is entirely on the side of cutting down the display of the wedding, and his own personal feelings are against receiving any civil list for the very reasons you give. I have, however, persuaded him that he should take something.' Mountbatten explained that Philip had virtually no money beyond his navy pay and that his 'little two-seater' (his beloved MG) made 'a big hole in his private fortune'. 'As a future Prince Consort, however,' he went on, 'I think you will agree that Third-class travel would be regarded as a stunt and a sixpenny tip to a porter as stingey . . . It really amounts to this: you have either got to give up the Monarchy or give the wretched people who have to carry out the functions of the Crown enough money to be able to do it with the same dignity at least as the Prime Minister or the Lord Mayor of London is afforded.'

As it turned out, Philip was not destined to be Prince Consort. It would be ten years, in fact, before he would become a prince of the United Kingdom. At the outset of his marriage, he did not go entirely without honours, however. The wedding was set for 20 November 1947. At the beginning of the month, the King reported to Queen

Mary: 'I am giving the Garter to Lilibet next Tuesday, November 11th so that she will be senior to Philip, to whom I am giving it on November 19th. I have arranged that he shall be created a Royal Highness & that the titles of his peerage will be: Baron Greenwich, Earl of Merioneth & Duke of Edinburgh . . . It is a great deal to give a man all at once, but I know Philip understands his new responsibilities on his marriage to Lilibet.'

Mountbatten (who had become a Knight of the Garter himself at the end of 1946) returned from India for the wedding. On the eve of the great day, Mike Parker organised a stag night for Philip at the Dorchester Hotel. He told me about it: 'It was a great night. Everyone was in naval evening dress. Mountbatten was the senior guest, alongside David Milford Haven and captains and 1st lieutenants of the 27th Destroyer Flotilla, the flotilla that wound up in Japan at the end of the war. It was a very happy occasion. It was an evening of comrades. Philip was an orphan of sorts and we were family.[90] Philip was happy and we were happy for him.' At the beginning of the evening, the gentlemen of the press were invited to take photographs of the guests. When they had done so, Mountbatten suggested that the guests might now borrow the press cameras to take a group photograph of the gentlemen of the press. Having done so, the guests, at Parker's bidding, removed the flash bulbs from the cameras and smashed them against the wall, so preventing any further photography. 'We were just having fun,' Parker told me. 'It was a good-humoured evening all round.'

At the time, that's how the newspapermen saw it, too. Over the years, however, the incident has been cited, time and again, as an illustration of Philip's fundamental hostility towards the press. He denies it absolutely. He has said to me more than once, 'I go out of my way to line people up for the photographers, to make sure everyone in the group is in the picture, to make sure the photographers have got what they need. I always have.' He knows they will never be satisfied. 'Of course, they always want one more. They're never satisfied. But I do my best. I do try to help.' On the morning of his wedding, seeing the

---

[90] The concept of fellow officers forming one's 'family' was best expressed for me by a soldier called John Kenneally, another orphan, the illegitimate son of a prostitute, who won the Victoria Cross in the final assault on Tunis in 1943. His regiment, the Irish Guards, were his 'family': 'It was a hard school to learn in. Without being over-sentimental, men can love each other. It is born of mutual suffering, hardships shared, dangers encountered. It's a spiritual love and there is nothing sexual about it. It's entirely masculine, even more than brotherly love, and it's called comradeship.'

photographers huddled in the cold outside Kensington Palace, he ordered cups of hot coffee and tea to be sent out to them.

There is some additional confusion about the eve-of-wedding stag night, confusion inadvertently caused by Larry Adler[91] who, in interviews reproduced in several books, and used in a recent Channel Four documentary about Prince Philip, said: 'I was at his bachelor party the night before his wedding to Princess Elizabeth.' He wasn't. Adler was at a different dinner, an earlier event, organised by the photographer Baron Nahum (always known simply as 'Baron') who had met Philip at Broadlands when he had been taking photographs of the Mountbattens, had become a friend of Philip's and was to take the official photographs of the royal wedding. When, not long before his death in 2001, I asked Larry Adler about the stag-night he remembered, he said: 'I may have got the date wrong, but I've not forgotten the occasion – or the atmosphere. There were about twenty to thirty guys there, all cracking jokes at Philip's expense – you know, dirty jokes, ward-room stuff. I couldn't join in because it wasn't comfortable. Philip wasn't comfortable. He was getting married and he was scared. His face was white. He was beginning to realise what he'd let himself in for.'

Philip and his best man, David Milford Haven, spent the night before the wedding at Kensington Palace. John Dean, the Mountbattens' butler who became Philip's valet, said, 'Their rooms were astonishingly poor and humble – floors scrubbed boards with worn rugs.' (Robin Dalton recalls her boyfriend David's room being 'in the servants' attic'. 'We had a flat together in Chelsea,' she told me, 'but in the run-up to the wedding it was thought advisable that David, as Philip's best man, move in with his grandmother. I remember David and me, on our nights together, creeping up the back stairs of her apartment at Kensington Palace as silently as possible.') John Dean recalled bringing Philip his early-morning tea promptly at 7 a.m. and finding his young master in happy form and not the least bit nervous.

Patricia Mountbatten's recollection is a little different. 'I saw him just after breakfast that morning,' she told me. 'We were alone together

---

[91] Larry Adler (1914–2001) was an American-born, London-based virtuoso mouth organ player. He was both gifted and preposterous, a name-dropper on an epic scale (Gershwin, Churchill, Einstein, he had known them all) and a raconteur who rarely stopped. Once, when he was very old, he was a guest on a radio show I was presenting, and inadvertently slipped off his chair and fell to the floor. Flat on his back, feet in the air, he carried on talking. Many regarded him as a bore. I liked him, even if – like Prince Philip – I would not rate him as an altogether reliable witness.

– we were cousins and we knew each other very well – and I said something about what an exciting day it was and, suddenly, he said to me, "Am I being very brave or very foolish?"' I asked Lady Mountbatten what she thought he meant by that. 'He was apprehensive,' she said. 'He was uncertain – not about marrying Princess Elizabeth, but about what the marriage would mean for him. He was giving up a great deal. In many ways, nothing was going to change for her. Everything was going to change for him.'

For a start, that very morning, he stopped smoking cigarettes. The King was a heavy smoker. (It was a family habit: Queen Mary was a smoker, too.) Princess Elizabeth saw the effect cigarettes had on her father and did not want her husband to smoke. Philip was happy enough to oblige his bride-to-be – and disciplined enough to be able to do so overnight. At 11 a.m., fortified by a gin and tonic, dressed in naval uniform, sporting the insignia of a Knight Companion of the Order of the Garter and wearing the ceremonial sword that had belonged to his grandfather, Prince Louis of Battenberg, Philip, accompanied by his best man, set off for Westminster Abbey.

Over at Buckingham Palace, Elizabeth, too, had an early start. It was still dark when Bobo brought her little princess a cup of tea. 'I don't think any of us had very much sleep,' reported Crawfie. 'I went along to Lilibet's room very early, and found her in her dressing-gown, peeping excitedly out of the windows at the crowds.' Despite the bitter cold, people had slept out overnight to secure their view. Along the Mall and down Whitehall, the pavements were packed, fifty people deep. 'I can't believe it's really happening,' Lilibet told Crawfie. 'I have to keep pinching myself.'

Norman Hartnell, who had designed the Princess's wedding dress, delivered it personally to the Palace the night before. At 9 a.m. he and his entourage were on parade again for the final fitting. It took an hour and a quarter. 'She looked so beautiful,' recalls Margaret Rhodes, who was one of the eight bridesmaids. 'We were all dressed by Mr Hartnell, too. It was very exciting. There was rationing, of course, and we used up all our clothes coupons.' The bride's dress alone absorbed three hundred coupons and cost £1,200. Given the prevailing austerity, the extravagance was considered controversial by some. Most, however, went along with the Leader of the Opposition, Winston Churchill, who welcomed the wedding and all that it involved as 'a flash of colour on the hard road we have to travel'. Norman Hartnell used to enjoy telling the story of how his manager – who had travelled far and wide gathering materials for the dress – was stopped at customs on his return from a buying trip to the United States and asked if he had anything to declare. 'Yes,' the man replied, 'ten thousand pearls for the wedding dress of Princess Elizabeth.' The dress was made of ivory silk, decorated with pearls arranged as white roses of York, entwined with ears of corn embroidered in crystal. The effect was ravishing.

Inevitably, there were last-minute dramas, 'the tensions common to any home on a wedding morning', according to Crawfie. The bride's bouquet was lost. A footman remembered receiving it and bringing it upstairs, but what happened to it after that, he couldn't recall. Panic ensued and then, suddenly, happily, the footman remembered he had placed it in a cool cupboard nearby for safe-keeping. Next, the precious tiara given to the Princess by Queen Mary snapped as it was being put on her head. More panic, until nervous hands managed to repair the damage. Finally – and most dramatically – the Princess went to put on the double string of pearls that her parents had given her as a wedding present – and realised that they were half a mile away at St James's Palace where all the wedding presents were to go on public display.

The Princess's recently appointed private secretary, Jock Colville, was summoned to her sitting room. 'She stood there, radiant and entrancing in her wedding dress,' he recalled. Could he, somehow, make his way to St James's Palace and retrieve the necklace, she asked. 'I looked at my watch,' he said. 'I rushed along the corridor. I galloped down the Grand Staircase and into the main quadrangle of Buckingham Palace. Take any car, the Princess had called after me. So I ran towards a large Royal Daimler. "To St James's Palace," I cried to the chauffeur, and I flung open the door of the car. Before I could leap in, a tall elderly man, ablaze with Orders and Decorations, began to emerge. It was King Haakon VII of Norway. "You seem in a hurry, young man," he said. "By all means have my car, but do let me get out first."' When Colville reached St James's, the detectives guarding the royal wedding gifts were not inclined to believe his story. He pleaded with them. He asked them to telephone Buckingham Palace. The line was dead. With his heart beating and the minutes ticking by, he told them his name and, when they discovered it printed in the official Wedding Programme, reluctantly, they allowed him to escape with the necklace. Pushing his way through the crowd, apologising as he went, 'with one hand firmly pressed against the pocket of my tunic where the pearls lay', Colville made his way back to the car and reached Buckingham Palace with only moments to spare.

At 11.15 a.m. the Princess, carrying her bouquet, wearing her parents' pearls, her grandmother's tiara and Mr Hartnell's fairy-tale dress, clambered into the Irish state coach. Her father, slight and pale, but smiling, dressed in his uniform as an Admiral of the Fleet, sat next to her. Together, escorted by the Household Cavalry in full ceremonial dress uniform for the first time in six years, father and daughter travelled along the Mall and down Whitehall towards Westminster Abbey, crowds, up to fifty people deep, cheering them all the way. 'The King looked unbelievably beautiful,' Sir Michael Duff wrote to his friend, the photographer Cecil Beaton, 'like an early French King and HRH the Bride a dream.' It was a poignant journey for them both, but more so for the King than his daughter. For Lilibet a new life was about to begin; for George VI an era was coming to an end. 'It is a far more moving thing to give your daughter away than to be married yourself,' the King told the Archbishop of York later that day.

The Archbishop, Cyril Garbett, officiating alongside the Archbishop of Canterbury, Geoffrey Fisher, described the wedding – to the congregation of two thousand in the Abbey, to the few thousand more watching a film of the occasion on fledgling television in the evening and to the millions tuned in to the live broadcast on the wireless around the world – as 'in all essentials exactly the same as it would have been for any cottager who might be married this afternoon in some small country church in a remote village in the Dales'. Well, up to a point, Lord Archbishop. The Princess had chosen traditional hymns ('The Lord is my shepherd', sung to the tune of Crimond, was Crawfie's favourite moment) and vowed, until death, to 'love, honour and obey' her husband, 'for richer for poorer, for better for worse', so the essentials were certainly familiar, but everything else was truly beyond the ken of the average British cottager of the period. For a start, there were eight bridesmaids (led by Princess Margaret, walking alone, three paces ahead of the other bridesmaids, in recognition of her rank), two kilted page boys (Prince William of Gloucester and Prince Michael of Kent), and the guests – the men in uniform and morning suits, the women in full-length dresses with long white gloves and glittering tiaras – included a remarkable array of royalty, some still reigning, others retired, hurt. On Lilibet's side of the family, her Uncle David and his American wife, the Duke and Duchess of Windsor, were conspicuous by their absence, and, on Philip's side, the principal non-invitees were his three sisters and their German husbands. It was only two years since the end of the war, too soon for the British Royal Family to be seen extending the hand of friendship to the enemy. (Philip's youngest sister, Sophie, had three brothers-in-law still awaiting denazification, one of them still interned.)

Alice wrote a twenty-two-page description of the wedding for her daughters, to 'console them for their absence'. She was there, of course, seated with her mother, the Marchioness of Milford Haven, and her sister, Louise with her husband, Crown Prince Gustaf of Sweden, and her brother, Dickie, who, with Edwina, had come home briefly from India for the occasion.

From Philip's father's side of the family the contingent was smaller: of Andrea's seven brothers and sisters, all but one was dead. Philip's uncle, Big George, was there from Paris, with his wife, Marie Bonaparte, and their daughter, Eugénie, alongside assorted first cousins, second cousins and cousins by marriage, including Queen Helen of Romania, Queen Alexandra of Yugoslavia and Queen Frederika of Greece.

There were so many foreign royals in the best seats for the wedding that members of the British Parliament had to draw lots to secure access to the 'parliamentary enclosure'. Chips Channon was one MP who managed to get in. 'I thought Princess Elizabeth looked well,' he noted in his diary, 'shy and attractive, and Prince Philip as if he was thoroughly enjoying himself.' (Five days later, Channon gave a spectacular post-wedding party – 'a great, great success' by his own account: 'I "laced" the cocktails with Benzedrine, which I find always makes a party go' – and entertained some of the royalty who were in town, including the Queens of Spain and Romania. 'I am sorry that Queen Freddie [of Greece] and the Duchess of Kent [Princess Marina, Philip's first cousin] could not come,' he told his diary: 'They are on a secret visit to the affronted German relations to tell them about the Wedding.' They took Alice's twenty-two page account with them.)

Noël Coward was at both Channon's party and at Westminster Abbey, where he found, to his surprise and pleasure, that he was placed in the fourth row, next to Beatrice Lillie. Coward recorded in his diary: 'A gala day . . . The wedding was most moving and beautifully done. English tradition at its best.' The Coward verdict was the general one. As the young couple left the Abbey, Philip bowing smartly to the King and Queen, Elizabeth dropping a low, slow curtsy to her parents, they looked like figures from a story book: a fairy-tale princess with her prince from a foreign land, destined to live happily ever after. Jock Colville was one of those who, in the run-up to the marriage, had been sceptical about its prospects. 'As the day drew nearer,' he confessed, 'I began to think, as I now sincerely do, that the Princess and Philip really are in love.' That's what the cheering crowds thought, too, as the Abbey bells pealed, and the bride and groom, beaming and waving, were taken back to Buckingham Palace in the Glass Coach.

At the Palace, Baron took the official photographs and luncheon was served. It was billed as an 'austerity' wedding breakfast, a modest affair for just 150 guests: family, close friends and courtiers. Crawfie was excited to be included:

> It was a gay and merry lunch party. The tables were decorated with smilax and white carnations, and at each of our places there was a little bunch of white heather, sent down from Balmoral. The famous gold-plate and the scarlet-coated footmen gave a fairy-tale atmosphere to it all, and I was in a veritable dream. The skirl of the bagpipes warmed the hearts of those of us who came from north of the Tweed. The French gentleman seated next to me, however, winced from time to time, but he bore it with fortitude.
>
> There were no long speeches. The King hates them and has always dreaded having to make one. He was brevity itself. The bridegroom, another sailor, had just as little to say. It was a very large room and there were no microphones, so few people even heard the little that *was* said. The French gentleman kept hissing in my ear, '*Qu'est ce qu'il dit?*' I was unable to help him.

The younger members of the family, and their nannies, had a quiet lunch and 'a nice lie down' in another part of the Palace. According to Crawfie, the page boys, Prince William and Prince Michael (the six- and five-year-old sons of Lilibet's uncles, the Dukes of Gloucester and Kent), were 'thoroughly overtired', 'grew peevish' and almost came to blows: 'Shocked nannies enveloped them in those vast white shawls royal nannies always seem to have handy. Like sheltering wings! They were borne off, but not before they had made ceremonious bows to the King and Queen. In royal circles manners are taught young.'

The little ones reappeared to see the bride and groom set off on their honeymoon. Mr Hartnell was especially proud of his going-away outfit for the young Princess: a love-in-the-mist crêpe dress with blue velvet cloth travelling coat, and blue felt bonnet trimmed with ostrich pompom and curved quills in two tones of blue. It needed to be warm because the November weather was bitter and, for the benefit of the crowds, the newlyweds were to travel from Buckingham Palace to Waterloo Station (en route for Winchester and their first stop at

Broadlands, the Mountbattens' country house in Hampshire) in an unheated open landau. (It was foggy, but at least it wasn't raining and, under their lap rugs, discreet comfort was provided by hot-water bottles and Lilibet's favourite corgi, Susan.) As, hand in hand, the newlyweds came down the Palace staircase, the family, cheering, gathered round and threw rose petals. As the couple's carriage trundled through the Palace gates, the King and Queen stood watching, holding hands. Princess Alice kept waving until the carriage disappeared from view. In some ways, perhaps it was like any cottager's wedding. All three proud parents had tears in their eyes.

A few days later, back in Athens, Alice wrote to Philip: 'How wonderfully everything went off & I was so comforted to see the truly happy expression on your face and to feel your decision was right from every point of view.' And, from London, the King wrote, touchingly, to Lilibet, as she embarked on married life and he contemplated a future without his elder daughter at his side:

> I was so proud of you & thrilled at having you so close to me on our long walk in Westminster Abbey, but when I handed your hand to the Archbishop I felt that I had lost something very precious. You were so calm and composed during the Service & said your words with such conviction, that I knew everything was all right.
>
> I am so glad you wrote & told Mummy that you think the long wait before your engagement & the long time before the wedding was for the best. I was rather afraid that you thought I was being hard-hearted about it. I was so anxious for you to come to South Africa as you knew. Our family, us four, the 'Royal Family' must remain together with additions of course at suitable moments!! I have watched you grow up all these years with pride under the skilful direction of Mummy, who as you know is the most marvellous person in the World in my eyes, & I can, I know, always count on you, & now Philip, to help us in our work. Your leaving us has left a great blank in our lives but do remember that your old home is still yours & do come back to it as much & as often as possible. I can see that you are sublimely happy with Philip which is right but don't forget us is the wish of
> Your ever loving & devoted
> Papa

The newlyweds began their honeymoon at Broadlands, not far from

Winchester, by the River Test. They were not alone. As well as Lilibet's corgi, Susan, the young lovers' entourage included a personal detective, a personal footman, Bobo MacDonald (the princess's nurserymaid turned dresser and confidante), and John Dean. John Dean and Cyril, the footman, looked after the luggage: the bride had fifteen cases, the groom just two. The detective did his best to keep the public at bay. At Winchester station, there were crowds waiting to cheer the young couple. At Broadlands, there were more sightseers gawping at the gates. Despite the cold, eager rubberneckers (loyal subjects as well as representatives of the press) hovered, day and night, at the edge of the estate hoping for glimpses of the happy pair. On Sunday morning, when the couple went together to a service at Romsey Abbey nearby, frantic royal-watchers scrambled across tombstones to get a better view. Several came equipped with chairs and stepladders to enable them to peer through the windows into the Abbey itself. For the royal newlyweds, life in the goldfish bowl had begun.

A few years ago, when visiting Broadlands as a tourist,[92] I recollect there was some sniggering among our party when we were shown the bedroom in which Elizabeth and Philip spent their wedding night. A fellow visitor reached over the security cordon to touch the nuptial bed and announced happily, 'The Queen is very keen on sex, you know.' I didn't know, but I was happy to hear it. And I have heard it said by others, quite often, since. I recall Lord Longford telling me, 'The Queen enjoys sex, as I do. People who ride tend to. It's very healthy.' Lord Longford was a Knight of the Garter, a God-fearing man, wholly honest and utterly devoted to Her Majesty, but I do wonder: how did he know? Sarah Bradford, in her comprehensive and compelling biography of the Queen, states boldly, but without giving us any authority for the assertion: 'Elizabeth was physically passionate.' I don't doubt it, but I do ask myself: who told Mrs Bradford? I have not raised the matter with Her Majesty, and I would be very surprised if anyone else has either.

Thanks to servants' tittle-tattle (reliable in this instance) we do know that Prince Philip, in the early days of his marriage, did not wear pyjamas. We are told, too, by Patricia Mountbatten, that once, when she remarked on Lilibet's flawless complexion, Philip laughed and said to his cousin, beaming, 'Yes, and she's like that all over.' One of David

[92] A visit is highly recommended. The house – a grey-brick Palladian villa – was once the country home of Lord Palmerston, features a fascinating exhibition on the life of Earl Mountbatten of Burma and is usually open to the public from 12 noon to 5.30 p.m. between June and September. Call 01794 505010 for details.

Milford Haven's friends told me David had told her that Philip had told him that Lilibet was 'very keen on sex, quite a goer'. Well, for both their sakes, let us hope so – but let us not pretend that we know. I can just about visualise Prince Philip giving a nod and a grin to David Milford Haven in response to a jocular enquiry on the subject, but I do not think he is the sort of man who would – for a moment – discuss the most intimate aspects of his married life with his men friends, now or then.

What happened between the sheets on the night of the royal wedding I cannot tell you. I was not there. However, I can report, because there were witnesses, that the evening at Broadlands was not especially peaceful. The telephone rang incessantly; the staff at Broadlands (in the absence of the Mountbattens in India) were not as well organised as they might have been; Bobo and Cyril and John were exhausted. The day had been a long one. The bridal couple retired as soon as supper was over: they looked weary but very happy, Lilibet especially so.

By several accounts, the bride and groom certainly had a jollier evening in Hampshire than the groomsman and bridesmaids had in London. Elizabeth's cousin, Margaret Rhodes, was one of the bridesmaids and she told me, 'We didn't have a girl's party before the wedding, but, on the day itself, we did have the traditional evening where the best man entertains the bridesmaids. It was not a success. The best man was Milford Haven, not my favourite man. Let's not talk about him.'

'Why not?' I asked Mrs Rhodes.

She assumed a very pinched look and said, rapidly, stubbing out her cigarette, 'We went to somewhere like Quaglino's and he was much keener on some dolly-bird at the other table than he was on us. He was not my idea of a gentleman.'

Milford Haven's girlfriend at the time, Robin Dalton, fears that she was probably the 'dolly-bird at the other table'. Looking anything but pinched, she told me, smiling into her Bloody Mary, 'I think the party was at Ciro's in Orange Street, not Quaglino's. I do remember Princess Margaret getting cross because David was spending too much time with me. I was only at the wedding because David got me a ticket in a special stand for unofficial guests. I had been married, albeit briefly. I was a divorcée, so not a suitable bride for a descendant of Queen Victoria. I couldn't accompany him into the Royal Enclosure at Ascot, even had I wished to. I loved David. He was so sweet and we had five happy years together. Then, understandably, and very suddenly, David got married to someone else, through the mistaken idea that she was very rich, leaving me with his dog, his car and both of us in tears.[93] As a wedding present, I think Philip gave David a pair of cuff links Philip had been given by the Duke of Gloucester.'

As best man, David's present to Philip and Lilibet was something both practical and sought-after: the most up-to-date (and expensive) record player on the market, the new 'Deccola'. According to Robin Dalton, 'David and Philip had very little money. They survived on their naval pay, and £5 a week each from Lord Mountbatten. One night at a dinner party, I sat next to a businessman who proudly told me he was manufacturing the Deccola. By the end of dinner, I had procured, free for David, the very first one off the production line and the manufacturer had procured valuable publicity because all the wedding presents went on prominent display.'

Philip and Elizabeth received around 1,500 wedding gifts, ranging from five hundred cases of tinned pineapple from the Government of Queensland to a turkey from a woman in Brooklyn who had heard that 'they have nothing to eat in England'. 'The people of Kenya' generously gave the royal couple a hunting lodge; the people of Britain generously sent Lilibet dozens of pairs of nylon stockings. The Aga Khan pleased Elizabeth with his present of a thoroughbred filly; Mahatma Gandhi impressed Philip with his gift of a personally woven piece of cloth, intended as a cover for a tea tray. As she toured the exhibition of the presents displayed at St James's Palace, Queen Mary, not an admirer of Gandhi, decided the material was intended as a loincloth and was not amused. Philip protested, but the old Queen did not want to be enlightened. She muttered, 'What a horrible thing' and, lips pursed, moved quickly on.

One gift that seems not to have been put on display was that of a tiny

---

[93] Milford Haven's first marriage – to Romaine Simpson – ended disastrously. (It did not begin too well, either: his mother, Nada, decided the prospects were so poor she could not bear to attend.) He then became infatuated with the Hungarian film starlet Eva Bartok, before marrying Janet Bryce, the mother of the 4th and current Marquess. Lord Brabourne told me, his wife nodding assent: 'David was awfully nice. We liked him. Girls adored him. But he was hopeless. He was gullible. He died young.' He left the navy, he drank too much, he got involved in unfortunate financial ventures, he died in 1970, aged fifty, running to catch a train. When Prince Philip and David Milford Haven came to Windsor over Christmas 1943, the King's private secretary, Sir Alan Lascelles, sized them both up and came to a definite conclusion: 'I prefer the latter.'

gold bicycle, apparently given to Prince Philip by a French friend of his and David's, a hotelier from the South of France called Félix. During the summer before the wedding Philip joined David at Nada's holiday home above Cannes. Every day during the holiday (so the story goes), Philip would borrow a bicycle from Félix to ride over to the home of a certain married lady . . . Félix thought the little gold bicycle would be an amusing souvenir of the bachelor prince's last summer holiday as a 'free man'.

After five nights at Broadlands, the honeymooners returned briefly to London for lunch at Buckingham Palace with the King and Queen before setting off by train for Scotland and a further two weeks of honeymoon at Birkhall on the Balmoral Estate.[94] Here, the young couple had a quieter, cosier, more secluded time. They went for walks in the snow. They warmed themselves by roaring log fires. They got to know one another. They had time alone – or, as much time alone as you get when there are servants always hovering. It is the privilege of princes to be waited on, but the price they pay for that privilege is a heavy one: someone is always close at hand, waiting, watching, listening, standing in silent judgement; sometimes reporting this and that to others in the servants' hall; occasionally reporting that and this to the world at large. Marion Crawford (governess), John Dean (valet), Paul Burrell (footman turned butler), in their way, in their day, showed real dedication as royal servants. They served their mistresses and masters with devotion, and then repaid the royal trust placed in them by spilling the beans in best-selling books, protesting their continuing loyalty all the way to the bank.

Philip had had an odd childhood, but, at boarding school and in the Royal Navy, he had to some extent lived in 'the real world', fending for himself. Lilibet, on the other hand, was a girl, born before the era of

---

[94] You too could honeymoon on the Balmoral Estate. The Estate – which was purchased by Prince Albert for Queen Victoria in 1851 – is owned and funded by the Queen personally (rather than as Sovereign) and Her Majesty lets out a number of holiday cottages: for details see www.balmoralcastle.com. Overall, the estate comprises 18,659 hectares owned between Balmoral, Birkhall and Glen Doll, 2,940 hectares of grouse moor at Corgarff and 4,688 hectares of sporting rights rented from a neighbour. The land is poor (mainly granitic) and most lies over 1,000 feet above sea level. There are seven Munros (mountains over 3,000 feet), 3,000 hectares are forested and 190 hectares are arable or pasture, of which ninety are farmed by a tenant and a hundred by the Estate with twenty-nine Highland cows, their progeny, and the Queen's Highland, Fell and Haflinger ponies.

female emancipation, brought up as a princess, living in palaces and castles, surrounded by servants. She, more than Philip, was wholly accustomed to being fed, and bathed, and dressed, and watched over, by others. At Broadlands, at Birkhall, at Buckingham Palace, the entourage was always there: the detective, the driver, the footman, the valet, and Bobo. Especially Bobo.

Margaret MacDonald was the daughter of an Inverness railway worker. As a child she lived by a railway line in a small railway company cottage. At twenty-two – in 1926, when Princess Elizabeth was born – she joined the Yorks' household as nurserymaid and assistant to Alah Knight, the royal nanny. When Princess Margaret Rose was born in 1930, Alah, naturally, concentrated on the new baby, and Bobo (as Miss MacDonald was soon nicknamed) began what would become a lifetime of single-minded devotion to Princess Elizabeth. When Lilibet was a little girl, Bobo shared her bedroom. When the Princess grew up, Bobo became her dresser, confidante and friend. John Dean described her as 'a small, smart, rather peremptory Scots woman' whose years with the royal household 'seemed to be imprinted on her face and stature'. She was formal – 'We have to keep a certain standing in the house', was her line – and seemed formidable to some, but, according to Dean, she was 'quite friendly when thawed'. She was a redhead when young. Dean reported: 'She was a lovely dancer and very good fun, with a nice sense of humour, but even when we were staying in some village, and were out socially in the local pub, she always addressed me as "Mr Dean". She always referred to Princess Elizabeth as "My Little Lady".' In private, with the Princess, Bobo would call her mistress 'Lilibet', one of the very few outside the Royal Family to feel comfortable doing so. (Playfully, Princess Margaret occasionally called her sister 'Lil'.)

Officially, Bobo was simply Elizabeth's dresser. She looked after the royal wardrobe. She dealt with the royal dressmakers: Mr Hartnell, Hardy Amies, and, later, Ian Thomas. She kept them in their place, both by the manner with which she handled them, and by not allowing any one of them complete control over Elizabeth's appearance. 'You're here for the clothes not the accessories,' she would tell the designers, firmly. Bobo was a personally disciplined, conservatively inclined, frugally minded Scotswoman: she saw no virtue in Lilibet being kitted out with expensive handbags. Officially, Bobo looked after Elizabeth's wardrobe. Unofficially, Bobo looked after Elizabeth. Her devotion was absolute, her commitment total, her access almost unlimited. By the time she died, in 1993, aged eighty-nine, she had become a legendary figure in royal circles: the one person to whom the Queen always listened.

For sixty-seven years, Bobo lived for Elizabeth. She loved her, protected her, respected her. She was wholly loyal and ever-present. I imagine, at times, she must have got on Prince Philip's nerves. Mike Parker said to me, 'Let's face it, he had a hell of a time with her. Miss MacDonald was *always* there. And in charge. Princess Elizabeth was Bobo's baby and that was that. But I don't think he ever complained. Anyway, he didn't to me. He didn't say a word. Not a word. He just put up with it.' Patricia Mountbatten told me that Bobo would prepare Lilibet's bath and then potter in and out of the bathroom while she was having it, effectively keeping Philip at bay: 'He couldn't share the bathroom with his wife, because Bobo saw it as her territory and I don't think Princess Elizabeth had the heart to say, "Bobo, please go away." I think Philip must have found it quite irritating.'

After two weeks at Birkhall, the honeymoon was over and Elizabeth and Philip (and the detective and the dresser, the footman and the valet, the seventeen cases and the corgi) returned to London in time for the King's fifty-second birthday on 14 December. 'The Edinburghs are back from Scotland,' Jock Colville noted in his diary. 'She was looking very happy, and, as a result of three weeks of matrimony, suddenly a woman instead of a girl. He also seemed happy, but a shade querulous, which is, I think, in his character.'

I think it is, too. In many ways, Prince Philip is remarkably good-humoured and long-suffering. He put up with Bobo; he has shrugged off his press coverage; he has endured more than half a century of footling royal flummery and thousands of hours of mind-numbing small talk with strangers and civic dignitaries. But he is 'a shade querulous'. He can be difficult. He can be scratchy. His impatience sometimes shows. And he is always contradictory.

In 1947, Princess Elizabeth was twenty-one and, though self-possessed, still quite shy. I asked her cousin Margaret Rhodes – who is fairly tentative now and, I imagine, was even more so then – what she made of Philip when she first got to know him in the 1940s. 'I used to dread sitting next to him,' she told me, pulling a rather anxious face. 'He'd be so contradictory. You'd say something just to say something, and he'd jump down your throat. "Why do you say that? What do you mean?" Quite frightening, until you got used to it. I think he's always had that de-bunking element in him. It was just his way.'

Was he like that with Elizabeth, I asked.

'Yes,' said Mrs Rhodes, 'he was like that with the Queen. He'd say, "Why the bloody hell? What the bloody hell?" I think she did sometimes find it very disconcerting.'

Patricia Mountbatten – whose manner is more robust than that of Mrs Rhodes: she is her father's daughter – told me that while, in her experience, the Queen did not respond to her husband's intemperate outbursts in kind, she enjoyed it when others did. 'I remember a big party at Balmoral,' said Countess Mountbatten, 'a shooting party, when, at dinner, Philip and I had a right old ding-dong about South Africa. It was a terrific argument and the Queen kept encouraging me. "That's right, Patricia," she said, "you go at him, nobody ever goes at him."' (When the Duke is critical of his wife, berating her for paying attention to the dogs when she should be listening to him, or wondering out loud why she spends so much time on the telephone, or telling her she is wearing the wrong clothes for a shooting expedition, the Queen is quite capable of answering back, saying to him, 'Oh, do shut up.' According to family and friends, she has become bolder with him, and he gentler with her, over the years.)

Why is Prince Philip a touch querulous? His cousin Patricia Mountbatten says, 'He has a very similar character to my father. He's a dynamo. He wants action. He wants to get things done. He likes getting his own way and it's frustrating for him when he doesn't.'

'And life at court was very, very frustrating for him at first,' according to Patricia's husband, Lord Brabourne. 'It was very stuffy. Lascelles was impossible. They were absolutely bloody to him. They patronised him. They treated him as an outsider. It wasn't much fun. He laughed it off, of course, but it must have hurt. I'm not sure that Princess Elizabeth noticed it. She probably didn't see it. In a way, marriage hardly changed her life at all. She was able to carry on much as before. In getting married, she didn't sacrifice anything. His life changed completely. He gave up everything.'

According to Margaret Rhodes, 'He's mellowed a lot in recent years.' He must have done. When I first became involved in the work of the National Playing Fields Association in the 1970s, I was warned that Prince Philip was a 'hands-on' president, but not always easy. He could be abrupt, I was told. He would be demanding, he might be rude. I certainly found him challenging – he questions everything: whatever you say, he counters it with 'Yes, but . . .' – and, occasionally, impatient ('Why hasn't this happened? What are you waiting for?'), but never rude. Now and again, he will indicate his disapproval with a sigh, or a raised eyebrow, or a weary shake of the head, but, on the whole, with the general public, and with those he meets undertaking his extraordinary array of public duties, he is surprisingly equable: easy-going, unaffected and good-humoured. I have seen him looking grouchy now and again (and kept my distance), but I have only once seen him positively bad-tempered. He expected to find a folder of papers in their usual place on the desk in his study at Buckingham Palace. A footman had moved the papers. Philip gave him short shrift. I blanched. The footman retreated, chastened and abashed. Lord Brabourne said to me of Philip: 'He's naughty now. He shouts at people sometimes.' Gina Kennard said to me: 'Let's face it, he can be really quite bad-tempered.'

Jock Colville's assessment of the mood and manner of the royal couple in 1947 is borne out by other witnesses: the bride was very happy: the groom, happy but a touch querulous. Philip still did not have a home to call his own. The plan had been for the newlyweds to have a country home at Sunninghill Park in Windsor Great Park and a London home at Clarence House, next to St James's Palace, over-looking the Mall. Unfortunately, the substantial house at Sunninghill Park burnt to the ground before the Edinburghs could move in, and Clarence House was in need of substantial refurbishment and repair.[95] Eventually, they rented a comparatively small country house, Windlesham Moor, in Berkshire (just two floors: four reception rooms, five bedrooms, plus staff quarters) and, in May 1949, eighteen months after their wedding, moved into their London home, a handsomely restored Clarence House.[96] Meanwhile, they perched briefly at Clock House in Kensington Palace (the home of the Earl and Countess of

[95] Clarence House was built in the late 1820s for Queen Victoria's uncle, who was Duke of Clarence until he became William IV in 1830. Queen Victoria's son, the Duke of Connaught, lived there until his death in 1942, aged ninety-one. During and after the Second World War, it was used by the Red Cross and the Ministry of Works. Sunninghill Park eventually became the site of a new house, mocked in the media as a ranch-style house in the tradition of the TV series *Dallas* and *Dynasty*, the home of the Queen and Prince Philip's second son and his wife, the Duke and Duchess of York.

[96] The restoration cost £78,000, rather more than the £50,000 voted for the work (somewhat grudgingly) by parliament. The Edinburghs were in residence from 1949 until George VI's death in 1952, when the new Queen moved back to Buckingham Palace and Clarence House became the home of the Queen Mother. It is now the London home of the Prince of Wales, who has undertaken further restoration work, and opened part of the house to the public for the first time. For details see: www.princeofwales.gov.uk

Athlone, who were on a three-month trip to South Africa), and then spent a year living with the King and Queen at Buckingham Palace, Windsor, Balmoral and Sandringham. For Elizabeth, Buckingham Palace was 'home from home'. For Philip, given a bedroom and sitting room of his own alongside his wife's established apartments, the arrangement was less satisfactory.

There was one area in which Philip, however, was able to do as he pleased: the appointment of his first equerry-in-waiting. He chose his friend, contemporary and fellow naval officer, Mike Parker. 'I was honoured,' Parker told me, 'and I felt I could do the job. Philip and I were mates and I felt I could be a useful ally to him at court. The King was fine, very friendly, very helpful, but the traditional courtiers weren't always so easy. I had been planning to return to Australia, but my wife, Eileen, who was Scottish, didn't want to leave the UK, so it worked out all round.' Parker was Philip's right-hand man – equerry, ADC, secretary, friend – for ten years, until 1957, when the 'scandal' of his divorce from Eileen obliged him to resign.

Princess Elizabeth's private secretary, Jock Colville, was chosen for her by the King's private secretary, Tommy Lascelles. Born in 1915, educated at Harrow and Trinity College, Cambridge, Colville was a career diplomat who started out (as personable and bright young men from the Foreign Office sometimes do) as an assistant private secretary in Downing Street. He worked for Chamberlain, Churchill and Attlee in turn, so he knew his way around the corridors of power. He was also wholly at home with the Palace culture. His mother, Lady Cynthia Colville, was a lady-in-waiting to Queen Mary. As a boy, he was a Page of Honour to George V. In 1948, he married Lady Margaret Egerton, known as 'Meg', daughter of the 4th Earl of Ellesmere, who had been recruited by Princess Elizabeth as one of her first ladies-in-waiting. He was a class act, as smooth and British as Parker was rough and Australian, but they rubbed along well and came to see one another's strengths.

Completing the team, as Comptroller and Treasurer to the Edinburgh household, was an older man, Lieutenant-General Sir Frederick 'Boy' Browning, born in 1896, a dashing war hero, considered by Baron to be the handsomest man he ever photographed, married to the novelist Daphne du Maurier, and Chief of Staff to Philip's uncle, Louis Mountbatten, on his South-East Asia Command. Mountbatten recommended Browning to his nephew unreservedly: 'Boy has drive, energy, enthusiasm, efficiency and invokes the highest sense of loyalty and affection in his subordinates. His judgement is absolutely sound, and he would sooner die than let his boss down . . . he is not a "yes man" or even a courtier and never will be. He will fearlessly say what he thinks is right . . . Frankly, Philip, I do not think you can do better.'

It was a strong team. It had to be. The Princess and the Duke, aged twenty-one and twenty-six respectively, were about to embark on a curious and exhausting adventure: a relentless, endlessly repetitive roller-coaster ride of royal duties and good works, from which only death or revolution could release them. When I asked Prince Philip if he felt frustrated that his marriage had ultimately curtailed his naval career, he said: 'In 1947 I thought I was going to have a career in the Navy, but it became obvious there was no hope. The royal family then was just the King and the Queen and the two princesses. The only other male member was the Duke of Gloucester. There was no choice. It just happened.' Philip had joined the family firm: he had to play his part in the family business. 'You have to make compromises,' he said to me. 'That's life. I accepted it. I tried to make the best of it.'

For the first four and a quarter years of his marriage, the Duke combined his royal duties with his naval ones. He had plenty of energy, a well-run office and an enviable ability to successfully juggle the competing demands of the Admiralty and Buckingham Palace. He worked hard; he played hard; he slipped quite easily into the role of supportive consort and interested royal visitor. He had – he has – the ability to live in the moment, to concentrate intently on the job in hand. He is good at compartmentalising his life, switching from one interest/duty/activity to another in an instant, as required. In a day, he might wear several hats (metaphorically) and several uniforms (literally): he seems quite at home in each of them. In the space of sixteen hours he can move from parade ground to business meeting to memorial service to charity lunch to factory tour to award ceremony to state banquet, changing kit four times, appearing up-to-speed throughout, but not letting the agenda or mood of one engagement affect the next. It is a useful skill to acquire – if you aspire to the royal life. (It also, I think, explains something that those who become friendly with royalty sometimes find puzzling. I have a number of 'showbusiness friends' who have enjoyed the company of Prince Philip – or Prince Charles or Prince Andrew – at charitable events, felt they were getting on famously, even been invited over to Windsor Castle or Highgrove House for a meal, and then been disconcerted because the camaraderie of the moment isn't sustained. The royal is being thoroughly jolly –

really friendly, intimate and confidential – and then, suddenly, he's gone. It's 2.45 p.m., the car is waiting, he gets up, he goes: he may not even say goodbye. That's it – until next time. And, on the whole, *you* cannot organise next time: the ball is in their court. The royal life provides opportunities for countless brief encounters, many of them happy, some of them intense: it is not conducive to forming and sustaining a wide range of everyday friendships.)

In 1948, with the Edinburghs living at Buckingham Palace, Philip could walk to work, and did. He started the year with a desk job at the Admiralty, as an operations officer 'pushing ships around'. Later in the year, he went on a Staff Course at the Royal Naval College, Greenwich, and chose to spend the week in Greenwich, coming home to Lilibet at weekends. Spending nights, and weeks, and sometimes months, apart from your spouse, is the lot of married servicemen and women. It may be unsatisfactory: it may cause tensions and difficulties in a relationship: but it is not unusual: in the navy especially, it is the way things are. In the years to come, the time Elizabeth and Philip would spend apart would give rise to comment: to them it was simply an inevitable fact of life.

Understanding the lives of other people is not easy if their way of life is very different from your own. I have spent my entire married life sharing a bedroom – and a bed – with my wife. If we started to sleep in separate rooms, I would be dismayed: I would see it as the beginning of the end. The truth is it might be more comfortable and convenient sometimes to sleep apart, but we don't – we never have. Why? Because we are middle-class, and comfortably married middle-class couples of our generation always share the same bedroom. That's the way it is. Among the upper classes, especially three or four generations ago, it was different. Men and women led much more separate lives: they lived in larger houses: they had separate (if adjacent or adjoining) bedrooms. That's just the way it was. When Elizabeth and Philip moved into Clarence House they had separate but communicating bedrooms. It was what they – and their staff – would have expected. In his memoir, the Duke's valet, John Dean, described the arrangement as though it was the most natural thing in the world. Of an evening, John would be assisting Philip in his bedroom, while Bobo would be tending to Elizabeth in hers, and the royal couple 'would joke happily through the left-open door'.

In July 1982, an intruder (a thirty-one-year-old schizophrenic named Michael Fagan) found his way into Buckingham Palace and disturbed the Queen, alone, asleep in bed. This alarming incident prompted a double dose of outrage from the tabloid press: why was the Palace security so lamentable and where was Prince Philip? Why was he not on hand to come to his wife's rescue? Indeed, the 'revelation' that the Queen and her husband did not appear to share a bedroom caused more comment in certain quarters than the fact that a lunatic could wander off the street into the Sovereign's bedroom without let or hindrance. The Queen, who, at the time, handled the intrusion with commendable calm, was nevertheless shaken.[97] The popular press had the answer: 'Give her a cuddle, Philip' instructed one newspaper headline. Although it is really none of your business (or mine), I am able to tell you that, customarily, when sleeping under the same roof, the Queen and Prince Philip do share the same bed. It just happened that on the morning of Fagan's intrusion, Philip had a crack-of-dawn start for an out-of-town official engagement and so spent the night in his own quarters.

In May 1948, the young couple undertook their first official foreign assignment: a four-day visit to Paris, a trip designed – as had been the King and Queen's French tour in 1939 – to burnish the *entente cordiale*. It did the trick. The programme was packed and predictable: Versailles, Fontainebleau, a night at the Opéra, a trip down the Seine. There were lunches, dinners, receptions and a banquet – the stuff of every royal tour. The French press was charmed: the Princess was beautiful, the Duke was handsome, and they both spoke surprisingly good French – he, thanks to his decade in Paris as a child; she, thanks to the tutoring

---

[97] Gina Kennard, told me, 'At Balmoral that year – after that man got into her bedroom – the Queen began snapping at Philip. She was really quite snappy with him. Which was unusual for her. Not for him, of course. He's always been a bit snappy. But the man getting into her room was horrid.' It was. The man had a broken glass ashtray in his hand and was bleeding. The intrusion occurred at around 7.15 a.m. on 9 July 1982. The Queen pressed the alarm button by her bed, but her overnight police guard had gone off duty at 6.00 a.m. and her footman was out walking the corgis. The intruder simply wandered in, wholly unhindered, drew the curtains and sat on the bed. He wanted to share his troubles with Her Majesty. (Later, he told police he had planned to cut his wrists in front of the Queen.) Eventually, when he asked for a cigarette, the Queen managed to manoeuvre him out of the bedroom and the alarm was raised. The incident prompted a much-needed review of Palace security, which was, in the words of the intruder himself, 'diabolical'. This was not Fagan's first dawn raid on the Palace: on the previous occasion he had stolen a bottle of wine. The Home Secretary at the time was Willie Whitelaw. Ultimately, he was responsible for the Metropolitan Police and the Queen's security. He offered his resignation. It was declined. Some years later, he told me, his eyes brimming with tears, 'I felt utterly ashamed, utterly miserable. It was the worst moment of my public life.'

of Antoinette de Bellaigue. 'In four hectic days,' Jock Colville noted, with satisfaction, 'Princess Elizabeth had conquered Paris.' Forty years before the phrase 'the Diana effect' became common currency, Colville watched Elizabeth going about her business and described what amounted to the same phenomenon: 'Quite mysteriously, a visit by a young princess with beautiful blue eyes and a superb natural complexion brought gleams of radiant sunshine into the dingiest streets of the dreariest cities. Princes who do their duty are respected, beautiful Princesses have an in-built advantage over their male counterparts.'

One of the things that saddened – and worried – the Queen and Prince Philip about Diana, Princess of Wales, was not that she was popular, but that she allowed her popularity to go to her head. Elizabeth was adored once, too – as much as Diana was, perhaps even more so. In the late 1940s and early 1950s, in Britain, in France, in countries around the world, thousands – tens of thousands, sometimes *hundreds* of thousands – turned out to cheer her. Once upon a time, Philip and Elizabeth were seen – and talked about – and written up – as characters from a fairy-tale. The difference between them and Princess Diana, I think, is that they did not take it personally. When I discussed this with Prince Philip in his library at Buckingham Palace, he said to me, 'You won't remember this, but in the first years of the Queen's reign, the level of adulation – you wouldn't believe it. You really wouldn't. It could have been corroding. It would have been very easy to play to the gallery, but I took a conscious decision not to do that. Safer not to be too popular. You can't fall too far.'

The four-day trip to Paris was the Edinburghs' first overseas triumph. As a diplomatic and public relations exercise it was an unqualified success. At a personal level it was hell. The weather was unbearable: it was the hottest Whitsun weekend of the century. The schedule was alarmingly crowded: the couple were allowed one night off – 'a private evening' – and it was not a success. According to Jock Colville: 'We went to a most select three-star restaurant; the French had been turned out, so we found a table, just a party of us all alone in this vast restaurant. Prince Philip spotted a round hole in a table just opposite us, through which the lens of a camera was poking. He was naturally in a frightful rage. We went on to a night club, again the French all turned out. One of the most appalling evenings I have ever spent. Everybody dressed up to the nines – nobody in either place – except the lens.'

Philip was in a rage and he had an upset stomach. Elizabeth stayed calm, but she felt quite as queasy. She was three months pregnant.

(*Above*) The best of times: surveying the harbour at Malta, 1949. (*Below*) Baron's photograph of the sponsors at Prince Charles's christening in the Music Room at Buckingham Palace, 15 December 1948. Seated, l–r, The Dowager Marchioness of Milford Haven, Elizabeth and Charles, Queen Mary; standing, l–r, Patricia Brabourne, Philip, George VI, David Bowes-Lyon (Queen Elizabeth's brother), the Earl of Athlone (Queen Mary's brother), Princess Margaret

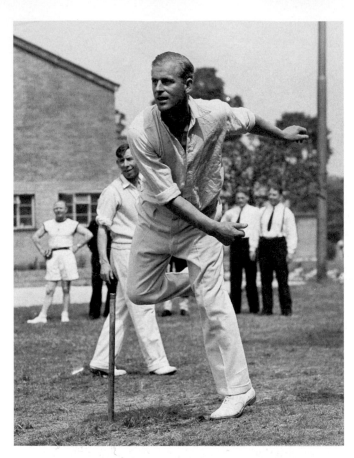

Philip, bowling in the nets at Corsham, 1947

The Thursday Club cricket match, 1948, with Baron and Philip, seated centre, in top hats, and James Robertson-Justice, in back row, far left

Princess Anne's christening, 21 October 1950: a page from Queen Mary's photograph album

Elizabeth and Philip at the Royal Windsor Horse Show, May 1949

Summer holiday: Philip and Elizabeth with Charles and Anne, August 1951

Taking command: Philip, Captain of HMS *Magpie*, Malta, 1951

Letting go: Philip, water-skiing in the Mediterranean, August 1951

(*Above left*) 14 November 1951: George VI, 'recovered' from his operation, pictured eleven weeks before his death, with Prince Charles on his third birthday, Princess Anne and Queen Elizabeth. (The Edinburghs were returning from their American tour.) (*Above right*) 6 February 1952, the day George VI died: Princess Alice, Philip's mother, arriving in Chicago and telling reporters, 'The King looked exceptionally well when I last saw him on January 16th.'

7 February 1952, the new Queen Elizabeth, dressed in mourning for her father, arriving at Heathrow Airport on her return from Kenya

Happy and glorious:
Coronation Day, 2 June 1953

Off duty: Charles and Anne with Elizabeth II at Balmoral Castle, September 1952

On duty: Charles, saluting, and his sister Anne, with Princess Mary, the Princess Royal, and her sister-in-law, Queen Elizabeth the Queen Mother, at Buckingham Palace, June 1953

THE DUKE & THE QUEEN

Chapter Nine

'Love does not consist in gazing at each other,
but in looking together in the same direction.'
Antoine de Saint-Exupéry (1900–1944), *Wind, Sand and Stars*

'Her Royal Highness the Princess Elizabeth, Duchess of Edinburgh, was
safely delivered of a Prince at 9.14 o'clock this evening. Her Royal
Highness and the infant Prince are both doing well.'

On Sunday 14 November 1948, at a little after 11 p.m., Commander
Richard Colville, RN – a cousin of Jock Colville's, but an older man and
less subtle, who had joined the Palace as press secretary to the King the
year before – took the formal announcement, written out in his own
neat hand, and, accompanied by Jock, scrunched his way across the
Buckingham Palace courtyard to fix it to the Palace railings. The
waiting crowd – some three thousand strong – greeted the news with
sustained cheers and an impromptu chorus of 'For he's a jolly good
fellow'.

By daybreak, word had spread across the nation – and the world. In
the United States, radio programmes were interrupted with the news.
In South Africa and India, in Kenya and Canada, in Australia and New
Zealand, guns were fired, bells were rung, bonfires were lit. In the streets
of London, news vendors cried, 'It's a boy!' and across the mountain
ranges of Wales a chain of beacons was lit. On the high seas, the ships
of the Royal Navy – every one of them – put out more flags and, on the
River Thames, the humblest boats were festooned with celebratory
bunting. In homes, and pubs and clubs and churches, there was – in a
way that seems incredible to us now – genuine rejoicing. At
Westminster Abbey, the bells rang out with a peal of five thousand
changes. In the chamber of the House of Commons, the Prime
Minister, Clement Attlee, on behalf of a grateful nation, saluted the

virtues of the constitutional monarchy 'which have won the hearts of the people' and spoke of the 'great responsibilities' that would one day settle on the shoulders of the infant Prince. The Leader of the Opposition, Winston Churchill, now seventy-four, rose to the occasion with a typical rhetorical flourish:

> Our ancient monarchy renders inestimable services to our country and to all the British Empire and Commonwealth of Nations. Above the ebb and flow of party strife, the rise and fall of ministries and individuals, the changes of public opinion and fortune, the British monarchy presides ancient, calm and supreme within its functions, over all the treasures that have been saved from the past and all the glories that we write in the annals of our country. Our thoughts go out to the mother and father and, in a special way, to the little prince, now born into this world of strife and storm.

At the very moment of the little Prince's birth, his father was in the Buckingham Palace squash court, having a game with his friend and equerry, Mike Parker. The Prince and Parker had had more than one game that evening – and a swim in the Palace pool. Princess Elizabeth's confinement – in the Palace Buhl Room, specially converted into a well-equipped surgery – had been a painfully long one. The King's private secretary, Tommy Lascelles, brought the good news hotfoot from the Buhl Room to the squash court. Philip raced back, with Lascelles and Parker trailing, on the way picking up the carnations and champagne he had at the ready, and went in to congratulate his young wife and admire his new son. 'It takes a man to have a son!' was the signal Philip sent to Parker when Parker's first child was born. Parker told me, 'Philip was thrilled to have a son. He was over the moon. Absolutely delighted.' That same night Philip sent a telegram bearing the glad tidings to his mother in Greece.

Princess Alice, now aged sixty-three, had recently moved to the Greek island of Tinos. She planned, she told her family, to 'withdraw from the world' and found 'a religious sisterhood of Martha & Mary', training girls to become nursing sisters. She was not a nun herself, but she dressed as one, and rose early every morning to attend to her devotions. Prince Philip says, 'Wearing the habit meant that she did not have to worry about clothes or getting her hair done.' She led a life of comparative simplicity, in a modest house, where the electricity supply was erratic and there was no telephone. She was thrilled to receive her son's telegram. She wrote to him at once: 'I think of you so much with a sweet baby of your own, of your joy & the interest you will take in all his little doings. How fascinating nature is, but how one has to pay for it in the anxious trying hours of the confinement.'

Princess Elizabeth recovered quickly from her confinement. She spent ten days in bed recuperating (as new mothers were encouraged to do) and breast-fed her son from the start. The Princess wrote to her former music teacher: 'The baby is very sweet and we are enormously proud of him. He has an interesting pair of hands for a baby. They are rather large, but with fine long fingers quite unlike mine and certainly unlike his father's. It will be interesting to see what they become. I still find it hard to believe I have a baby of my own!'

The first cotside report to reach the public came from one of Elizabeth's aunts, her mother's younger sister, Rose, now Countess Granville, who told a gathering of Girl Guides in Northern Ireland that the new mother was 'wonderfully well and radiantly happy' and the new prince 'could not be more angelic looking': 'He is golden-haired and has the most beautiful complexion, as well as amazingly delicate features for so young a baby . . . The Queen says that she thinks the baby is like his mother, but the Duke is quite certain that the baby is very like himself.' After a few days, in small clusters, palace servants were allowed to gather round the royal crib ('done up in buttercup yellow silk, with lace trimmings', according to Crawfie: 'The Royal Family do not observe the old tradition of pink and blue') and coo and ooh and ah at the bonny little Prince, who had weighed in at a satisfactory seven pounds six ounces. John Dean described the infant as 'a tiny red-faced bundle, either hairless or so fair as to appear so'. Crawfie thought that, like all royal babies in her experience, he bore a strong resemblance to George V, with 'an absurdly mature look, and ridges under his eyes'.

After the initial excitement of the royal birth – four thousand congratulatory telegrams were received at Buckingham Palace within twenty-four hours of the news first breaking, closely followed by an avalanche of cards, letters, flowers and assorted gifts, from teddy bears to hand-knitted bootees – a macabre rumour started. Around the land the whisper went: something is wrong with the child: he is disfigured, he might not live. Crawfie later wrote, 'The stories that went around at that time about him were entirely without foundation of any kind.' Crawfie believed the root cause of the stories was the Royal Family's own obsession with privacy, what she called a 'strange campaign of secrecy': 'For a long time no pictures were issued, and even the household did not know what the baby's names were to be.'

There was a news vacuum and on the streets it was filled with wild speculation. The baby might be 'healthy and strong, and beautifully made', as Crawfie insisted, 'with a flawless, silky skin', but, if so, why not show him off to the world? And why not name him? The answer to both questions, it seems, was a simple desire on the part of the Princess for privacy. Just as fifty years later, on the death of Diana, Princess of Wales, the Queen's first instinct was to shield her grandsons, protect their privacy and keep her own counsel, so, in November 1948, on the birth of Prince Charles, Princess Elizabeth instinctively wanted to guard her baby son's privacy. There would be photographs – of course[98] – and the baby's names would be made known – naturally – but all in good time . . . Why should the Heiress Presumptive and her little boy have to dance at once to the public's tune?

Throughout her life the Queen has fulfilled her public duty conscientiously and with complete commitment, and has hoped, as a consequence, to be allowed some private space for her private life. Do we really need to know how the infant Prince took to the breast (quite well, apparently), or whether and when he was circumcised (yes, on 20 December 1948, it seems: Dr Jacob Snowman performed the operation)? Of course we don't need to know. It is none of our business. And yet, we are curious.

From the birth of her son to the present day, Elizabeth II has struggled to maintain a degree of privacy for herself and her children. It has not been easy. Hugh Dalton, the Labour MP and sometime Chancellor of the Exchequer, wrote in his diary in the week that Prince Charles was born: 'If this boy ever comes to the throne . . . it will be a very different Commonwealth and country he will rule over.' Dalton was prescient. Elizabeth had been born in the reign of George V, King-Emperor. She grew up in an age of deference and discretion, when bowing and curtsying to royalty was automatic, when you did not speak to a royal unless first spoken to, when her Uncle David could conduct an open affair with a married divorcée and know that it would go unreported by a self-denying press. The world has changed. The Empire has gone, deference has disappeared and newspapers will print what

[98] And the first were taken by Cecil Beaton, who reported to his diary: 'Prince Charles, as he is to be named, was an obedient sitter. He interrupted a long, contented sleep to do my bidding and open his blue eyes to stare long and wonderingly into the camera lens, the beginning of a lifetime in the glare of public duty.'

they damn well like – and the more intimate and salacious it is, the more they like it. When Edward VIII and his girlfriend, on holiday together, swam naked off the coast of Albania, there were no paparazzi hiding on the hillside. When, half a century later, the Duchess of York, on holiday with her boyfriend in the South of France, appeared topless by their swimming pool, the revealing photographs, taken with telephoto lenses from the adjacent hillside, appeared on front pages in Britain and around the world. Nothing is sacred any more. For a high-profile public figure, a wholly private life is next-to-impossible nowadays.

For Princess Elizabeth in 1948, the desire for privacy was more than a matter of personal preference and natural reticence. Famously, in 1867, Walter Bagehot, writing about the role of the monarchy in *The English Constitution*, declared: 'We must not let daylight in on magic.' Bagehot believed that sustaining the mystique of the monarchy was essential to its authority – and survival. Elizabeth had studied Bagehot, and Commander Colville, who was the Palace press secretary from 1947 until 1968, believed in Bagehot's maxim completely. When Colville got the job he had no experience of press relations: he had been in the navy for twenty-two years. For the next twenty-one years he dealt with the press in a manner that suggested that relations with them were the very last thing that either he or the Royal Family desired.

According to Kenneth Rose, a journalist and biographer who dealt with him on a regular basis, Commander Colville did not discriminate between hacks: 'All were made to feel that their questions were impertinent if not downright vulgar.' Colville would supply information about the Sovereign's public engagements, and that was all. In his view, as he explained to the Press Council, the Queen was 'entitled to expect that her family will attain the privacy at home which all other families are entitled to enjoy'. Somewhat impertinently, the Press Council begged to differ, maintaining that 'the private lives of public men and women, especially royal persons, have always been the subject of natural curiosity. That is one of the consequences of fame or eminence or sincere national affection. Everything therefore that touches the Crown is of public interest or concern.'

All their adult lives, Elizabeth and Philip have been wary of the press. Take it from all who know her, the Queen is a delightful person – amusing, engaging and intelligent – but she is not comfortable with journalists. She has never given an interview and has no desire to do so. When she comes face to face with a journalist or broadcaster, at a public event or a private reception, she watches her words. She is determined to give nothing away. Jennie Bond was the BBC's royal correspondent for fourteen years. When she gave up the job in 2003, she told me, 'I never got to know the Queen. I barely got to meet her. As a royal reporter, you don't. You are kept at arm's length. And on the rare occasions when you are admitted to the royal presence, the small talk is very desultory. When the Queen went to South Korea, I covered the visit for the BBC and met Her Majesty briefly at a reception. She said, "Oh, have you come here specially?" I felt like saying, "No, I just happened be in South Korea and thought I'd drop by." I think it's sad that, after fourteen years, I still had the most distant relationship with the Queen and Prince Philip. I think, from their point of view, it's bad public relations. From my point of view, I didn't dislike them. I just didn't get to know them. There were endless opportunities when they could have made their mark with the media, and they simply didn't take them. They avoid journalists. They walk away from them. They dismiss them. The Duke's even worse than the Queen. He's really perfected the art of saying hello and goodbye in the same handshake.'

Prince Philip, in fact, is almost invariably good company and, in my experience, usually goes out of his way to be agreeable to strangers. He doesn't trust the press, however. 'If I'm doing something I care about,' he once said to me, 'I really hope the press won't come along too, because I know they'll only ruin it.' When I reminded him that he was the member of the Royal Family who, in the 1950s, first talked to the press, giving a series of newspaper, radio and television interviews, he said, 'Yes, I made a conscious decision to talk to the media – but not about me, only about what I'm doing, what I'm supporting.' When I told him that, fifty years on, that was no longer enough, that the modern media need something more sexy, they need 'personalities', he nodded. 'Yes,' he said, with a sigh, 'the press have turned us into a soap opera.'

In 1948, the soap opera had something of the fairy-tale about it. A month and a day after the royal birth came the royal christening. On the morning of Wednesday 15 December, in the White and Gold Music Room at Buckingham Palace, wearing the flowing silk and lace christening robe his mother had worn for her christening twenty-two years before, the infant Prince was baptised into the Church of England and named Charles Philip Arthur George. His godparents included the King, Queen Mary, the King of Norway, Prince George of Greece, the Dowager Marchioness of Milford Haven, Elizabeth's uncle, David Bowes-Lyon, and Dickie's daughter, Patricia Brabourne. Patricia told me that she thought Philip and Elizabeth chose 'Charles' as a name simply because they liked it. Boy Browning was one of those who felt the name was 'bad news', given the precedents of Charles I and II, to say nothing of the unhappy fate that befell Charles Stuart, 'Bonnie Prince Charlie'. Princess Margaret, however, was delighted with the choice of name, explaining that henceforward she would be known as 'Charley's Aunt', 'probably my finest title'.

After lunch, and the taking of the formal photographs (including a fine study of the sleeping Prince in the crisply starched arms of his nurse), Queen Mary invited the assembled company to gather round Queen Victoria's photograph albums to decide who among his forebears the new Prince most closely resembled. She decided, without doubt, it was Prince Albert. Queen Mary took the keenest interest in family history. Her christening gift was a silver cup and cover given by George III to a godson in 1780, 'so that', she noted in her diary, with allowable satisfaction, 'I gave a present from my great-grandfather to my great-grandson 168 years later'. Queen Mary entertained few doubts about her family's place in history. Baby Charles's other great-grandmother, Victoria Milford Haven, was more circumspect. She wrote to Dickie of her 'latest & important great-grandson': 'Let us hope he may live in a more peaceable & prosperous time than we & live to be some sort of reigning king.'

Alice did not attend the christening, but she received news of her new grandson's progress from other members of the family. She got a full report from her younger sister Louise, which she shared with Dickie:

> She says that Lilibet was looking so well & fresh, a good recovery after a hard time she had, 30 hours in all. The baby is sweet with a well-shaped head, an oval face & a little bit of fair fluff of hair. She says he is like Philip, but Marina says he is like Lilibet, so you can choose. I am so happy for Philip for he adores children & also small babies. He carries it about himself quite professionally to the nurse's amusement.

By every account, Prince Philip was – and is – wonderful with babies and small children. 'They like him and he likes them,' according to Countess Mountbatten. 'No question about it, Philip was a very good father to his children when they were young.' According to Lady Kennard, 'He was a wonderful parent. He played with his children, he read them stories, he took them fishing, he was very involved. I remember we stayed with them in Scotland when Charles must have been about one. The three of them were so happy together, easy and relaxed. Philip has been marvellous with his grandchildren, too. He's just good with the little ones.' In the summer of 2002, when the Prime Minister, Tony Blair, and his wife, Cherie Booth, went to stay at Balmoral, Philip took a special shine to the Blairs' two-year-old son, Leo. Proudly, Leo sang the whole first verse of the National Anthem to Philip and Philip responded happily by singing Leo the second verse. Cherie Blair, who, I imagine, is not an instinctive monarchist, told me, 'I have to say that both the Queen and Prince Philip are really, really good with little children. You couldn't fault them.'

Philip and Lilibet were very happy with their new baby. Parenthood suited them. According to all of their friends to whom I have spoken – friends who have known them across more than half a century – the first few years of their marriage were, in many ways, the happiest. 'Perhaps inevitably,' Gina Kennard said to me. 'Princess Elizabeth was not yet Queen, Philip was still in the navy. They were young, they were relatively carefree.' And they were cosseted. They were devoted to little Prince Charles, but they did not have to tend to him unaided. He had two Scottish nurses in constant attendance: Helen Lightbody, who arrived on the recommendation of the Duchess of Gloucester, whose sons she had looked after, and Mabel Anderson, who placed an advertisement in a nursing journal and was amazed to find herself invited to Buckingham Palace for an interview with the Princess.

Before Charles was born, Elizabeth had declared, 'I'm going to be the child's mother, not the nurses.' Well, she was – but, inevitably, because she was a princess as well as a mother, because 'royal duty' called and all her life Elizabeth has made answering the call of royal duty her first priority, and because it was the way of her class and her time, much of the nitty-gritty of childcare was left to Mrs Lightbody and Miss Anderson.[99] Until Clarence House was ready for the family to move in to in July 1949, the baby lived and was looked after in the country, at Windlesham Moor, only seeing his parents when they came down from London at weekends. (The breast-feeding had stopped in January, when Charles was not quite two months old. Elizabeth had contracted measles and the doctors advised that, until she was better, mother and child should stay apart.)

---

[99] Both nurses were maiden ladies. Because Helen Lightbody was the more senior, she was given the courtesy title of 'Mrs' as Alah Knight had been in her day.

The Edinburghs rented Windlesham Moor from a Mrs Warwick Bryant. It had useful grounds – fifty acres and a fine garden noted for its azaleas – but the house itself – two storeys, five bedrooms, four reception rooms, plus staff quarters – was by no means a mansion. According to John Dean, Philip was particularly happy there: 'I believe that in those early days the Duke was uneasy in the atmosphere of the Palace with its formalities, and that this heightened his pleasure in having a country home that was so different.' Clarence House, of course, was much grander, but, again according to Dean, Philip made it 'his own'. The Duke, reported the valet, loved 'home-making' and was particularly keen on every kind of new-fangled labour-saving device. The facilities for the staff were 'wonderful', said Dean, 'as near ideal as could possibly be imagined'. Even so, the turnover in the ranks of the junior members of the household was quite high. The hours were long – when the royals were in residence, staff got just one half-day a week free and alternate Sundays off – and the wages were modest. The Edinburghs were not extravagant. The Princess was a 'considerate employer', according to Dean, concerned about the health and welfare of her servants,[100] but, overall, the Duke was in charge, the undoubted captain of the domestic ship, 'pleasant and courteous to servants', but quite demanding, and liable to speak his mind 'in naval fashion'. When the Duke called Dean 'a stupid clot', master and servant did not speak to each other for several days.[101] Dean did not find Philip altogether easy to work for. 'He is difficult to dress,' he complained, 'because he's not interested in clothes and is set on his own ideas – he wears suede shoes with evening dress and he simply cannot tie a tie.' The Princess, in her dressing-room, would hear her husband and his valet

---

[100] Paul Burrell, who first went to work at Buckingham Palace as an under-butler in the 1970s and later became one of the personal footmen to the Queen, told me that when once he asked Her Majesty how many servants she had, she replied, 'I have many members of staff, but no servants.'

[101] Who would be a servant? Burrell also tells of the time when, as butler to the Princess of Wales, servant and mistress fell out and were not on speaking terms for a matter of *weeks*. 'Silence,' someone said, 'is the unbearable repartee.' But it may be preferable to verbal abuse. More than one royal servant has reported being barked at by the Duke of Edinburgh and Burrell, in his book *A Royal Duty*, 2003, gives a hair-raising account of a book being thrown in his direction by a ranting, screaming and foot-stamping Prince of Wales, who, minutes later, apologised shame-facedly, only to be told by Burrell, as he picked up the missile from the floor, 'If you can't vent your feelings on me, Your Royal Highness, who can you vent them on?'

arguing next door. 'Listen to them, Bobo,' she would say to her own, ever-present dresser, 'they're just like Papa and Jerram [the King's valet]. Only sometimes I think they're worse.'

In fact, the Edinburgh household was a contented one. At Windlesham Moor, Mr Huggett, the head gardener, and an ex-guardsman, playfully encouraged the Princess to take an interest in his team's handiwork, saying, 'Ma'am, from one Grenadier to another, I think you ought to come round the garden after church', while Philip encouraged general team spirit by getting the staff of all ranks to come together to play cricket on summer Sunday afternoons. At Clarence House, when films were shown in the Edinburghs' home cinema, the members of staff were invited to join the guests for the show. In the staff sitting-room at Clarence House, there was even a television set.

In 1949, there were very few households in Britain that could boast of having a television set, fewer still that could boast of having two. In an age of austerity, the Edinburghs wanted for nothing. Their country house was thoroughly comfortable; their town house was unostenta-tiously palatial. The high-ceilinged reception rooms were filled with elegant eighteenth-century furniture. The Princess's bedroom was freshly decorated in pink and blue (with a crowned canopy over the royal bed); the Duke's bedroom and bathroom featured light wood panelling, red furnishings, and framed photographs of the ships in which he had served; Prince Charles's nursery was all in white, with blue trimmings. The young couple took an active interest in the detail of the refurbishment of Clarence House. The Duke chose and arranged all the pictures, and personally supervised the installation of the kitchen and laundry-room equipment. The Princess helped mix the light lime-green paint for the dining room walls with her own hand and offered her own practical solution to the problem of the lingering smell of paint: 'Put a bucket of hay in there and that'll take it away.'

Yes, these were the golden years. Elizabeth conceived her second child towards the end of 1949. Princess Anne Elizabeth Alice Louise was born at Clarence House at 11.50 a.m. on Tuesday 15 August 1950. Elizabeth reported to a friend: 'Both Philip and I are very thrilled about the new baby and we only hope that Charles will take kindly to it. He has only seen Fortune Euston's baby at close quarters and he then tried to pull her toes off and poke her eyes out, all of which she took very kindly, having a brother of 2 who presumably did the same.'

Elizabeth and Philip were proud parents and happy ones. They were good parents, too. That is certainly the impression I get, speaking to, say, the Duchess of Grafton (Fortune Euston, as was) or Countess Mountbatten (one of Prince Charles's godmothers), but it is not the impression you will have gained if you have read any of the many books that have touched on the matter. Every one of them – without exception, I think – portrays Elizabeth as a well-intentioned but somewhat distant mother and Philip as a forbidding, formidable and usually absent father. Sarah Bradford, for example, in her widely acclaimed portrait of the Queen, says of the young mother's relationship with baby Charles: 'Elizabeth, although fond of him, was not particularly maternal.' Anthony Holden, in his acclaimed biography of Charles, describes the young children's routine at Clarence House in this way:

> The royal nursery settled into a rigid daily routine in the care of the two nannies, 'Mrs' Lightbody and Miss Anderson. Charles and Anne were got up each day at 7 a.m. sharp, dressed, fed and played with in the nursery until nine, when they enjoyed a statutory half-hour with their mother. They rarely saw her again until teatime, when Elizabeth would try to clear two hours in her day. She liked to bath the children herself when her schedule permitted, after which they were dressed up again to be introduced to distinguished visitors. Even before his third birthday, Charles had learned to bow before offering his cheek for a kiss from 'Gan-Gan', Queen Mary, and not to sit down in the presence of his grandfather. It was a formidable introduction to the complexities of any child's life – basking but sporadically, and unpredictably, in the attentions of his mother, with his father all but a stranger. Already a pattern was being set that would come to haunt Charles's life even in adulthood, even at times of his greatest need.

The tone and content of this account of nursery life at Clarence House is accepted as a reflection of the truth by nearly one and all – including Prince Charles who, in 1994, allowed his authorised biographer, Jonathan Dimbleby, to reveal that the Prince felt 'emotionally estranged' from his parents and, all his life, had yearned for the kind of affection that, in his view, they were 'unable or unwilling to offer'. Charles's strictures hurt his parents. (That he chose to make them in public angered them as well.) All that Prince Philip will say to me on the record about his and his wife's parenting skills is, 'We did our best.'

In fact, Elizabeth saw her young children as much as any aristocratic mother of her generation and more, perhaps, than many busy working mothers today. And Philip, on the evidence of those who witnessed him in action as a young father in the late 1940s and early 1950s, far from being distant and forbidding, was hands-on and loving – more so than many of his stiff-upper-lip, Eton-educated, Guards officer contemporaries. The royal couple did not spend as much time with their children as they might have liked for the simple reason that, as well as being parents, Elizabeth was Heiress Presumptive to an ailing King and Philip was a serving officer in the Royal Navy.

George VI was fifty-three when Prince Charles was born in November 1948. He looked much older. In the preceding eighteen months he had lost seventeen pounds in weight. He was, he said, 'in discomfort most of the time', suffering from numbness and cramp in his feet and legs. He carried on with his duties – standing, in considerable pain, at the Remembrance Day service at the Cenotaph in Whitehall and reviewing the Territorial Army in Hyde Park – but summoned his doctors. Two days before Charles's birth, he was diagnosed as suffering from arteriosclerosis, a condition brought on by his chronic smoking. Two days after the birth, he agreed, reluctantly, to postpone a planned tour of Australia and New Zealand. In March 1949, he underwent an operation to help regulate the blood supply to his legs, and felt much better. Because of the continuing danger of a sudden thrombosis, he was advised to reduce his commitments, to rest more and worry less. He did his best. He promised his mother that he was trying to 'worry less about political matters' – he was an inveterate worrier – and avoid the bursts of bad-temper – his notorious 'gnashes' – that were brought on by frustration and irritation. 'Since he has become a recognised invalid,' a courtier told Harold Nicolson, 'he is as sweet and patient as can be.'

As the King curtailed his workload, so the pressures on the young Princess increased. 'It was inevitable,' Prince Philip said to me. 'You've got to remember that the Royal Family then was just the four of them: the King and the Queen and the two Princesses. It's very different now. Now we have to avoid tripping over one another, so Charles goes off and does the arts, Anne does the prisons, and so on. Then, there was just the four of them – and the Duke of Gloucester – for everything. Because of the King's health, it was inevitable that we did more. There was no choice.' But there were compensations. As well as dutiful days, there were glamorous nights. To mark Elizabeth's twenty-third birthday in April 1949, they went to see Laurence Olivier and Vivien Leigh in *The School for Scandal* at the New Theatre and then went on for supper and dancing with the Oliviers at the Café de Paris off Leicester Square.

The American entertainer Danny Kaye, then the toast of the town, danced attendance on them – literally. (John Dean reported watching the star of *The Court Jester* 'capering round Princess Elizabeth' at Windlesham Moor.)

They consorted with stars of stage and screen (as royalty has often done) and they had a lot of fun, too, in their own way with their own set. Gina Kennard told me, 'I remember lots of laughter, lots of old-fashioned gaiety. Country weekends. Shooting – not hunting in Philip's case. We used to pot at rabbits. Serious shooting, too, of course. Shoot suppers. Hunt balls. Proper house parties. With tennis. And croquet. And dancing. They are both wonderful dancers. You should have seen Philip's samba! And games. Sardines. Hunt the Thimble. So much fun.' And some dressing-up, too. At the American ambassador's fancy-dress ball, Philip came as a waiter and Elizabeth as a maid.

In the summer of 1949, the world was an uncertain place. The Cold War was upon us. The Soviet Union was testing the atomic bomb. In China, Shanghai had just fallen to Mao Tse-tung's People's Liberation Army. The British Empire was no longer what it once had been. India and Ireland had become republics. There were race riots in Durban. In Britain, the economy was enfeebled. The Chancellor of the Exchequer spoke of 'the crushing difficulties' faced by the British people as he prepared to devalue the pound sterling by a staggering 30.5 per cent. But at Windsor Castle the champagne still flowed. At the end of Royal Ascot, a royal ball. They danced till dawn. There was magic in the air. In his diary, Chips Channon described the scene:

> The rooms were banked with flowers . . . Windows were open on to the terrace . . . the doors were flung open, and we saw the King and Queen waiting to receive us, side by side: he seemed brown and she, though unfortunately very, very plump, looked magnificent in a white satin semi-crinoline number with the Garter and splendid rubies . . . We walked along a long passage with magnificent Canalettos and Zoffanys, by the dozen, many of which have been rehung and cleaned since the war . . . The King had his foot up on a foot stool to rest, though he seemed quite well and often danced . . . The Edinburghs made a somewhat late appearance (he had been to the Channel Islands or somewhere) and they looked divine. She wore a very high tiara and the Garter – he was in the dark blue Windsor uniform, also with the Garter. They looked characters out of a fairy tale . . . At a quarter to five, [the Queen] told the band to

stop; everyone bowed and curtseyed to the remaining Royalties and we left, and drove back in the dawn – looking back, the Castle rose romantic in the pink morning light. I was enchanted with the evening.

Philip had boundless energy. He could indeed make a flying visit to the Channel Islands ('or somewhere') and then dance till dawn. Patricia Mountbatten said to me, 'He was a dynamo.' Mike Parker told me, 'He crackled with energy. He made things happen. He made things jump.' As well as fulfilling his naval and his royal duties, he was beginning to take on a range of 'good works' – starting with the presidencies of the London Federation of Boys' Clubs and the National Playing Fields Association. He was not inclined to be a docile figure-head: he wanted to be pro-active and hands-on. Mike Parker said to me: 'He wanted to make a difference and, if necessary, he was ready to make a noise.'

Elizabeth was altogether quieter. She was still quite shy. She didn't have her husband's ability to swing into a room of strangers and talk easily to anybody. She sometimes felt, as they went out on official visits together, that the crowd would prefer to see the Duke than the Princess. She was wrong, of course. She was beautiful and she was the Heiress Presumptive. She knew her duty, and did it conscientiously. Encouraged by Jock Colville, she was now regularly reading Foreign Office telegrams because – as Colville put it to the King's private secretary, Tommy Lascelles – they 'would give HRH an idea of world affairs which she cannot possibly get from the newspapers'. She was also making speeches – speeches drafted by Colville and Lascelles – whose content, when not simply anodyne, reflected the essentially conservative views and values of the Establishment of the day. In October 1949, for example, the young princess and mother, aged twenty-three, addressed a massed meeting of the members of the Mothers' Union in Central Hall, Westminster, and, in her thin, high-pitched voice, deplored the 'current age of growing self-indulgence, of hardening materialism, of falling moral standards' and nailed her colours firmly to the unshakeable, unbreakable matrimonial mast: 'We can have no doubt that divorce and separation are responsible for some of the darkest evils in our society today.'

The same October, Philip, now twenty-eight, was appointed 1st lieutenant and second-in-command of HMS *Chequers*, the Leader of the 1st Destroyer Flotilla in the Mediterranean Fleet at Malta. The appointment was a good one – Philip was the youngest of the 1st lieutenants in the Flotilla – and reunited him with his old friend from HMS *Valiant*, the future First Sea Lord and Chief of the Defence Staff, Terry Lewin. 'I found him doing the job of Flotilla Gunnery Officer,' Philip recalls. 'We served together until August 1950 in what was a very happy Wardroom, four of whose members were destined to become Flag Officers.'

The posting also brought Philip back into daily contact with his uncle, Dickie Mountbatten, recently translated from Viceroy to Vice-Admiral. Mountbatten, having overseen the end of Empire in India, was reconnecting with the Royal Navy in Malta in a relatively humble role as Commander of the First Cruiser Squadron. Philip arrived on his own in Malta and went to stay with Dickie and Edwina at the house they were renting, the Villa Guardamangia. The two men took a little while to get used to one another again. Philip, according to Dickie, was 'very busy showing his independence'. Within three weeks, however, everything was much jollier. 'Philip is right back on 1946 terms with us,' Mountbatten reported in a letter to his daughter, Patricia, 'and we've had a heart-to-heart in which he admitted he was fighting shy of coming under my dominating influence and patronage!' Mountbatten's joy was wholly unconfined when, towards the end of November, Princess Elizabeth came out to Malta to join her husband. 'Lilibet is quite enchanting,' declared Mountbatten, 'and I've lost whatever of my heart is left to spare entirely to her. She dances quite divinely and always wants a Samba when we dance together and has said some very nice remarks about my dancing.'

This is the period in Elizabeth's adult life that can perhaps be described as the most 'normal' – or, at least, 'the least unreal', the most like that of other young couples of Philip's and Elizabeth's generation. He was a serving officer: she was a naval wife. Buckingham Palace was a thousand miles away: the British press left them largely unmolested. 'It was a good time,' according to Philip. 'It was a fabulous time,' according to Mike Parker. 'I think it was their happiest time,' said John Dean: 'They were so relaxed and free, coming and going as they pleased.' Of course, the very fact that Parker, as equerry, and Dean, as valet, were in Malta as well, is a reminder that, when it comes to royalty, nothing is ever entirely 'normal'. The Princess arrived in Malta comfortably attended: as well as Parker and Dean and the inevitable police officer, there was the ever-faithful Bobo MacDonald and a new lady-in-waiting, Lady Alice Egerton, sixth and youngest daughter of the

4th Earl of Ellesmere and sister of Meg Egerton, who had recently married Jock Colville.[102]

The Edinburghs, plus retinue, stayed with the Mountbattens at the Villa Guardamangia where the indoor help included a butler, a housekeeper, three cooks, six stewards, two housemaids, two cleaning ladies and a valet. 'We are not too grossly overstaffed,' protested Dickie, who was accustomed to living on a fairly grand scale. Clearly, however, he felt a little sheepish about the valet, writing to Edwina: 'I fear you think I'm very spoilt wanting a valet and I do admit I am, but if one is working hard it does help if there is a second man in the house who can look after my clothes.'

John Dean, who was there looking after Philip's clothes, paints a very sunny portrait of the Edinburghs in Malta. There were parties and picnics, swimming expeditions and boat trips. Elizabeth went out for coffee and shopping and visits to the hairdresser with the other young officers' wives. Philip – encouraged by his uncle – took to the polo field and discovered one of the great sporting pleasures of his life. I once asked Prince Philip if much of his life had been fun. He did not like the question. He pulled a dismissive face. 'I don't think I think very much about "fun",' he said, a little irritably. Then he pondered. 'The cricket matches for the Playing Fields were fun,'

---

[102] Alice Egerton was born on 7 August 1923 and died on 7 October 1977. She committed suicide. She was a lady-in-waiting to Princess Elizabeth until 1952 and a Woman of the Bedchamber to the Queen from 1953. In 1957 she was appointed a Commander of the Royal Victorian Order. In 1996, Sarah Bradford, in the first edition of *Elizabeth: A Biography of Her Majesty The Queen*, suggested that Lady Alice, who was unmarried, committed suicide after being dismissed as a lady-in-waiting for telling the Queen of the Duke of Edinburgh's infidelities. When the book was published, Lady Alice's brother, the 6th Duke of Sutherland, issued a denial. In November 2003, as an admirer of her meticulously researched biographies, I went to see Sarah Bradford. She said to me: 'I believed my information had come from a reliable source, but Lady Alice's family told me that, in fact, Lady Alice had suffered from depression over a number of years and it was her depression that led to her suicide. I accepted that, apologised to Lady Meg, and took the suggestion out of the paperback edition of the book.' There was something about the way Sarah Bradford smiled as she told me this that made me think, 'What she believes now is that, yes, Lady Alice did suffer from depression, and that was the cause of her suicide, but there is something in the story nevertheless . . .' As I understand it, Lady Alice suffered from manic depression and her behaviour was consequently erratic. Interestingly, in the 1950s, she became a particular friend of Prince Philip's mother, Princess Alice, who, of course, had her own experience of manic depression in the 1930s. Meg Egerton, Lady Margaret Colville, died, aged eighty-five, in May 2004 and the Queen, unusually, attended her memorial service.

he said, after quite a pause. Then he beamed: 'The polo was entirely fun.'

Princess Anne was conceived in Malta. Prince Charles, of course, was just one year old and back in England, being looked after by his nurses and devoted grandparents. The King sent a progress report to Lilibet: 'He is too sweet for words stumping around the room.' Elizabeth had been in London for Charles's first birthday on 14 November. Six days later she flew to Malta to join Philip and, after a few duty nights as a guest at the Governor's residence, settled in happily to life at the Villa Guardamangia, 'although', according to John Dean, 'she was probably a little sad at leaving Prince Charles behind'. She was away from her boy for five weeks. She stayed in Malta until 28 December when Philip and HMS *Chequers* (along with six other warships) were sent on manoeuvres to patrol the Red Sea. Neither Philip nor Elizabeth was with Charles for his second Christmas, and, when Elizabeth did get back to England, she did not rush immediately to Sandringham to be reunited with her little boy. She spent four days at Clarence House, attending, apparently, to 'a backlog of correspondence', and fulfilling a number of engagements, including a visit to Hurst Park races where she had the satisfaction of seeing 'Monaveen', a horse she owned jointly with her mother, winning at 10–1. I suspect Prince Charles, even now, is resentful about this. His memories of his childhood are not happy ones and go back a long way. He told Anthony Holden that he could still recall his first pram, 'lying in its vastness, overshadowed by its high sides'. Charles believes he was neglected by his parents when he was small. His parents, understandably, see it differently. Philip recalls that he was serving in the Royal Navy and that servicemen and their families are often apart. Elizabeth believes that, all her life, she has done her best to balance the range of her responsibilities – as a princess and monarch, as a mother and wife – but, of course, it has not always been easy. She was with Charles for his birthday. That was important. She was with Philip in Malta. That was important, too. And, please remember, Charles was far from being either neglected or unloved: when he was not with his parents, he was with doting nurses and grandparents who adored him.

Elizabeth spent three months in England before returning to Malta – again without Charles – on 28 March. On her twenty-fourth birthday, 21 April 1950, at 8.45 a.m., in her bedroom at the Villa Guardamangia, her telephone rang. When she picked up the receiver she was greeted with a rousing chorus of 'Happy Birthday to You' performed by a group of young naval officers accompanied by some of the band of HMS

Liverpool. According to Bobo, who was there (of course), 'Lilibet was wildly excited and kept saying, "Oh! Thank you, thank you! That was sweet but who are you?"' She was answered by a second chorus of the song, harmonised by the officers' Glee Club, then a burst of bagpipes. Bobo reported to Dickie Moutbatten – whose Flag Officer had been responsible for organising the surprise birthday greeting – that 'Lilibet first went white, then quite red, and ended up with tears in her eyes'. Mountbatten was enchanted with the birthday girl: 'I think she's so sweet and attractive. At times I think she likes me too, though she is far too reserved to give any indication.' Elizabeth's birthday treat was to watch her husband and her uncle playing polo.

The young wife spent six weeks with her husband in Malta and then returned to England on 9 May and did not see him again for three months until he, too, came home, for five weeks' leave, at the end of July. Princess Anne was born on 15 August at Clarence House. The birth was a cause for general rejoicing. Among the first callers was Philip's mother, Princess Alice, who had come over specially from Greece, determined not to miss the birth of her latest grandchild. She was dressed in her nun's habit and spotted by a sharp-eyed reporter from the *Daily Mail* who decided to describe her, intriguingly, as 'one of the few remaining mystics in the Greek church'.[103] It was a happy time for the whole family – with the possible exception of Prince Charles. This is how Sarah Bradford puts it in her biography of the Queen:

> For Prince Charles, the return of his father closely followed by the appearance of a new baby must have been something of a shock. A photograph of the time shows him peering into the cradle with a slightly puzzled air. He was two years old and had not seen his father for nearly a year, his mother only at intervals. Now the appearance of a new sister as the focus of everyone's attention must have been very confusing; only his loving grandparents and his unchanging nursery retinue provided stability. His father left again for Malta on 1 September and in December his mother went out to join him. At Christmas Prince Charles and his new sister went as usual with their grandparents to Sandringham.

[103] Earlier, in January 1949, when the *Daily Mail* first learnt about her and the home and religious school for district nurses that she planned to found on the island of Tinos, they sent a reporter to interview her. He did not get very far. 'I don't like talking about my work,' she said. 'Duty is its own reward. I am not a politician or a film star. Taking pictures of me at work would be posing.'

Philip and Elizabeth do not dispute the facts. What they find frustrating is the gloss. There is another photograph of Charles, taken at the time, looking quite content. Elizabeth was devoted to her son and knew that when she went away – always after several months at home and usually for no more than four or five weeks at a time – her boy was in good hands – the best. Coping with a young sister might be a challenge for Charles, but it is one that millions of other children have had to contend with in the long history of the world. That Philip was based in Malta might not be ideal, but what choice did he have?

In July 1950, a few weeks before Princess Anne was born, Philip was promoted to the rank of lieutenant commander and given his first command: the frigate HMS *Magpie*. The promotion was not automatic: it involved an exam, part of which the Duke failed, first time around. Apparently, the Commander-in-Chief was all for overruling the examiner. Philip was having none of it. 'If they try to fix it,' he said, 'I quit the Navy for good.' He took the exam again and, according to Mike Parker, 'went through like a breeze'. Parker told me, 'Philip was first-class at his job and popular with his men.' Terry Lewin agreed: 'They admired him because he was good.' Some did not admire him. According to Sarah Bradford, 'One said he'd rather die than serve in that ship again, while another described him as "stamping about like a — tiger".' The Duke's biographer, Tim Heald, probably has the balance about right: 'His command of *Magpie* was a success. He was tough, hard, mucked in with everybody, and if he had a fault it was a tendency to intolerance. It is not just his enemies who have commented on this last trait.'

Philip was ambitious and fiercely competitive. He was determined that *Magpie* would be the smartest, sharpest frigate afloat, and that her eight officers and 150 men pull their weight at all times. He led from the front. He demanded the best and gave his all. In the annual Mediterranean Fleet regatta, the officers and men of *Magpie* rowed to victory in six out of the ten races, with 'Dukey', as he was known to his men, rowing at stroke in the Destroyer Command Officers' race – which they won (of course) by half a length from a field of fifteen. As well as taking part in routine naval manoeuvres, *Magpie* – or 'Edinburgh's Private Yacht' as some called her – was sent on sundry ceremonial exercises. In December 1950, when Elizabeth came to Malta, there was an expedition to Athens to call on Philip's cousins, King Paul and Queen Frederika. Princess Elizabeth travelled on board the Commander-in-Chief's Despatch Vessel, HMS *Surprise*. One morning there was a jovial exchange of signals between the ships:

Surprise to *Magpie*: Princess full of beans
Magpie to *Surprise*: Can't you give her something better for breakfast?[104]

Happy days. But the fun – and Philip's career – did not last. The King's health was gradually deteriorating. On 4 May 1951, when George VI and Queen Elizabeth went to the official opening of the Festival of Britain on the south bank of the Thames,[105] the King looked grey and weak. Three weeks later, on 24 May, at Westminster Abbey, at the installation of the Duke of Gloucester as Great Master of the Order of the Bath, the King appeared seriously ill. His doctors diagnosed 'catarrhal inflammation' on the left lung and prescribed a course of penicillin injections. The King felt relieved, confident, he told his mother, that the condition would resolve itself with treatment. In the event, his condition worsened. In July he started to undergo a series of tests that would eventually establish the presence of a malignant tumour in his lung. In July, too, the Edinburghs returned from Malta. The Princess and her husband were required for public duty. Elizabeth had revelled in the relative freedom she had enjoyed as a naval officer's wife. 'They're putting the bird back in its cage,' said Edwina Mountbatten. Philip had relished his brief year in command of his own ship. 'That's that,' he said to Mike Parker. 'It was bloody for him,' Mike Parker said to me, 'Absolutely bloody.' 'No,' Prince Philip said to me, 'it's what happened. That's all. It happened sooner than might have been expected, but it was inevitable. I accepted it. That's life.'

That autumn the King and Queen had planned to make a visit to

---

[104] The exchange fairly reflects the family sense of humour, which tends to be broad rather than subtle. There also appears to be a family weakness for practical jokes. When Queen Frederika came to dinner on board Mountbatten's ship in the summer of 1949, she made him an apple-pie bed. Six months later, when Mountbatten was staying with Queen Frederika and King Paul, he had his revenge. 'Put packet of brown sugar in Freddy's bed,' he noted, gleefully, in his diary.

[105] The King and Queen arrived at the Festival's centrepiece, 'The Dome of Discovery', described at the time as 'Morrison's Folly', in honour of the Labour government minister, Herbert Morrison, who was responsible for promoting the Festival. Forty-eight years later, Morrison's grandson, Peter Mandelson, was a member of the Labour government that presided over the Millennium Dome, also sited south of the Thames, and officially inaugurated by George VI's daughter, Elizabeth II, on 31 December 1999.

Canada and the United States. The Princess and the Duke were sent in their place. They were due to leave on 25 September, sailing on the liner *Empress of Britain*, but their departure was postponed as the King's condition deteriorated further. On Sunday 23 September, in a two-hour operation at Buckingham Palace, the King had his left lung removed. A crowd of five thousand waited outside the Palace for news and, when it came at 5 p.m., the bulletin, written in black crayon, encased in a picture frame and hung on the Palace gates, told the truth, but not the whole truth: 'The King underwent an operation for lung resection this morning. Whilst anxiety must remain for some days, His Majesty's immediate post-operative condition is satisfactory.' In 1951, cancer was a word rarely spoken above a whisper.[106] On 24 September, Harold Nicolson wrote in his diary: 'The King pretty bad. Nobody can talk about anything else – and the Election is forgotten. What a strange thing is Monarchy!'

Clement Attlee, the Prime Minister, had already told the King that he proposed dissolving parliament at the beginning of October to hold a general election on the last Thursday in the month. Despite the King's frailty, on 25 October the election went ahead. Attlee's Labour Party lost. The Liberals were routed. Winston Churchill and the Conservatives were returned to office with a majority of seventeen. Churchill was coming up to his seventy-seventh birthday and had suffered a stroke. He was hard of hearing, not altogether mobile and not always wholly alert. He had no doubt, however, that he was ready for office.

The King was coming up to his fifty-sixth birthday and far from well. Lord Moran (Winston Churchill's doctor) reckoned 'he can scarcely live more than a year', but since the King himself was not told he had cancer, he was ready to believe the operation had cured him. He did all

---

[106] In fact, it was a word rarely spoken at all. Because cancer, in those days, almost invariably spelt death, the word was taboo. Some talked euphemistically of 'the big C'; most avoided the subject – like the plague. And even when relatives of a patient were told 'the worst', the patient himself was usually kept in the dark. This approach – 'fearing' the disease, 'protecting' the patient – continued at least until the 1960s. (When, in the 1970s, my aunt was dying of cancer, my parents travelled to Lourdes to collect some holy water. They wanted to give it to my aunt in the hope of a miracle cure, but because her doctor had not told her of her condition, my parents were unable to administer the water openly. Instead, they used the water to make my aunt a cup of instant coffee. She died soon afterwards. The local priest explained that the expected miracle had not occurred because my parents, by boiling the Lourdes water, had steamed the efficacy out of it.)

he could – mentally and physically – to rally his strength and determined on a policy of business as usual. On 8 October, with his blessing and encouragement, Princess Elizabeth became the first member of the Royal Family to fly the Atlantic when she and Philip went ahead with their postponed North American tour. It was essentially a visit to Canada – George VI was King of Canada, after all – with a brief foray into the United States thrown in for good measure. When the royal couple reached Washington DC, the thirty-second President, Harry S. Truman, introduced the young Princess to his elderly and nearly deaf mother-in-law. 'Mother!' boomed the President, 'I've brought Princess Elizabeth to see you!' The old lady beamed at the young Princess. 'I'm so glad your father has been re-elected,' she said.

Travelling with the Edinburghs on the thirty-five day, twelve-thousand-mile, cross-continental tour was the Princess's new private secretary, Martin Charteris. Jock Colville, having completed his two-year secondment to Clarence House (and happily married one of Elizabeth's ladies-in-waiting) had returned to the Foreign Office in 1949.[107] Charteris had come on board because he knew Jock Colville and because his wife was friendly with the King's private secretary, Sir Alan Lascelles. 'It was as simple as that,' he told me, forty years later, still chuckling. 'No vetting, no board interviews, no security clearance, no qualifications required, no training given. That's the way it was.' Certainly, Charteris had no technical qualifications for the job – he was neither a courtier nor a diplomat – but he was evidently the right kind of chap. His background was thoroughly sound: born 1913, second son of Lord Elcho (killed in action, 1916), grandson of the 11th Earl of Wemyss; educated at Eton and Sandhurst, he was a career soldier who had a decent war, much of it spent in the Middle East, where he eventually wound up running Military Intelligence in Palestine. He went to work for Princess Elizabeth in January 1950 and stayed at her side for twenty-seven years. He loved her – in the best sense – and loved

---

[107] He did a two-year stint as the Head of Chancery at the British Embassy in Lisbon before being summoned back to 10 Downing Street to serve as Joint Principal Private Secretary to Churchill from 1951 to 1955. When I met him in the 1970s, he was in his sixties and a director of Hill Samuel, the merchant bank. Urbane, discreet, with matchless connections, he padded contentedly about the corridors of power. He was also a very elegant writer and kindly gave me a copy of what he called his 'memories', *Footprints in Time*, a volume of 'vignettes' of some of the many extraordinary figures he encountered during his enviable career. (The book, published by Collins in 1976, is long out of print, but well worth chasing up.)

to talk about her – in the best way. He was wholly loyal (he was devoted to her), but his anecdotes about her, while always affectionate, were both well observed and usually revealing.[108] He liked to tell the story of the day he went for his first interview with his prospective employer and how impressed he was by her style before they even met. Charteris arrived early at Clarence House for his 11.30 a.m. appointment. At 11.25 a.m., Boy Browning rang through to the Princess. 'Major Charteris is here to see you, Ma'am. Shall I bring him in?' 'Yes,' said the Princess, coolly, 'at half-past eleven.' Charteris told me – and anyone else who cared to listen – that the moment he set eyes on her he was smitten. 'She was wearing a blue dress and a brooch with huge sapphires. I was immediately struck by her bright blue eyes and her wonderful complexion. She was young, beautiful, and dutiful. I knew at once that I would be proud to serve her.'

She was dutiful, and prepared for the worst. On the flight to Montreal on 8 October 1951, Charteris took with him the documents of accession in case they should be required. The Princess was already privy to a range of state papers. Throughout her time in Canada, she carefully monitored the news from home, conscientiously reading the air-mail edition of the London *Times*.[109] The tour was not an unmitigated triumph. The programme was exhausting – it took in every province in the dominion – and the Princess was anxious about her father. The Canadian press, who had been bowled over by the effortless charm of Queen Elizabeth when she and the King had toured the country twelve years before, complained that the twenty-five-year-old

---

[108] The older he got the less discreet he became. He died just before Christmas 1999, aged eighty-six. I met him properly at the beginning of the 1990s when I was set to succeed Sir Peter Morrison as MP for the City of Chester. Lord Charteris of Amisfield, as he then was (and Provost of Eton, President of the Prayer Book Society, a director of Claridge's and the Connaught hotels, and an amateur sculptor, among other things) came to Chester to give a talk to the local Conservative Association about his life with the Queen.

[109] These were the days when *The Times* was still owned by the Astor family and regarded as 'the newspaper of record'. Nowadays, the Queen and Prince Philip read the *Daily Telegraph* and, whenever possible, the Queen completes both the *Telegraph*'s daily crossword puzzles. Given the Duke of Edinburgh's open contempt for the newspapers owned by Rupert Murdoch, I am always surprised that, when you go to Buckingham Palace, the two papers provided in the waiting room at the Privy Purse entrance are *The Times* and the *Telegraph*. The Queen has six national daily newspapers laid out for her to scan at breakfast-time each day: *The Times*, *Telegraph*, *Mail*, *Express*, *Mirror* and *Racing Post*. By all accounts, she reaches for the last first, rarely sees the *Sun* and never sees the *Daily Star*.

Princess was shy and unsmiling. 'Please smile more, Ma'am,' pleaded Charteris. 'But my jaws are aching,' sighed the Princess. (Exactly fifty years later, accompanying the Queen on a tour of the West Country, the Duchess of Grafton told me, 'She does find this constant smiling very exhausting, you know. After a day like today, her jaw really aches.') The royal couple did their best, of course. They scored well when – kitted out like characters from *Oklahoma!* by the ever-present Bobo and John Dean – they gave their all dancing a Canadian square dance. Philip did less well when – hoping to be humorous – he nonchalantly referred to Canada as 'a good investment'. Forty-nine years later, in October 2002, when the royal couple were back in Canada for an eleven-day golden jubilee tour, Canadian newspapers were still quoting the remark.

Martin Charteris said to me, 'It was a long trip and it wasn't plain sailing. It wasn't easy for either of them.' Is it true, I asked him, that, at breakfast one morning on the Governor-General's train, the Duke called the Princess 'a bloody fool'. 'He might have done,' said Charteris, smiling. 'He had a naval turn of phrase.' Was he often ratty with the Princess, I asked. 'Not so much ratty,' said Charteris, 'as restless. He was impatient. He was frustrated. You must remember he had just turned thirty and he was obliged to give up a promising career in the Navy to do – what? He hadn't yet defined his role, found his feet as consort. He was certainly very impatient with the old style courtiers and sometimes, I think, felt that the Princess paid more attention to them than to him. He didn't like that. If he called her "a bloody fool" now and again, it was just his way. I think others would have found it more shocking than she did. Although she was very young, she had a wise head on her shoulders. She has always understood him – and his ways. And valued his contribution – which has been immense and is underestimated. I believe history will come to judge him well.' (When, in 2003, to discuss this book, I had lunch with the Queen's present private secretary, Sir Robin Janvrin, in referring to Prince Philip he used almost the same phrase: 'Whatever the papers say about him now, I have no doubt at all that history will come to judge him well.')

I happen to be writing this on Thursday 20 November 2003, during the state visit to the United Kingdom by George W. Bush, forty-second President of the United States. Today is the Queen and Prince Philip's fifty-sixth wedding anniversary. Last night, the royal couple hosted a state banquet in honour of George and Laura Bush at Buckingham Palace. During the reception, before dinner, there was a telling moment. On one side of the room stood the Queen and the President, alone, chatting quietly – amiably but with little animation – while two yards away, on the other side of the room, stood Prince Philip at the centre of a small group that included the First Lady, Laura Bush, and the American Secretary of State, Colin Powell. They were all laughing. Prince Philip was leaning forward, gesticulating with his hands, entertaining his guests, telling a funny story. This – exactly this – has been going on for more than half a century. She makes intelligent, interested small talk, always amiably, but sometimes a little awkwardly. He keeps the party going. 'He has done the state some service,' Martin Charteris said to me. 'I think the Queen appreciates his sense of humour, and values it.'

On the long train ride across Canada back in the autumn of 1951, Philip did his best to entertain his wife with a range of practical jokes. According to John Dean, these included surprising her with a booby-trapped can of nuts and chasing her down the corridor wearing a set of joke false teeth. When they flew to Washington, DC, on 31 October, the smiles were rather more forced when, at the British Embassy reception in their honour, they were expected to shake hands with each of the 1,500 guests. In terms of public relations, however, the brief visit to the nation's capital was an unqualified success. 'We have many distinguished visitors here in this city,' declared the President, welcoming his British visitors to the White House Rose Garden, 'but never before have we had such a wonderful couple, that so completely captured the hearts of all of us.' Sir Oliver Franks, the British ambassador, reported to the King that when the sixty-seven-year-old President appeared with the twenty-five-year-old Princess in public he gave 'the impression of a very proud uncle presenting his favourite niece to his friends'. According to Martin Charteris, 'Truman fell in love with her.' Truman was captivated, certainly. Memorably, he said, 'When I was a little boy, I read about a fairy princess, and there she is.' When the royal couple had returned to Canada to complete their tour, the President wrote himself to the King in England, 'We've just had a visit from a lovely young lady and her personable husband . . . As one father to another we can be very proud of our daughters. You have the better of me – because you have two!'

The Princess and the Duke returned to England by sea in the middle of the month, missing Prince Charles's third birthday on 14 November. In a birthday photograph, taken at Buckingham Palace, the toddler prince and his grandfather, sitting on a sofa side by side, look very much at ease. The photograph when it was published, combined with the King's determination to think positively and the Queen's ability to avoid the unpleasant by ignoring it (what Martin Charteris later called her capacity for being 'a bit of an ostrich'), encouraged the public to believe that the King's health was on the mend. On 2 December a day of national thanksgiving for the Sovereign's recovery was celebrated in churches throughout the kingdom. When, early in November, Princess Elizabeth, in a transatlantic call from Canada, had spoken to her father on the telephone, she reported that he sounded 'much better'. When she saw him on her return home, later in the month, he 'looked awful', according to Charteris, 'quite dreadful'.

The King had hoped to travel to Australia and New Zealand in the spring of 1952, to undertake the antipodean tour his health had forced him to postpone in 1948. Now he knew that would be impossible. Again, Elizabeth and Philip would go in his place. On their return from Canada, by way of tribute to what they had already achieved, he made them both Privy Councillors. His own hope for the New Year was to enjoy a recuperative holiday in South Africa in March. First, there was Christmas and the ordeal of the 3 p.m. Christmas Day broadcast. Customarily, the King gave the broadcast live so that he could speak 'directly' to his people. Because of its significance, and because of his stammer, it was a ritual he dreaded. One Christmas morning he barked at his family: 'I can't concentrate on anything because I've got that damned broadcast coming up this afternoon.' This year, his difficulty with breathing precluded a live broadcast. A BBC engineer, Robert Wood, came to Buckingham Palace on 21 December and, over two hours, painstakingly pieced together the ten-minute recording. Wood said afterwards: 'It was very, very distressing for him, and the Queen, and for me, because I admired him so much and wished I could do more to help.'

Christmas at Sandringham was a family affair and, by all accounts, the King – particularly because he did not have the cloud of 'that damned broadcast' hanging over him – was in mellow mood throughout. He was well enough to go shooting. He showed a revived interest in the business of the estate. He caught up with official correspondence, writing to, among others, President Truman and his successor, General Eisenhower. He began the New Year in a positive and determined frame of mind. On 29 January he travelled to London and saw his doctors who, remarkably, pronounced themselves 'very well satisfied' with their patient's progress. The next day, by way of celebration, there was a family outing to the theatre. The King and Queen took their daughters and their son-on-law (and the King's equerry, Peter Townsend) to the Theatre Royal, Drury Lane, to see a performance of *South Pacific*. Next day, Thursday 31 January, the King and Queen, with the prime minister in attendance, went to Heathrow airport to see Elizabeth and Philip off to Kenya, on the first leg of their journey to Australia and New Zealand. They were due to be away for almost six months. In photographs of the farewell, the King, standing on the tarmac, windswept, hat in hand, looks gaunt and bleak and lonely. But Churchill, who was there, said he was 'gay, and even jaunty, and drank a glass of champagne'. 'I think,' Churchill added, 'he knew he had not long to live.'

On 1 February, the King returned to Sandringham. It was the end of the shooting season. On 5 February he was out on the estate shooting hares and rabbits. In the evening there was a jolly dinner with the Queen and Princess Margaret, and members of the royal household, and one or two shooting friends. At 10.30 p.m. the King retired to bed. At midnight he was seen by a watchman in the garden standing at his bedroom window. At some time in the early hours of Wednesday 6 February, he died, in his sleep, of a coronary thrombosis. 'He died as he was getting better,' said Princess Margaret.

When George VI died, the Heiress Presumptive was in East Africa, in Kenya, about one hundred miles north of Nairobi, at Treetops, a three-bedroom 'hotel' set, amazingly, in the branches of a giant fig tree, overlooking a salt lick, a unique vantage point for observing the wild animals ranging below. 'She became Queen,' Harold Nicolson wrote in his diary, 'while perched in a tree in Africa watching the rhinoceros come down to the pool to drink.' In fact, at the very moment of her father's death, Elizabeth was either asleep, or taking a photograph of the sunrise, or having breakfast, watching, not watering rhino, but a troop of playful baboons who had captured paper rolls from the Treetops lavatory and were throwing them over the branches. The news from England did not reach her for several hours.

At Sandringham, the King's death was discovered by his valet at 7.30 a.m. when he took in his early morning tea. The Queen, a widow at only fifty-one, was heartbroken. 'He was so young to die,' she wrote to her friend Osbert Sitwell, 'and was becoming so wise in kingship. He was so kind too, and had a sort of natural nobility of thought & life which sometimes made me ashamed of my narrower & more feminine point of view. Such sorrow is a very strange experience . . .'

The King's private secretary, Sir Alan Lascelles, telephoned the assistant private secretary, Edward Ford, in London and instructed him to break the news to the King's mother and to the prime minister. At 10 Downing Street, Ford found Churchill, propped up in bed, cigar in hand, surrounded by paperwork. 'I've got bad news,' Ford said. 'The King died this morning. I know nothing more.' 'Bad news?' said Churchill. 'The worst.' He threw aside the papers he had been working on. 'How unimportant these matters seem,' he said. Later, when Jock Colville arrived, he found the prime minister in tears. Colville said that he tried to console Churchill with the thought of how well he would get on with the new Queen, but 'all he could say was that he did not know her and that she was only a child'.

The child meanwhile, still unaware that she was now Queen, had finished breakfast at Treetops, clambered to the ground down the rickety ladders (she was wearing jeans), and, with Philip and the rest of her party, had driven the ten or so miles back to Sagana Lodge – the royal couple's wedding present from the people of Kenya – to spend the rest of the morning fishing for trout in the Sagana River before preparing for the onward journey to Mombasa and the boat that was due to take them on to New Zealand and Australia via Ceylon. The party included Bobo and John Dean, Pamela Mountbatten as lady-in-waiting, Mike Parker as equerry and the celebrated local 'white hunter', Jim Corbett, armed with a high-velocity rifle, to guard the Princess both from rampaging elephants and the possibility of an attack by local Mau Mau terrorists. Martin Charteris was staying nearby, at the Outspan Hotel in Nyeri, once the home of Robert Baden-Powell. It was at the Outspan, at lunchtime, that Charteris got the news – given to him, in a garbled version, by a local newspaper reporter. The King's secretary at Sandringham had sent a telegram to Charteris in Nyeri, but it never reached him.[110] From the Outspan, Charteris telephoned Parker at Sagana Lodge. Parker found a wireless, fiddled with the dial and, eventually, tuned in to the BBC. Philip was having a siesta. Parker woke him and gave him the news.

'I never felt so sorry for anyone in all my life,' said Parker. 'He looked as if you'd dropped half the world on him.' The Duke said nothing, according to Parker, 'nothing at all. He just breathed heavily, in and

---

[110] Edward Ford thinks this is because the telegram was in the form of a pre-arranged coded message: 'Hyde Park Corner', three words that would signify the King's death to those in the know. Ford reckons the telegraphist mistook the message for the address.

out, as though he were in shock.' Philip found Elizabeth and took her into the garden. He told her what had happened. Did he hold her, I asked Parker. 'I can't remember,' he said. 'We were all in a state of shock. But she was quite calm, I do remember that. She said very little. They were out on the lawn together, alone, away from the rest of us. They walked slowly up and down the lawn, up and down, up and down, while he talked and talked and talked.'

When Martin Charteris arrived back at Sagana, he found them in the sitting room. 'I can still picture the scene,' he told me, 'the Queen, sitting at her desk, pencil in hand, making notes. She was sitting upright, erect, utterly resolved. Her cheeks were a little flushed, but there were no tears. Philip was lying back on a sofa, silent, holding a copy of a newspaper wide open over his face.' Parker was busy making the arrangements for their immediate return to London. The new Queen was anxious to send messages back home and to Ceylon and New Zealand and Australia. She apologised for all the inconvenience she was causing. 'I'm so sorry we've got to go back,' she said to Pamela Mountbatten. 'I've ruined everybody's trip.' Martin Charteris asked her what name she wanted to use as Queen. 'My own name, of course,' she told him. 'Elizabeth.' Charteris said later, 'I never imagined that anyone could grasp their destiny with such safe hands.'

They changed, they packed, they got into their cars and drove to Nanyuki airport. By now, reporters and photographers had arrived at Sagana. 'I asked them not to take any pictures,' Charteris told me, 'and, as our cars left the Lodge, though the world's press lined the road, not a photograph was taken.' They flew first to Entebbe. There they were reunited with the rest of their luggage, flown up from Mombasa – including the black mourning clothes which Bobo and John Dean had carefully packed against this very eventuality. For two hours they waited in the airport lounge while a storm abated and then, at last, climbed aboard the BOAC Argonaut aircraft for the long flight home. Little was said on the journey home. John Dean recalled that he saw the Queen get up once or twice and return to her seat looking as if she had been crying. Martin Charteris told me, 'We slept for much of the first part of the journey. I discussed some of the details of the accession with Her Majesty. She was completely calm, utterly composed. For a long time she simply gazed out of the window.'

It was mid-afternoon on Thursday 7 February when the plane touched down at Heathrow. Waiting to greet his new Sovereign was her Prime Minister, Winston Churchill, who had first become a member of parliament more than fifty years before, when Victoria was Queen. Elizabeth II, Victoria's great-great-granddaughter, a tiny figure in black, solemn and self-possessed, came down the aircraft steps alone. Philip lingered inside the aircraft door, hidden, watching and waiting until the new Queen had touched British soil. Only then did he emerge and come down the steps to join her. 'Oh yes,' he said to me, 'when the late King died, everything changed.'

Chapter Ten

'A King is a thing men have made for their own sakes, for quietness' sake. Just as if in a family one man is appointed to buy the meat.'

John Selden (1584–1654), *Table Talk*

'When King George died,' I asked Prince Philip, 'did you know what to expect?'

'No,' he said, laughing a little bleakly. 'There were plenty of people telling me what *not* to do. "You mustn't interfere with this." "Keep out." I had to try to support the Queen as best I could without getting in the way. The difficulty was to find things that might be useful.'

'But there was the example of Prince Albert, the Prince Consort,' I suggested. 'You'd read biographies . . .'

'Oh, yes.' An exasperated sigh. 'The Prince Consort . . .' A pause. 'The Prince Consort's position was quite different. Queen Victoria was an executive sovereign, following in a long line of executive sovereigns. The Prince Consort was effectively Victoria's private secretary. But after Victoria the monarchy changed. It became an institution. I had to fit in with the institution.'

The institution had its own momentum and Philip had very little authority of his own. As darkness descended on that cold, dank February afternoon, the new Queen and her husband were driven from Heathrow airport to Clarence House where they found the old King's private secretary, Sir Alan Lascelles, already waiting for them. Only, of course, he was not waiting for Philip. He was waiting for the Queen. He had a sheaf of state papers that he needed Her Majesty to sign. Within the hour, Queen Mary also came to call. She was eighty-four and frail, full of dignity and grief. The day before, her son, the King, had died.

Today, she had come, not to hug her granddaughter, but to curtsy to her new Queen. 'Her old Grannie and subject must be the first to kiss her hand,' she said. Elizabeth's eyes pricked with tears as she accepted her grandmother's obeisance. Martin Charteris told me, 'For the young Queen, it was a moment that must have sorely tested her reserve and her resolve, but she loved her father and wanted to carry herself courageously as he would have done.'

Elizabeth said as much the following day, at St James's Palace, where her Privy Councillors gathered for the formal meeting of the Accession Council – many of them, according to Hugh Dalton, a former Chancellor of the Exchequer, who was there, 'people one didn't remember were still alive, and some looking quite perky and self-important'.[111] The Queen, looking 'very small', according to Dalton, entered alone and read the Declaration of Sovereignty in a 'high-pitched, rather reedy voice'. 'She does her part well,' said Dalton, 'facing hundreds of old men in black clothes with long faces.' Harold Wilson, another of the Privy Councillors and one of her future prime ministers, said it was 'the most moving ceremonial I can recall'. When she had read the formal Declaration, she added, 'My heart is too full for me to say more to you today than that I shall always work as my father did.'

Outside, on the ramparts of the Palace, the Garter King of Arms, in Tudor tabard, proclaimed the Accession: 'Queen Elizabeth the Second, by the grace of God Queen of this Realm and of all Her other Realms and Territories, Head of the Commonwealth, Defender of the Faith.' Inside, Philip, only eight weeks a Privy Councillor himself, stepped forward to take his sovereign by the hand and escort her out of the chamber and down to her waiting car. 'In the back of the car,' according to Sarah Bradford's biography of the Queen, 'she finally broke down and sobbed.' Someone who was there at the time said to me, 'The

---

[111] The Privy Council was originally an active advisory council to the sovereign. As a body, the Privy Council is no longer asked to give advice, but members of the Cabinet must be Privy Councillors (and some other senior ministers are as well) and Orders in Council and Proclamations are still approved by the Sovereign in the presence of three Privy Councillors (enough to form a quorum). On leaving the Cabinet, individuals remain Privy Councillors for life, entitled to style themselves 'The Right Honourable' – unless (like Jonathan Aitken on his imprisonment for perjury) they resign from the Council in disgrace. Other 'eminent persons' – archbishops, senior members of the judiciary, the Queen's private secretary, etc – are also appointed to the Privy Council, which is only summoned in full 'upon the demise of the Crown'.

Queen may have cried – that would only be natural, the experience was overwhelming – but I assure you that she did not "break down and sob". That is not her way. Why does everything have to be exaggerated?'

There is no need to exaggerate the national sense of grief at the passing of George VI or the degree of admiration bordering on adulation expressed for the new Queen. When news of the King's death was broadcast, drivers stopped their cars, got out and stood to attention as a mark of respect. When his body lay in state in Westminster Hall, more than three hundred thousand people filed slowly past in tribute. 'The world showed a large and genuine measure of grief,' said Jock Colville. 'The King was universally loved and respected,' said Martin Charteris, 'He gave his life for his country.' 'The King's outstanding quality,' said Dean Acheson, the US Secretary of State, was 'his selfless dedication to duty.' 'He was a grand man,' President Truman noted in his diary, 'Worth a pair of his brother Ed.' George VI had been King through the six long years of the Second World War and had not flinched. At his funeral at St George's Chapel, Windsor, the card accompanying Winston Churchill's wreath bore just two words, the inscription to be found on the Victoria Cross: 'For Valour.'

In his broadcast on the night of the King's death, Churchill, as Prime Minister, paid tribute to the courage and fortitude of the late King and then, with typical Churchillian bravura, heralded a new Elizabethan age: 'Famous have been the reigns of our Queens,' he rumbled prophetically. 'Some of the greatest periods in our history have unfolded under their sceptre.' Churchill might not yet know Elizabeth well, might consider her no more than a child, but, very quickly, he became utterly enchanted by her. 'You've got to remember,' Charteris said to me, 'Churchill was nearly eighty and the Queen was no more than twenty-five, but it was not simply her youth and beauty that entranced him. He was impressed by her. She was conscientious, she was well-informed, she was serious-minded. Within days of her Accession she was receiving prime ministers and presidents, ambassadors and High Commissioners – all those who had come to London for the King's funeral – and doing so faultlessly. She had authority and dignity as well as grace.' Within a year, Churchill was confiding to his doctor, Lord Moran: 'All the film people in the world, if they had scoured the globe, could not have found anyone so suited for the part.'

Meanwhile, the Duke of Edinburgh, when he was being noticed at all, was not being so rapturously received. Within three weeks of the

Accession, Churchill had received a formal letter of complaint about the Duke from a Conservative MP, Enoch Powell. Philip had visited the House of Commons to listen to a debate – something, according to Powell, a royal consort had not done since 1846 – and, while sitting observing the proceedings from the peers' gallery, the Duke was deemed to have expressed his own opinions about the matters under discussion below, in a manner neither seemly nor constitutional. The government chief whip endorsed Powell's complaint: Philip's demeanour had not been 'exactly poker-faced'. Philip was quietly reprimanded. 'It kept happening,' according to Patricia Mountbatten's husband, Lord Brabourne. He told me, 'Philip was constantly being squashed, snubbed, ticked off, rapped over the knuckles. It was intolerable.' Mike Parker told me, 'The problem was simply that Philip had energy, ideas, get-up-and-go, and that didn't suit the Establishment, not one bit.' In his diary, another, more senior Conservative MP, Harold Macmillan (another of Elizabeth's future prime ministers) summed up the 'Establishment's' reservations succinctly: 'I fear this young man is going to be as big a bore as Prince Albert. It was really much better when royalty were just pleasant and polite.'

Among the many who came to London for the lying-in-state and funeral of the late King was his older brother, David (or 'Ed' as President Truman had called him), whose abdication as Edward VIII, of course, had led to George VI's reign. The Duke of Windsor, as he had become, was now fifty-seven and destined to live a further twenty years. Queen Elizabeth, privately, may have blamed her brother-in-law's selfishness for her own husband's premature death, but now she entertained him to tea and spent some time alone with him. He reported to his duchess – who, diplomatically, had stayed behind in New York – that the widowed Queen had 'listened without comment' (they are very practised at that) '& closed on the note that it was nice to be able to talk about Bertie with somebody who had known him so well'. 'Officially and on the surface,' David told Wallis, 'my treatment within the family has been entirely correct and dignified.' Superficially, he acknowledged, he was handled impeccably by courtiers and relations alike – 'But gee,' he added, 'the crust is hard & only granite below.' Unsurprisingly perhaps – given that he had lived away from the court for sixteen years, and that most of those at court had little affection and still less respect for him – he found the mood and way of life at Buckingham Palace stiff and uncompromising. 'Gosh they move slowly within these Palace confines,' he said. He found the tone and atmosphere at Clarence House, the Edinburghs' base camp, much more congenial. 'Clarence House was informal and friendly,' he reported to Wallis. 'Brave New World, full of self-confidence & seem to take the job in their stride.'

According to Martin Charteris, 'the operation at Clarence House was a good one'. 'We were a good team,' said Mike Parker, 'Philip ran a tight ship.' As well as being the Edinburghs' office, Clarence House was also their home – and Philip's first and only family home since he had last lived with his parents in Paris when he was ten. Philip wanted to go on living there. He put his thoughts on paper in a note to Boy Browning. He proposed that Queen Elizabeth the Queen Mother – as she decided she wished to be known – should remain at Buckingham Palace and that the new Queen and her family should remain at Clarence House. One day, he suggested, Clarence House might also be an appropriate London home for Prince Charles. (It now is.) The business of the monarchy could be conducted from Buckingham Palace, while the family of the monarch could continue living where they were. Sir Alan Lascelles was having none of it. 'God, he was bloody,' says Lord Brabourne, fifty years on. Lascelles was adamant: the traditional home of the British monarch was Buckingham Palace: it always had been: it should remain so. In fact, the Palace – built by the Duke of Buckingham in 1703 and rebuilt between 1825 and 1837 – had only been the official London residence of the Sovereign since Queen Victoria's reign, but Lascelles, as the Queen's private secretary, had authority that Philip, as the Queen's husband, lacked, and – significantly – he also had the backing of the prime minister. Churchill said, 'To the Palace they must go.' So, to the Palace they went.

At the same time, in another, even more sensitive matter, the young Queen did as her private secretary and prime minister advised, rather than as her husband wished. She decided that her children – and her children's children – should bear her family name rather than his. Philip was incandescent. 'I am nothing but a bloody amoeba,' he protested. 'I am the only man in the country not allowed to give his name to his own children.'

'It hurt him, it really hurt him,' Patricia Mountbatten said to me when I went to see her. Sitting facing her and her husband, John Brabourne, in their drawing room at Mersham half a century after the event, from the pained expressions on their faces you would think the wound had been inflicted yesterday. 'Can you imagine doing such a thing?' asked Lord Brabourne. 'It so hurt him,' repeated Countess

Mountbatten. 'He had given up everything – and now this, the final insult. It was a terrible blow. It upset him very deeply and left him feeling unsettled and unhappy for a long while.' 'A long while,' echoed Lord Brabourne. A silence fell in the room. The fire crackled. Suddenly, jointly, the Brabournes seemed to sense that they had gone too far. 'Of course, I don't blame the Queen,' said Lady Mountbatten. 'It was Churchill,' said Lord Brabourne, emphatically, 'encouraged by Lascelles. They forced the Queen's hand.' Lady Mountbatten said: 'I remember hearing the Queen say herself that she was in favour of the name Mountbatten-Windsor.'

The issue arose when it did, as it did, because, at a house party at Broadlands, within days of the old King's death and the new Queen's accession, Dickie Mountbatten was heard to declare 'that the House of Mountbatten now reigned'. Prince Ernst August of Hanover, who was there, swiftly reported this boast to Queen Mary – whose own husband, of course, George V, had created the House of Windsor in 1917. Queen Mary, outraged, summoned the prime minister's secretary, Jock Colville. Colville duly reported the dowager Queen's concerns to Churchill, who had his own reservations about Mountbatten – and was by no means alone. The Duke of Windsor, after the King's funeral, wrote to Wallis: 'Mountbatten – one can't pin much on him but he's very bossy & never stops talking. All are suspicious & watching his influence on Philip.'

Churchill decided on 'action this day' and immediately raised the issue with his senior ministers. According to the Cabinet minutes of 18 February 1952, 'The Cabinet's attention was drawn to reports that some change might be made in the Family name of the Queen's Children and their descendants. The Cabinet was strongly of the opinion that the Family name of Windsor should be retained; and they invited the Prime Minister to take a suitable opportunity of making their views known to Her Majesty.' The prime minister did exactly that and, within six weeks, despite her husband's furious protestations, the Queen made her position plain before the Privy Council: 'I hereby declare My Will and Pleasure that I and My children shall be styled and known as the House and Family of Windsor, and that my descendants who marry and their descendants shall bear the name of Windsor.'

'Philip was not happy,' said Charteris. 'Philip was spitting,' said Mike Parker. 'Personally,' reflected Dickie Mountbatten, 'I think it was Beaverbrook's hatred of me coupled with Winston's disenchantment with what I did in India that brought all this about.' Certainly,

Beaverbrook had Churchill's ear and, not long before George VI's death, John Gordon, the editor of the *Sunday Express*, had reported to his newspaper's proprietor that a member of the Greek royal family had told him that those 'dangerous people', the Mountbattens, were 'determined to be the power behind the throne when Elizabeth succeeds', though he sensed they would not prevail as 'Elizabeth was developing into a strong-minded woman who would not be controlled by him'. Gordon told Beaverbrook that the Mountbattens were plotting to get Philip pronounced King or King Consort. But Arthur Christiansen, the editor of the *Daily Express*, who knew Philip through their shared membership of the photographer Baron's Thursday Club (of which more anon), assured Beaverbrook that Philip 'sees through his uncle and fully realises how great are the Mountbatten ambitions'.

There is no evidence that Philip ever wanted to be called Prince Consort – let alone King Consort or King – and I do not believe he was particularly concerned about the actual name 'Mountbatten'. It was not his father's name. It was not his mother's name. It was the anglicised version of his maternal grandfather's name. What concerned Philip was the principle that a father be allowed to pass on his surname to his children. He believed he had precedent on his side. Victoria of Hanover had married Albert of Saxe-Coburg-Gotha: their son, Edward VII, had reigned as a member of the House of Saxe-Coburg-Gotha.

He also, unfortunately, had precedent against him. During the First World War, George V showed that a sovereign could change the name of the Royal House at will.

'What the devil does that young fool Edinburgh think that the family name has got to do with him?' asked Queen Mary in the spring of 1952. In the spring of 1953, ten weeks before the Coronation, Queen Mary died. In the summer of 1953, shortly after the Coronation, Tommy Lascelles retired. In April 1955, Winston Churchill, aged eighty, resigned as Prime Minister. On 8 February 1960, eight years to the day after her Accession Council, and shortly before the birth of Prince Andrew, the Queen issued a new declaration of her 'Will and Pleasure':

> While I and my children will continue to be styled and known as the House and Family of Windsor my descendants, other than descendants enjoying the style, title or attributes of Royal Highness and the titular dignity of Prince or Princess, and female descendants who marry and their descendants, shall bear the name Mountbatten-Windsor.

It was a compromise. 'The Queen has always wanted,' announced the Buckingham Palace press office, 'without changing the name of the Royal House established by her grandfather, to associate the name of her husband with her own and his descendants. The Queen has had this in mind for a long time and it is close to her heart.' She had certainly been brooding about it. Harold Macmillan, her Prime Minister between 1957 and 1963, liked to tell the story of calling on the Queen at Sandringham and encountering the old Duke of Gloucester in the hall. 'Thank Heavens you've come, Prime Minister,' says the Duke. 'The Queen's in a terrible state. There's a fellow called Jones in the billiards room says he wants to marry her sister, and Prince Philip's in the library wanting to change the family name to Mountbatten.'

It was a compromise – and kindly meant – but it did not amount to much. Essentially, the Queen's descendants, if non-royal, could be called Mountbatten-Windsor. Dickie, delighted to find the door even slightly ajar, did his best to push it further open. In 1973, Princess Anne married Captain Mark Phillips. In June that year, Mountbatten wrote to Prince Charles: 'When Anne marries in November, her marriage certificate will be the first opportunity to settle the Mountbatten-Windsor name for good . . . if you can make quite sure . . . that her surname is entered as Mountbatten-Windsor it will end all arguments. I hope you can fix this.' It seems he did, for – though clearly contrary to the stipulations of the Queen's declaration of 1960 – it was as a Mountbatten-Windsor that Princess Anne was married.[112]

Mountbatten was obsessed with the issue of the Mountbatten name. 'His vanity, though child-like, was monstrous,' wrote his biographer,

---

[112] By chance, the first properly named Mountbatten-Windsor – the Queen and Prince Philip's seventh grandchild – happens to have been born in the very week that I have been writing this. Lady Louise Alice Elizabeth Mary Mountbatten-Windsor, born on 10 November 2003, is the daughter of the Earl and Countess of Wessex. The child's Christian names nicely reflect both the Windsor and the Mountbatten heritage. Princess Louise (1848–1939) was the sixth child of Victoria and Albert; Princess Louise of Hesse-Cassel (1817–98) married Christian IX of Denmark and was grandmother to Prince Andrea, Prince Philip's father; Philip's maternal aunt, Louise (1889–1965) became Queen of Sweden in 1950. Prince Philip's mother was Alice; the Queen's mother was Elizabeth; the Earl of Wessex's great-grandmother was Queen Mary; the Countess of Wessex's mother is Mary Rhys-Jones. The Mountbatten family's delight in the arrival of the first unquestioned 'Mountbatten-Windsor' may have been a little dented by the Buckingham Palace spokesman who, having announced the new royal baby's full name, added: 'She will, however, be generally known by the more easily remembered title of Lady Louise Windsor.'

Philip Ziegler, 'his ambition unbridled.'[113] I think Philip always had the measure of his uncle. He loved him, liked him, respected him, admired him – and was grateful to him. But (in my experience at least) Prince Philip speaks with equal affection – and gratitude – and almost as frequently – of his other maternal uncle, George Milford Haven. Dickie was a great achiever (and a great operator), but at times he had to be taken with a pinch of salt. Philip always understood that. Elizabeth understood it, too. They knew Mountbatten's strengths and his weaknesses and his foibles – and were enormously fond of him. In 1974, five years before he was murdered by the IRA, they took him on a cruise aboard the Royal Yacht. He was seventy-four, and delighted to be in *Britannia* once more, 'but what moved me most of all', he wrote in his diary, 'is the increasing kindness of Lilibet and Philip who treat me more and more as a really intimate member of their immediate family'. They understood him and he, perhaps, understood them, too. When the cruise was over, Mountbatten wrote to Philip: 'You sometimes seemed rather disappointed, perhaps frustrated would be a better word, but I feel you underestimate your effect on the U.K, and especially the Commonwealth. I hear more and more praise and appreciation from people in all walks of life.'

For Philip, in 1952, frustration and disappointment were already the order of the day. His children were not to inherit his name. He was not happy about that. He was obliged to move house. He was not happy about that. He was treated as something of an extraneous nuisance by both the court and the prime minister – and there was very little he could do about that. Mike Parker said to me, 'There were a lot more of them than there were of us.' At Clarence House, Philip and Elizabeth had essentially shared a secretariat, and Philip was head of the household. It was his domain. At Buckingham Palace, it was very different. Elizabeth was Queen. The Palace was the sovereign's domain. Naturally, she inherited her father's Household (huge and hidebound), to which she added Martin Charteris (more flexible and fun, but still relatively inexperienced), leaving Philip, pretty isolated, with just Parker and Boy Browning. 'You can imagine,' Countess Mountbatten said to me, 'Bobo MacDonald sitting by the bath-tub' – and 'Tommy

---

[113] Ziegler's official biography of Mountbatten, first published in 1985, is a wonderful book, sympathetic, scrupulous and gripping. When writing it, there was a point when Ziegler became so frustrated by aspects of his subject that he found it necessary to place on his desk a notice that read: REMEMBER, IN SPITE OF EVERYTHING, HE WAS A GREAT MAN. If you read *Mountbatten*, you will be in no doubt of that.

Lascelles sitting in judgement', chipped in Lord Brabourne – 'it can't have been easy.'

It was not easy. In most households in Britain in the early 1950s, the husband and father was the dominant figure. He was the head of the household, the breadwinner, the law-maker; he ruled the roost, he was the cock of the walk. For Philip, it was not like that. 'It was bloody difficult for him,' said Mike Parker. 'In the Navy, he was in command of his own ship – literally. At Clarence House, it was very much his show. When we got to Buckingham Palace, all that changed.' 'It was an unsettling time for him,' said Martin Charteris. 'He had no defined role, while the Queen's role was clearly defined and she assumed it with an extraordinary and immediate confidence and ease. For the rest of us, it was wonderful to behold, but I can see that he might have found it somewhat disconcerting.'

According to Elizabeth Longford, soon after her Accession the Queen told a friend: 'I no longer feel anxious or worried. I don't know what it is – but I have lost all my timidity somehow becoming the Sovereign and having to receive the Prime Minister.' She was now leading a life from which her husband was necessarily – constitutionally – excluded. When the prime minister came to the Palace for his weekly audience with the Sovereign, the old man and the young Queen would sit together, alone, sometimes for up to an hour. 'What do you talk about?' Jock Colville asked Churchill. 'Oh, mostly racing,' answered Churchill, with a twinkle. And polo, apparently. And the state of the world, of course.

The Queen was – and is – supplied, daily, with a mass of 'state papers': Cabinet minutes, Foreign Office telegrams, documents, briefs, drafts – boxes of 'secret' documents relating to all manner of United Kingdom, Commonwealth and international affairs. Philip has never had access to any of these. When I told him that, as a Lord Commissioner of the Treasury, I used to sign mandates that were then sent to Her Majesty for counter-signature, he was bemused. 'I had no idea she did that,' he said. 'I've no idea what goes on.'

When he says this, it is not to complain. He is simply stating it as a matter of fact. 'I was told "Keep out" and that was that.'

'So, what did you do?' I asked him.

'I tried to find useful things to do,' Philip said to me. 'I did my best. I introduced a Footman Training Programme. The old boys here [at Buckingham Palace] hadn't had anything quite like it before. They expected the footmen just to keep on coming. We had an Organisation and Methods Review. I tried to make improvements – without unhinging things.'

The Organisation and Methods Review involved the Duke and Mike Parker treading on a number of toes. 'Some of the old guard weren't too happy,' Parker told me. 'We met with a fair bit of resistance. But I think we made a few improvements, dragged some of them into the twentieth century. We explored the whole Palace. We didn't find a wicked fairy in a turret with a spinning wheel, but we did discover the wine cellar. It's deep underground and goes on for miles and miles. There were some great old vintages and menus dating back to the early days of Queen Victoria.'

When I suggested to Prince Philip that he is an instinctive moderniser, and always has been, he interrupted me: 'No, no, not for the sake of modernising, not for the sake of buggering about with things in some sort of Blairite way. I'm anxious to get things done. That's all. I'm interested in the efficient use of resources.'[114]

I said to him, 'Weren't you the first member of the Royal Family to use a helicopter?'

'Yes,' he said, 'in the run-up to the Coronation.' He was Chairman of the Coronation Commission. It was a real job and he took it seriously. Large numbers of Commonwealth and Colonial troops arrived in the country to take part in the event and were stationed in barracks across the land. The Duke decided to visit them all. He and Mike Parker looked at the logistics and reckoned they should go by helicopter. They borrowed one from the Royal Navy. 'It was just more practical,' the Prince explained to me, 'but it caused a ruckus. I didn't go through the proper channels. There was a lot of pettifogging bureaucracy.' Parker was hauled before the prime minister and given a severe dressing down.

The Coronation when it came – on 2 June 1953 – was more than a logistical triumph. 'Never has there been such excitement,' wrote Jock Colville, 'never has a Monarch received such adulation.' The day itself was dank and overcast, but the mood was universally jubilant.[115]

---

[114] I am writing this on the morning after the 2003 Royal Variety Performance. Last night, during the interval, Prince Philip was introduced to some of the team involved in putting the show together. 'But I've already met these people,' he protested. 'We were introduced when we arrived. Shouldn't we meet some new people? Let's use the time we've got usefully.'

[115] Of course, there were a few republicans with reservations, but, sensibly, they kept their heads down. And the Duke of Windsor stayed away because he was not wanted. Elizabeth felt his presence would be inappropriate. He came to England to attend his

Everest had been conquered and Elizabeth was to be crowned![116] Hundreds of thousands of people – happy and curious – braved the drizzle and filled the streets of London. Millions more – in Britain and around the world – followed the day's events on television. (Never before in human history had so many people witnessed the same events at the same time.) Philip was chairman of the Coronation Commission, but most of the detail was out of his hands. The pageantry was largely in the gift of his vice-chairman, Bernard Fitzalan-Howard, the 16th Duke of Norfolk, hereditary Earl Marshal and Chief Butler of England, a seasoned campaigner whose family titles dated back to 1139 (when Stephen was King) and whose past personal triumphs included the management of the funeral of George V and the coronation of George VI. The Duke was a 'character'. When asked by a peer if his invitation to the Coronation might be prejudiced because of his divorce, Norfolk replied, 'Good God, man, this is a Coronation, not Royal Ascot.' When asked if it was true that the peers were hiding sandwiches inside their coronets during the service, he answered, 'Probably. They're capable of anything.' When one of the Coronation rehearsals was running behind schedule, his voice echoed round Westminster Abbey: 'If the bishops don't learn to walk in step, we'll be here all night.'

The Queen attended several of the Abbey rehearsals herself and learnt her moves from the Duchess of Norfolk who also acted as her stand-in. At Buckingham Palace – where the ballroom was marked out with ropes and posts replicating the Abbey's floor plan – she put in hours of extra practice on her own. She listened to recordings of her father's Coronation. She walked the course with sheets pinned to her shoulders representing the robes she would wear. To become accustomed to its weight, she sat at her desk wearing the actual St Edward's crown first used at the Coronation of Charles II in 1661. It was heavy – five pounds – and its weight was of significance,

mother Queen Mary's funeral on 31 March, but felt he had not received a warm welcome. Elizabeth would not pay him the £10,000 a year allowance he had been given by her father. A family dinner was held at Windsor Castle following Queen Mary's funeral. He was not invited. He wrote to his wife: 'What a smug, stinking lot my relations are and you've never seen such a seedy worn-out bunch of old hags most of them have become.'

[116] The 29,002-foot summit of the world's tallest mountain had been reached at 11.30 a.m. on 29 May. The news reached London on the morning of the Coronation. The triumphant mountaineers were a New Zealander, Edmund Hillary, and a Nepalese Sherpa, Norgay Tensing, but the leader of the expedition, John Hunt, was British and the feat was hailed as a British achievement.

symbolising, according to the Archbishop of Canterbury, the burden of the demands that would be made upon her 'to her life's end'.

The Archbishop, Dr Geoffrey Fisher, a muscular Christian (at Oxford he was a noted footballer, rugby player and oarsman), went to great lengths to ensure that the spiritual significance of the Coronation was not obscured by the pomp and pageantry. In the run-up to the great day, he gave a series of sermons exploring and explaining the Coronation liturgy. He was an experienced teacher (he had been headmaster of Repton) and in Elizabeth, of course, he had a willing pupil. Martin Charteris said to me, 'People will have their own memories of the Coronation – of the pageantry, the processions, the Queen of Tonga in her open carriage[117], the street parties and what have you – but for the Queen herself, the coronation was not about celebration, it was about dedication. It was a religious event.' A few days after the event, the Archbishop looked back on it in awe: 'The wonder of it, the unforgettable bearing of the Queen, the overwhelming sense of dedication to God, of worship of God, consecration by God and communion with God, embracing everyone in the Abbey.' And beyond. In the United Kingdom in 1953, the Anglican faith was alive and well – and popular. In London in the early 1950s, more than 40 per cent of all adults regularly attended church. Today, fewer than 3 per cent do.

Westminster Abbey, the setting for Elizabeth's Coronation, was where William the Conqueror was crowned on Christmas Day, 1066. The essential elements of the ceremony were much as they had been for a thousand years. For the Queen, the most significant part of the service was the Act of Anointing, the moment, in the Archbishop's phrase, that brought her 'into the presence of the living God'. It was a moment, both intimate and sacred, that, at her own request, was neither filmed nor televised. As she sat on the Coronation Chair, under a canopy held by four Knights of the Garter, the Archbishop made a sign of the cross on each of her hands, on her breast and on her head. 'Be thy Head anointed with holy Oil,' he said, 'as kings, priests and prophets were anointed. And as Solomon was anointed King by Zadok the priest and Nathan the prophet, so be thou anointed, blessed and consecrated

---

[117] Queen Salote of Tonga was a huge lady and she travelled to the Abbey in an open carriage sitting opposite the comparatively diminutive Sultan of Kelantan. Someone asked, 'Who is that with Queen Salote?' 'That,' said Noël Coward famously, 'is her lunch.'

Queen over the Peoples, whom the Lord thy God hath given thee to rule and govern.'

For Philip, the most significant part of the service came a little later. This was, in every sense, the Queen's day – and, in truth, hers alone. He was there as her attendant lord. Dressed in the uniform of an Admiral of the Fleet,[118] he accompanied her to and from the Abbey in the great Gold State Coach. He shared in the waving, not the crowning. This was her Coronation, not theirs. In the Abbey, she processed alone. She took the Coronation oath alone. She alone was anointed with holy oil. She alone was crowned. When the Coronation was done – when St Edward's crown had been placed upon her head – the nobility paid homage to their Queen. The first to do so was the Lord Archbishop of Canterbury. Next was the Duke of Edinburgh. He stepped forward and knelt before her. He placed his hands between hers and said, 'I, Philip, Duke of Edinburgh, do become your liege man of life and limb, and of earthly worship; and faith and truth will I bear unto you, to live and die, against all manner of folks. So help me God.'

He said it and he meant it. When, once, I asked Prince Philip what his life had been about, he narrowed his eyes and flinched away from the question. I decided to persist. 'Supporting the Queen,' I suggested, 'isn't that what it's all been about?' He looked away – which is unusual for him: normally, he looks directly at you – and said, very slowly and almost inaudibly, 'Absolutely. Absolutely.' He may have been disappointed that his naval career was cut short. He may have been angered that he could not give his own name to his own children. He may have been infuriated by the way he was patronised by some of those he met at court. But never – not once – in more than fifty years – has he flinched in the performance of what he sees as his one, essential duty: to support the Queen.

Margrethe, the Queen of Denmark – who is another direct descendant of Queen Victoria – said to me, 'I think people in your country undervalue Prince Philip because he makes what is a very difficult job look so easy. He does it so well people don't realise what a complicated and difficult job it is. It has not been easy for my husband being Prince Consort and it has not been easy for Prince Philip. Philip does have one advantage. He comes from a royal family. He has always

---

[118] On giving up his active naval career, Philip had been appointed Admiral of the Fleet – and Field Marshal and Marshal of the Royal Air Force. When Mountbatten was promoted Admiral in February 1953, Philip sent him a telegram: 'Congratulations on your promotion. Keep it up – you may catch up one day!'

understood what monarchy is about.' Margrethe's husband is a Frenchman and former diplomat. Philip is the grandson and nephew of kings. All his life he has had royalty all around him. He has never questioned his place at the Queen's side, one step behind her. He has never complained about that. From start to finish, he has taken that 'as read'. At her Coronation, the Queen stood at the altar, laid her hand on the Holy Bible and swore, 'The things which I have here before promised, I will perform and keep. So help me God.' And Philip knelt before his sovereign, and with his hands in hers, vowed to become her 'liege man of life and limb, and of earthly worship . . . So help me God.' In 2005, in a largely Godless country where the hereditary principle – for more than a thousand years, central to our governance – only survives in the case of the Royal Family, the ritual of the Coronation will seem to many archaic and absurd, the words used an almost meaningless mumbo-jumbo from a bygone age. In June 1953, Elizabeth and Philip understood what they were saying and meant every word. Uncle David would not have done, which is why Elizabeth did not want him there. She kissed the Bible and signed the Coronation oath. Philip promised her 'faith and truth'. For neither of them was any of this a hollow ritual.

When Philip had completed his homage, he stood up, touched the Queen's crown and kissed her left cheek. Next to pay homage were the Dukes of Gloucester and Kent, followed by the senior peers in turn, including England's premier baron, Mowbray Segrave and Stourton, whose titles dated back to 1283 (when Edward I was King) and whose appearance provided some unexpected light relief. The Archbishop recalled: 'He came down from his homage all over the place, bunching up his robe and, as the Queen said, with moth balls and pieces of ermine all over the place.' When the homage was over, the trumpets sounded and the congregation – 7,500 strong – called out: 'God Save Queen Elizabeth, Long Live Queen Elizabeth, May the Queen Live for ever.'

As the choir sang a valedictory *Te Deum*, the Queen stepped down from her throne. In the St Edward's Chapel, she changed her velvet robes once more – the ceremony had involved a lot of dressing and undressing – and swapped the historic St Edward's crown for the slightly lighter, but undeniably fancier, Imperial State crown, studded with many of the most precious stones on earth – including the Black Prince's ruby, Elizabeth I's pearl earrings and Charles II's sapphire. Bearing the crown jewels, carrying the sceptre in her right hand and the orb in her left, while the congregation sang the National Anthem,

Elizabeth II processed through the Abbey to the West Door where the Gold State Coach again awaited her. She clambered aboard, accompanied by Philip, and, drawn by eight grey horses, the coach – a proper fairy-tale affair, over the top, baroque and bedazzling, with door panels painted by Cipriani in the 1760s – took them, slowly and steadily, on a circuitous seven-mile route back to Buckingham Palace. They were cheered, long and loud, by hundreds of thousands of the Queen's subjects, many of whom had camped out for several nights, in the cold and wet, to secure a good view of the passing parade. They were escorted by twenty-seven further carriages, twenty-nine military bands and thirteen thousand troops. The Chairman of the Coronation Commission reckoned it 'not a bad show'.

Back at the Palace, in the Green Drawing Room, Cecil Beaton was waiting to take the official photographs. 'In came the Queen,' he recorded in his diary, 'with her ladies, cool, smiling, sovereign of the situation.' Beaton is a useful witness because he has a photographer's eye and an artist's sensibility. 'The Queen looked extremely minute under her robes and Crown, her nose and hands chilled and her eyes tired. "Yes," in reply to my question, "the Crown does get rather heavy." She had been wearing it now for nearly three hours.' His description of Philip rings especially true:

> The Duke of Edinburgh stood by making wry jokes, his lips pursed in a smile that put the fear of God into me. I believe he doesn't like or approve of me. This is a pity because, although I'm not one for 'Navy-type' jokes, and obviously have nothing in common with him, I admire him enormously, and think he is absolutely first-rate at this job of making things comparatively lively and putting people at their ease. Perhaps he was disappointed that his friend, Baron, was not doing this job today; whatever the reason he was definitely adopting a rather ragging attitude towards the proceedings.

Beaton was homosexual, and camp in manner, and his favourite royal sitter on Coronation Day – on any day, come to that – was Queen Elizabeth the Queen Mother, always the queens' favourite Queen. He found her in 'rollicking spirits' and so immediately warm and helpful towards him that, at once, all his 'anxieties and fears' were dispelled:

> The Queen Mother, by being so basically human and understanding, gives out to us a feeling of reassurance. The great mother figure and

nannie to us all, through the warmth of her sympathy bathes us and wraps us in a counterpane by the fireside. Suddenly I had this wonderful accomplice – someone who would help me through everything. All at once, and because of her, I was enjoying my work. Prince Charles and Princess Anne were buzzing about in the wildest excitement and would not keep still for a moment. The Queen Mother anchored them in her arms, put her head down to kiss Prince Charles's hair, and made a terrific picture.

Prince Charles (who is not homosexual, despite what you may have heard) would endorse every word of Beaton's description of his grandmother. In the Abbey, Charles, not yet five years old, in white silk shirt and shorts, had watched the Coronation from the Royal Box, perched between his aunt and his grandmother. His other grandmother, Princess Alice, was nearby, 'a contrast to the grandeur', Beaton noted, 'in the ash-grey draperies of a nun'.

For Alice, it was a wonderful experience, moving and exciting. She ordered a special, brand-new nun's habit for the occasion. (She was an interesting mix: she craved the simple life, but travelled widely; mostly she lived modestly, but sometimes she was immoderately extravagant; she advocated self-discipline, but she smoked like a chimney.) For the Queen Widow (as Beaton called the Queen Mother) it was a more poignant occasion. At the Palace she was 'dimpled and chuckling, with eyes as bright as any of her jewels': at the Abbey, in her expression 'we read sadness combined with pride'. Martin Charteris told me that he believed that the Queen Mother was jealous of her daughter. 'Queen Elizabeth was not yet fifty-two when the King died,' he reminded me. 'She was accustomed to being centre-stage, the focus of attention, universally loved. She was still loved, of course, and admired, but she was no longer the star of the show and I don't think she found that easy. In the early days of the new Queen's reign, there was an awkwardness about precedence, with the Queen not wanting to go in front of her mother and Queen Elizabeth, of course, accustomed to going first.'

I want to quote one last time from Cecil Beaton's diary for two reasons: to illustrate Elizabeth's sense of humour (which is rarely seen in public) and to suggest something about the Queen Mother's attitude to her son-in-law. Beaton had not expected to be asked to take the Coronation pictures. Because Baron, 'a most unexpected friend of Prince Philip's', had been taking all the recent royal photographs, Beaton assumed that Baron would get this special assignment, too.

When he didn't, and when, in early May 1953, Beaton learnt that the job was going to be his, after all, the news came 'as an enormous relief':

> The same night that this message was relayed to me, at a ball at the American Embassy, I saw the Queen for a brief moment and thanked her. 'No, I'm very glad you're going to take them,' she said, 'but, by the time we get through to the photographs, we'll have circles down to here' (she pointed halfway down her cheeks), 'then the Crown comes down to here' (to the eye), 'then the court train comes bundling up here, and I'm out to here' (sticks stomach out). 'There are layers upon layers: skirt and mantle and trains.' She spoke like a young high-spirited girl.
>
> I also had a short opportunity to thank the Queen Mother for what I am sure must have been her help in bringing about this 'coup' for me. She laughed knowingly with one finger high in the air.

I can picture her. She could be very naughty. Philip was the chairman of the Coronation Commission. He might well have preferred to have the official Coronation photographs taken by his friend, Baron, but, if so, he was thwarted. Beaton secured the assignment, not only because he was an exceptional photographer who wooed Queen Elizabeth with flattery and flowers,[119] but also because Baron was Philip's man and Philip was someone Queen Elizabeth did not entirely trust. When first he had appeared on the scene, she had had her misgivings about him – encouraged by her brother David and his set – but, according to several of Philip's friends, her doubts and reservations about her son-in-law persisted until the end of her very long life.

Philip always behaved towards Queen Elizabeth with punctilious courtesy. At around the time of her one hundredth birthday, I happened to interview Prince Philip (seventy-nine himself at the time) for ITN Radio and tried to nudge him into saying something about his mother-in-law. Apart from insisting that he had no desire to live so long himself, he would not be drawn. I have had no reports of his having ever made any disparaging remarks about her, but several people have told me how, within their hearing, Queen Elizabeth made slighting comments about Philip and referred to him – not entirely humorously – as 'the Hun'. One of Philip's close female friends told me that the

---

[119] 'I took enormous care to choose a bouquet of all the first spring flowers to be sent to that adorable human being living in that cold, bleak Palace.' You couldn't make it up!

coolness between Prince Philip and Prince Charles was, in part, a by-product of the unspoken tension between Philip and his mother-in-law. Charles adored his grandmother and Queen Elizabeth was extravagantly, effusively, fond of Charles. There was an intimacy and mutual sympathy between them that Philip did not share. 'She laughed knowingly with one finger in the air.' She could be *very* naughty.

On Coronation Day, Cecil Beaton described Princess Margaret at Buckingham Palace, sailing towards him, 'her purple train being held aloft by four pages', 'with pink and white make-up and a sex twinkle of understanding in her regard'. Perhaps Beaton knew her secret. Margaret was twenty-two and in love with a married man sixteen years her senior.

Group Captain Peter Townsend was born in 1914, at the outset of the First World War, and, in 1940, in the Battle of Britain, became one of the heroes of the Second World War. He was a fighter pilot who led the 'B' Flight of Hurricanes in the celebrated No. 43 Squadron. He was mentioned in despatches. He won the DFC and bar. But the war took its toll: he had a nervous breakdown. 'I knew in my bones that I should never again be the pilot I once had been,' he confessed in his memoirs. 'I had gone too far down the hill ever to get to the top again . . . The more I flew, and there could be no relenting, the more fear, stark, degrading fear, possessed me. Each time I took off, I felt sure it would be the last.' By 1944, he was no longer flying, but he was still a hero, and when the King expressed the desire to have an RAF officer as an equerry for the first time, Townsend seemed a first-rate choice. He was handsome, agreeable, distinguished and came from a solid, if middle-class, background. (His brother, Michael, a naval captain, served with Philip in HMS *Chequers*.) He was also complex, troubled and deeply religious. The King took to him at once and Townsend was immediately sympathetic to the King: 'The King did not try, or even need, to put me at my ease . . . the humanity of the man and his striking simplicity came across warmly, unmistakably . . . sometimes he hesitated in his speech, and then I felt drawn towards him . . .' Townsend was said to be the only member of the Household who could successfully soothe the King when he was overwhelmed by one of his 'gnashes'. He arrived at Buckingham Palace anticipating a three-month attachment. He remained in the King and Queen's service for nearly ten years. On the day he came for his initial interview, in February 1944, Lilibet and Margaret, then aged seventeen and thirteen, saw the beautiful, brown-haired, blue-eyed hero, who was just twenty-nine, arrive at the Palace, and, as he came into view, so the story goes, Lilibet whispered to her younger sister, 'Bad luck. He's married.'

Townsend married young and unluckily. Rosemary Townsend was attractive, vivacious and flirtatious. She was also socially aspirational. She liked to flirt with the King. (Women did. One does.[120]) According to Townsend, when he secured the job as equerry, his wife's immediate reaction was: 'We're made.' In fact, they were undone. Townsend gave his all to the Royal Family: he was devoted to the King, charmed by the Queen, and, before very long, innocently enamoured of the teenage princess:

> One day after a picnic lunch with the guns, I stretched out in the heather to doze. Then, vaguely, I was aware that someone was covering me with a coat. I opened one eye to see Princess Margaret's lovely face, very close, looking into mine. Then I opened the other eye, and saw behind her, the King leaning on his stick, with a certain look, typical of him: kind, half-amused.

In 1947, when the Royal Family took their three-month trip to southern Africa, Townsend was in attendance, of necessity leaving Rosemary behind. Rosemary had an affair with a young Guards officer and then another, with John de László, son of the painter Philip de László. Townsend's marriage was breaking down and he was falling in love with the second-in-line to the throne. He was sixteen years older than Margaret and a married man. He should have known better. He should have resisted temptation. But he didn't. He was besotted:

[120] I know. Ludicrously, I have attempted to flirt with several heads of state. Once, at a reception at Buckingham Palace, I attempted to flirt with the Queen. She looked at me in silence, bemused and appalled. At the same party, I watched her son, Prince Andrew, flirting – fairly outrageously – with almost every female he met, and, whenever I caught sight of Prince Philip, the Queen's husband was talking to an attractive younger woman and the flirtation was more subtle and evidently mutual. Not everybody flirts. At the same party, the Duke of Kent was mixing nicely, simply chatting in a considerate, congenial way. Prince Edward is not a natural flirt. (It takes one to know one.) Once, at a dinner, twenty years ago, when we were both younger, I found myself seated next to Princess Anne. Because the table was crowded, and because of the unfortunate position of the table leg, the Princess and I had no choice but to spend the whole meal with our thighs pressed together. When I said, 'I'm not trying to be deliberately flirtatious', the Princess gave me a withering look of which her mother would have been proud – and I spent the rest of the evening with a constricted torso to ensure as much space between our upper bodies as possible.

What ultimately made Princess Margaret so attractive and lovable was that behind the dazzling façade, the apparent self-assurance, you could find, if you looked for it, a rare softness and sincerity. She could make you bend double with laughing; she could also touch you deeply. There were dozens of others; their names were in the papers, which vied with each other, frantically and futilely, in their forecasts of the one whom she would marry. Yet I dare say that there was not one among them more touched by the Princess's *joie de vivre* than I, for in my present marital predicament, it gave me what I most lacked – joy. More, it created a sympathy between us and I began to sense that, in her life too, there was something lacking.

When the King died, Margaret was twenty-one years old and bereft. 'He was so kind and brave all his life,' she said, 'the very heart and centre of our family and no one could have had a more loving and thoughtful father.' His death left a void and Townsend filled it. Having served as the King's equerry, he was now appointed Comptroller of the Queen Mother's Household. At the end of 1952, he secured a divorce from Rosemary on the grounds of her adultery. He was the innocent party; he was the wronged husband; he was now a free man and he wanted to marry the new Queen's sister. With a sense of timing that, according to their detractors, serves to illustrate Townsend's naivety and Margaret's selfishness, in the spring of 1953, in the immediate run-up to the Coronation, the young Princess told her sister and her mother that she and Townsend were in love and wished to marry. Townsend later recalled: 'If they were disconcerted as they had every reason to be, they did not flinch, but faced it with perfect calm and, it must be said, considerable charity.'

Sir Alan Lascelles, the new Queen's private secretary, who was set to retire after the Coronation, was less understanding. 'You must be either mad or bad or both,' he told Townsend when he heard the news. Martin Charteris, then the Queen's assistant private secretary, said to me, 'I don't think he was mad or bad, but he was naive. Incredibly so. He was a commoner and a divorcé. Rightly or wrongly, divorcees were not presented at court, were not invited to garden parties, were not formally introduced to royalty. I don't think there was ever a serious prospect of a marriage. If the King had still been alive I don't believe the matter would have arisen. I don't think Townsend would have dared.'

Queen Elizabeth the Queen Mother seemingly put the matter out of her mind – 'the old ostrich approach' as Charteris had it. The young

Queen, not yet crowned, put the matter on hold. 'Under the circumstances,' she said, 'it isn't unreasonable for me to ask you to wait a year.'
In the event, Margaret and Townsend waited more than two years
before bowing to the inevitable.

Elizabeth wanted Margaret to be happy. As their cousin, Margaret
Rhodes, put it to me, 'Margaret drove the Queen mad frequently, but
she was her sister and she loved her.' Philip was not unsympathetic,
either. He was infuriated by the amount of publicity the romance
generated, and annoyed, especially, that it was a report from
Westminster Abbey on Coronation Day – telling of Margaret brushing
Townsend's lapel 'with a tender hand' – that triggered the worldwide
media interest in the story, but there is no evidence to support repeated
press suggestions that he was positively hostile towards Townsend.
When stories of his alleged plotting against his would-be brother-in-law
appeared in the papers, Philip bleated, despairingly, 'What have I done?
I haven't done anything.' In truth, he tried to keep out of the way. As
he said to me once, with reference to his own children's marital
difficulties: 'I try to keep out of these things as much as possible.' Martin
Charteris said to me, 'Prince Philip had a sort of ragging, joshing way
with Princess Margaret, treated her as the wayward younger sister, but
I don't believe he interfered in any way. The Queen was naturally
sympathetic towards the Princess, but I think she thought – she hoped
– given time, the affair would peter out. Townsend really was
unsuitable. He was older, he had two sons already. It just wasn't going
to happen. Churchill wouldn't wear it. Salisbury wouldn't wear it. The
Commonwealth wouldn't wear it.[121] It wasn't going to happen.'

It didn't. For two years the issue simmered on, with the publicity
surrounding it coming to the boil at regular intervals. In the hope that
distance might lessen enchantment, under pressure from Lascelles and
Churchill the Queen agreed that Townsend be 'let go' from court. He
was despatched to the British Embassy in Brussels as air attaché.

---

[121] Under the Royal Marriages Act of 1772, the Queen's sister required the Queen's
blessing before she could marry. If the Queen decided not to sanction marriage,
Princess Margaret could wait until her twenty-fifth birthday and then marry without
the Sovereign's consent provided she could secure the approval of parliament. In 1953,
when Margaret was still twenty-three, Churchill, whose momentary first instinct had
been that 'the path of true love must be allowed to run smooth', quickly advised against
the marriage. Lord Salisbury, a senior figure in the government, was adamantly
opposed. The Commonwealth prime ministers, when consulted, expressed their
misgivings. The Queen was Supreme Governor of the Church of England: her sister's
union with a divorced man was not to be condoned.

Margaret took up her public duties. She accompanied her mother on a tour of Rhodesia. Alone, she undertook a tour of the West Indies. For nearly two years the lovers remained apart, but in touch. They were love-sick and the malady lingered on. It all came to a head in the summer and autumn of 1955, as Margaret approached and passed her twenty-fifth birthday. At twenty-five, she would be free to marry without the Sovereign's consent. The new Prime Minister, Anthony Eden (himself, incidentally, a divorcé), advised the Queen that the government still could not sanction the union – Lord Salisbury, for one, would resign if it attempted to do so – and, while the legislation required to enable the marriage to take place might be passed by parliament, it would necessitate the Princess sacrificing her right of succession. Margaret was third in line to the throne. Eden advised the Queen that 'neither the proposed marriage nor her renunciation of her right to the Succession need in themselves affect her style and title as Her Royal Highness Princess Margaret or the provision made for her under the Civil List', but, inevitably, if she married Townsend, her status would be changed, irrevocably.

In the end, Margaret decided against the sacrifice. She met with Townsend on 22 October. 'We were both exhausted,' he recalled, 'mentally, emotionally, physically.' He knew his Princess loved her life as a princess. He knew he could not expect her to abandon it for a life in Brussels as the not-quite-as-royal-as-once-she-was second wife of a middle-aged air attaché. They met again. 'We looked at each other,' he said, 'there was a wonderful tenderness in her eyes which reflected, I suppose, the look in mine. We had reached the end of the road.'

On 31 October, they met at Clarence House and had a last drink together, toasting the happiness they had shared and the future they would not. At 7 p.m. that same evening the young Princess issued a public statement that, within hours, became the lead story on front pages around the world:

I would like it to be known that I have decided not to marry Group Captain Peter Townsend. I have been aware that, subject to renouncing my rights of succession, it might have been possible for me to contract a civil marriage. But, mindful of the Church's teaching that Christian marriage is indissoluble, and conscious of my duty to the Commonwealth, I have resolved to put these considerations before any others.

I have reached this decision entirely alone, and in doing so I have been strengthened by the unfailing support of Group Captain Townsend. I am deeply grateful for the concern of all those who have constantly prayed for my happiness.

Sarah Bradford, in her biography of the Queen, says, when she reaches this point in the story: 'Amazingly, the royal family did not rally round Margaret on the night of her formal renunciation. She dined alone while her mother kept an official engagement at London University. The Queen Mother did not say goodnight to her daughter on her return. For some time they had barely been on speaking terms; for the Queen Mother, the Townsend affair had been as traumatic as the Abdication had for Queen Mary. Elizabeth telephoned for a brief conversation, after which Margaret returned to watching boxing on television. The King's death and his widow's subsequent withdrawal, Elizabeth's marriage and Margaret's romance had weakened the family bonds that had linked "us four" so closely together.' Certainly, the 'family dynamic' had changed, but I believe that, today, the Queen – who, I understand, admires Sarah Bradford's biography of George VI – would quarrel with the implications of the Bradford account of 'the night of the formal renunciation'. Of course, the Queen Mother fulfilled a long-standing official engagement. Duty always comes first. Of course, the Queen telephoned her sister, but the conversation was neither cursory nor unsympathetic. The Queen's position – and her lack of any kind of anonymity – mean that she cannot simply jump into the car and go round to see people on a whim. Consequently, many of her closest and most important relationships are sustained through the telephone. Prince Philip occasionally claims to be bemused by the amount of time his wife spends on the telephone.

Townsend did not entirely disappear from Margaret's life. He went around the world, slowly, to help himself forget her, but found himself unable to do so. He contacted her once more in the spring of 1958. They met again at Clarence House, apparently with the Queen Mother's somewhat uncertain blessing. This was in March 1958, when the Queen and the Duke of Edinburgh were on a state visit to the Netherlands. Unfortunately, news of the reunion reached the press, and salacious, sensationalised coverage of the Princess's tryst at Clarence House quite eclipsed more responsible reporting of the Sovereign's visit to Holland. Elizabeth and Philip were not amused. Margaret and Townsend knew there was no hope, and parted for a final time. Within a year, Peter Townsend, aged forty-five, was engaged to a

Belgian girl, aged nineteen. Marie-Luce Jamagne looked uncannily like the teenage Margaret.

In May 1960, Princess Margaret, approaching thirty, married a man her own age ('and almost her own height' quipped friends: in fact he was several inches taller): Tony Armstrong-Jones, a gifted theatre and society photographer, and one of the most alarmingly charming people a girl (or boy) could hope to meet. They did not live happily ever after. Far from it. Their marriage was a roller-coaster ride: at times exciting, at times quite frightening: ultimately disastrous. As personalities they had much in common: both were charismatic, creative, charming, manipulative, selfish and self-absorbed. Their marriage was turbulent almost from the start, characterised by self-indulgence, recrimination and mutual infidelity. And yet, as parents, they seem to have been enormously successful. As adults, the Snowdon children have been happy and fortunate in their relationships in a way that the children of Philip and Elizabeth, on the whole, have not been. The Snowdon children – children of a broken home – made good marriages and got on well and easily with both their parents. Three of the children of the Queen and the Duke of Edinburgh have had failed marriages, and their relationship with their eldest son is notoriously uncomfortable. It is interesting to ponder why.

I talked about this with Margaret Rhodes. She is quite shy, a little nervy, but with a sensible head on her shoulders and a countrywoman's values. She also has a beady eye. She has seen all conditions and types of relationship in her long life. She can sense what works and does not work. Of the Queen and Prince Philip's marriage, she said to me at once, and emphatically, and convincingly: 'On the whole, it ranks as one of the most successful marriages. One of the most successful.'

'And as parents?' I asked.

'I've seen Philip being absolutely sweet with his children's babies,' said Mrs Rhodes, 'absolutely sweet.' She paused and poured out more coffee. She sighed. 'But with their own children it hasn't been easy. There's no use denying it. Things have gone slightly awry with Prince Charles. I've been at Birkhall when he's been there. He's very conscientious, very committed. He'll have dinner, and go back to work. He works so hard, but then he's so extravagant.' Another pause. 'The Queen finds Prince Charles very difficult. He is extravagant and she doesn't like that.'

Mrs Rhodes lit one more cigarette and looked at me. 'It's incredibly sad,' she said. 'It's a fractured family. Terribly sad.'

'Why do you think that is?' I asked. 'What's at the root of it?'

'Philip can't bring himself to be close with Charles,' said Mrs Rhodes. 'Perhaps you don't learn to give love if you haven't had love.'

We talked for a while about Prince Philip's childhood and the years when he barely saw – or heard from – either of his parents.

'But what about the Queen?' I asked. 'Her childhood was very loving, wasn't it?'

Mrs Rhodes pondered for a moment. 'The Queen was always reserved, even as a child. And when she became Queen that did add to her reserve, very definitely. But you're right. The King adored both his daughters. And Queen Elizabeth was brimming with love.' At this point, Margaret Rhodes, who is by nature a woman of restraint, flung her arms wide open to illustrate the warmth and breadth of the Queen Mother's embrace. She smiled and looked again directly at me. 'Perhaps,' she said, 'having married someone who is like Philip, it is difficult to go on expressing emotion to an unemotional person. You find, in time, you can't express love any more. Princess Margaret could. Completely. And her children have been so successful.'

MA & PA

Chapter Eleven

'To marry is to domesticate the Recording Angel. Once you are married, there is nothing left for you, not even suicide, but to be good.'

Robert Louis Stevenson (1850–94), *Virginibus Puerisque*

Gina Kennard, a childhood friend of each of them, who has known them both almost all her life (and is godmother to Prince Andrew), said to me, 'The Queen and Prince Philip were good parents, *really* good parents, *always* interested in their children and *always* actively involved. Whatever Charles says about it now, Philip was a wonderful father. He used to read them stories, play with them, go fishing – the lot. So much nonsense is talked about the Queen and her family. We saw quite a lot of them in the 1950s. They were a young family, full of energy and life, and a very happy one. I remember lots of fun and games, lots of laughter.'

Martin Charteris, a trusted courtier, who was close to Elizabeth from 1949 onwards, told me, 'There's this myth that the Queen cares more about her dogs and her horses than she does about her children. I believe it was fuelled when someone who had written to Her Majesty commiserating on the death of one of her corgis received a four-page hand-written response. Certainly, the Queen is devoted to her animals – absolutely devoted: they're what help keep her sane – but she loves her children deeply, as any mother would. Both she and the Duke of Edinburgh did their level best to give their children a normal family life. Not always easy, under the circumstances.'

Elizabeth II was Queen, after all. In November 1953, Elizabeth and Philip, without their children, embarked on a five-and-a-half-month post-Coronation Commonwealth tour. They took in Bermuda, Jamaica, Fiji, Tonga, the Coco Islands, Aden, Uganda, Malta and

Gibraltar. They spent three months in Australia and New Zealand, and ten days in Ceylon. As Ben Pimlott put it in his biography of the Queen, 'Such a marathon of travel, speeches, national anthems, handshakes, troop inspections, Parliament openings, performances, banquets, bouquets and gifts, had never been before undertaken by a British Head of State – or perhaps by anybody.' 'I can't remember much about it,' Prince Philip said to me, laughing, 'but I can tell you the crowds were incredible, the adulation was extraordinary. You wouldn't believe it, you really wouldn't.' It was reckoned that three-quarters of the entire population of Australia turned out to see the Queen in person.

While their parents were away, Charles and Anne, aged five and three, were looked after by their grandmother, the Queen Mother. At the end of the grand tour, the children were to be reunited with their parents in Malta, where their great-uncle, Dickie Mountbatten, was now Commander-in-Chief of the Mediterranean Fleet. The children, sent from England in the newly-commissioned Royal Yacht *Britannia*, arrived in Malta ten days ahead of their parents. Mountbatten was not amused to receive a message from Boy Browning – his one-time Chief of Staff who had become Comptroller of the Edinburghs' Household in 1948 – to the effect that Mountbatten should submit a programme of proposed 'excursions for the children' to be laid before Her Majesty for her approval. Understandably indignant, Mountbatten reported the request to his wife, Edwina, telling her he had told Browning that Lady Mountbatten, the children's great-aunt (and, incidentally, mother of Pamela Mountbatten, who was accompanying the Queen on the royal tour as lady-in-waiting) 'would organise the trips, etc., as desirable each day. Really!'

When you become Sovereign, nobody treats you quite as they did before. According to Sonia Berry, perhaps Lilibet's closest childhood friend, 'She would never have chosen to be Queen. She would much rather have lived in the country with horses and dogs and been a normal housewife.' Lilibet and Sonia's friendship did not end with the Queen's Accession, but its nature changed. Suddenly there was a new formality – a sense of strain and distance – in the air. Overnight, the old, easy intimacy disappeared. Letters and invitations were no longer sent to 'you', but to 'Your Majesty'. When Philip was away, the Queen might come to Sonia's for tea or dinner – 'She used to say how nice it was to get out of Buckingham Palace' – but informality and spontaneity were no longer possible. Security was required. Guest lists had to be checked. Curtains had to be drawn so that the sovereign might not be observed. 'Once she arrived, she was completely at ease,' says Sonia Berry. But for everybody else, inevitably, having the Queen in your midst is an honour, may be exciting, can be exhilarating, but, as experiences go, is rarely wholly comfortable. Sonia Berry says now, 'Looking back, perhaps the formality was a mistake, but it takes time to change.'

On her Accession, Elizabeth II was in no mood for change. Naturally shy, instinctively conservative, she was content to follow in her father's footsteps, to do her duty as he had done his. Her court had much of the character – and personnel – of his. Soon after her Coronation, her private secretary, Sir Alan Lascelles, who had been the late King's private secretary also, was succeeded by Sir Michael Adeane, who had joined the royal household in 1937, aged twenty-seven, as an assistant private secretary to George VI. Adeane, on his mother's side, was a grandson of Lord Stamfordham, assistant private secretary to Queen Victoria and influential private secretary to George V as Prince of Wales and King. Adeane had the traditional courtier's manner: he was effortlessly courteous, he had a nice sense of humour, he understood the ways of the world. Like his father (who was killed in action in 1914), he was an officer in the Coldstream Guards, and, while he was no radical, he was no fool either: he got a First in History at Cambridge.[122] For nineteen years, until 1972, he served the Queen with intelligence, quiet efficiency and complete devotion. He was cautious, he was careful, he was kindly: Her Majesty liked his style. It suited her own.

---

[122] In *Who's Who*, he listed his recreations as shooting and fishing (naturally) and his clubs as Brooks's and the Beefsteak (of course). I was still a teenager when I first met him and was much impressed. He seemed to me the epitome of courtliness: formal yet easy, and wholly unpatronising. (Perhaps he was accustomed to dealing with children. He once said, 'Because you happen to be in Whitehall terms the equivalent of a Permanent Under-Secretary, it is no use thinking you are a mandarin. One moment you may be writing to the Prime Minister. The next you are carrying a small boy's mac.') The humorist Basil Boothroyd (who was writing an authorised biography of Prince Philip at the time) liked to tell the story of the morning he encountered Adeane crossing the forecourt at Buckingham Palace. Boothroyd was arriving, Adeane was departing. Boothroyd paused to greet the Queen's private secretary. Pleasantries were exchanged. Courtesies were extended. The weather was discussed, the Queen's blooming health was touched on, the vigour and charm of the Queen Mother marvelled at, progress on Boothroyd's book reported – then Adeane threw in gently: 'If you'll forgive me, I must be on my way now. I've just heard that my house is on fire. I wouldn't mind, but as it's part of St James's Palace . . .'

As monarch, the Queen had role models: her father and grandfather. According to Martin Charteris, 'She took on the mantle of monarchy as to the manner born – which, of course, she was. Right from the start, she performed all her duties, not only conscientiously – never chafing against her lot – but with a quiet confidence that was moving to behold. Remember, she was not quite twenty-six at the start of her reign.' Dutifully, and thoroughly, she read through her 'boxes', absorbed Cabinet minutes, digested Foreign Office telegrams, signed state papers, met her prime minister, gave audiences to ambassadors, judges, generals, held meetings of the Privy Council, conducted investitures. Her husband was involved in none of this. As consort, the Duke of Edinburgh had no role models (Prince Albert died sixty years before Prince Philip was born) and – in a way – no role. As he put it to me, 'I had to find a way of supporting the Queen, without getting in the way.'

According to Patricia Mountbatten, Philip in the 1950s was 'a dynamo, an absolute dynamo – he was very like my father at the same age'. In her autobiography, Wallis Simpson described Dickie Mountbatten as she found him when they first met and Dickie was in his early thirties: '[He] bubbled with ideas on every conceivable subject – housing, relieving unemployment, new strategies of attack in polo, or how to cure the chronic maladies of the British Exchequer. The more baffling these problems, the more convinced Dickie was that he had a fundamental contribution to make and was determined to make it.' According to Mrs Simpson, the hyperactive Dickie 'bombarded' her lover, then Prince of Wales, 'with pamphlets, books, and clippings, all carefully annotated or underlined and all urgently commended to the Prince's attention'. Philip – equally bubbling with ideas and initiative – might have liked to 'bombard' the Queen, as his uncle had once 'bombarded' hers, but he chose not to. He knew there was no point. It did not occur to the Queen to involve her husband in affairs of state: it would not have been constitutionally appropriate, and Her Majesty, a firm believer in the value of precedent, tradition and continuity, has always been one for observing the proprieties.

Besides, as Prince Philip put it to me, her advisers made his position crystal clear. 'Keep out,' they said, 'you mustn't interfere with this.' Lord Brabourne, Patricia Mountbatten's husband, told me that, at the time, Philip found the traditional courtiers' hostility towards him 'intolerable and deeply frustrating'. Fifty years on, the Duke of Edinburgh simply shrugs and says to me: 'I had to fit in. I had to avoid getting at cross-purposes, usurping others' authority. In most cases that was no problem. I did my own thing.'

To get a flavour of Philip's 'own thing' turn to page 402 and scan the list of his 'involvements and offices', as supplied to me by his current secretary, Miles Hunt-Davis. It is a long list – and extraordinarily varied – and each line represents many hours, weeks and months of activity: meetings, minutes, briefings, speeches, arm-twisting, fundraising, travelling hither and yon. As you will see from the list, 1956 was an especially fruitful year. Philip was just thirty-five. As well as publishing a collection of speeches (his thoughts on competitive sport, science, technology, and the environment), he initiated the Commonwealth Study Conferences[123] that year, and, with Sam Hordern, founded the Royal Agricultural Society of the Commonwealth, and, with Kurt Hahn, founded the Duke of Edinburgh Award Scheme. The Award Scheme is arguably Philip's 'great achievement', both because of its impact and influence (the concept has spread to fifty countries; started from scratch in 1956, two and a half million young people have since taken part), and because the qualities the Award encourages – self-reliance, compassion, fitness, skill, enterprise, endeavour – are among those Philip values most.[124]

Some years ago, as I was making the smallest of small talk with the Queen at a drinks reception (where she wasn't drinking, or eating the nibbles, so nor was I: paying court is not easy), the subject of the National Playing Fields Association came up. The Queen is the charity's

[123] His own idea: three-week-long, high-powered international conferences, held every six years, and designed to take a big issue, examine it, worry it, look at it in depth and from different perspectives. The first conference, in 1956, focused on work and the changing demands of industrial society. In 1998, the conference was held in Canada and the theme was the impact of technology in a global 'infodustrial' society. The ninth conference was held in October 2003 in Australia and New Zealand. The theme was 'People First in the Global Century'. Because of a clash of commitments, Prince Philip could not attend: the Princess Royal went in his place.

[124] There are some 11,000 books on Prince Philip's library shelves, all carefully arranged and catalogued. The collection is both predictable and surprising: more than a thousand books on wildlife and conservation, six hundred books on matters equestrian (including two by HRH), 494 on sport, a complete run of cartoon annuals by Giles, more than two hundred volumes of poetry, 990 books on art. Not many novelists are represented on the Duke's shelves, but C. S. Forester is one of them. The heroes of the Hornblower stories exemplify the virtues Philip values – decency, daring, discretion, courtesy, comradeship, kindliness, loyalty, courage – and that the youth organisations he has headed (such as the Award Scheme and the Outward Bound Trust) are, in part, designed to foster.

patron, the Duke of Edinburgh its president. 'I don't know very much about the Playing Fields, I'm afraid,' Her Majesty said to me, with a slightly apologetic laugh. 'That's Prince Philip's department. He doesn't tell me much about it. He has his departments, I have mine.'

Inevitably, since the Queen's Accession, she and her husband have, to an extent, led separate, parallel lives. She is Head of State and does what heads of state must. (She is also Head of the Commonwealth, of course, and Head of the Church of England.) He is her consort and, as consort, dutifully, and with some style, does whatever is required. And, when not required, he does his own thing. She has her role, her duties, her enthusiasms, her friends. He has his obligations, his interests, his enthusiasms, his friends. Frequently, they overlap: often, they do not.

From the start of her reign (when the courtiers surrounding the young Queen were of a type, and it was not Philip's type[125]), while Elizabeth was required to exclude her husband from affairs of state, and content to do so (and ready, too, to take the established order's side instead of his in the matter of the name of the House of Windsor), she was ready – anxious, even – to allow him full sway on the home front, in their domestic and private life. Readily, she bowed to his wishes in the matter of her children's upbringing and education. (Prince Charles followed in his father's footsteps to Cheam School and to Gordonstoun – and was not at all happy, as we shall see.) She positively encouraged her husband to take on her late father's role and responsibilities in the active management of the royal estates.[126] Elizabeth wore the crown, but Philip wore the trousers.

In public, he walked one step behind her. In private, he treated his wife much as any strong-willed, independent-minded, intelligent, able and energetic naval husband of his temperament and generation might. He questioned her judgement, he called her 'a bloody fool', he swore at her and them when he tripped over a clutch of her corgis. Martin Charteris said to me, 'It sounds worse in the telling than it actually was.

---

[125] Mike Parker, Philip's private secretary until 1956, said to me, 'They were old school – Eton, Oxbridge, the Brigade of Guards – which Philip was not, and which I most definitely was not. I think he had the measure of them, but I'm not sure they had the measure of him.'

[126] See the list of the Prince's activities supplied to me by his office on page 406. It covers work on the houses and gardens at Windsor, Sandringham and Balmoral, ranging from the replanting of Queen Anne's Ride at Windsor to building log cabins at Sandringham to replacing the 'tin wing' at Birkhall. The Prince is proud of these achievements. They have given him satisfaction.

He can be grumpy. He is outspoken. He can be argumentative. But it's just his way. If she hadn't been Queen, you wouldn't have noticed.' But she was Queen and people did notice. Lord Mountbatten liked to tell the story of driving with the Queen and Prince Philip through Cowdray Park. Philip was at the wheel and driving far too fast. The Queen started drawing in her breath and flinching at the way her husband was driving. Philip turned to her and said, 'If you do that once more I shall put you out of the car.' When the hair-raising journey came to an end, Mountbatten asked the Queen why she hadn't protested. 'But you heard what he said,' replied the Queen. 'And he meant it.' Martin Charteris recalled an unhappy half-hour once in the Royal Yacht *Britannia*. 'I'm not going to come out of my cabin until he's in a better temper,' said Her Majesty. 'I'm going to sit here on my bed until he's better.'

Philip can be irascible – even with his wife. 'It means nothing,' Mike Parker insisted when I raised the subject with him. 'Philip is an outspoken kind of a guy. Everyone knows that. He might use colourful language talking privately with the Queen – for all I know, they might have the odd barney, as couples do – but he is devoted to Her Majesty, absolutely devoted, don't be in any doubt about that.' And, according to several reliable witnesses, as the years have gone by, the Queen has got increasingly better at holding her own with Prince Philip and, on occasion, giving as good as she gets. Martin Charteris smiled impishly when I tackled him on the matter. 'Have I heard Her Majesty say, "Oh, do shut up, Philip, you don't know what you're talking about"?' he asked, tapping his chin with his forefinger. 'Possibly,' he said. 'More than once?' I persisted. 'Perhaps.'

In public and on parade – and the Duke of Edinburgh is relentlessly on parade with Her Majesty: at the State Opening of Parliament, at the Cenotaph on Remembrance Sunday, at the distribution of the Royal Maundy, at the Queen's Birthday Parade, at Royal Ascot, at the Garter Ceremony, at the Thistle Service, at the Braemar Royal Highland Gathering, at garden parties and state banquets: the royal calendar is nothing if not predictable – towards his Sovereign, Prince Philip's manner and his manners are impeccable. Mike Parker said to me, 'From day one, he was clear that his duty was to support the Queen, first, second, third and last. That's what he's there for. That's what he does. And I don't believe he has failed in his duty. Ever.'

Together, the Queen and the Duke have undertaken many thousands of engagements within the United Kingdom and, overseas, have so far completed 253 visits to 128 different countries. Their travels have ranged from the Cocos Islands (5.4 square miles, with a population of 655) to the People's Republic of China (3.7 million square miles, with a population of 1.25 billion).[127]

At the beginning of 1956, the royal couple spent three weeks in Nigeria, where, shaded from the African sun by an elegant canopy designed in London by Norman Hartnell, their programme included a spectacular Durbar at Kadona and countless cheerful encounters with colourfully clad and broadly-beaming tribal chiefs. In Lagos, ten thousand masked 'tribal warriors' danced for them, and a crowd, conservatively estimated at a million-strong, chanted 'Our Queen! Our Queen!' with apparently heartfelt enthusiasm. (Within a decade Nigeria was a republic and soon after embroiled in a devastating civil war: the 'tribal warriors' turned tribal warriors.) In April of the same year, Nikita Khrushchev and Nikolai Bulganin, the new leaders of the Soviet Union, visited Britain, took tea with the Queen and Philip at Windsor Castle, and presented Her Majesty with a thoroughbred horse as a thirtieth birthday present. Khrushchev, General Secretary of the Soviet Communist Party, and once a farmhand, plumber and locksmith, had expected 'haughtiness' from a queen, but, to his surprise, found her 'completely unpretentious', 'the sort of woman you would be likely to meet walking along Gorky Street on a balmy summer afternoon'. In June, Queen and Duke paid a state visit to King Gustaf VI Adolf and Queen Louise of Sweden (Philip's aunt) and, in July, received a state visit from King Faisal of Iraq (no relation).

The Queen rarely travels abroad without the Duke[128], but the Duke frequently undertakes overseas assignments without Her Majesty. Between the beginning of 1952 and the end of 2003, on behalf of the United Kingdom, the Commonwealth and the range of causes he supports, he has taken part in 612 overseas visits to 141 different countries.

He set off on his single longest tour in October 1956. He was away for four months – 124 days to be precise. His travels took him to Australia, New Zealand, Ceylon, the Gambia, Antarctica, and the Falkland Islands. The tour was controversial. To an extent, it still is. In

---

[127] For a comprehensive list of state and Commonwealth visits, see p. 389.

[128] Her solo foreign forays are usually related to her interest in horse breeding. She has enjoyed private visits to stud farms in Normandy in France and to Kentucky in the United States, where her host has been William Farish, Texan racehorse owner and breeder and US ambassador to London, 2001–5.

1999, Channel Four screened a two-part television documentary, produced by an independent company, Seven Sisters Productions, entitled *The Real Prince Philip* and designed to reveal just that. The Prince and his office cooperated with the film-makers, giving the programmes' researchers a long list of names to contact (including mine) in the hope that – in the words of Prince Philip's private secretary, Miles Hunt-Davis – 'they would be able to produce a fair and honest portrayal of His Royal Highness'. In the event, the Prince and his team were disappointed – 'extremely disappointed' – by the result. Miles Hunt-Davis took particular exception to the second programme and wrote to the film's producers to say so:

> Your portrayal of the 1956/57 World Tour in *Britannia* in Programme 2 was marred, firstly by implying that the journey was undertaken in order to get away from The Queen and the Court and secondly that it was a spree. This is totally wrong. The journey was planned to allow His Royal Highness to open the Olympic Games in Melbourne and the use of *Britannia* was specifically planned to enable Prince Philip to visit as many of the remote British Dependent Islands as possible. Most of these were only accessible by sea and had never before been visited by a Member of the Royal Family. The result of this trip was that Prince Philip had visited more of the then British Empire than any other member of the Royal Family.

The timing of the tour was unfortunate. In July 1956, on the fourth anniversary of his overthrow of King Farouk, President Gamal Abdel Nasser of Egypt announced that he was nationalising the Anglo-French-controlled Suez Canal Company, declaring that if the imperialist powers did not like it they could 'choke to death on their fury'. In August, while she was attending a race meeting at Goodwood, the Queen was required to approve a proclamation, to be read out in the House of Commons that very afternoon, ordering twenty thousand army reservists to be called up for service in the Canal zone. In October, as the Duke of Edinburgh, Mike Parker and their party in *Britannia* were sailing east of Trincomalee, on the north-east coast of Ceylon, one of the world's outstanding natural harbours, in the Middle East British and French bombs – and paratroops – were dropping on to Egypt. In the event of war, *Britannia* was designated a hospital ship. There was momentary uncertainty about whether or not the tour could proceed.

It did. Within days, international uproar and United States' opposition to the Anglo-French action in Egypt brought about a cease-fire. The crisis was resolved. Anti-British riots in Singapore meant abandoning a proposed stopover at the south end of the Malay peninsula, but, other than that, the royal itinerary was unaffected. On 22 November, in Melbourne, as planned, the Duke of Edinburgh formally opened the sixteenth Olympic Games, the first to be held south of the equator.

The length of the tour was unusual, but, as Prince Philip points out, the scope of the tour was ambitious. 'We were reaching parts of the Commonwealth that, in some cases, had never before been visited by a member of the Royal Family. And they seemed quite pleased to see us.' To some in 1957 (and, perhaps, to many in 2004), for a young husband and father to be separated from his wife and family for four months may seem out of the ordinary, but to a naval officer – especially one with experience of war – a sixteen-week tour of duty is not so remarkable. Philip regarded the tour of 1956/57 as a duty to be done and a job worth doing. The Queen agreed and encouraged him to go. As she said in her Christmas message that year: 'If my husband cannot be at home on Christmas Day, I could not wish for a better reason than he should be travelling in other parts of the Commonwealth.'

Almost half a century later, it infuriates His Royal Highness (and Her Majesty) that this arduous tour is still being portrayed as something of a princely 'jolly' and being used – by the Channel Four film-makers among others, including those now preparing obituaries for newspapers and television – as the platform from which to launch a raft of what Miles Hunt-Davis calls 'innuendoes about Prince Philip's private life which [are], in my view, overstated and unbalanced'.

Back at the beginning of 1957, what first set the rumour-mill a-grinding – and allowed 'innuendo' to be translated from a whisper behind the hand to a headline on the front page – was really nothing to do with Prince Philip at all. It was a classic case of 'guilt by association'. Mike Parker was being sued for divorce by Eileen, his wife of fourteen years. 'We should never have got married in the first place,' Parker said to me. 'It was a wartime romance, exciting at the time, but we weren't suited long-term. And Eileen wasn't suited to royal life either.' She called her memoirs *Step Aside for Royalty*. 'I didn't behave that well,' admitted Parker. 'It was a helluva mess.' And a mess made public when news of Mrs Parker's petition for divorce was published in February 1957, just as *Britannia* – with Parker and his boss on board – was cruising calmly towards Gibraltar on the final leg of the world tour.

'When we reached the Rock,' said Parker, 'the world's press was waiting. It was not a pretty sight.'[129]

Parker told me, 'I decided to get back to London as soon as possible. We had been on this remarkable voyage, testing the newly-commissioned *Britannia*, visiting Ascension Island, Tristan da Cunha and goodness knows where, but all that was instantly forgotten. I'd become the story – and a liability to Philip.' Surrounded by rapacious hacks ('Literally – I think they bought every other seat on the plane'), Parker, unusually tight-lipped, and accompanied by his solicitor, flew from Gibraltar to London. At Heathrow airport he found yet more of the world's press awaiting him – together, surprisingly, with the habitually tight-lipped Commander Richard Colville, the Queen's press secretary, who had motored down from London, not to give the Duke of Edinburgh's friend and secretary a helping hand, but to say to him this, and nothing more: 'Hello Parker, I've just come to let you know that from now on, you're on your own.' (Colville made this excursion to Heathrow on his own initiative. Parker was not 'on his own' as far as the Queen and the Duke were concerned. 'The Duke saw me off at the airport in Gibraltar and the Queen was wonderful throughout,' Mike Parker told me. 'She regarded a divorce as a sadness, not a hanging offence. Her prime minister at the time was a divorcee, after all.[130] The Queen telephoned me and could not have been more sympathetic.' Initially, Parker – and his employer – hoped he might be able to weather the storm. 'But pretty damn quickly I could see it wasn't going to be possible. It was going to take a year for my divorce to come through. I had to resign. I had no choice.' The Queen was sorry to see him go and appointed him a Commander of the Royal Victorian Order in recognition of his years of loyal service to her husband.)

---

[129] At a later date, Prince Philip, visiting Gibraltar, gazed up at the Rock, covered with the limestone promontory's celebrated monkeys, and saw a posse of newsmen and photographers awaiting his arrival. 'Which are the monkeys?' he asked. Philip and Parker shared a sense of humour. One year, Commander Parker listed his 'recreations' in *Who's Who* as follows: 'enjoying young people, including himself, de-pomping, promoting style in anything, sailing in the Pacific and through red tape and tennis anyone?' He told me his address in Queensland was 'Banana Creek – great address, isn't it?'

[130] In fact, Sir Anthony Eden, Prime Minister since April 1955, had resigned on grounds of ill health on 9 January 1957. He was married first to Beatrice Beckett in 1923, divorced in 1950, and, in 1952, married Clarissa Spencer Churchill who said, famously, of the autumn of 1956: 'For the past few weeks I have really felt as if the Suez Canal was flowing through my drawing room.'

Parker flew to London, but Philip remained on board *Britannia*. Since it was now the beginning of February and he had been away from hearth and home since mid-October, the *Sunday Pictorial*, for one, wanted to know why. The Royal Family, the newspaper reminded its readers, 'is loved and envied throughout the world because it *is* a family.' Why wasn't Philip at home with the kiddies? Anne was six and Charles was eight. 'How can you expect youngsters to understand that Daddy is so near yet cannot come home?'

The reason that Philip remained where he was was simple. It was convenient. And he was not about to dance to the *Sunday Pictorial*'s tune. As planned many months before, the Queen was scheduled to pay a state visit to President Craveiro Lopes of Portugal between 18 and 21 February and Philip was due to join her. He did. 'But,' as they sigh wearily at Buckingham Palace to this day, 'why let the boring facts get in the way of the salacious innuendoes?' Fairly or unfairly, the collapse of the Parker marriage combined with Philip's prolonged separation from his wife and children created a flood of speculation – and eventually the dam burst. The *Baltimore Sun* – the premier newspaper of Wallis Simpson's home town – broke 'the story', with the paper's London correspondent reporting that the British capital was awash with rumour that the Duke of Edinburgh was romantically involved with an unnamed woman whom he met on a regular basis in the West End apartment of a society photographer. 'Report Queen, Duke in Rift Over Party Girl' ran the headline.

According to Mike Parker, 'The Duke was incandescent. He was very, very angry. And deeply hurt. There was no truth in the story whatsoever.' The Queen was equally dismayed, and, surprisingly (given her instinct to follow precedent and the unwritten rule that royalty never answers back), authorised the normally uncommunicative Commander Colville to issue an official and complete denial: 'It is quite untrue that there is any rift between the Queen and the Duke.' Having received the Palace's reassurance, *The Times*, *Daily Telegraph*, *Mail* and *Sketch* did the decent thing and ignored the story altogether: if it wasn't true it wasn't to be reported. (Those were the days!) The *Daily Express*, *Mirror* and *Herald* were less circumspect, however, and splashed the Palace denial on their front pages. On 11 February, from New York, for the *Manchester Guardian*, Alistair Cooke reported to his readers, no doubt accurately: 'Not since the first rumours of a romance between the former King Edward VIII and the then Mrs Simpson have Americans gobbled up the

London dispatches so avidly.' Tongues were wagging, all over the world.[131]

The Queen and the Duke did their best to rise above it. They were reunited at Lisbon's military airport. The scene was a memorable one, and when the movie comes to be made is sure to feature. During part of the tour, Philip had grown a full set of naval whiskers. Photographs of the bearded traveller had found their way back to London. When Philip, now clean-shaven in anticipation of the state visit to Portugal, bounded up the steps of the Queen's plane in Lisbon, he was greeted by an extraordinary sight: his wife and her entire entourage, sitting in their seats, all sporting false ginger beards! (This is a family that is fond of practical jokes, remember.) Minutes later, when the royal couple emerged from the plane, both were beaming, and an eagle-eyed reporter, with a sentimental streak, was sure he spotted a tell-tale smudge of lipstick on the Duke's cheek.

Her Majesty decided to deal with the rumour-mongers' cheek as well. In 1947, when Philip became a naturalised British subject, he ceased to be a prince of Greece and, technically at least, a 'prince' of any kind at all. On his wedding day, 20 November 1947, George VI created him Baron Greenwich of Greenwich, Earl of Merioneth and Duke of Edinburgh. The late King had made his son-in-law a Royal Highness, but not a prince. In March 1955, Sir Winston Churchill, a month before his retirement as Prime Minister, proposed to the Queen, 'in informal conversation', that she might like to consider making her husband 'a prince of the United Kingdom'. She agreed, but, at the time, did nothing about it. Two years later, in February 1957, Harold Macmillan, a month after his appointment as Prime Minister, put forward the same proposal. Her Majesty warmly welcomed the suggestion and, this time, took action. On 22 February, the day following their return from the state visit to Portugal, Queen Elizabeth II announced that, henceforward, His Royal Highness the Duke of Edinburgh would carry 'the style and dignity of a prince of the United Kingdom'. This was not merely 'in recognition of the great services

---

[131] This was the week, incidentally, when Bill Haley and his Comets (with record sales of twenty-two million) landed in London for the first time. Haley, twenty-nine, told the British press, 'Everyone wants to get into the act.' He was referring to rock and roll rather than royal rumour-mongering, but the media, anxious to find a royal angle to any story wherever possible, declared that 'See you later, alligator / In a while, crocodile', catchphrases from one of Haley's hit songs, had now become 'popular greetings within Princess Margaret's set'.

which His Royal Highness has provided to the country', but also – and pointedly – 'of his unique contribution to the life of the Commonwealth, culminating in the tour which he has just concluded'. And that should have been the end of that.

But it wasn't. The rumours rumbled on. They rumble still. I have seen a number of the newspaper obituaries already prepared in anticipation of the Duke's death, and, for the BBC, ITN and Sky News, among others, I have recorded contributions to assorted post-mortem tributes currently in preparation. Each of them, without exception, makes reference to Prince Philip's life as 'a ladies' man'. In the various print and television obituaries I have seen, no specific allegations are made, but there is plenty of what the Prince's private secretary calls 'fact obscured by innuendo'. By dint of knowing winks and nudges, and the use of apparently telling photographs, the distinct impression is left that Philip was a man who, publicly, supported the Queen through thick and thin, but at the same time, albeit discreetly, managed to play the field.

Prince Philip is sensitive to this. I know because I have discussed it with him. Publicly, he brushes it off. Privately, he broods. He knows what people say. He told me that, a few years ago, an interviewer (from a notionally respectable broadsheet weekend magazine) had informed him that it was commonly believed – and would he care to confirm this or deny it? – a) that he had several illegitimate children[132], b) that his second son was fathered by someone else, and c) that he had had a homosexual relationship with Valéry Giscard d'Estaing, the former President of France! (At this juncture, His Royal Highness would be using two or possibly three exclamation marks!!) You might think that, after all these years in the public eye, and knowing how people just love to gossip, and seeing the way the press is nowadays (and not only the tabloids), he could shrug his shoulders and laugh it off. Well, to an extent he does. But his laughter is weary and tinged with frustration and anger. These stories damage his reputation, chip away at it insidiously. He does not like them. He should not listen to them, of course – we know that! – but he does. He is more sensitive, more vulnerable, than sometimes he seems. These stories hurt him. And they hurt the Queen.

Once, he showed me a photocopy he had made of ten pages from an

---

[132] In 1995, a German newspaper reported that Prince Philip had twenty-four illegitimate children and that this had been confirmed by Buckingham Palace. It transpired that the newspaper had misinterpreted the word 'godchildren'.

Australian magazine, *Woman's Day*, that on its front page promised readers a full exposé of 'Prince Philip's torrid sex life' with 'famous lovers named'. Inside – under the banner headline: 'Philip's Outrageous Affairs' – Australian readers were offered a 'sizzling extract' from a book 'they daren't publish in Britain'. The book's author, Nicholas Davies, purported to reveal 'a shocking world of royal adultery, passion and betrayal' and stated – as fact, not surmise – that the Duke of Edinburgh's liaisons with his cousin, Princess Alexandra, with the film star Merle Oberon, and with the Duchess of York's mother, Susan Barrantes (among others!) were the reason 'why the Queen banned her husband from her bed.'

It's the most terrible tosh, but it's out there, in print, between hard covers, and available to one and all. And some of those who read it may believe it. And those who don't believe it all may think, 'Well, there's no smoke without fire . . .' (The book itself is not published in the UK, but it is available here, via the internet, and, internationally, it has enjoyed wide circulation. In the United States, according to *Publishers Weekly*, the initial print-run was fifty thousand copies.) What can Philip do about it? He knows his only defence would be to sue for libel, but that is a ponderous and expensive business and might involve him in having to give evidence – and would, in any event, provide further, valuable, publicity for the book. What is more, the problem for any individual suing for libel in such a case is that they have to specify which are the statements claimed to be libellous. This means that if any statement is not complained about, it could be taken as being true!!

What is the truth? Why do we need to know? Is it any of our business? As the great Cervantes puts it in *Don Quixote*: 'Suppose they were lovers, what's that to me? Plenty of people expect to find bacon where there's not so much as a hook to hang it on.' And surely, as Dr Johnson insists, 'A man is to have part of his life to himself'? Well, yes. And no. Prince Philip is in a special position. He is the Queen's consort, and Her Majesty is Supreme Governor of the Church of England. At her Coronation, he knelt before her, placed his hands between hers, and vowed, 'I, Philip, Duke of Edinburgh, do become your liege man of life and limb, and of earthly worship; and faith and truth will I bear unto you . . .' Privately, Prince Philip has been critical of the Prince of Wales, disapproving of his son's adultery with Camilla Parker Bowles. Publicly, Prince Philip is a role model – especially to the young and those in the armed services. He is founder of the Duke of Edinburgh Award Scheme and patron of the Outward Bound Trust.

He is a Colonel or Colonel-in-Chief, Field Marshal, Admiral and Air Commodore forty-two times over. He takes these appointments seriously. Honour, duty and example count with him. Is he a hypocrite? Is he a philanderer?

I think we can take it as read that the Queen has been faithful throughout her married life. There are those who persist in believing that Prince Andrew's natural father was the Queen's racing manager, Henry Porchester, 'Porchey', 7th Earl of Carnarvon, suggesting the conception occurred at some point between 20 January and 30 April 1959 when Philip was away on another of his long sea voyages in *Britannia*. Never mind that the dates don't stack up (Andrew was born on 19 February 1960, a happy by-product of the Queen and Philip's post-*Britannia* reunion): the idea of the Queen committing adultery is simply preposterous. I asked Geordie, 8th Earl of Carnarvon, if his father and Her Majesty knew of the rumour and what they made of it. Were they amused? 'They knew all about it,' Geordie told me, 'and were not in the least amused. They were angry. My father was very annoyed by it, and embarrassed. It was dreadful.' The Queen and Porchey were best friends. They had known each other all their adult lives: they shared a passion for racehorses and a sense of humour. They may even have been a little in love – in the nicest possible way – but the idea of a romance between them is risible. 'Both my parents were friends of the Queen and Prince Philip,' Geordie told me. 'Obviously my father saw a lot of the Queen throughout the year, but in October he used to invite them to Highclere [the Carnarvon family estate, near Newbury in Berkshire] for a shooting weekend – partridge shooting. Prince Philip sometimes came, not always. He's an extremely good shot. And the Queen, of course, has always been good at working dogs. On Saturday night, my mother would do dinner, the best of English country house cooking, using old recipes of my great-grandmother's. And on Sunday my father and the Queen might walk round the stables or visit Highclere stud. The Queen adored going on the gallops early in the evening. It was just a perfect, relaxing weekend. My father died in 2001, but last year [2003] we reinstated the weekend, and the Queen came again, and Prince Philip, too. Without my father it couldn't be quite the same, but it was very jolly.'

In the United Kingdom, as I write, there are two 'republican movements' (self-styled) which have taken to the world wide web to demand DNA testing to establish the true paternity of not one but two of the Queen's children. Republic.org.uk and Throneout.freeserve.co.uk, not content with suggesting that Porchey fathered Prince Andrew, also allege that the Queen's youngest child, Prince Edward, born in 1964, was the product of the union between Her Majesty and the Deputy Master of her Household, Patrick, 7th Baron Plunket. Patrick Plunket was a delightful individual, good-looking and good-humoured, born in 1923, so only three years older than the Queen, and more like a brother than a lover. His parents were 'characters'[133] and great friends of Elizabeth's parents, dating back to the days when they were still the Yorks. In 1938, when Patrick was not yet fifteen, they were both killed in a plane crash on their way to a party William Randolph Hearst was giving in their honour in California. Educated at Eton and Cambridge, Patrick joined the Irish Guards, rose to the rank of lieutenant colonel and became an equerry to George VI in 1948. He had charm and taste (he was a trustee of the Wallace Collection and the National Art Collections Fund), and, as the Queen's Deputy Master of the Household from 1954 until his early death from cancer in 1975, masterminded the Queen's official entertaining with style and devotion. Martin Charteris told me, 'Patrick Plunket's death was a real loss to the Queen, a personal loss. He was a life-long courtier, but he wasn't a stuffed shirt. He was great fun. He had a wonderful flair for entertaining, of course, but he was also very good at human relations. He was very easy with the Queen and she was very relaxed with him. He treated her almost as an equal, certainly as a friend. If you wanted to say something awkward or difficult to Her Majesty, you could do it through Patrick. When he died a bright light went out in her life.' The Queen mourned the loss of Patrick Plunket: he was a true friend, but he was not the father of Prince Edward. Lord Plunket was a confirmed bachelor: in many ways, that was part of his attraction.

[133] Terence 'Teddy' Plunket, 6th Baron, was an Anglo-Irish charmer (of Wilton Crescent, SW1, and Old Connaught House, Bray, County Wicklow) who, in 1922, married Dorothé, a petite beauty, and noted dancer. Dorothé's mother was Fannie Ward, actress and protégée of Cecil B. de Mille. Officially, her father was Joseph 'Diamond Joe' Lewis (who had made a fortune in South Africa in the diamond rush), but, biologically, it seems she was fathered by Lord Londonderry. When Dorothé married Teddy Plunket, she was the widow of Captain Jack Barnato, a First World War air ace (and son of 'Babe' Barnato, another South African diamond king) who died in the great influenza epidemic of 1918. They had three sons. When the Plunkets were killed in 1938, Queen Elizabeth wrote to Lady Londonderry: 'They both gave so much happiness to so many people . . . Those dear little boys make one's heart *ache*.'

Given her nature and her upbringing, you would expect the Queen to be wholly faithful to her marriage vows. Her role models, after all, were her mother and father and her grandparents, George V and Queen Mary. There were stories about George V when he was a young Duke of York – he was rumoured to already have a wife and three children at the time of his engagement to Mary of Teck[134] – and George VI, as a young Duke of York, was briefly led astray by his older brother, the Prince of Wales, but, as husbands, George V and George VI were continent and loyal, and, as wives, Queen Mary and Queen Elizabeth were, without doubt, above reproach. Lilibet, as a child and adolescent, had a stable and happy home-life and the example of parents who were as devoted and loving to their children as they were to one another. The black sheep of the family was the Duke of Windsor: his love-life as Prince of Wales had been chequered: his married life, living in exile with a double divorcée, was not a bed of roses. Elizabeth II is not judgemental – Prince Philip says his wife's most singular virtue is her tolerance – but she is observant. Her younger sister's love-life may have been more colourful than her own – it was certainly more varied and adventurous – but the Queen will have noticed that Princess Margaret's romantic relationships, and her marriage to Tony Snowdon, while they brought her undoubted 'highs', did not provide her with lasting happiness.

Who were Prince Philip's role models? What is the pattern – the template – within his immediate family? His royal grandfather, King George I of Greece, had a good marriage, but apparently allowed himself some light romantic relaxation during his annual holiday (without the Queen) in the French spa town of Aix-les-Bains. Philip's uncle, King Constantine I of Greece (King George's eldest son), had a less happy

---

[134] 'I say, May,' he told his fiancée in the spring of 1893, 'we can't get married after all. I hear I have got a wife and three children . . .' In the original rumour the 'wife' was American and living in Plymouth. 'Why there I wonder?' pondered the Prince. At first, he found the story 'really very amusing'. The rumour rumbled on and gathered momentum. When, eventually, it appeared in print, the year was 1910, the Duke of York was King, and the charge was specific. E. F. Mylius, in an article headed 'Sanctified Bigamy', published in a republican paper in Paris and sent to every British MP, alleged that in 1890, in Malta, the future King had married an admiral's daughter who bore him several children: 'Our very Christian King and Defender of the Faith has a plurality of wives just like any Mohammedan Sultan.' His Majesty found this less amusing and decided to nail the lie. The Crown issued libel proceedings and Mylius was sentenced to twelve months' imprisonment.

marriage, holiday dalliances similar to those his father enjoyed, and, at the climax of the Balkan war in 1912/13, caused consternation at home and a scandal at court by conducting an almost open affair during his wife Sophie's sixth and final pregnancy. Philip's father, Constantine's younger brother, Andrea, was not a philanderer, but he was attractive to women, and, as we have seen, following his separation from Princess Alice in the 1930s, eventually settled with a lady-friend in the South of France. As a young man, Prince Philip's maternal grandfather, Louis of Battenberg, was a self-confessed Lothario. His memoirs of his bachelor days included a page marked '*NOT FOR MY DAUGHTERS*'. So lively was his love-life, and so notorious, that Queen Victoria, fearing that he might have been contemplating marriage with her youngest daughter, Princess Beatrice, instructed the Admiralty to send him abroad – and keep him there. In due course he made a good marriage to Queen Victoria's granddaughter, Princess Victoria, and had four children: Princess Alice, Prince Philip's mother; Princess Louise, Prince Philip's aunt; and George and Louis, Prince Philip's uncles.

Georgie, 2nd Marquess of Milford Haven, and his wife, Nada de Torby, were a charismatic couple. In the 1930s, Georgie acted as Philip's guardian. Philip stayed with Georgie and Nada during the school holidays. They were two people of considerable personal charm, but their marriage was not conventional. Nada had a reputation as a bisexual and Georgie as a collector of pornography. Louis Mountbatten, 'Dickie', and his wife, Edwina Ashley, were a charismatic couple, too – and charming also. And glamorous, rich, restless and achieving as well. In its imperfect way, their marriage was a good one, though, again, not unduly constrained by the letter of their wedding vows.

'Edwina and I spent all our married lives getting into other people's beds,' Mountbatten once confessed to a friend. Philip Ziegler, Mountbatten's official biographer, while accepting that Edwina was, in every sense, 'a goer', doubts that Mountbatten was promiscuous. He conducted two protracted love affairs outside his marriage, but, according to Ziegler, 'though he liked to imagine himself a sexual athlete, he seems in fact only to have had slight enthusiasm for the sport.' Mountbatten's daughter, Patricia, told me she concurred with Ziegler's conclusion that her father 'loved the company of women, sought their affection and had an almost irresistible urge to use them as confidantes', but that his real energy – his colossal life-force – was channelled into his working life: 'If asked to choose between seduction by the most desirable of houris and a conversation about service matters with a person of influence, he would unfailingly have chosen the latter. Never would he have sacrificed his career for lust.'[135]

In May 1945, as the Second World War reached its climax in Europe, Mountbatten was Supreme Allied Commander in South East Asia. The professional challenges he faced were formidable. On 8 May he confided to his daughter, Patricia: 'I do feel the need of opening my heart to a woman and not another man when I'm worried.' Now and again, though not very seriously, he had contemplated a divorce, simply to give Edwina her freedom (he was extraordinarily understanding and tolerant of his wife's passionate commitment to other men), but, that spring, when Edwina's current lover suddenly announced his engagement to another woman, it seems the Mountbattens decided to make a concerted effort to clear the air and come to a mutual understanding. On 7 May Dickie wrote to Edwina: 'I am so glad that you felt as happy as I did about our new-found relationship. I have always wanted to have you as my principal confidante and friend, but as long as A. was yours – it made it literally impossible for me. I hope you don't mind about my mentioning about my girl-friends – it was only to show you that they have never meant to me what A. meant to you, and so can never come between us, provided you no longer make difficulties about my seeing them, within reason, as you were apt to do in the old days!!'

Is Prince Philip like his uncle? Or his father? Or his grandfather? 'Men,' says my wife, 'they're all the same', but, in truth, they are different, aren't they? Some men find fidelity impossible; others find it hugely rewarding. Margaret Thatcher told me that President Reagan once told her that his single-minded devotion to his wife, Nancy, had given him 'strength and freedom'.[136] President Clinton's

---

[135] Ziegler also concludes that there is no evidence whatsoever to suggest that Mountbatten was homosexual. He had a number of homosexual friends, like Noël Coward, but, despite a raft of rumours, no homosexual life himself. A gay friend of mine introduced me to him, at the Garrick Club in London one night in the 1970s. Because Mountbatten happened to be with Sir Richard Attenborough that evening, my friend exclaimed, 'Ah, the two Dickies together at last!' Mountbatten appeared amused. He put his hand on my shoulder and kept it there, but only, I think, because he was old and I was young and he liked the company of young people. My friend took me on for a nightcap to a gay club nearby called 'Heaven'. Lord Mountbatten did not join us.

[136] In 1971, Reagan wrote a letter of advice to his son, Michael, who was twenty-six and about to be married: 'You have entered into the most meaningful relationship there is

marriage, by contrast, seems to have enjoyed strength and freedom of a different sort. Some men of distinction, leading public lives, seem to me to take extraordinary risks with their own reputations – and with their marriages. Clinton is a spectacular example: he risked impeachment for lust. John Major is another. When Major's illicit affair with a fellow MP was revealed, he said he had 'long feared' it would be made public and it was 'the one event in my life of which I am most ashamed'. Lord Jenkins of Hillhead, another high-achieving politician, another happily married man, told me that he had enjoyed a number of affairs while holding office, adding, emphatically, and with the broadest of grins, 'I've done nothing of which I'm ashamed.'

Decent men do have affairs and sustain successful marriages. I happen to be writing this on the day of the funeral of the 11th Duke of Devonshire. Andrew Cavendish was a quintessential English gentleman: effortlessly courteous, urbane, tolerant, good-humoured, self-deprecating, gently eccentric. For sixty-three years he was married to Debo, the youngest of the celebrated Mitford sisters. 'She is on the bossy side,' he told me, 'but I like that in a girl.' He acknowledged a weakness for 'fast women and slow horses'. The degree of his soft-spot for the ladies was exposed in 1985 when three blank cheques were stolen from his house in Mayfair. At the trial following the theft, his former butler gave evidence about the duke's habit of handing out cheques to ladies who came to call. When the judge asked him if the ladies were young, middle-aged or elderly, the duke was forced to admit that they tended to be young, and that he was on holiday with one of them at the time that the robbery occurred. The duchess was apparently unperturbed by this revelation.

in all human life. It can be whatever you decide to make it. Some men feel their masculinity can only be proven if they play out in their own life all the locker-room stories, smugly confident that what a wife doesn't know won't hurt her. The truth is, somehow, way down inside, without her ever finding lipstick on the collar or catching a man in the flimsy excuse of where he was till 3 a.m., a wife does know, and with that knowing, some of the magic of this relationship disappears . . . Any man can find a twerp here and there who will go along with cheating, and it doesn't take all that much manhood. It does take quite a man to remain attractive and to be loved by a woman who has heard him snore, seen him unshaven, tended him while he was sick and washed his dirty underwear. Do that and keep her still feeling a warm glow and you will know some very beautiful music.'

The duke confessed to me that he feared it might cost him the Garter. It didn't.[137]

The Order of the Garter, of course, is the most senior and the oldest British Order of Chivalry and was founded by Edward III in 1348. The origin of the emblem of the Order, a blue and gold garter worn just below the Knight's left knee, is obscure. Tradition says it was inspired by an incident which occurred while the young King, fresh from his triumph against the French at Crécy and celebrating the capture of Calais, danced at court with Joan, Countess of Salisbury. As King and countess danced, the lady's garter fell to the floor: the King retrieved the garter and tied it to his own leg. The courtiers watching the scene were apparently amused, but the King admonished them with the words, '*Honi soit qui mal y pense*' – 'Shame on him who thinks evil of this.' The phrase has been the motto of the Order ever since.[138] The Duke of Edinburgh has been a Knight of the Garter since 1947. Should we be ashamed of giving time and attention to the innuendoes about his private life?

On the record His Royal Highness is not about to dignify tittle-tattle with comment of any kind. When the journalist from the Sunday broadsheet suggested to him that he might have a raft of illegitimate children and have enjoyed a liaison with the President of France, he sat impassively, gazing steadfastly into the middle distance, incensed but silent. Privately, he will say, 'How could I? I've had a detective in my company, night and day, since 1947.' He points out that he is accompanied everywhere he goes, that his face is not entirely unknown,

[137] He was appointed a Knight of the Garter in 1996, aged seventy-six. He told me it gave him 'real joy every hour of every day': 'I know I don't deserve it, but it is our oldest order of chivalry and I take the idea of English chivalry seriously. It's important.' He also told me: 'English girls are the loveliest in the world and an Englishman should marry an Englishwoman, without a doubt. As to a dalliance? Well, the French have their strengths and the Italians are very agreeable, but if you want my advice stick to English women. They know the rules.'

[138] Less romantic historians reckon it is more likely that the Order was inspired by the strap used to attach pieces of armour, and that the motto referred to critics of Edward's claim to the throne of France. For those who want to learn more on the subject, I recommend *Royal Orders: The Honours and the Honoured* by Hugo Vickers, 1994. Hugo gave me my copy of his book on a memorable morning in 2000 when, for a TV documentary I was making on the honours system, we visited Spink, suppliers of medals and orders since 1666, and tried on a variety of decorations. The one I would have liked to take home was the Ugandan VC. Spink, as I recall, had created just six of these, at the behest of Idi Amin, when he was President of Uganda. Only one was ever awarded – by Amin to Amin.

and that, over five decades and on three continents, reporters have been trying to dig up some dirt on him that will stick and, thus far, have come up with bugger all!

Mike Parker told me, 'Philip has been one hundred per cent faithful to the Queen. No ifs, no buts. Take it from me, I know.' Lord Charteris said, 'I am aware what people say, and have said for years, but I know of no evidence of any kind, no evidence at all, and, if there were any, I rather think I would.' Geoff Williams, Prince Philip's former pilot, who accompanied his boss to fairly faraway places, put it even more succinctly: 'I have no information that would make two lines in the *Sun.*' And yet the murmuring goes on. 'When I see the tabloids,' Prince Philip once sighed to Patricia Mountbatten, 'I think I might as well have done it.'

Well, has he or hasn't he?

Countess Mountbatten is in no doubt. 'He has been completely faithful to the Queen,' she said to me. 'I'm sure of it, completely and utterly sure.' Just as her father, Lord Mountbatten, would never – in his biographer's phrase – 'sacrifice his career for lust', so her cousin, Prince Philip, would never betray the Queen for a mere roll in the hay. 'Supporting the Queen has been his life,' Countess Mountbatten reminded me. 'He wouldn't endanger his reputation or betray her trust. How could she retaliate? He simply would not allow himself to humiliate her in that way. He wouldn't risk it. He wouldn't want to. He is bound to the Queen by duty – and by love.' But when I raised the issue with Margaret Rhodes, she was less certain. 'I don't know,' she said to me, brow furrowed, staring into her coffee cup, 'I just don't know.' Perhaps, if she reads on, she will find out. I am going to try to nail the issue once and for all.

Buckingham Palace first put the matter of the royal marriage into the public domain in February 1957, with Commander Colville's question-begging official statement flatly denying 'any rift between the Queen and the Duke'. As we have just seen, what prompted the unfortunate statement was the torrent of speculation unleashed by the *Baltimore Sun*'s story that London was awash with 'whispers' that 'the Duke of Edinburgh had more than a passing interest in an unnamed woman and was meeting her regularly in the apartment of a court photographer'. The 'court photographer', of course, was Baron, Philip's friend, who would, in fact, have been with the Duke, and Mike Parker and company, in *Britannia* on the 1956/57 world tour, as 'official photographer', had he not gone into hospital for a hip operation at the beginning of

September 1956 and died unexpectedly on the operating table, aged only forty-nine.[139] Almost all the lurid 'stories' about Philip, from the late 1940s through the 1950s, revolve in some way around Baron and his 'set'.

Baron Henry Stirling Nahum – known to all as 'Baron': 'Lordly by name and lordly by nature' said one obituary – was born in 1907. His family were Italian Jews from Tripoli who settled in Manchester and made a success in the Lancashire cotton trade. Baron and his twin brother, Jack, came to London at the turn of the 1930s and cut a dash: Baron as a society photographer, Jack as a barrister. According to Robin Dalton, the film producer, who knew Baron well ('he was one of my dearest friends; he gave me away at my wedding; was godfather to my daughter; we spoke every day on the telephone until his death'), his success was due to 'his talent, his unique and lovable personality, and his connections': 'In the late 1920s he and Dickie Mountbatten had both been in love with a fascinating Frenchwoman, Yola Letellier[140], and had met at her feet in Paris. They remained friends. In time, Uncle Dickie introduced Baron to his nephew Philip – I think it was when Baron was taking pictures of the Mountbattens at Broadlands – and then Philip introduced Baron to David [Milford Haven] and me. David and I were living together in a flat in the King's Road. It cost £8 per week. We paid half each.'

Robin Dalton, in her *Incidental Memoir*, acknowledges that Baron 'was reputed to be at the centre of a very disreputable world indeed'. 'With me,' she says, 'he was a loving and gentle friend,' but she admits 'one heard lurid tales of orgies.' Robin and Baron became proper friends when 'David had gone skiing for two weeks and asked Baron to look after me.' Meeting 'Baron's set' (or 'Baron's Court' as it was sometimes known) opened up what Robin Dalton, in her *Memoir*,

---

[139] Needing a replacement photographer for the tour, Mike Parker went round to Baron's studio to see if one of his assistants might be suitable. He met Tony Armstrong-Jones, then twenty-six, but decided 'the young man was far too bohemian' to join the royal party. Within four years, Armstrong-Jones had joined the Royal Family, marrying Princess Margaret and becoming the Earl of Snowdon. He said to me recently, 'I always feel so sorry for those people from Bohemia.'

[140] She does sound intriguing. She was married to a hotelier, Henri Letellier, who was also the Mayor of Deauville, when Mountbatten first met her in 1926. According to Philip Ziegler, she was Mountbatten's closest female friend until his death: 'Edwina was wise enough to make her into a friend; she once told her husband that she liked Yola very much but that he was not to marry her if ever he found himself a widower.'

calls: 'avenues of enjoyment: painters, writers, photographers – skimming the surface, I now realise, of a murkier world underneath of which I remained largely innocent'. Baron's gifted artist friends included Stephen Ward (who did a drawing of the Duke of Edinburgh, among others, and, more famously, in his capacity as an osteopath and social intermediary, introduced the call girl Christine Keeler to the government minister John Profumo[141]) and the painter Vasco Lazzolo. 'Lazzolo,' Robin Dalton remembers, 'discovered a magic pill which was supposed to make us all madly sexy. You put it underneath your pillow and at the crucial moment of intercourse you were supposed to pop it and inhale. David and I tried it once, but as we were madly sexy anyway it didn't appear to do more than slow up proceedings. We were always losing the pills under the pillow. I think they were yellow and I expect they were the first primitive precursors of amyl nitrite.'

Having met at Broadlands in 1947, Baron and Philip became friends. Philip asked Baron to take his wedding photographs, and Baron invited Philip to join his informal luncheon club. The Thursday Club, as it was

---

[141] Profumo, who lied to parliament about his association with Keeler, resigned in June 1963. Ward was then charged with living 'wholly or in part on the earnings of prostitution'. He took an overdose on the final night of his trial and never recovered. He was found guilty on two charges, but died without sentence being passed. Ward's drawings of Philip and other members of the Royal Family were put up for sale to help defray his legal costs: Sir Anthony Blunt, Surveyor of the Queen's Pictures since 1945 (and a Soviet spy since 1936), bought them, privately, to save the Royal Family public embarrassment. The press, nevertheless, contrived to embroil the Duke in 'the Profumo affair' – albeit briefly. Ward hosted parties at which a feature was that 'the man who serves dinner' – in the words of Lord Denning's official report into the affair – 'is nearly naked except for a small square lace apron round his waist such as a waitress might wear. He wears a black mask over his head with slits for eye-holes. He cannot therefore be recognised by any of the guests. Some reports stop there and say that nothing evil takes place. It is done as a comic turn and no more. This may well be so at some of the parties. But at others I am satisfied that it is followed by perverted sex orgies: that the man in the mask is a "slave" who is whipped.' Was Philip 'the man in the mask'? On 24 June 1963 the *Daily Mirror* filled its front page with a huge headline, 'PRINCE PHILIP AND THE PROFUMO SCANDAL', and managed to get the best of both worlds, opening the story with the words, 'The foulest rumour which is being circulated about the Profumo Scandal has involved the Royal Family', adding, immediately, a much smaller headline: 'Rumour is utterly unfounded.' Since 1963, John Profumo has kept his own counsel and devoted himself to good works. He became a CBE in 1975 and, in 1995, at the dinner held at Claridge's to mark Margaret Thatcher's seventieth birthday, Mr Profumo was seated at the Queen's right hand.

known, met originally in an upstairs room at Wheeler's Restaurant in Old Compton Street, Soho. The purpose of the club was purely convivial: an excuse to start the weekend early, eat Wheeler's finest fish (Bernard Walsh, the restaurant's proprietor was a founder member), and drink Wheeler's cheap-and-cheerful house white wine – and plenty of it. According to Robin Dalton, 'Thursday night was a lost cause if you happened to be the wife or girlfriend of any of the members.' Dalton's boyfriend, David Milford Haven, joined the club, as did Philip and Mike Parker. The members (all male) included Baron's brother, Jack, artists like Vasco Lazzolo, newspaper editors (Arthur Christiansen of the *Daily Express*, Frank Owen of the *Daily Mail*), actors (James Robertson-Justice, David Niven), scriptwriters (Don Stewart, Monja Danischewsky), amusing men about town: Compton Mackenzie, Peter Ustinov, Lord Glenavy (better known as the stammering raconteur and columnist, Patrick Campbell), Larry Adler. The gatherings were high-spirited, occasionally raucous, but never debauched. There was gossip and banter, but no birds – other than the cuckoo . . .

The cuckoo became notorious. It lived inside a cuckoo clock in the room where the lunch was held. Predictably, it emerged on the hour and the half-hour, but its appearances on the half-hour were inevitably brief. One day, by way of an amusing wager, the club members bet Baron that he and his camera would not be quick enough to take a snapshot of the cuckoo when it popped out at half past one. Baron rose to the challenge – and failed. Next week, he tried again – setting his camera on a tripod, this time. He failed again: Mike Parker, apparently, nudged him as the cuckoo appeared. At the third attempt, Baron insisted that none of the club members be allowed within reaching distance of him or his camera. He was foiled once more: Parker had come equipped with three thunder-flashes – small, safe, lightly-explosive smoke bombs, used in military training, and useful for japes like this. Just as the hands of the cuckoo clock reached half past one, Parker, Philip and either James Robertson-Justice or Arthur Christiansen deployed the thunder-flashes: one burst immediately under Baron's camera, one landed on a table and the third ended up in the fireplace, where its explosion prompted a downfall of soot from the chimney. There was laughter – and blackened faces: the Duke was right by the fireplace – but when the smoke cleared and the police arrived, general agreement that perhaps it was time to call off the wager.

'We had fun at those lunches,' Parker recalled, 'plenty of laughter, but nothing *louche* or lewd, I assure you.' Parker also claimed that, even then, at the beginning of his public life, Philip had 'an instinct for self-preservation'. 'He was always correct,' Parker told me, 'always kept just that little bit of distance, never went too far. Most of the chaps were absolutely above board, but we had a nose for those that weren't.' They were always wary of Larry Adler,[142] and Parker said, from the outset, he thought there was 'something unsavoury' about Stephen Ward. When Kim Philby turned up as a guest one Thursday lunchtime (some time before his exposure as a Soviet spy), Parker's nose twitched, but only because 'he was the dullest man in the place'.

Courtiers of the Old School (the likes of Tommy Lascelles) always had their doubts about Mike Parker. He was Australian, after all, brash and breezy, and inclined to sail too close to the wind. They had their reservations about Baron, too. 'Baron was a gambler,' said Peter Ustinov, shortly after Baron's death, 'and it sometimes seemed to me as I watched him at work and at play that for him the whole of existence was a pastime with a score.' He took risks, and he knew all types and conditions of men – and women. It was Baron who introduced the Duke of Edinburgh to the first of the 'leading ladies' with whom he is supposed to have had an affair. Pat Kirkwood was an actress, singer and celebrated pantomime principal boy. The critic Kenneth Tynan (who knew about these things) once described her legs as 'the eighth wonder of the world'. In 1948 she was twenty-seven and starring in a musical revue called *Starlight Roof* at the London Hippodrome. According to Miss Kirkwood, one night, after the show, Baron (who, by his own

---

[142] Many found Larry Adler tiresome: he talked too much, he had a weakness for exaggeration, and his capacity for name-dropping rivalled my own. (This may be why I was in sympathy with him.) I met a number of other Thursday Club regulars in the 1960s. James Robertson-Justice (1905–75), actor, was the first grown man I ever saw stark naked. I knocked on his door at the Randolph Hotel, Oxford, and disturbed his pre-prandial snooze. He answered, 'Come!' I entered the room and found him spread-eagled on the bed, unadorned except for a hip flask which was nestling in the thicket of silver hair on his chest. Monja Danischewsky (1911–94), film producer and scriptwriter, wrote an hilarious autobiography (*White Russian, Red Face*, 1966), kept pigs (explaining, since he was Jewish, that he was sure, as a matter of honour, they would never attack him) and introduced me to the Famous Last Words of the Fatted Calf: 'I hear the young master has returned . . .' I shared a literary agent with Patrick Campbell (3rd Baron Glenavy, 1913–80) and appeared on *Call My Bluff* as a member of his team. When the other team captain, Frank Muir, was telling us (at length) about how he had recently been made captain of his local rifle club, Campbell muttered to me, under his breath, 'Small bore, I suppose.' These were funny men, and, in the best sense, men of the world. It must have been amusing to have had lunch at the Thursday Club when they were there and on song.

admission, was besotted with her) turned up with Philip and an equerry, and the four of them went off to dine. They had a late supper at Les Ambassadeurs in Mayfair and then went dancing at the Milroy nightclub nearby. Philip asked Pat to dance. And she did. 'But nothing happened,' she insists. 'Nothing happened at all. Then, or later. It was innocent fun. He was out on a night with the boys and I just happened to be there.' At the nightclub, she recalls, people stopped and stared, and there was some tut-tutting and disapproving looks, and Philip responded by pulling a face – but that is as shocking and outrageous as his behaviour got. When the dancing stopped, they went back to Baron's place for scrambled eggs. And then it was time for bed. Philip went off with his equerry, and Baron drove Pat home to her mother in St John's Wood.

Pat Kirkwood did meet Prince Philip twice more – once, in the early 1950s, in the official line-up after a televised command performance, and then, in the late 1960s, in another line-up, after a charity concert at the Theatre Royal, Drury Lane. On each occasion friendly handshakes and brief pleasantries were exchanged. And that's it. That is the long and the short of it. There is nothing more to tell. Yet on the fragile foundation of one night of dancing and two handshakes rests a massive mountain of myth that has managed to sustain itself across almost sixty years. It's quite amazing.

'Actually, it's quite hateful,' says Katie Boyle, another celebrated beauty from the 1950s who is regularly mentioned in despatches as one of Philip's flings. According to the book the Duke of Edinburgh brought to my attention, 'Philip's affair with Katie was very steamy. They had the most extraordinary times together.' On one occasion, claims author Nicholas Davies, when Katie Boyle – a blonde, glamorous television personality, seven years the Duke's junior – 'entertained Philip at her London home, she received an urgent message that her husband had returned unexpectedly and was on his way home. Philip rapidly exited through the back entrance just as Katie's husband put his key in the front door.' 'Yes, I've met Prince Philip several times,' Katie Boyle told me, when I raised the story with her. 'I think he's the most fantastic man. I love his dryness. But an affair? It's ludicrous, pure fabrication. When it appears in print, people believe it. You can't take legal action because it fans the flames, so you just have to accept people telling complete lies about you.'

I have known Katie Boyle since I was a small boy. I know her quite well. I believe her completely. I believe Hélène Cordet, too.

In the 1950s, in Britain, Hélène Cordet was celebrated, in a moderate way, as a cabaret artiste, television performer and the hostess of another chic Mayfair nightclub, the Saddle Room in Hamilton Place. In the 1920s, in France, Hélène Foufounis, as she then was, and Prince Philip of Greece were childhood friends. The Foufounis family were Greeks in exile, royalist to the core, comfortably off, with a country house and farm near Marseilles and a seaside holiday home at Berck Plage near Le Touquet in Normandy. Philip's mother and Madame Foufounis were friends; Philip's English nanny, Emily Roose, and the Foufounis's English nanny were allies. On holiday, in the country and at the seaside, Philip and the younger two of his older sisters, Cécile and Sophie, played with Hélène and her brother, Iaini, and her sister, Ria. Apparently, Ria, an invalid, bedridden with a diseased hip, was especially fond of Philip. (I can believe it: I have seen a photograph taken of them together at Berck Plage: she looks adoring, he looks adorable: he must have been about four at the time.) Hélène was four years older than Philip and, more than sixty years later, recalled, 'I was very jealous of him when he was a small boy. I don't think he disliked me as much as I disliked him, but my feelings were more jealousy than anything. Everyone adored him so much, particularly my mother, because he was so good-looking. My father had died when I was very small and I felt as if I wasn't loved by my stepfather, and was the least loved of all my family. So when this blond, blue-eyed German-looking little boy came along, and my mother paid so much attention to him, I was livid. And he and my brother Iaini used to gang up on me.'

Philip and Hélène were childhood friends. They met again a few years later, in London, when Philip was fourteen or fifteen. Hélène's stepfather had died, and the family fortune had taken a tumble, and she and her mother were living in a flat in Bayswater: 'I thought "Oh God!" He had been so beautiful as a child and now he was growing up. It gave me a bit of a shock.'

Hélène was growing up, too. Aged just twenty, she married her first husband, an Oxford undergraduate, William Kirby. The civil ceremony took place in Oxford, followed by a blessing at the Greek Orthodox Church in Bayswater, with Philip, aged sixteen, in attendance. According to Hélène, 'He was the best man *and* gave me away at my first wedding.' He also, apparently, trod on her veil. The marriage to William Kirby failed and the young Hélène sought consolation in the arms of a French airman, Marcel Boisot. Hélène and Marcel had two children: a son, Max, born in December 1943, and a daughter, Louise, born in February 1945, shortly after their marriage at Paddington Register Office in January 1945. It is these two children that many of the rumour-mongers would have you believe were fathered by Prince Philip. (The rumour-mongers have even gone to the trouble of dating Philip's wartime shore leave to prove it might be possible.) Philip is godfather to both Max and Louise and, over the years, has taken an interest in them. He encouraged Hélène to send Max to Gordonstoun (rather than Winchester) and Hélène's grandson, named Philip, went to Gordonstoun, too.

Philip and Hélène were friends, not lovers. He is not the father of her children. The rumours started because, when Max was born, Hélène was still married to William Kirby, though they had lived apart for two years. At the time, no one knew about Marcel Boisot. Hélène allowed the paternity of her children to remain a mystery. Even in her memoir, *Born Bewildered*, published in 1961, years later, she does not name him. I get the impression (though she denied it) that Hélène Cordet (sometime Foufounis, Kirby and Boisot) rather relished the *frisson* created by the rumours surrounding her friendship with Prince Philip. I get the impression Prince Philip thinks so, too, and it irritates him. She said, when the rumours were at their height, that she sought his advice about how best to handle the situation: 'It used to make me really mad, not so much for me, as for the Royal Family. It wasn't right, that chit-chat. So I said to Philip, "What do I do?" He said, "Look, if you like you can sue them, but I don't think it's worth it. On the contrary, it will just stir up more trouble." '

Is that, in fact, what I am doing now, stirring up more trouble, reheating old stories under the pretext of dismissing them, creating a whole new sensation while claiming to be throwing a wet blanket over old ones? I hope not, but I am aware of the risk. I am taking that risk, nonetheless, partly because I am interested in the phenomenon of how a raft of rumours-without-foundation can become immovably embedded in the public imagination, and partly, too, because I recognise that a general policy of *never* commenting, explaining or denying stories (which has much to commend it) can sometimes encourage even good people to think, perhaps, there is some truth in a lie. For example, recently, the writer Graham Lord published an entertaining and carefully researched biography of the actor David Niven. In the book, Lord writes that Niven, an occasional attendee at the Thursday Club lunches, was 'very proud of his friendship with the Duke of Edinburgh'. Lord goes on, 'According to actress Lauren Bacall,

Niven and his Hollywood pal, Douglas Fairbanks Jr, lent themselves as "beards" to cover up the Duke's alleged dalliances in the early years of his marriage to the Queen. "Philip always had women," Bacall told me, "and they covered for him and pretended that his women were their women."' It simply is not true, though it may well be what Niven told Bacall at the time and the impression she got on the few occasions in the late 1940s and early 1950s when there was a London showbusiness party and Philip was there.

In his book, published in 2003, Graham Lord makes much of the fact that he approached Buckingham Palace hoping to talk to Prince Philip about Niven and was rebuffed. Niven and the Duke were friends, insists Lord. Prince Philip's private secretary responds coolly that the Duke recalls meeting David Niven a couple of times. Lord then attempts to prove the depth of the friendship by quoting a letter – brief but thoughtful – sent by the Duke of Edinburgh to Niven in the aftermath of the murder of Lord Mountbatten. The Duke's letter begins 'Dear David' and is signed 'Philip'. It is a courteous and friendly response to Niven's letter of condolence. It does not make the Duke of Edinburgh and David Niven bosom friends.

Lord, I suspect, thinks that the Duke does not want to talk about his friendship with Niven because he has something to hide, because there is possibly some truth in Lauren Bacall's suggestion that Niven and Fairbanks Jr were the young Duke's 'beards'. Lord misunderstands the situation and misreads the Duke. Many do. Prince Philip has the widest range of acquaintanceship of any man I know: Nelson Mandela, the Pope, Frank Sinatra – he's met them all. People in the armed services, in the Church, in the voluntary sector, in the entertainment business – industrialists, environmentalists, athletes, academics, politicians – year in year out, the Duke of Edinburgh is meeting, greeting, saluting, chatting to, talking with, encouraging, challenging, teasing, annoying, pleasing, all manner of men, women and children. They *always* recollect meeting him, and remarkably, more often than might seem possible, he recalls meeting them – especially on second or third encounter; particularly if he has read about them or seen them on TV; notably, of course, if their particular occupation or achievement is in an area that already engages him. He is affable and chatty, unself-conscious and at ease with himself. He is good (much better than the Queen) at picking up a conversation or a relationship at exactly the point where it was left off – whenever that was: a month, a year, even a decade ago. He is good at living in the moment, appearing (and being) interested in who you are and what you have to say. If he is concentrating, and giving you his full attention, he can establish a sense of intimacy that is deceptive.

Prince Philip is a great letter-writer. (He has told me he will never write an autobiography, but I would like to persuade him to publish a collection of his letters.) I have quite a number of letters from him. They are addressed 'Dear Gyles' and signed 'Philip' and so – like his letter to David Niven – give an exaggerated impression of familiarity. As he has no surname, he has no choice but to sign his letters 'Philip'. As he is unstuffy, he addresses people he knows by their first name. He does have close friends – his first secretary, Mike Parker, was one; Sir Brian McGrath, his secretary from 1982 until the mid-nineties, is another; Lord Buxton of Alsa (television executive, conservationist, wildfowl enthusiast) is a third – but I am not one of them. Nor was David Niven. On the whole, as the former Prime Minister James Callaghan shrewdly observed, 'What the Royal Family offers you is friendliness, not friendship.'

Like the Queen, the Duke of Edinburgh is remarkably self-contained. Unlike the Queen, he may grumble and growl, and occasionally snap, but, like her, as a rule, he keeps his true feelings under wraps. And, even with those with whom he is intimate, he is still guarded. Mike Parker told me, 'Philip did not discuss his feelings – at least, not with me. I certainly did not know about him and Princess Elizabeth until virtually the day of the engagement. He's not one to let it all hang out. That's not his style.'

In the public arena, the Prince Philip you see – the outer man – is accessible (if a little forbidding), confident, bantering, outspoken. The private Prince Philip – the inner man – is much more difficult to reach. He is, from all I have seen myself and heard from those who know him well, more sensitive, more thoughtful, kinder and more tolerant than the well-known caricature would suggest, but he keeps these things hidden. His manner appears open, but his instinct is watchful. Whoever you are, he does not let you get too close. It's safer that way. He is careful of his reputation and conscious of his position, and of the responsibility it brings. And he has been, from the day he married Princess Elizabeth. As I write, I am looking at a photograph, taken in 1948, at a Thursday Club cricket lunch: it is a picture of a dozen of the regular club members, some with wives or girlfriends, seated at a long table, out of doors, in the sunshine, waiting for lunch. It is an informal shot – we are among friends: there is laughter, joshing, David Milford

Haven's dog, Simon, has his paws on the table – but one figure stands out from the crowd: in the centre of the picture sits the Duke of Edinburgh, just a tad more formal than the rest, looking straight at the camera, smiling, spruce, present and correct, knowing, in truth, that though this is just a snapshot, he is still the focus of attention.

In his diaries, Kenneth Tynan gives an account of a memorable evening in the mid-1960s, when, at his house after dinner, by way of entertainment, he rigged up two screens 'to show some American experimental films simultaneously with outtakes from British nudipix (cf. scenes when the model accidentally dropped towel, bra or knickers) and Jean Genet's erotic film *Chant d'Amour*'. Tynan's guests that night included Peter Cook, the comedian, Harold Pinter, the playwright, and the Queen's sister, Princess Margaret, and her husband, Tony Snowdon. 'I had warned Tony that there would be some pretty blue material,' recalled Tynan, 'and he said, "It would be good for M."' At first, apparently, the nudie picture show went well – 'the English bits were amateurish and charming,' according to Tynan, 'with odd flashes of nipple and pubic bush' – but when Jean Genet's homo-erotic fantasy crackled into life 'the atmosphere began to freeze'. The 'unmistakable shots' of male members, many and various, in assorted states of arousal, rapidly brought a 'gelid silence' to the room: 'no one was laughing now'. Happily for Tynan, Peter Cook came to the rescue, by suddenly improvising a spurious commentary for the film, 'treating the movie as if it were a long commercial for Cadbury's Milk Flake Chocolate . . . Within five minutes we were all rocking with laughter, Princess M included.'[143] My point in relating this story is this: the Duke of Edinburgh would never have allowed himself (let alone his wife!) to have been put into a position like this. He is careful where he goes and what he does. Baron, and some of Baron's friends, might have had a darker side to them – a side that wasn't quite cricket – but, if they did, Philip never joined them there.

The Duke is no prude, but neither, in my experience, is he given to off-colour humour or lewd behaviour. More than once, I have seen him, with a look or a raised eyebrow, silence someone, a little in their cups, who might have been on the edge of telling a story that went 'too far'.

[143] How times change. Kenneth Rose tells the story of Princess Margaret's grandparents, George V and Queen Mary, staying with Lord Derby in 1921 and also being offered post-prandial cinematic entertainment. However, according to Rose, 'The royal party were spared the impropriety of watching a nature film in which a duck laid an egg. The egg episode was cut out.'

In several accounts of the Duke, I have read reports of him appreciatively eyeing up shapely women and simultaneously making suggestive remarks. In my experience, while he evidently enjoys the company of good-looking women, his manners are impeccable. In the 1980s, when I was Appeals Chairman of the National Playing Fields Association, as fundraisers we organised a number of royal charity evenings at the pantomime. After the show, backstage, I would escort Prince Philip along the line-up of charmingly shapely and scantily clad chorus girls. The Prince shook them firmly by the hand and looked them only in the eye. At the Royal Variety Performance a couple of years ago, while the Queen's equerry and I nudged one another knowingly and agreed that Jennifer Lopez was indeed a fine figure of a woman (petite but perfectly formed), the Duke of Edinburgh directed his small-talk entirely at J-Lo's forehead. He is careful. He is no fool. And he is not interested in showgirls, actresses[144] and starlets. On that Sarah Bradford and I are agreed.

I bring Mrs Bradford[145] into the narrative at this point because, of all the more distinguished and reliable royal biographers, she is the only one who speaks openly, in terms and without equivocation, of 'the fact that Philip has not remained faithful' throughout his marriage. In the revised edition of her acclaimed biography of the Queen, published in 2002, she writes of the royal couple: 'Theirs is a very royal marriage; Elizabeth's generation was not brought up to expect fidelity but loyalty. Affairs are one thing, passion another. Philip is not the man to fall hopelessly in love; his affairs make no difference to a marriage as firm and indeed fond as theirs.' Other royal biographers hedge their bets and write of Philip's 'friendships with women' (Ben Pimlott) and 'supposed romances' (Robert Lacey); Mrs Bradford, alone, writes boldly, baldly, of his 'affairs'.

Because Mrs Bradford's work is widely respected and meticulously

---

[144] One actress often mentioned in association with him (notably by *Private Eye*) is Anna Massey. It turns out that she met Philip just once, in the 1950s, when her uncle, Vincent Massey, was Governor-General of Canada. (Incidentally, when I asked Prince Philip to tell me about the most impressive people he had met in his life, he began by naming Vincent Massey and Sir Robert Menzies [Australian Prime Minister, 1939–41, 1949–66] before saying, 'No, no, a list would be invidious.')

[145] Sarah Bradford, born 1938, married to the 8th Viscount Bangor, is an Oxford-educated historian who has written biographies of Cesare Borgia, Benjamin Disraeli, Sacheverell Sitwell, Princess Grace of Monaco and Jacqueline Kennedy Onassis, as well as the Queen and King George VI.

researched, I went to see her, to discover why she is so uncompromising in her assertion of Prince Philip's infidelity. We met on a winter's evening at her house in Fulham – in Britannia Road, appropriately. She was open, friendly and hospitable. By candlelight, over a glass of wine, she told me, 'There is no doubt in my mind at all. The Duke of Edinburgh has had affairs – yes, full-blown affairs and more than one. Not with Pat Kirkwood or Merle Oberon or any of those people. You're quite right, all that was nonsense, complete nonsense. I don't think there was ever anything in any of that. But he has affairs. And the Queen accepts it. I think she thinks that's how men are. He's never been one for chasing actresses. His interest is quite different. The women he goes for are always younger than him, usually beautiful and highly aristocratic.' In her book, Sarah Bradford puts it like this: 'Philip has learned to carry on his flirtations and relationships in circles rich and grand enough to provide protection from the paparazzi and the tabloids.'

In her drawing room, as the candles splutter, and her husband sits in the kitchen watching the early evening television news, Sarah Bradford recounts what she believes is a telling story of a private party given in Scotland and attended by the Queen and Prince Philip. The Queen, apparently, was seated at a table by the dance floor, talking to friends about racing, but, as she talked, her watchful eyes were elsewhere, gazing across the dance floor, observing her husband as he danced very close – too close – to their hostess's daughter. 'Well,' I said (fully understanding for the first time why Philip pulled that face on his one night of dancing with Pat Kirkwood back in 1948), 'by all accounts he's a great dancer and the Queen is the Queen – she can't really get up and dance as he might. I think we can excuse – even understand – a little light flirtation with the hostess's daughter on the dance floor.' Sarah Bradford did not agree. 'I wouldn't like it if William [Viscount Bangor] behaved like that,' she said.

I told Sarah Bradford that one of the reasons I admired her books was because of the amount of authenticated detail she provides. I asked her, if she was so certain about these 'affairs', why she had not named any names in her book. 'I wanted to give an accurate picture without hurting people,' she said, reasonably enough. The problem, of course, is this: if you make a highly charged assertion, but do not back it up with evidence, or give your sources, or name the names of any of those who might be involved, it is very difficult to make your assertion stand up. I told Mrs Bradford I was trying to get to the bottom of the raft of rumours about Prince Philip and his love-life – either to establish them as fact or scotch them once and for all. 'How do you know you are right about this?' I asked. 'I do know,' she said, smiling. 'Believe me.' 'Who are these women?' I persisted. 'You know who they are,' she said. 'They're the ones people talk about.' 'You mean, women like Sacha Abercorn,' I suggested. 'Yes,' said Mrs Bradford, putting down her wine glass. 'She is certainly one of them.'

Sacha Abercorn is tall, slim and striking. She is quietly spoken: intelligent, articulate and thoughtful. She was born in 1946, the daughter of Lt Col. Harold Pedro Joseph Phillips (known as 'Bunnie', a friend of Dickie Mountbatten, and sometime lover of Edwina) and Georgina Wernher (now, of course, Lady Kennard, known to friends as 'Gina' and to Prince Philip, when they were children, as 'George'). Sacha was christened Alexandra Anastasia – her Russian heritage is important to her. Her mother's mother was Zia Wernher, married to Sir Harold Wernher, but born Countess Anastasia Mikhailovna, elder daughter of His Imperial Highness Grand Duke Mikhail Mikhailovich, the grandson of Tsar Nicholas I. In a collection of prose poems she published in 2003,[146] the 'biographical note' reads in full: 'Sacha Abercorn is the founder of the Pushkin Prizes Trust. She received an Honorary Doctorate from the University of Ulster in 2003. She is a descendant of the Romanovs and of Alexander Pushkin, the great Russian poet.' Her husband is James, 5th Duke of Abercorn, twelve years her senior, an officer in the Grenadier Guards, briefly an Ulster Unionist MP, and for the past forty years, a force for good and a power to reckon with in the social and economic life of Northern Ireland. The Abercorns' family home (since 1612) in Omagh, County Tyrone, is called Baronscourt[147] – a very different milieu from the Baron's Court that surrounded Prince Philip's photographer friend, Baron, the founder of the Thursday Club. In 1999 James Abercorn became a

---

[146] *Feather from the Firebird* by Sacha Abercorn, published by the Summer Palace Press, County Donegal, 2003. The poems are short, powerfully felt, highly evocative, beautifully observed. Many of them feel autobiographical, coded tributes to people she has known and loved and lost: her younger brother, Nicholas, who committed suicide in 1991, her father, who died in 1980, her father's friend, Lord Mountbatten, murdered in Ireland by the IRA in 1979.

[147] 'Through hills at the foot of Bessy Bell . . . we come to Baronscourt, Lord Abercorn's magnificent seat . . . the great number of fine oaks and three long lakes which ornament this place give it an air of great grandeur . . .' Daniel Beaufort (1739–1821).

Knight of the Garter. (Sacha's younger sister, Natalia Ayesha, known as Tally, is married to Gerald, 6th Duke of Westminster, who became a Knight of the Garter in 2003.)

I went to see Sacha Abercorn at her London mews house, near Victoria Station, a stone's throw from Buckingham Palace. She was just back from a trip to Russia. She was in happy form, fielding telephone calls from her mother and her daughter, while making me tea. We moved from the kitchen to the drawing room and, sat, facing one another, perched on the edge of sofas. Notebook and pen in hand, I asked her when she first remembered meeting the Queen and Prince Philip.

'When I was a child,' she said. 'I must have been eight or nine. It was in the 1950s. We lived in Leicestershire, at Thorpe Lubenham, and they came to stay. They came with Charles and Anne, who were a bit younger than us. What do I remember best? I think the fun we all had – so much fun. The adults and the children all playing together. I remember dressing up as monsters. I remember huge bonfires and cooking potatoes in the ashes.

'In the evening, indoors, in the dark, after tea, we played a wonderful game called Stone. Do you know it? All the lights are turned out – you are in total darkness. Someone is chosen to be "He" and, in the darkness, when you are touched by "He" you have to stand absolutely still – like stone. There was fear and fun. It was fantastic. The Queen and Prince Philip loved it. They used to play it at Balmoral – all the grown-ups.' Sacha laughed, and covered her mouth with her hand, and said, 'I shouldn't tell you this, but once, my father was "He" and, in the dark, he felt this figure hidden behind the curtains – and then the Queen giggled and he realised who it was. Can you imagine? The Queen hiding behind the curtains and my father feeling her up and down?'

I asked Sacha how the Queen and Prince Philip seemed to relate to their own children. 'Then?' she asked. 'Yes,' I said. 'Really well. Really, really well. Philip was wonderful. I remember how he used to help Charles with his Go-Kart. And he used to tell them stories that he'd invented. I can't recall any gruff words – ever. Or any tension. I would go with my parents to Balmoral and their children would be there too. It was always fun and jolly. I loved the picnics. They were good times. I remember, once, in the stables, there was a dog fight and the Queen arrived and calmed it immediately. She's intrepid. She doesn't get thrown by things. They were good times for us and, I think, good times for them – human times, filled with good humour. They don't get that much time off, you know. The heavy duty is relentless.'

I asked Sacha how she had got to know Prince Philip, not as a family friend of her parents but as a personal friend of her own. She smiled and sat back and thought for a moment. 'I remember going to Cowes one year,'[148] she said. 'My parents were going to go, but my father had cancer and couldn't come, so I went on my own.' While Queen Victoria's favourite home was at Osborne House in East Cowes, as a rule the Queen did not accompany Prince Philip to Cowes Week. 'It was the chaps who did the sailing,' Sacha explained. 'I think the girls were there to have fun. It was great fun. All the secretaries from his office were there. And I remember Princess Anne and myself, dressed up as serving wenches. It was hilarious. I remember Uffa Fox telling stories – telling endless, endless stories. I suppose I was seventeen or eighteen, in that funny in-between world.

'And then I got married – at twenty – in 1966. The Queen and Prince Philip came to the wedding. Oh, yes, everyone was there. They all rolled up. It was extraordinary. It was in Westminster Abbey. It really was amazing. And then we would see them, now and again, at weekends, particularly in November, when they came to Luton Hoo.[149]

---

[148] Cowes, on the north coast of the Isle of Wight, is the headquarters of the Royal Yacht Squadron (founded 1812) and home of the annual 'Cowes Week' yachting regatta, held every August. In 1947, the Island Sailing Club of Cowes gave Philip and Princess Elizabeth a Dragon-class yacht as a wedding present. It was painted dark blue and Philip named it *Bluebottle*. For several years, he sailed her competitively in Cowes Week, with a regular crew that included the larger-than-life local character, yachtsman and boat-builder, Uffa Fox. Fox and Philip became firm friends. Fox persuaded the people of Cowes to give Philip one of the first of the small Flying Fifteen yachts, which Fox designed and Philip christened *Coweslip*. Probably the best known of Philip's yachts was *Bloodhound*, a pre-war, twelve-metre yacht designed for ocean racing. He raced her at Cowes and, for several years, cruised the west coast of Scotland in her with Prince Charles and Princess Anne. He ended his years of competitive sailing in a series of yachts called *Yeoman*, all owned by another friend and fellow sailing enthusiast, Sir Owen Aisher, founder of the Marley Tiles business and 'Yachtsman of the Year, 1958'.
[149] Luton Hoo, one mile south of Luton in Bedfordshire. Set in a thousand acres of parkland (laid out by Capability Brown), the original house, built by Robert Adam in 1767, was destroyed by fire in 1843, rebuilt and bought by Sacha's great-grandfather, Julius Wernher, in 1903. Wernher was a railway engineer's son who made his fortune as a young man in the South African diamond rush of the 1870s and used it to acquire Luton Hoo, decorate it in lavish French style and fill it (to bursting) with jewellery, porcelain, paintings and *objets d'art*. Julius's son, Harold (1893–1973), added to the collection, the best of which is now on public display (loaned to the British

They came each year for their wedding anniversary. My grandparents were there, and uncles and aunts. And the Brabournes. There were ten or twelve in the house party. There was shooting as usual and then, in the evening, some great entertainment. I remember Victor Borge particularly. And I remember the dinners – my grandmother being bossy, my grandfather bringing his heart and soul with him. The talk was always interesting. I remember my grandfather talking, and Prince Philip. I remember when they spoke, they took it in turns, they gave each other time, and we gave them full-blast attention. It was good.

'But it was later that we became close. I think it was at The Gables – when Nicky was running the shoots – that we particularly got interested in each other. What brought us together? Jung. Yes, Jung.[150] I've always been interested in Jung, his work, his ideas. And Philip is interested in Jung. Prince Philip is always questing, exploring, searching for meaning, testing ideas. We had riveting conversations about Jung. That's where our friendship began.'

The Duke of Edinburgh is not the caricature to which we are accustomed. The Duke of Edinburgh reads Jung, T. S. Eliot, Shakespeare, the Bible. Since the 1950s his interest in psychology, philosophy and religion have developed and deepened, and become increasingly intermeshed with his interest in the natural world and the environment.

His interest in life's spiritual dimension was given additional focus in 1962, with the appointment of Robin Woods as 'Dean of Windsor, Domestic Chaplain to the Queen and Register of the Most Noble Order of the Garter'. Woods (son of a bishop; chaplain to the forces, mentioned in despatches, 1944; 'interests: sailing, shooting, painting') and Philip became friends. With the Duke's active support and involvement, Woods developed St George's House at Windsor as a training college for clergy and a conference centre where clergy and laity could meet to explore issues and ideas. St George's held its first weekend 'consultation' in October 1966. The theme: 'The Role of the

---

people for 125 years) at the Ranger's House in Greenwich Park. Luton Hoo itself is now a luxury hotel: you can sleep where the Queen slept. For further details see www.elitehotels.com.

[150] Carl Gustav Jung (1875–1961), the great Swiss analyst, who eschewed Freud's obsession with sex and the power of the sexual impulse, and focused instead on what he termed the inherited 'collective unconscious' with its universal ideas or images: the 'archetypes'. Jung also wrote on subjects as diverse as nature, mythology and religion – subjects of deep interest to the Duke of Edinburgh.

Church in Society Today'. In 1970, Woods moved on from Windsor to become Bishop of Worcester,[151] to be succeeded briefly by Launcelot Fleming, sometime Antarctic explorer and Bishop of Norwich, and then, in 1976, by Michael Mann, whose background, in several respects, echoed that of Woods (he, too, had been mentioned in despatches) and whose education – at Harrow, Sandhurst, Wells Theological College and Harvard Business School – and range of experience – as an officer in the King's Dragoon Guards during the war, as a colonial administrator in Nigeria for nine years before his ordination in 1957 – made him a figure Philip could reckon with and relate to.

Together, the Duke of Edinburgh and Michael Mann embarked on a series of intellectual and philosophical adventures, and their collaboration and friendship led to the publication of three books. The first, *A Windsor Correspondence*, is simply an exchange of letters, between Duke and Dean, sparked by a lecture given by the astronomer Fred Hoyle entitled 'Evolution from Space'. The themes they touch on are science and Christianity, fundamentalism, evolution and morality. The second is *A Question of Balance*, and explores 'the crucial part that human nature plays in every aspect of communal life'. The Duke evidently has reservations about some of what the Church of England gets up to, but his conclusion is clear: 'religious conviction is the strongest and probably the only factor in sustaining the dignity and integrity of the individual.' The third book is called *Survival or Extinction: A Christian Attitude to the Environment*.[152] In 1986, the twenty-fifth anniversary of the World Wide Fund for Nature was celebrated with a conference held, at the Duke's suggestion, at Assisi, in Umbria, home of St Francis, patron saint of birds and animals. The aim was to forge 'a permanent alliance between conservation and religion'. By all accounts, the Buddhists stole the show, but, at the conference end, Hindus, Muslims, Jews and Christians each issued 'Declarations on Nature'. The World Wide Fund was later appointed

---

[151] Philip wrote to him: 'It has been simply marvellous having you at Windsor and your help and guidance for us and for our children has been invaluable.' Woods paid tribute to Philip as a 'man I had come to respect very deeply, not only for the integrity of his religion but for his ability to judge men and situations'.

[152] These three books, published by Michael Russell, in the 1980s, give a useful insight to the Duke's way of thinking. The other books of which he is author reflect the range of his enthusiasms, from *Birds from Britannia* (Longman, 1962) to *Competition Carriage Driving* (Horse Drawn Carriages Ltd, 1982).

'consultant to the Roman Catholic Church in programmes related to nature conservation' and the Duke went to Rome for a private audience with His Holiness Pope John Paul II. In *Survival or Extinction* the Duke and Michael Mann explore some of the themes touched on at the Assisi conference. The book also distils thoughts and ideas contributed at seven separate 'consultations' held at St George's House and includes a list of the various participants, beginning with 'Her Grace the Duchess of Abercorn, Counsellor in Transpersonal Psychology'.

Back in her mews house in Victoria, Sacha Abercorn poured me another cup of tea and continued with her story. 'It began with Jung,' she said. 'Philip was having these consultations at Windsor, and he said, "Could you get some of your Jung people to come along?" And I did. These consultations went on for three years. Michael Mann was very involved and, between them, they brought together a really interesting pool of thought.' Sacha sat forward on her sofa and said, with feeling, 'Prince Philip cares about the environment. He has a feeling for nature – in a practical way. He is totally a sentient human being – in a practical way. I saw that at first hand when we travelled with him several times in *Britannia* – James and myself, Aubrey Buxton and Kay [Buxton's second wife]. We went to Borneo, Sarawak, the Galápagos. Philip's feeling for the environment is not sentimental – not sentimental at all. It's emotional and practical.

'He's always asking questions, searching for answers. I think it was at Lubenham, and my mother and he were walking back to the house from church, and she said something like "I don't believe in anything". That made him stop, suddenly, and ask out loud, "What is it? What's behind it all?" He asks the difficult questions and that's what drew me to him. I remember, in the 1980s sometime, we were staying at Windsor for Royal Ascot, and I had just discovered Anthony Stevens' book on *Archetypes*[153] and I told Prince Philip about it and he was riveted. Riveted. We both were. One of the things that Stevens writes about is

---

[153] *Archetypes: A Natural History of the Self*, 1982. Stevens, a British Jungian with thirty years' experience as a practising psychiatrist, used the book to explore ways in which 'the archaic' influences our lives in fundamental areas – e.g. the development of attachment bonds, the maintenance of group solidarity, the contribution of myth, ritual and religion to the development of personality. He also began to link basic Jungian concepts with the structural elements of the brain. In 2003 he published *Archetype Revisited: An Updated Natural History of the Self*, described by one admiring reviewer as 'the overdue marriage of Darwin and Jung'.

left-brain/right-brain theory. [In a nutshell, the left hemisphere of the brain controls logic and language: the right controls creativity and intuition.] People think of Philip as being 'left-brain', but he is so full of 'right-brain'. Yes, he is practical, unsentimental and logical, but he is also emotional and intuitive. He is deeply sensitive. Deeply sensitive. His senses are so super-charged.'

Sacha was sitting forward now, smiling, her eyes shining. 'Our friendship was very close. The heart came into it in a big way. There's a hugely potent chemical reaction in him. It's a highly charged chemistry. We were close because we understood one another. He felt he could trust me and I felt I could trust him.'

Silence fell in the little drawing room and the tea had gone cold. 'In Eluthera,' I said – the Abercorns have a beautiful holiday home on the island of Eluthera in the Bahamas – 'In Eluthera, someone told me they had seen you and Prince Philip on the beach holding hands.'

Sacha smiled and said, without any awkwardness, 'It was a passionate friendship, but the passion was in the ideas. It was certainly not a full relationship. I did not go to bed with him. It probably looked like that to the world. I can understand why people might have thought it, but it didn't happen. It wasn't like that. He isn't like that. It's complicated and, at the same time, it's quite simple. He needs a playmate and someone to share his intellectual pursuits.'

'Do you think he sleeps with his other playmates?' I asked.

'I doubt it, I doubt it very much.' She paused and thought a moment and said, 'No, I'm sure not. But he's a human being. Who knows? I don't. Unless you are in the room with a lighted candle, who knows?'

'And what about the Queen?' I asked.

Sacha Abercorn smiled and said, 'She gives him a lot of lee-way. Her father told her, "Remember, he's a sailor. They come in on the tide."'

'Do you see much of him nowadays?' I asked, as Sacha began to stack up the tea things and I put my pen and notebook away.

'Not really. He used to come to Eluthera. And he'd come carriage-driving at Baronscourt with Penny [Romsey], but we've stopped having the carriage-driving. It was too expensive. I am sorry I don't see him properly any more. Really sorry. He is a very special man.'

As I walked away from Sacha's house, along Buckingham Palace Road, over Grosvenor Place, past the Royal Mews, I thought back on what she had told me – and the way she had told it to me: easily, fluently, without any sense of defensiveness or artifice – and I said to myself, 'Yes, that's it. That is all we need to know. It makes sense.'

It makes sense of the story told, nearly fifty years after the event, by Norman Barson, a royal footman, a former Grenadier guardsman, who worked for Philip and Princess Elizabeth at Windlesham Moor, the house, near Ascot, that was their weekend home at the beginning of their marriage. According to Barson, Philip would visit Windlesham Moor midweek, usually on a Tuesday or a Wednesday, early in the evening, and he would come, driving himself in his beloved MG convertible, accompanied by a young lady who was not the Princess. She was young, slim, pretty, well-spoken. Philip made no secret of the visits. He telephoned in advance to say he was coming. Barson prepared them beef sandwiches and gin and orange. 'He always poured the lady's drink,' said the footman. 'He hardly drank at all. I could later hear them laughing and joking, but I never once heard him refer to her by name . . . I never saw them kiss or canoodle. I remember thinking he acted exactly the same with her as with the Queen. He was charming to both of them. He stared into their eyes with his head on one side and made them laugh.'

It makes sense of the late Sir Angus Ogilvy – the delightful husband of Princess Alexandra, granddaughter of George V, fifteen years Philip's junior and long-reported as one of the Prince's 'romantic interests' – coming up to me at a party in 1999 (at the home of the newspaper publisher Conrad Black – in his glory days) and congratulating me on an article I had written about the Duke of Edinburgh. Ogilvy knew full well what people used to whisper about his wife and the Duke (indeed, I understand he once raised the matter with Martin Charteris, seeking his advice), but did it no longer trouble him because he understood the Duke and the nature of the Duke's relationship with his women friends? Sir Angus said to me, 'Prince Philip's a good man, a really good man, hopelessly misreported, misrepresented and misunderstood.' The Queen appointed Princess Alexandra as one of only a tiny handful of Lady Companions of the Order of the Garter in 2003.

It makes sense of Penny Romsey. Dr Johnson once said, 'If I had no duties, and no reference to futurity, I would spend my life in driving briskly in a post-chaise with a pretty woman.' The Duke of Edinburgh has duties, and an eye to the future, but he is nevertheless wholly at ease carriage-driving with Penny Romsey, thirty years his junior, because he knows the Queen knows that Penny is his playmate, not his mistress.

The Queen would like us to know it, too. The Queen makes a point of being on parade to cheer her husband and his carriage-driving companion as they take part in competitions. One Saturday evening, not long ago, on a day when the *Daily Mail* had carried photographs of her husband and his friend at a carriage-driving event – photographs with captions dripping with innuendo – the Queen said to Penny Romsey, who was staying for the weekend, 'Penny, are you planning to go to church in the morning? If you are, would you like to come to church with me?' The Queen was ready to send out a signal, happy to be pictured on her way to church with her husband's much younger friend. She is the Queen's friend, too, of course. Penny Romsey married Dickie Mountbatten's grandson, Norton, in 1979. The Romseys have two children, Nicholas and Alexandra. They had another daughter, a little girl called Leonora, who died of cancer in 1991, aged five. The last time I had lunch with Prince Philip (it was a fundraiser for the Playing Fields Association, held in the Cabinet War Rooms, earlier this year) he told me that evening he was going to the theatre, to Drury Lane, to see *Anything Goes*, with the Queen and Lord and Lady Romsey. These people are kith and kin, cousins as well as friends.

Penny Romsey's mother-in-law, Countess Mountbatten, said to me when I went to see her, 'Philip is a man who enjoys the company of attractive, intelligent younger women. Nothing wrong in that. He's always had somebody there, sharing one or other of his particular pursuits. He has special friends, like Penny. But I am quite sure – quite sure – absolutely certain – he has never been unfaithful to the Queen.'

What lies at the root of these passionate friendships, these unconsummated *amitiés amoureuses*? Countess Mountbatten would say it was the old Mountbatten energy, that Philip is like his Uncle Dickie: a dynamo who needs the occasional confidential companionship of a sparky, larky girl who is flattering, intelligent and fun. A respected Freudian analyst (like his Uncle George's wife, Princess Marie Bonaparte, or my friend Brett Kahr) would say he is recreating what he had – and loved and lost – in early childhood: the company of adoring girls, devoted playmates like his four older sisters or the Foufounis girls. A wise young woman, only born in 1981, would say that these friendships are what keep him young. Jessica Hay used to go out with Nicholas Knatchbull, the Romseys' only son, and, when she was still a teenager, stayed at Broadlands for a weekend shoot. 'The Queen's a fantastic shot,' she recalled. 'She shot more partridge than anyone else that day. At one point my trousers got caught as I climbed over a stile and I got stuck. Everyone had gone but Philip. He came back and helped me. Then he said, "What am I going to get in return?" He's got a twinkle in his eye. He knows he won't get the younger women, but I think the flirting keeps him young.' At dinner, Jessica sat next to Philip. 'I wouldn't call the royals affectionate,' she said, 'but they are very thoughtful towards one another. At dinner Prince Philip would always check that the Queen was all right, although you still got the sense that she is the one in control of their relationship.' (Well, the Queen is the Queen, after all.)

This is the chapter in my book that the Duke of Edinburgh's private secretary will feel is 'somewhat unnecessary'. I am uneasy about it myself, but only because I know the ways of the media: this is the chapter that will be serialised first and quoted, repeatedly, out of context. In context, I have few qualms about it. It is here as part of the story. It is here to set the record straight.

The Duke of Edinburgh has spent a lifetime being talked about and being misunderstood. He knows it. 'I've just got to live with it,' he said to me: 'It happens to a lot of people.' It happened to Charles Dodgson – the Victorian writer Lewis Carroll, creator of Alice in Wonderland. Dodgson had many girlfriends: children and young women who were his playmates, his special friends. In 1893, his sister, Mary, wrote to him about the gossip that was attached to these relationships. On 21 September 1893, he replied to his sister: 'You need not be shocked at my being spoken against. *Anybody* who is spoken about at all, is *sure* to be spoken against by *somebody*: and any action, however innocent in itself, is liable, and not at all unlikely, to be blamed by *somebody*. If you limit your actions in life to things that *nobody* can possibly find fault with, you will not do much!' (I am surprised he did not run to a double exclamation mark.) Lewis Carroll told his sister that as a result of his experience he was convinced 'that the opinion of "people" in general is absolutely worthless as a test of right and wrong'. He said that, for him, there were only two tests when 'having some particular girl-friend as a guest': did he have her family's '*full* approval for what I do'? And did he 'feel it to be entirely innocent and right in the sight of God'? Lewis Carroll told his sister his conscience was clear. The Duke of Edinburgh's conscience is clear, also.

And how about the Queen? How does she feel about all this in the dark watches of the night? She cannot say, fully, freely, as Robert Browning says in his poem, *By the Fireside*: 'We stood there with never a third.' But Robert Browning was a sentimentalist, which the Queen is not. She knows her man, loves him, admires him and accepts him as he is. She is also Sovereign of the Order of the Garter. *Honi soit qui mal y pense.*

Chapter Twelve

'Children begin by loving their parents. After a time, they judge them. Rarely, if ever, do they forgive them.'

Oscar Wilde (1854–1900), *A Woman of No Importance*

Dr Johnson was characteristically clear-cut in his advice to those about to embark on matrimony. 'Now that you are going to marry,' he said, 'do not expect more from life than life can afford.' His definition of the family was to the point, as well: 'A family is a little kingdom, torn into factions and exposed to revolutions.'

Princess Elizabeth, in fact, was brought up within a family unit that was small, close-knit, loving and giving – 'us four' as George VI put it. Elizabeth was an adorable child: she was adored by both her grandfathers, and adored them in return. George V died, aged seventy, in 1936, when Elizabeth was ten; 'Grandfather Strathmore', the 14th Earl, died eight years later, in 1944, aged eighty-nine. 'Grandma Strathmore' died suddenly, in the summer of 1938, aged sixty-five. Her daughter, Queen Elizabeth, wrote to the Prime Minister, Neville Chamberlain:

> I have been dreading this moment ever since I was a little girl and now that it has come, one can hardly believe it. She was a true 'Rock of Defence' for us, her children, & Thank God, her influence and wonderful example will remain with us all our lives.
>
> She had a good perspective of life – everything was given its true importance. She had a young spirit, great courage and unending sympathy whenever and wherever it was needed, & such a heavenly sense of humour. We all used to laugh together and have such fun.

George VI died in February 1952, aged only fifty-six, followed within fourteen months, by his mother, Queen Mary, aged eighty-five, formidable and forbidding in appearance, frail and in pain at the end, heartbroken by her second son's early death. In the year of her Coronation, the new young Queen, at the age of twenty-six, was left with just two of her immediate family: her mother, then aged only fifty-two, and her sister, aged twenty-two. Happily, both lived on for almost half a century more.

Elizabeth II had a good relationship with her mother – 'loving and normal' is how Margaret Rhodes described it to me. Queen Elizabeth the Queen Mother was blessed with many of the virtues she recognised in her own mother: a good perspective on life, a young spirit, a heavenly sense of humour. Elizabeth II loved her mother, respected her, *liked* her. She might occasionally shake her head when contemplating her mother's insouciant extravagance,[154] she might, now and again, express an envy of her mother's extraordinary capacity for avoiding all unpleasantness, but, fundamentally, mother and daughter were good friends, on the same wavelength, with mutual interests (especially horses), comfortable in each other's company, each looking forward to their regular, easy, uncomplicated chats on the telephone. The Queen recognised her mother's special star quality and had no desire to compete with her. Queen Elizabeth recognised her daughter as an exemplary Sovereign and was always careful to show due deference. (On the occasions when she momentarily forgot herself – stepping through a doorway ahead of the Queen, for example – she was always quick to apologise.) Margaret Rhodes' description of the Queen coming by to have a drink with Queen Elizabeth on a Sunday morning after church would be the envy of many a mother and daughter. 'There was mutual respect and deep affection,' said Mrs Rhodes, 'but, most of all, they just got on really, really well.'

Mrs Rhodes' description of the Queen's relationship with Princess Margaret is less dewy-eyed. 'The Queen was sometimes infuriated by Margaret, inevitably,' she told me. 'She found her behaviour exasperating at times, of course she did. But Margaret was her sister and she loved her.' From all the people I have spoken with who are close

---

[154] At the time of her death, her overdraft at Coutts was reported to be in the region of £4 million. She was supposed to have said at a dinner party once, 'Golly, I could do with £100,000, couldn't you? Had such an awful afternoon today with my bank manager scolding me about my overdraft.'

to the Queen – courtiers, friends and family members – I get the impression of someone who, though conservative by upbringing and conventional in her own life, is not judgemental when it comes to others. She looks for the best in people and hopes for the best from them and for them. When things go wrong, she prays (on her knees, with her hands folded together) that they will go better. She is sure of the values, principles and beliefs that have guided her life, but she is neither prescriptive nor dogmatic with regard to the lives of others. She may be Queen, but she does not lay down the law. She is reluctant to interfere in the private lives of members of her family, although she has done, now and again, in the case of her children, as we shall see. She was sorry to be depicted, as she felt she was, in a series of articles published in the *Daily Telegraph* in the run-up to her golden jubilee,[155] as someone who is emotionally inhibited, buttoned-up, psychologically repressed, awkward when it comes to being loving and giving. She may not express her emotions in the manner of the Princess Diana generation, but that does not means she is unfeeling.

The Queen was profoundly fond of her younger sister, for all Princess Margaret's waywardness. The Queen really loves Margaret's two children, David and Sarah, and sometimes seems more at ease in their company than she does in the company of one or two of her own offspring. In the 1950s, when Margaret Rose wanted to marry her father's equerry, Peter Townsend, the Queen was not unsympathetic. It was just a very difficult situation. When, in 1960, Princess Margaret married the photographer, Tony Armstrong-Jones, the Queen hoped they would live happily ever after. That they didn't was, from the Queen's point of view, a matter for sadness, not recrimination. Again, it was not easy. Divorce is commonplace nowadays (almost routine in the case of the Queen's children), but a generation ago things were different. The Duke of Windsor had married a divorcée in 1937, but it was not until thirty years later that someone in line to the throne (albeit eighteenth in line!) was divorced themselves. In 1967, George, the 7th Earl of Harewood, aged forty-four, became the first of George V's direct descendants to be divorced. His wife sued him on the grounds of his adultery with an Australian violinist, which he acknowleged. He wanted to marry his mistress (also a divorcée, and the mother of his son – oh yes: what a mess!) and to do so, under the

---

[155] Articles, based on a wide-ranging series of interviews by Graham Turner, published in book form as *Elizabeth: The Woman and The Queen*, 2002.

terms of the Royal Marriages Act, required the Sovereign's consent. The Queen sighed a sad sigh and, having taken advice from the Privy Coucil, granted it. Lord Harewood sighed a different sort of sigh and slipped discreetly out of the country (to the United States) to marry for the second time.[156]

The Queen loved her sister. And she liked Tony Snowdon. (It would be hard not to – he is talented and engaging and, always, went out of his way to be solicitous to both the Queen and his mother-in-law, Queen Elizabeth.) When the Snowdon marriage began to deteriorate, as early as the mid-1960s, the Queen was dismayed, and concerned, especially for the Snowdon children, but there was little or nothing she could do, except hope and pray – which, we can be sure, she did. The Snowdons had relationships beyond their marriage and rows within it. By 1976, the position was untenable, separation unavoidable. The Queen was saddened by what had happened, but when her press secretary declared, 'There has been no pressure from the Queen on either Princess Margaret or Lord Snowdon to take any particular course', he was speaking nothing but the truth. The Queen would have liked her sister to have had a happier, more fulfilled, less complicated life. In the 1970s and early 1980s, she read in the newspapers – you couldn't not – about her sister's relationship with young Roddy Llewellyn – a sandy-haired charmer (a gentleman gardener and garden designer) eighteen years Princess Margaret's junior – and, no doubt, felt that the publicity was not very good for the Royal Family and that the romance would, all too probably, end in tears.[157] She was right on both counts. She was concerned for her sister, but her attitude was

---

[156] Lord Harewood's first wife, Marion, subsequently married the Liberal politician, Jeremy Thorpe, later tried and acquitted on a charge of conspiracy to murder.

[157] It did, after seven years. Roddy moved on (and married, happily); Margaret lived on, but ended her life without a partner – though not without friends. I did not know her, but I know both Roddy Llewellyn and Tony Snowdon and they are each delightful: gifted, engaging, playful, funny. (Kenneth Williams heard Roddy tell a story over dinner at my house and recorded in his diary that he had never heard a story better told.) Princess Margaret did not treat her body as a temple: she smoked and drank and paid the price. She was spoilt, she could be self-indulgent, the stories of her rudeness and bad behaviour are too many not to have had some truth to them. However, from all I have heard of her, from her husband, from her lover, from her friend Angela Huth, among others, it is clear that, at her best, she was great fun: witty, giving, thoughtful, musical and gay. She was loyal to the Queen, proud of her country and did her duty, as and when required. Several said to me that she never quite recovered from the death of her father in 1952.

sympathetic, sometimes despairing, but never 'holier than thou'. Sarah Bradford, in her biography, quotes the Queen as referring to 'my sister's guttersnipe life'. Those who know the Queen well tell me that does not sound like the Queen they know. It simply is not her kind of turn of phrase.

While the drama of the disintegrating Snowdon marriage unfolded, the Duke of Edinburgh stayed out of the way – figuratively speaking, and, often, literally, too. 'I don't go looking for trouble' is how he put it to me. In terms of education, upbringing, experience, attitude, temperament and physique, Prince Philip and Lord Snowdon could not be more different, but each seems to have made it his business to be on relatively good terms with the other. (To this day, Lord Snowdon has a small, framed, solo portrait of the Duke standing on his desk.) Doubtless, like the Queen, Philip had reservations about the somewhat rackety nature of the extra-marital adventures of his in-laws (and the attendant publicity), but was there anything very helpful he could do in the matter? Not really. Besides, he had his own sisters and mother to think about.

Throughout their lives, Prince Philip maintained a fond and active interest in his sisters and their families. Cécile, the third of his four sisters, her husband and their three children, all died in and after the tragic air crash of 1937. Sophie, known as 'Tiny', the youngest of the four, lived on into the twenty-first century, dying, aged eighty-seven, in November 2001. She was widowed in 1943, and left with the title of Princess but no very princely income and the challenge of bringing up five small children on her own. In 1946, aged thirty-two, 'pretty little widow Tiny' (as Queen Mary called her) married Prince George Wilhelm of Hanover,[158] aged thirty-three, headmaster of Salem School (reckoned a sound appointment by Kurt Hahn), and went on to have three more children. Theodora, known as 'Dolla', Philip's second sister, had married Berthold, Margrave of Baden,[159] in 1931, and had three

[158] For his biography of Princess Alice, Hugo Vickers interviewed Prince George of Hanover who told him of his mother-in-law's habit of having a ready answer for everything: 'She would say: "That is because . . ." and then she would pause until she came up with the answer!' Prince Philip is certainly his mother's son.

[159] 'Margrave, a German nobleman of rank equivalent to an English marquis' – *Chambers Dictionary*. 'Baden, bounded S and W by the Rhine, contains the Black Forest and part of the Swabian Jura. Formed (1771) from the Margraviates of Baden-Baden and Baden-Durlach. Became a Grand Duchy 1806. In 1952 in the new arrangement of *Länder* ('States') it became part of Baden-Württemberg' – *Penguin Encyclopedia of*

children. Berthold died, aged fifty-seven, in 1963. Dolla died six years later, in 1969, aged sixty-three. (Philip was on an official tour of Canada and the United States at the time and, as duty comes first, decided he could not return for her funeral. Prince Charles, recently invested as Prince of Wales, was despatched to Salem to represent him.) Dolla's health had been poor for several years. Even before her husband's death, when she was still in her fifties, Dolla was described by Alice (in letters to Philip) as looking 'old & haggard', with a bad heart, 'arteries narrowing', walking with a stick. Philip's eldest sister, Margarita, born in 1905, married Prince Gottfried of Hohenlohe-Langenburg, known as 'Friedel' Hohenlohe, another German princeling and descendant of Queen Victoria, in 1931. They had four sons and two daughters and a handsome home at Langenburg, one of seven Hohenlohe castles that now feature on the 'Castle Trail' promoted by the Rhine Valley Tourist Board. Friedel died in 1960, aged sixty-three, and not long after, Margarita suffered a further loss, when, in January 1963, an extensive fire at Langenburg destroyed much of the castle and all of her personal possessions. She died in 1981, aged seventy-six.

Before the war, Philip visited his sisters and their husbands in Germany. After the war, he was again in regular touch. The fear of anti-German sentiment meant that they were not invited to Philip and Elizabeth's wedding in 1947 – about which they were unhappy and not wholly understanding – but they were very much on parade at Elizabeth II's Coronation. Within weeks of the accession, Margarita reported to Uncle Dickie that the sisters had firmly 'fixed that in Philip's mind!!'. Philip saw them when he could and corresponded with them regularly. He paid private visits to them in Germany and regularly invited them to visit Britain, to stay with him and the Queen in Scotland. In 1965, twenty years after the end of the war in Europe, the Queen and Prince Philip paid their first official state visit to Germany and the ten-day programme allowed time for a number of unofficial excursions: Philip took Elizabeth to Wolfsgarten, the Hesse-Darmstadt family heartland; to Salem for a weekend with Dolla; to Langenburg to visit Margarita. They kept in touch. They were his family. He keeps in touch with nephews and nieces and a multitude of cousins, still.

Philip's mother was an unusual lady. More than once, in response to letters of condolence, Philip described her life as one 'of wars,

Places. Berthold was the son of Max of Baden, former Chancellor of the German Empire, and co-founder, with Kurt Hahn, of Salem School. Berthold and Theodora (and Philip) were related in sundry ways, including being descendants of George III.

revolutions, separations and tragedies'. She was a survivor. She had many strengths: she was intelligent, thoughtful, kind-hearted, honest, honourable, determined. She could also be infuriatingly wilful and contrary. She had visionary qualities and a spiritual dimension that was always sincere, if occasionally difficult to pin down. There is evidently much of her in her only son. In the 1930s, her mental breakdown and her separation from her husband destroyed her family life, but she recovered and soldiered on. During and after the war she lived in Greece, relatively modestly, travelling, when it became possible, and travelling widely – to Britain, to Germany, to Sweden, around Europe, even to India and the Middle East. Philip saw as much of his mother as their unusual lives allowed. For example, in the summer of 1966, visiting Sophie in Germany, Alice was taken ill with liver and heart problems and admitted to a hospital in Munich. Philip paid the hospital bills and, then, eight weeks later, returning to Balmoral from the Commonwealth Games in Jamaica, and hearing that his mother was well enough to travel and anxious to get home, immediately flew himself from Scotland to Germany, collected his mother, and flew her on to Athens, where he spent the night to settle her in, and then flew immediately back to Scotland. Again, early in 1967, travelling to and from Australia on official business, he visited her in Athens, this time bringing some new carpet with him for her flat.

Later in 1967, the aftermath of the 'Colonels' Coup' of 21 April – which led, effectively, to the end of the Greek monarchy – and her own failing health forced her to accept her son and daughter-in-law's invitation to come to live at Buckingham Palace. She had been reluctant to leave the country she regarded as home for the land of her birth, but when she was told the invitation had come from 'Lilibet personally', she said, 'We go this afternoon.'

According to Stephen Barry, another royal servant who disobliged his former employers by publishing a volume of reminiscences,[160] the Palace staff found the Duke's mother, in her grey nun's habit, 'strange but likeable'. She was, said Barry, 'eccentric and deaf, and smoked like a chimney. If we could tell when the Queen was coming by the

[160] *Royal Secrets*, 1985. The book does not quite live up to its enticing title, but I enjoyed it. Then again, I enjoyed the telltale books by Marion Crawford, John Dean and Paul Burrell (the governess, the valet and the butler), while understanding how infuriating and intrusive the Royal Family will have found them. I am grateful to Mrs Thompson (the Brandreth family's lone cleaning lady) for her discretion over more than twenty years.

pattering of the corgis' feet, we always knew when Princess Andrew was about from the clouds of smoke that followed her. And the coughing. The poor lady coughed incessantly as she lit another cigarette. Not surprisingly, she was often in hospital with bronchitis.'

Alice died at Buckingham Palace, in her sleep, on 5 December 1969, aged eighty-four. Her granddaughter, Princess Anne, who had just turned nineteen, asked to see her and later told Princess Alice's biographer, Hugo Vickers, 'I am glad I did that. She looked very peaceful. All the lines in her face had gone and for the first time I could see the resemblance to the de László portrait.' Philip de László's handsome portraits of Prince Philip's parents, painted when Edward VII was King and they were still in their twenties, hang in Philip's study at Buckingham Palace to this day. Philip almost never speaks of his parents, but he guards their memory and, in my experience, brooks no criticism of them, of any kind. He is fiercely loyal. They are his family.

'We are a family,' the Duke repeated to me, somewhat exasperated when I was quizzing him about his relationships with his children and their partners. 'We are a family,' he said. 'What do you expect?' You expect ups and downs, good times and bad – that's the truth. And we all know it. The Queen and Prince Philip have a family life that is complex and sometimes complicated. That is true of most of us. Need more be said? The Queen and Prince Philip are weary – 'thoroughly fed up' is the Prince's phrase – of the media's apparently insatiable appetite for the meanest morsel of tittle-tattle about their own and their children's and their grandchildren's private lives, not only because much of what gets published is simply inaccurate, but also because, as individuals, the Queen and the Duke belong to a more discreet generation. There are some things you just don't talk about.

The Emperor Napoleon – whose younger brother Lucien was the forebear of Princess Marie Bonaparte, who married Prince Philip's father's older brother, Prince George (Big George) of Greece: this is, in every sense, a family saga – used to say that if you truly want to know a person you should think of the world as it was when that person was twenty. When Philip and Elizabeth were twenty the world was not as it is now. Couples had their problems, families had their feuds, but, on the whole, and as a rule, they were not much discussed at home, and never broadcast abroad. You simply did not wash your domestic dirty linen in public. Now we let it all hang out. The Duke of Edinburgh has complained to me more than once that 'the media have turned us into a soap opera'. Well, like it or not, this is the age of the soap opera. Flick through the popular magazines and newspapers of the 1940s – the decade in which Philip and Elizabeth each turned twenty – and you will read about war, history, travel, fashion, home-making, hobbies. Flick through the most popular publications of today and you will read, almost exclusively, about celebrity, sex and 'relationships'. We are gripped by 'relationships'.

Within the Queen and Prince Philip's immediate family there is only one relationship that presents them with real difficulty: their relationship with their eldest son, Prince Charles. When, once, talking with the Duke of Edinburgh about him being somehow at odds with Prince Charles, I began to say that I found it strange because they seem to me to be remarkably similar, similar in mannerisms, similar in interests. The Duke interrupted me. 'Yes,' he said, 'but with one great difference. He's a romantic – and I'm a pragmatist. That means we do see things differently.' He paused and shrugged, and said, with a slightly despairing laugh, 'And because I don't see things as a romantic would, I'm unfeeling.'

In my experience, Prince Philip is pragmatic and unsentimental, but far from unfeeling. Prince Charles begs to differ. He still recalls – he still talks about – the mortifying day when his father came to Gordonstoun, to see his son, just turned seventeen, play the title role in the school production of *Macbeth* – and laughed. 'It was the "Scottish play",' remembers Prince Charles. 'I had to lie on a huge, fur rug and have a nightmare. My parents came and watched, along with other parents. I lay there and thrashed about and all I could hear was my father and "ha, ha, ha". I went up to him afterwards and said, "Why did you laugh?" and he said, "It sounds like *The Goons*."'

You could fill a book with tales from the Prince of Wales of hurtful moments from his childhood – and, to an extent, he already has. In the early 1990s, Charles cooperated with the broadcaster Jonathan Dimbleby to produce a television film and biography that made plain that Charles was profoundly unhappy about his childhood. By now in his forties, going grey and with a pained expression, he let the world know that, as he was growing up, he felt that he was 'emotionally estranged' from both his parents, craving 'the affection and appreciation' from them that they were either 'unable or unwilling' to offer. His stories of small slights that left their scars are many and similar. When, as a little boy, he forgot to call his detective 'Mr' and simply used his surname, as he heard his parents do all the time, he was made to apologise. When he left a door open and a footman went to close it, Philip stopped the footman, barking, 'Leave it alone, man. The boy's got hands.' When, one winter on the Sandringham estate, young Charles was throwing snowballs at a police officer, Philip called to the policeman, 'Don't just stand there, throw some back!' When, again at Sandringham, Charles came back from playing in the grounds one afternoon, having lost a dog lead, his mother sent him straight out again, instructing him not to return until he had found what he had lost, reminding him, 'Dog leads cost money.' When, this time in London, young Charles was seen sticking his tongue out at the crowd watching him drive down the Mall, his father gave him a spanking.

Talking to Jonathan Dimbleby (and, before him, to those of his friends and family who cared to listen), Charles gave the impression that he regarded his father as a bully and a tyrant and his mother as distant and ungiving. As a little boy at Buckingham Palace, he passed his mother's study one day and asked her to come and play with him. Gently closing the door against him, she said, 'If only I could.' When his parents returned from their post-Coronation tour and Charles, aged five, was taken in *Britannia* to the port of Tobruk to greet them, the little boy attempted to join the line of dignitaries waiting to shake Her Majesty by the hand. 'No, not you, dear,' were the mother's first words to her son after five months of separation.

Charles felt neglected at home and abandoned at school. The Queen, educated at home, and, though Head of State herself, brought up traditionally to accept the father as the natural head of the family, was content to be led by her husband in the matter of her own children's education. 'The Queen and I,' said Philip in 1956, when Charles was seven, rising eight, 'want Charles to go to school with other boys of his generation and learn to live with other children, and to absorb from childhood the discipline imposed by education with others.' In September 1957, two months before his ninth birthday, Charles was despatched to his first boarding school, Cheam in Hampshire. The school had changed its location since Philip had been a pupil a quarter of a century earlier, but the school's spirit remained the same. Charles later reflected that his first weeks at Cheam had been the loneliest of his life. Five years later, in 1962, again following in his father's footsteps, Charles moved on to Gordonstoun, in Scotland, on the Moray Firth. His new school's spartan regime was not to his taste. 'It's absolute hell,' Charles wrote home. 'It's near Balmoral,' his father told him. 'There's always the Factor there. You can go and stay with him.[161] And your grandmother goes up there to fish. You can go and see her.' And he did, whenever he could. Queen Elizabeth the Queen Mother was a loving grandmother who always gave her favourite grandson an understanding shoulder to cry on and a warm bosom to embrace. Charles adored his grandmother. His distress at her death was pitiful to behold. He was bereft. 'She was quite simply the most magical grandmother you could possibly have and I was utterly devoted to her,' he said. 'For me, she meant everything, and I have dreaded, dreaded this moment.'

When asked how Prince Charles was getting on at Gordonstoun, Prince Philip replied, 'Well, at least he hasn't run away yet.' In fact, he stayed the course and did rather well. He became 'Guardian' (head boy) as his father had done before him (and Prince Edward would later do) and secured two A levels (Grade B in History, Grade C in French), becoming the first heir to the throne in British history to achieve a university place on the strength of academic credentials alone. He may not have enjoyed some of the rigours of the Gordonstoun routine, but he acknowledged that the school had developed his 'will power' and helped his self-discipline, 'not in the sense of making you bath in cold water, but in the Latin sense, of giving shape and form to your life'. The philosophy of Kurt Hahn that helped form Prince Philip, helped form Prince Charles, too. The values that inspired the Duke of Edinburgh Award Scheme and the Outward Bound Trust are not dissimilar from those that underpin the work of the Prince's Trust.

The Queen and Prince Philip admire their son's achievements. The Queen, in particular, has gone out of her way to praise him in public and to thank him – sincerely, and from the heart – both for the support he has given her over the years and for the range of good works he undertakes, with imagination and dedication, on behalf of the wider community. Privately, she grumbles about his extravagance. The Queen keeps her breakfast cereals fresher longer by storing them in Tupperware containers. The Prince of Wales does not. He has a style and taste and panache – and way with money – that reflect his maternal grandmother rather than his parents. He entertains, and entertains

---

[161] 'Factor, *n*, an agent managing heritable estates for another (*Scottish*)' – *Chambers Dictionary*. Charles sought comfort and companionship from family retainers. He was close to the nannies of his early childhood, Helen Lightbody and Mabel Anderson, and to his governess, Catherine Peebles, known as 'Mispy'. She recalled how sensitive and tentative Charles was as a small boy: 'If you raised your voice to him, he would draw back into his shell, and for a time you would be able to do nothing with him.'

royally. The Queen is reported to have said, 'The amount of kit and staff he takes about – it's obscene.' I think he thinks that's part of the point of being Prince of Wales. At a party at Highgrove, I thanked him for his superb hospitality and congratulated him on the wonderful way it was all done: the silver, the crystal, the lighting, the flowers – especially the flowers. 'They came from the garden,' he said. 'It's a joy to behold,' I murmured. 'Isn't it?' he said, beaming, 'I'm so glad you like it. I want you to like it. I'm so lucky to have all these lovely things around me. I simply want to share them. I want everyone to love my garden. It is a joy, isn't it? Such a joy.' That simply is not the way his parents talk.

The Queen, of course, does not talk to the press. The Duke of Edinburgh does. Indeed, I made the point to him once that he started it all, that he was the first senior member of the Royal Family to give any kind of extended interview. 'Yes,' he said, 'I made a conscious decision to talk to the media – but not about me, only about what I'm doing, what I'm supporting.' That Prince Charles should voluntarily talk to a broadcaster and journalist about family matters, about his private life, and let the journalist have access to his diaries and private correspondence, seemed to his parents sheer foolishness. The Queen and the Duke were appalled by the Dimbleby book. They could not see how their son's indiscretions – or special pleading on his own behalf – could serve his cause, or that of the Royal Family, in any way. They were also hurt by their son's public complaints about the quality of their parenting. They had meant well, they had done their best, and their recollection of Charles's childhood was rather different from his own. They recalled fun and games, bath-times, story-telling, picnics and bonfires, laughter not tears. Prince Philip remembers taking Charles and Anne, regularly, during the summer holidays, cruising in his twelve-metre yacht *Bloodhound* and believes that these were 'good times, happy days'.

I am on the Duke's side, but he is not above reproach. Charles may whinge about his childhood, but Philip cannot resist firing cheap shots at his son's expense. He does it all the time. It's a habit. He may not even realise how frequently he does it. For example, I recall, twenty years ago, happening to be with Prince Philip on his birthday. He had come to the headquarters of the National Playing Fields Association for a fund-raising event. Before meeting the multitude and working the crowd, he met up with the charity's small band of officers for a cup of tea and a chat. We presented him with a birthday present: three pairs of gloves – same make, same size, different colours – to wear while carriage-driving. He undid the wrapping paper and inspected the gloves. The brown ones he liked, the tan-coloured pair also met with his approval; but the lilac-coloured gloves he held out somewhat disdainfully, saying, with a smirk, 'I think we'll pass these on to the Prince of Wales.' Two years ago, I happened to be with him at Buckingham Palace, with the director of the Outward Bound Trust, at a meeting to discuss plans for his eightieth birthday celebration at the Albert Hall. Our meeting coincided with an outbreak of Foot and Mouth disease in England and Wales. Farms, fields and swathes of countryside were being closed to contain the spread of the disease. The director of the Outward Bound Trust reported proudly that none of the OBT's activities had yet had to be curtailed, while the Prince's Trust had already pulled the plug on an assortment of its outdoor enterprises. 'Doesn't surprise me,' said the Duke, with a chuckle. Gina Kennard, who has known him and his family all her life, said to me, 'He just can't resist coming out with these personal remarks. He can't stop himself. He's at his worst with Charles, but he could be quite sarcastic with Anne too, you know.'

That something went wrong in his relationship with Prince Charles is undeniable. Charles is a sensitive flower. He was shy. He was uncertain. As an adolescent, he bruised easily. The poet Kathleen Raine (1908–2003), only a little younger than his grandmother, met him when he was in his early twenties and thought, 'That poor young man – anything I can do for him, I will do, because he is very lonely.' The Queen Mother, not deliberately (though she was capable of mischief), but, effectively, made him feel that she understood him in a way that his parents did not. 'He is a very gentle boy,' she said, 'with a very kind heart, which I think is the essence of everything.' Queen Elizabeth offered Charles a safe haven and warm waters, away from the cool breeze of his mother and the harsh wind of his father. Gina Kennard said to me, 'When he was a little boy, there didn't seem to be a problem at all, but, as he was growing up, I think probably the Queen was too tolerant, and Prince Philip too tough.'

Countess Mountbatten, Philip's first cousin and one of Charles's godparents, said to me, 'You can see it from both sides, can't you? A resilient character such as Prince Philip, toughened by the slings and arrows of life, who sees being tough as a necessity for survival, wants to toughen up his son – and his son is very sensitive. It hasn't been easy for either of them.' Patricia Mountbatten paused and then added, with a dry laugh, 'Anne, of course, as a natural tomboy, presented no problems.'[162]

Anne is like her father. She will make no complaint of any kind about her upbringing. Father and daughter have always got on well. They are alike in many ways. They undertake their public duties in the same brisk, no-nonsense fashion; they compete with one another as to which can fulfill the more engagements in the year (Prince Philip and the Princess Royal are the most active members of the Royal Family by quite a margin); they vie with one another as to which has the more efficient private office. They have an easy, good-humoured, comfortable relationship. They don't brood about it: they just get on with it.

Philip was separated from his mother throughout his adolescence, but refuses – absolutely – to use that as an excuse for anything. He will not find fault with his mother, however hard you press him. Anne will not find fault with hers, either – whatever Charles may say. The idea that, as a mother, the Queen was remote and uncaring – an idea spread by Prince Charles via Jonathan Dimbleby in 1994, and fostered by anonymous courtiers quoted by Graham Turner in his golden jubilee portrait of the Queen in 2002 – is flatly rejected by the Princess Royal. 'I'm not going to speak for anyone else,' she says, 'but I simply don't believe that there is any evidence whatsoever to suggest that she wasn't caring. It just beggars belief. We as children may have not been too demanding, in the sense that we understood what the limitations were in time and the responsibilities placed on her as monarch in the things she had to do and the travels she had to make, but I don't believe that any of us, for a second, thought she didn't care for us in exactly the same way as any other mother did. I just think it's extraordinary that anybody could construe that that might not be true.'

Anne found her father demanding in a way that was encouraging and her mother tolerant in a way that allowed her children to find their own feet. 'If she'd been a disciplinarian,' says Anne, with a wry smile, 'and said "No" to everybody, we'd have all been psycho-analysed out of existence on the basis that we had too controlling a mother. We've all been allowed to find our own way and we were always encouraged to discuss problems, to talk them through. People have to make their own mistakes and I think she's always accepted that.'

[162] Mabel Anderson, who was nanny to both Prince Charles and Princess Anne, said: 'He was never as boisterous and noisy as Princess Anne. She had a much stronger, more extrovert personality. She didn't exactly push him aside, but she was certainly a more forceful child.'

'We are a family,' Prince Philip said to me. In much the same way, Princess Anne adds, 'Judging by some families, I think we are all on pretty good speaking terms after all this time, and that's no mean achievement for quite a lot of families. I think we all enjoy each other's company.'

The family grew in the early 1960s. Prince Andrew, now Duke of York, was born on 19 February 1960. Prince Edward, now Earl of Wessex, was born on 10 March 1964. (There is a lovely, informal photograph, taken in June 1964, of the Queen carrying baby Edward in her arms on their way by train to Balmoral. She looks anything but unmotherly.[163]) Martin Charteris told me that, when Andrew was conceived, 'the Queen and Prince Philip had been trying for another baby for quite a while.' 'How on earth do you know?' I asked him. 'Because Her Majesty told me so,' he chuckled. 'She wanted me to pass it on to President Nkrumah, you see.' I didn't see, so Lord Charteris, beaming broadly, obligingly explained: 'In late 1959, the Queen was due to visit Ghana. It was going to be a big thing. In May she discovered she was pregnant and realised that the Ghana trip would have to be put off. She knew that Dr Nkrumah was a sensitive chap[164] and might take offence unless he knew the whole story, so I was despatched to Accra to put him in the picture – which I did. At first, he was appalled, then he decided that if the Queen couldn't come to him, he'd go to her – at Balmoral – which he did. I have to say, she has a way with these Commonwealth leaders. They trust her. Absolutely.'

In due course, Andrew and Edward followed Charles to Gordonstoun – and survived. In 1979, aged nineteen, exactly forty years after his parents' celebrated encounter there, Andrew enrolled at Dartmouth Royal Naval College. At twenty-one, he qualified as a helicopter pilot and joined 829 Naval Air Squadron, flying Sea Kings from the carrier HMS *Invincible*. In April 1982, *Invincible* sailed for the

[163] In her biography, Sarah Bradford quotes the Queen telling an unnamed friend in 1964, 'Goodness what fun it is to have a baby in the house again! He is a great joy to us all, especially Andrew who is completely fascinated by him. In fact he considers him his own property, even telling Charles and Anne to "come and see *my* baby"!'
[164] Kwame Nkrumah (1909–72) studied theology in the United States in the 1930s, attended the London School of Economics in 1945, returning to his native Gold Coast in 1947 where he founded the Convention People's Party and spent two years in prison charged with 'political agitation'. In 1951 he was appointed first prime minister of the Gold Coast (known as Ghana from 1957) and became first president of the republic in 1960. His vanity was boundless. He created a one-party state and proclaimed himself 'Redeemer'. He was deposed in a military *coup* in 1966.

South Atlantic with the British naval task force set to recapture the Falkand Islands from the invading Argentines. He put his life on the line.[165] 'Prince Andrew is a serving officer,' said Buckingham Palace in answer to suggestions that the Queen might want to keep her son out of harm's way, 'and there is no question in her mind that he should go.' When Port Stanley was liberated and the conflict over, Andrew telephoned home. 'My mother was in,' he said, 'it was about the right time of evening.' She told him that she was relieved he was safe and how proud his parents were of him, and then, immediately, she asked him 'to pass on how proud she was of everyone and to say how marvellously the troops had done'.

In June 1986, Prince Edward, having graduated from Cambridge (with a respectable degree in modern history), joined the Royal Marines, notoriously the toughest billet in the armed services. Given his slight build and his reported ambition at the time to be an actor, it seemed an odd choice for the twenty-two-year-old to make, but he had signed up before going to university and was determined to make a go of it. He tried, and he failed. It was the psychological as much as the physical demands of the training that overwhelmed him. And, apparently, the attitude of his commanding officer was unsympathetic. In January 1987, with the acquiescence of his parents, Edward resigned his commission. His father (Captain-General of the Royal Marines) was disappointed, but coped. These things happen. That's life. You just have to get on with it.

Philip, in my experience, speaks of Edward with an ease and warmth that he does not evince when talking of the Prince of Wales – who, of course, having secured his own, adequate, degree from Cambridge (BA Hons, Class II, Division II), went on to serve in Her Majesty's armed services for six not unchallenging years. At the RAF training college at Cranwell, Charles showed immediately that he shared his father's aptitude for flying. He then followed his father to the Royal Naval College, Dartmouth, and served in a series of warships: *Norfolk*, *Minerva*, *Jupiter* and *Hermes*. At the time of the Falklands conflict,

---

[165] Two hundred and fifty-five British officers and men died in the conflict – and 652 Argentines, lest we forget. The senior members of the British Royal Family are impressively sanguine about putting their lives on the line. They live with the ever-present threat of assassination. In June 1981, twenty-two months after the murder of Lord Mountbatten, six shots were fired at the Queen as she rode on horseback down the Mall to attend Trooping the Colour. Her horse, Burmese, reared up, but Her Majesty brought the animal under control at once and rode on regardless.

Charles expressed regret that he had not been 'tested' in action as Andrew had been, but, throughout his years of service (1970–76) – culminating with a stint as a helicopter pilot in the Fleet Air Arm – he was as gung-ho and courageous as any father could wish. There is, however, something perverse about Prince Philip. He is not always easy. He likes to be contrary and, perhaps, just because nobody would expect it, he seems to prefer Edward, who flunked the Royal Marines, to Charles, who served in the services with distinction and pushed himself to the limit. Gradually, Edward has taken on a number of his father's commitments, notably as the front man for the Duke of Edinburgh Award. The Queen has already let it be known that, when Prince Philip dies, Prince Edward will be recreated as the new Duke of Edinburgh. Edward's first-born, Louise, is the first royal child to bear the surname Mountbatten-Windsor.

The youngest of the royal children has been the most indulged. In June 1987, a year after he joined the Royal Marines, Edward, now twenty-three and settled on a new career in entertainment, joined forces with the BBC and John Broome, the owner of the Midlands-based visitor attraction, Alton Towers, to present a spectacular royal version of the slapstick-and-games TV show, *It's A Knockout!*. According to Edward, 'Both the BBC and John Broome positively drooled at the idea.' Of course, they did! Edward persuaded his sister Anne, his brother Andrew and Andrew's new wife, Sarah Ferguson (who needed little persuading), to dress up in mock-Tudor costumes and lead teams of celebrities – Rowan Atkinson, Les Dawson and Barbara Windsor among them – as they competed in a series of silly fun and games loosely disguised as a medieval joust-about. It was well-meant, and useful sums were raised for charity, but *It's A Royal Knockout* did nothing for the dignity of the House of Windsor or the standing of the new generation of young royals. Everyone at Buckingham Palace at the time (from the private secretary to the press office) claims to have been against it, but Edward was determined (utterly determined) and the Queen did not have it in her to say 'No'. The embarrassment of the spectacle itself was compounded by Prince Edward's post-show press conference. The attendant hacks, hot and weary after a long day, not satisfied with the access they had been given to the 'royal celebrities', failed to show any enthusiasm for what Edward hoped the world would regard as his finest hour. Faced with the media's indifference, Edward made a couple of sarcastic remarks and stalked out of the press tent. 'Edward Storms Out After Game Show' ran one headline; 'It's a Walkout' ran another.

The press for the young Prince did not improve much as the years went by. They were relatively gentle with him when he worked as a backroom boy and production assistant for Andrew Lloyd Webber's Really Useful Group, but when he turned his attention to television film-making, and founded his own production company, Ardent, the gloves were off again. The films were rubbished; he was accused of exploiting his family name to get them made; Ardent was repeatedly reported to be making losses – losses of almost £2 million over seven years, according to the *Guardian*. The knock-out blow came in April 2001 and was delivered by the *News of the World*. (No wonder Philip is close to Edward: they both share a loathing for Rupert Murdoch's brand of tabloid journalism. Philip dates the decline in the tone and standards of Britain's popular press to Murdoch's arrival in the United Kingdom.)

In June 1999, Edward, aged thirty-five, had married Sophie Rhys-Jones, aged thirty-four, a pretty, wholesome, blonde public relations executive who appeared to have a sensible head on resolute shoulders. Appearances can be deceptive – as Sophie, now Countess of Wessex, found to her cost when, in the spring of 2001, on behalf of her PR company, she took a meeting with a potential 'client', an Arab 'sheikh', who turned out to be an undercover reporter for the *News of the World*. Sophie's small talk, as recorded by the 'sheikh', was hardly treasonable, but it was unfortunate. She referred to the Queen as 'the old dear' and the Queen Mother as 'the old lady' and described the Prince of Wales and Camilla Parker Bowles as 'number one on the unpopular people list', only likely to be married after the death of 'the old lady'. She was not discreet. She mocked the Prime Minister, calling him 'President Blair'; she poured scorn on the Prime Minister's wife, calling her 'horrid, absolutely horrid'; and she described the Leader of the Opposition (William Hague) as 'deformed'. Most damagingly, she let slip that, while her company's prestige and royal connections were not officially for hire, 'that is an unspoken benefit'.

When Sophie discovered the truth about the sting, on advice from Buckingham Palace, she sought to bury her indiscretions and buy off the *News of the World* by giving them 'a personal interview' – and promptly fell between two stools. Rival newspapers tumbled over themselves to publish edited highlights of her secretly recorded conversation with the 'sheikh' (leaked to them – goodness knows how!) and the *News of the World* carried a sensational interview that was as personal as anyone could hope for. 'My Edward Is Not Gay' ran the headline, above a story in which the Countess denounced the rumours of her husband's homosexuality and revealed that they were determined to have a baby and were even contemplating *in vitro* fertilisation in order to be able to do so.

And the consequence of all this was . . . well, you can see for yourself by checking out the official Buckingham Palace website at www.royal.gov.uk:

> The Earl of Wessex announced in 2002 that he and The Countess of Wessex had decided to concentrate on supporting The Queen during the Golden Jubilee and beyond, and helping the Royal Family shoulder some of the increasing workload into the future. They therefore withdrew from their respective companies, Ardent Productions and R-JH, in order to focus their energies more into supporting those organisations, charities, individuals and companies who deserve to be recognised for their effort, initiative and entrepreneurship.

Prince Edward features in a number of other, less dignified websites, where he is listed, variously, as a 'celebrity gay', 'a royal gay icon' and 'the Queen's queen'. He is not homosexual and never has been, though the rumour was rife in London throughout the 1980s. At the time, I was working at the breakfast television station TV-am, where, despite the assurances of Edward's best friend at the station (James Baker, son of the newsreader, Richard Baker) and the close (and charming) attention paid by Edward to our beautiful young weather girl, Ulrika Jonsson, we would not accept that the seventh in line to the throne was anything but a closet screamer. There was something about his mouth, his manner, his handshake, his hairline, his record – leaving the Marines, that petulant performance after the royal *It's A Knockout!* – that convinced us he was homosexual. Had he been, I believe his parents, born and brought up long before the decriminalisation of homosexual acts between consenting adults in private (which only happened in 1967), would nevertheless have coped – and coped quite well. The Queen is a devout and traditional Christian, the Duke of Edinburgh is very much a man's man, but neither betrays the least hint of homophobia. They are tolerant people: on the whole, they accept others as they find them. In the case of their children, and their children's choice in partners, they have done their level best not to interfere. It has not always been easy.

Princess Anne was the first of the royal children to be married. As far as her parents were concerned, she was free to marry anybody she chose. She chose to marry Lieutenant Mark Phillips, born 1948, educated at Marlborough and Sandhurst, a guardsman (The Queen's Dragoons), the soldier son of a soldier, and, more to the point, an achieving equestrian: a key member of the British three-day eventing team that had triumphed in the World Championships in 1970, the European Championships in 1971 and the Olympic Games in Munich in 1972. Anne, too, was an achieving equestrian: in 1971 she won the individual European Three-Day Event at Burghley; in 1976 she would be a member of the British Olympic Team in Montreal. On 14 November 1973 (Prince Charles's twenty-fifth birthday), at Westminster Abbey, before a congregation of a thousand and a television audience of many millions, Anne and Mark were married. 'I shouldn't wonder if their children are four-legged,' the Queen is supposed to have remarked.

Once upon a time, not so long ago, the only daughter of the Queen of England would have been expected to marry a prince of some kind – or, at least, a high-ranking aristocrat. There were sound reasons for this: he would know the rules, he would know his way around the court, he might even have land and money enough to keep the royal daughter in the style to which she was accustomed. The twentieth century changed all that. Gradually, over several decades, the rigid British class structure – so clear, so certain, in its own way, so helpful, when Queen Victoria's granddaughter, Princess Victoria, had married Prince Philip's grandfather, Prince Louis of Battenberg, in 1884 – began to collapse. The Great War changed much, the Second World War changed more. The invention of the refrigerator, the washing machine and the dishwasher, the 1944 Education Act, the arrival of television, the advent of the Pill, the Angry Young Men of the 1950s, the Beatles, the Rolling Stones, Harold Wilson – they all played a part. At the beginning of the Queen's reign, at royal investitures, as Her Majesty passed, everybody bowed or curtsied to the ground. Now, nobody does. The age of deference is dead. Old money has given way to new money. Meritocrats outrank aristocrats, and celebrities outclass them both.

The Queen and the Duke of Edinburgh helped their children adjust to this changing world quite effectively by sending them away to boarding school. Philip is as royal as they come, but he is nothing like an English aristocrat. He is an outsider; a European; in many ways, an iconoclast. Philip chose Gordonstoun – Kurt Hahn's Gordonstoun – for his sons – not Eton or Harrow. Anne went to Benenden, a girls' school in Kent, because Gordonstoun was not yet coeducational. (Both Anne's children, Peter and Zara, born in 1977 and 1981, went to Gordonstoun and then to Exeter University.) As a child, educated at home, Princess Elizabeth did not mix and mingle – let alone live and play – with the middle classes. At Benenden, Princess Anne did. At Gordonstoun and Benenden, the royal children met middle-class children, with middle-class values, and shared the middle class experience.

Mark Phillips was from solidly middle-class stock, thoroughly respectable, if a little unexciting. When I met him I liked him. He seemed on the shy side and sparing with the small talk – but what do I know about dressage? In royal circles, he was reckoned dull and a bit dim, and Prince Charles is credited with giving him the nickname 'Fog'. Four months after their marriage, however, Anne's new husband proved his worth. One night, in March 1974, as they were being driven along the Mall on their way back to Buckingham Palace after a charity film show, an armed man yanked open their car door and attempted to abduct the Princess. Shots were fired. The assailant pulled Anne frantically by one arm while she held tight to Mark with the other. Eventually, police arrived in sufficient numbers to subdue the attacker, who turned out to have a history of mental illness. The world was rightly impressed by the Princess's cool under fire. 'Her bravery and superb obstinacy were unbelievable,' Prince Charles recorded in his diary when he heard about the incident. 'My admiration for such a sister knows no bounds!' Anne was unhurt, but her personal protection officer was shot and wounded during the assault, and later awarded the George Cross for his bravery. Mark Phillips was appointed a Commander of the Royal Victorian Order and Anne was given the Grand Cross.[166]

[166] The Royal Victorian Order was founded on 21 April 1896 by Queen Victoria as a way of rewarding outstanding personal service to the Sovereign. The lowlier long-serving royal staff get the MVO; the Queen's private secretaries get the KCVO; ladies of the Royal House get the GCVO. Princess Alexandra, the Duchess of Kent and the Duchess of Gloucester all have the Order. Princess Michael of Kent does not have the Order, nor did Sarah, Duchess of York, nor Diana, Princess of Wales. The Queen has another personal order at her disposal: the Royal Family Order, created at the beginning of her reign. She has given it to almost every royal lady you can think of: her mother, her sister, assorted cousins and aunts; in 1969 she gave it to the Duchess of Kent and Princess Anne; in 1981 she gave it to the Duchess of Gloucester and the Princess of Wales. Conspicuously, she did not give it to the Duchess of York and has not given it to Princess Michael of Kent, but has given it to Edward's wife, Sophie, Countess of Wessex. Yes, the Queen (perhaps alone in the world) can give those who

Mark Phillips was a handsome husband, an outstanding horseman and a good father. He sired two fine bipeds and moved on. The marriage failed, as marriages do, and, since the passing of the Divorce Reform Act in 1969, nobody needed to take the blame. The couple separated in 1989, the marriage was dissolved in April 1992, and, on 12 December the same year, the Princess Royal married Commander Timothy Laurence, RN, at a private ceremony at Crathie Church, near Balmoral Castle in Scotland.

Tim Laurence, the naval son of a naval father, is also from solidly middle-class stock, thoroughly respectable, if a little unexciting. When I met him I liked him. He seemed on the shy side and sparing with the small talk – but what do I know about nautical manoeuvres? He is five years younger than Princess Anne. The couple met when he was the assistant navigating officer in the Royal Yacht *Britannia*. He was an equerry to the Queen, 1986–9, and is an MVO in consequence. Soft-eyed, rosy-cheeked and chinless, he is brighter and more determined than he looks. In July 2004, promoted to rear-admiral, he was appointed Assistant Chief of the Defence Staff, making him the armed services' highest-ranking member of the Royal Family since Lord Mountbatten was appointed Chief of the Defence Staff in 1959. Tim Laurence's marriage to Princess Anne has not been a bed of roses, but what marriage is? There have been ups and downs, and reported rifts and separations, but he is busy and she is busy (none busier: her commitment to duty is almost obsessive), and – at the time of going to press – they soldier on. Anne's parents were saddened by her divorce, but what could they do? They were hopeful that her second marriage would bring lasting happiness, but *che sarà sarà*. I know they worry about her. 'Things aren't easy for Anne,' said the Duke of Edinburgh, brow furrowed, earlier this year.

I imagine (I do not know) that Prince Philip has sent his daughter any number of letters, offering her encouragement, comfort and good advice. He is an assiduous correspondent. He types his letters himself. He writes with head and heart, and always to a purpose. It is his most effective means of personal communication. In conversation he can be hectoring and difficult to read. On paper, he seems calmer, more considered, more considerate. He uses letters to show he cares. He uses

have everything something they do not have. In 1987, Her Majesty accorded her daughter the title 'The Princess Royal'; in 1994, Anne became a Lady of the Garter; in 2000, in recognition of her fiftieth birthday and her years of public service, she became a Lady of the Thistle.

them, too, to think out loud, to explore, to question, to offer ideas and advice, and to say those things that, within a family, are sometimes more comfortably written down than spoken out loud.

At the beginning of 1981, when his eldest son was thirty-two and flirting with the idea of marrying Lady Diana Spencer, then nineteen, Philip wrote to Charles, as perhaps a father should write to a son, encouraging him to make up his mind. The girl was young and vulnerable, and the press speculation about a possible match was at fever pitch. The child was in the spotlight and Charles was dithering. He was, he admitted to himself, in 'a confused and anxious state of mind'. Seven years earlier, on Valentine's Day 1974, his great-uncle, Dickie Mountbatten, had written to Charles with his own brand of matrimonial advice:

> I believe, in a case like yours, the man should sow his wild oats and have as many affairs as he can before settling down but for a wife he should choose a suitable, attractive and sweet-charactered girl *before* she met anyone she might fall for. After all Mummy never seriously thought of anyone else after the Dartmouth encounter when she was thirteen! I think it is disturbing for women to have experiences if they have to remain on a pedestal after marriage.

By 1981, Mountbatten, whom Charles regarded as 'infinitely special', the one man in his life who combined the roles of 'grandfather, great uncle, father, brother and friend',[167] was no longer around to offer advice. Mountbatten was murdered by the IRA in August 1979, leaving Charles bereft, overwhelmed by 'a kind of wretched numbness', convinced that 'something' should be done about the IRA, but admitting to his diary that he felt himself to be 'supremely useless and powerless'. In January 1981, 'confused and anxious', he told his

[167] I get the impression that the Duke of Edinburgh sometimes regarded the 'infinitely special' relationship between his uncle and his son as somewhat self-indulgent on both their parts. The Duke is his own man. He is unsentimental and dispassionate. He is a cool, and, I reckon, shrewd, judge of character. He would never speak of anyone as Prince Charles speaks of Lord Mountbatten or Queen Elizabeth the Queen Mother. The Duke admired his uncle greatly, but he had the measure of him. And it irritates him that some people seem to think that he was virtually brought up by Mountbatten. He complained once, 'I don't think anybody thinks I had a father. Most people think that Dickie's my father . . .' He says that his grandmother, Victoria Milford Haven, probably had a greater influence on him than either of his uncles, Dickie or Georgie.

In the swing: Anne and Charles with their parents at Balmoral in 1955

Guiding spirits: Charles, coming ashore at Malta, with his great-uncle, Dickie Mountbatten, April 1954; Charles, with his grandmother, Queen Elizabeth, going to watch his father play polo in Windsor Great Park on 10 June 1957, Philip's thirty-sixth birthday

Together: Fortune Euston, Elizabeth II, Mike Parker and the Duke of Edinburgh, Nigeria, February 1956

Apart: Philip in Antarctica, on the Grahamland Peninsula, January 1957

Together: Elizabeth II and Philip, now a Prince of the United Kingdom, photographed at Buckingham Palace, July 1957. Behind the camera: Tony Armstrong-Jones

Behind the camera: Elizabeth II, with her sister and mother, and her subjects looking on, at the Badminton Horse Trials, April 1957

Hats on: Mexico, 1954

Hands on: Mexico, 1954

Action man: preparing for take-off in a Westland helicopter

Action man: getting from ship to ship by jackstay

Sailing at Cowes in *Bluebott[le]*
with Prince Charles an[d]
Uffa Fox, 195[ ]

Playing polo in Jamaica
with Prince Charles, 1966

A second family: The Queen, playing with Prince Edward, aged fifteen months, and Prince Andrew, aged five, at Windsor Castle, June 1965

Look at the time: The Queen with Prince Edward, aged five, and Prince Charles, aged twenty, April 1969

Princess Alice with her grand-children, Charles and Anne, on their arrival in Athens for the wedding of King Constantine of Greece, September 1964

Guiding hands: Charles and his grandmother, Queen Elizabeth, 1969; Charles and his great-uncle, Dickie Mountbatten, 1977

Philip and Elizabeth [dan]ce the Gay Gordons [at] the annual Ghillies' Ball at Balmoral, in the run-up to their silver wedding anniversary, 1972

The Queen, on Burmese, rides on after six blank shots are fired at her on her way to Trooping the Colour, June 1981

'We are a family': The Queen
with Princess Diana and her
bridesmaids, July 1981

Philip with Princess Beatrice,
aged three, the daughter of Prince
Andrew and Sarah Ferguson, May 1991

The Queen at work: on board the Royal Yacht *Britannia* with
her private secretary, Martin Charteris

The Queen at play: at the Derby with, centre, her friend and racing manager,
'Porchey', 7th Earl of Carnarvon

THE Sun 25p

Wednesday, November 25, 1992   25p   Audited daily sale for October 3,572,450   Today's TV: Pages 20 and 21

ONE'S BUM YEAR

Or as Queen admits: I've had an *Annus Horribilis*

I know how you feel Ma'am   Troubled John Major leans over the Lord Mayor to speak to the Queen

THE Queen opened her heart to the nation yesterday — and admitted 1992 has been one of her worst years ever.

In the most revealing speech of her 40-year reign, she said: "It has turned out to be an 'annus horribilis'" — Latin for a horrible year.

Her remarks came after a year in which she has seen

By RUKI SAYID

Charles' and Andrew's marriages hit the rocks, Anne's end in divorce and the blaze at her beloved Windsor Castle.

The Queen also signalled she is ready to start paying income tax on her estimated £6billion fortune.

Following the barrage of public criticism, she said: "This sort of questioning can act — and it should do so — as an effective engine for change."

Looking weary and fighting a heavy cold, the Queen made her astonishing speech at a banquet in London's Guildhall to mark her 40th year on the throne.

Guests including Premier John Major heard her say "1992 is not a year on which I shall look back with undiluted pleasure. In the words of one of my more sympathetic correspondents it has turned out to be an annus horribilis." In a

Continued on Page Four

'Annus horribilis'

Inspecting the fire damage at Windsor, 21 November 1992

Mourning Diana: outside Buckingham Palace in September 1997,
the week Princess Diana died

Mourning *Britannia*: at Portsmouth in December 1997, witnessing the decommissioning
of the Royal Yacht *Britannia*

Sad times, glad times:

The memorial service for those killed in the terrorist attacks of 11 September 2001, the day 'Porchey' also died

The funeral of Queen Elizabeth the Queen Mother, 9 April 2002

Aged seven weeks, Lady Louise Mountbatten-Windsor – the first correctly named Mountbatten-Windsor - with her parents, Edward and Sophie, Earl and Countess of Wessex, and her grandmother, the Queen, photographed at Sandringham by Prince Andrew, Duke of York, Christmas 2003

Mutual support: The Queen and Prince Philip at Westminster Hall for the
Commonwealth Parliamentary Conference, September 2000

Walkabout: The Queen meets her subjects in Wiltshire, December 2001;
the author in attendance (right)

50 Years On: Philip and Elizabeth together at 'Omaha' Beach in France, marking the fiftieth anniversary of the D-Day Landings of June 1944

diary he was 'terrified' of making a promise 'and then perhaps living to regret it'.

Throughout his twenties Charles appeared to have been following his great-uncle's advice. He had fallen in love ('whatever love means') a number of times. In the summer of 1971, at Smith's Lawn, the Guards' polo ground at Windsor, he had met Camilla Shand, a year older than him, already the girlfriend of Andrew Parker Bowles, but a game girl, with a reputation as something of a goer and proud to be the great-granddaughter of Alice Keppel, celebrated mistress to Charles's great-great-grandfather, Edward VII. Charles and Camilla had an affair – Uncle Dickie allowed them to use Broadlands for illicit weekends – but, in March 1973, Camilla announced her engagement to Major Parker Bowles. Charles heard the news while serving in HMS *Fox* somewhere in the Caribbean. He wrote to Uncle Dickie, mourning the end of an idyllic relationship, bleating that now he had 'no one' to return to in England, but, concluding, stoically, that 'the feeling of emptiness would eventually pass'. It did and it didn't. Other girls came and went – Mountbatten's granddaughter, Amanda Knatchbull, among them – but the yearning for Camilla never wholly disappeared and, in the aftermath of Uncle Dickie's murder, Charles turned to Mrs Parker Bowles for consolation. She was ready to give it, and her husband, an older man and not inexperienced in the ways of women, was ready to look the other way.

Uncle Dickie had indulged Charles at Broadlands, but, before he died, he had also cautioned his great-nephew against selfishness and self-indulgence. In April 1979, five years after sending Charles his Valentine's Day advice, Lord Mountbatten wrote to his great-nephew again, holding out before him this time, not the prospect of wild oats, but the fearful ghost of the black sheep of the family, Charles's other great-uncle, the Duke of Windsor. Uncle Dickie confessed to his great-nephew that his behaviour was the cause of sleepless nights: 'I thought you were beginning on the downward slope which wrecked your Uncle David's life and led to his disgraceful Abdication and his futile life ever after.'

Deep down, Mountbatten knew that Charles would not continue on what he called 'your Uncle David's sad course'. Charles knew it, too. In his diary entry of 29 January 1981, he recognised the absurdity of his own confusion: 'It all seems so ridiculous because I do very much want to do the right thing for this Country and for my family.'

That is all the Duke of Edinburgh wanted, too. What Mountbatten would have termed 'a suitable, attractive and sweet-charactered girl' was now on the scene. She was innocent and eligible, ready and willing. It was time for Charles to put up or shut up. He should either propose to Diana, counselled his father, so 'pleasing his family and the country', or release her. He really should not let her go on dangling in the wind like this.

Mountbatten's daughter, Patricia Brabourne, Charles's godmother, said to me when I went to see her, 'I take it you've seen the letter? It wasn't a bullying letter at all. It was very reasonable. It was fair. It was sensible.' That is not how it seemed to Charles at the time. Charles said that his father's letter made him feel 'ill-used and impotent'. Faced with what he regarded as a parental 'ultimatum', he felt emasculated, cornered, compelled almost, to do what he did next. He telephoned Diana and suggested they meet. On Friday 6 February, at Windsor Castle, the Prince of Wales, aged thirty-two, asked Lady Diana Spencer, aged nineteen, to marry him. Apparently, she giggled nervously, and said, 'Yes, yes, of course, yes.'

And the rest – well, you know the rest . . . or, if you don't, you must have been living on the planet Mars this past quarter of a century. Charles and Diana were married at St Paul's Cathedral on 29 July 1981. Fifteen years later they were divorced. The decree nisi was granted on 15 July 1996, the decree absolute on 28 August – the feast day of St Augustine of Hippo, the fourth-century divine, famous for his maxim, 'Audi partem alteram': 'Hear the other side'.

There are certainly two sides to the sorry story of the marriage of Charles and Diana, and, having friends who were good friends of each of them, I have heard both sides, in detail, ad nauseam. I imagine you have, too. Charles, according to Diana's camp, was selfish, self-indulgent, thoughtless, unsympathetic, uncaring and cruel. He made no effort to share her interests and took no trouble to like her friends. He was older than her and more experienced: he had a duty of care which he neglected, almost from the start. Faced with her frailty – her post-natal depression, her mood swings – he was unable to cope. Faced with her cries for help – her bulimia, her attempts at self-injury – he turned away and sought solace in the arms of the one woman he had loved all along, Camilla Parker Bowles. He was weak yet wilful, pathetic yet petulant. He behaved like a spoilt child. He lacked emotional intelligence and generosity of spirit. Above all, he was jealous of his young wife's popularity with the public.

Diana, according to Charles's friends, was a sad case, almost from the start. She was in love with the position not the Prince. She never came close to understanding her man – or trying to.[168] She was self-regarding, self-absorbed, self-obsessed. She resented her husband's range of interests: she demanded a cull of some of his closest friends. She came from a difficult background – a dysfunctional family with a history of marital and mental instability – and it showed. Diana was difficult, deceitful and manipulative. She made up stories, she told lies, she had affairs. She really was beyond the pale.

Interestingly, both camps – so pitilessly vituperative in their attacks on the integrity and character of their villain of choice – offer a guarded truce in the matter of the Wales's children. When it comes to William (born 21 June 1982) and Harry (born 15 September 1984), it seems to be agreed by both sides that both parents, in their different but equally loving ways, meant well and did their best. Interestingly, too, from our point of view (because this is a portrait of Philip and Elizabeth not of Charles and Diana), throughout the whole unhappy saga, Charles's parents meant well and did their best, too. They did not take sides and, at first at least, they tried not to interfere.

The tradition of the Prince of Wales having a difficult relationship with his parents is as old as Prince Hal. Edward VII, as Prince of Wales, fell foul of Queen Victoria and Prince Albert. Victoria blamed her son for her husband's premature demise. Edward VIII, as Prince of Wales, disappointed George V and Queen Mary. Her son's Abdication in 1937 blighted the rest of Queen Mary's life. The Queen and Prince Philip have their reservations about their eldest son – about his self-indulgence and tendency to self-pity, in particular – but they recognise and admire his many gifts and achievements, and they love him dearly and wish him well. They were delighted with his engagement to Diana and full of hope for the success of the marriage. When it began to go wrong and others said 'I told you so' – Charles's friend Nicholas Soames, Philip's friend Penny Romsey, the Queen Mother's friend Lady Fermoy (Diana's maternal grandmother), among them – Elizabeth and Philip said nothing. They kept their own counsel. They looked on, silent and dismayed. Unlike almost everybody else involved in the

---

[168] In March 1996, at the House of Commons, I happened to have dinner with Dame Barbara Cartland, the romantic novelist, long-standing friend of Lord Mountbatten, and mother of Raine, who married Diana's father, the 8th Earl Spencer, in 1976. Dame Barbara was full of concern for the plight of the Prince and Princess of Wales. 'It's so sad for them both,' she said. 'It's heartbreaking. Of course, you know where it all went wrong? She wouldn't do oral sex, she just wouldn't. It's as simple as that. Of *course* it all went wrong.'

drama, Philip and Elizabeth could see both sides of the story, and had some sympathy with both sides, too. They cared about Charles and they cared about Diana. They cared about their grandchildren, especially. And they cared about the Crown and the country, also.

Initially, as the marriage began to disintegrate, the Queen did not intervene because, in fairness, what could she do? Unlike Queen Elizabeth the Queen Mother, the Queen does not avoid unpleasantness by putting her head in the sand, but nor is she an interfering busybody. She is naturally reticent. Time heals so much and 'Least said soonest mended' is a policy that often pays dividends. She believes in prayer and patience and hoping for the best. Philip believes in steering clear of trouble – 'I try to keep out of these things as much as possible' is his line – unless he thinks he has something useful to contribute. By the summer of 1992, however, both Philip and Elizabeth reckoned 'something must be done'.

That June, the *Sunday Times* began to serialise Andrew Morton's book, *Diana: Her True Story*. Essentially, the book laid bare the devastation at the heart of her marriage. It portrayed Diana as a wronged woman, locked in a loveless union, psychologically battered by an unfeeling husband who refused to hear or respond to her cries of anguish. It was a gripping read – and everybody read it, or at least got the gist of it from the never-ending reports of what it both said and implied. Morton's sources were acknowledged to be Diana's friends. At Buckingham Palace, they suspected Diana herself. They were right, of course. Diana had not met Morton, but, through an intermediary – James Colthurst, an Old Etonian doctor with an excellent bedside manner and sympathetic ear – she poured her heart out to him, recording tapes in which she told her story her way and answering any supplementary questions that Morton (via Colthurst) fed back to her. Challenged by the Queen's private secretary, her own brother-in-law, Robert Fellowes[169] (who had married her level-headed older sister,

---

[169] Lord Fellowes of Shotesham since 1999. Born 1941, the son of Sir William Fellowes KCVO, land agent to the Royal Family at Sandringham, 1936–64. Robert (Eton, Scots Guards) was assistant private secretary to the Queen from 1977, deputy private secretary from 1986, private secretary from 1990 to 1999 – and, consequently, LVO 1982, CB 1987, KCVO 1989, PC 1990, KCB 1991, GCVO 1996, GCB 1998, QSO 1999. He once said to me that he thought his lasting legacy would be that he was the man who persuaded the Queen to allow herself to be painted by Lucian Freud. I don't think he was joking. I am sure that Andrew Parker Bowles hopes that he will be remembered by posterity, not as the man who gave his surname to Camilla, but as the subject of one of Lucian Freud's last great portraits.

Jane, in 1978), Diana flatly denied any involvement in Morton's book. When Prince Philip told her directly that many feared she had in some way cooperated with the book's author, she told her father-in-law, equally directly, that she had not. She lied.

That same June, during the week of Royal Ascot, the Queen and Prince Philip sat down with Charles and Diana at Windsor to listen to their woes and talk about the way ahead. According to Diana, the meeting was frank and, in the circumstances, almost friendly. Charles said very little, but Diana laid her cards on the table. Her husband's behaviour was unreasonable, unjust and unfair. She believed the time had come for a trial separation. The Queen and Prince Philip (again, according to Diana) listened sympathetically, but firmly resisted any suggestion of a formal separation. They counselled the unhappy couple to search for a compromise, to think less of themselves and more of others, to try to work together to make their marriage work, for their own sakes, for the sake of the boys, for the sake of Crown and country. The Queen and the Duke were totally as one. The Prince and the Princess were hopelessly at odds. The Queen hoped that the meeting had done something to clear the air and proposed a second meeting on the following day. Diana apparently agreed, but failed to turn up. The Queen, the Duke and Prince Charles remained at Windsor. Diana returned to Kensington Palace.

As his son's marriage teetered on the brink of total collapse, Philip initiated a correspondence with his daughter-in-law that he hoped might prove helpful. This correspondence has been the subject of much misunderstanding. A garbled version later appeared in the tabloid press, suggesting that Philip had written to Diana to scold and upbraid her. He was accused of calling her 'a trollop' and 'a harlot'. He was not amused. Nothing could have been further from the truth.

Five years ago, in May 1999, talking to the Duke about Diana, I said to him, 'The public view of you, for what it's worth, is of a grouchy old man, unsympathetic to his daughter-in-law, but I happen to know – not from you, but I know it – that when things were difficult you wrote to Diana – kind letters, concerned, fatherly, loving, caring letters from Pa, explaining how you knew, first hand, the difficulties involved in marrying into the Royal Family.' He smiled at me. 'The impression the public have got is unfair,' I said. He shrugged. 'I've just got to live with it,' he said. 'It happens to a lot of people.'

Philip's letters to Diana were typical of his correspondence overall. They were sympathetic, but unsentimental, direct, but to a purpose.

Here is a problem: let's worry it, let's unravel it, separate the strands, see if we can't make sense of them, come closer to a proper understanding of what's wrong in the hope of being able to do something towards putting it right. He did upbraid her for failing to come to the second meeting with himself and the Queen when they had set aside time for the purpose; he did ask her to look at her own behaviour and acknowledge that there had been faults on both sides; he did remind her that, while Charles was sometimes difficult, she was not always easy. He talked about the canker of jealousy, and the problem of Camilla. He did not condone his son's on-going relationship with Camilla – not for a moment – but he did want Diana to at least try to see the situation from Charles's point of view. Her post-natal depression and her irrational behaviour after Prince William's birth had not made her easy to live with. Her constant 'suspicion' of her husband was wearing. In his letters, Philip confronted his daughter-in-law with home truths: he invited her to face the facts. Essentially, he wanted to make Diana think about her marriage, long and hard. And he did. He also made her cry.

When Diana received the letters she was at her most vulnerable and volatile. As soon as one arrived, she opened it, scanned it, usually burst immediately into tears and then shared it, as soon as possible, with her closest friends. Rosa Monckton, then managing director of Tiffany's in London, and Lucia Flecha da Lima, wife of the Brazilian ambassador, were probably Diana's two closest girlfriends at the time of her death.[170] I had lunch with them both recently and they described to me the ritual of receiving, reading and replying to the Duke of Edinburgh's correspondence. 'When the letters came,' explained Rosa, 'they caused

[170] They were both older than Diana (by eight years and more) and, as well as being her girlfriends, had a sisterly/motherly relationship with her, pastoral as well as playful. (Diana's father, Earl Spencer, died in 1992. Diana's relationship with her own mother, Frances, was fraught, from the time her mother 'bolted' from home to run off with Peter Shand Kydd when Diana was only six; at the time of Diana's death mother and daughter were not on speaking terms.) In the weeks running up to her death, Diana had spent time with both Lucia (staying with her in Washington, DC) and Rosa (cruising together around the Greek Islands). Lucia and Rosa are now regarded as Diana's representatives on earth. It is not their fault. Diana was arguably the most celebrated woman of the twentieth century: her death eclipsed that of Mother Teresa. People still want a slice of Diana. I had supper recently with James Hewitt, one of Diana's lovers in the darker days of her marriage. He is very charming, very easy to be with: you can see why Diana fell for him. 'I hope I made her a little happier,' he said to me. 'That's all.' The point of the story is this: as we left the restaurant, people reached out to shake Hewitt's hand – they wanted to be close to him because he had been close to Diana.

excitement and alarm at the same time. Diana was very up and down. Something he said might make her cry, something might make her laugh. She very often got the wrong end of the stick, misinterpreting what he meant.' 'We went through each letter, so carefully, thinking about what he said, talking about it, explaining it to her,' Lucia recalled. 'We would get into the car and all go to the embassy [the Brazilian Embassy] and sit together and read the letters, line by line.' 'Then,' said Rosa, 'we helped her draft her replies. She took the correspondence very seriously.' The correspondence continued for some months. For a while, Philip's letters, carefully tied together with ribbon, were stored for safe-keeping in a box in the Brazilian ambassador's safe. 'They were good letters,' said Lucia, emphatically. 'He is a good man.' Rosa Monckton agreed. 'Actually, he was pretty wonderful,' she said to me. 'All he was trying to do was help. And Diana knew that.'

According to Paul Burrell, Diana found many of Philip's letters hard to take, describing them as 'brutal'. In his book, *A Royal Duty*, Diana's butler and much-advertised 'rock', maintained that 'the inherent problem of using Prince Philip as a mediator was that he rarely pulled any punches, and as someone who didn't understand the princess, he could hardly be expected to know how to handle her personality and temperament'. I think Burrell is wrong. I think Philip did understand his daughter-in-law and, acting *in loco parentis*, was offering her what she needed: tough love. He accepted that her bulimia was an illness and that consequently she could not always be answerable for her behaviour. He acknowledged that Charles was wrong to have returned to Camilla, but told her that she, too, was wrong to have taken other lovers, and asked her to reflect on why her husband had sought out his old flame. He praised her achievements, but invited her, also, to consider where and when she might have got it wrong. Some of his remarks were undeniably negative, but his underlying message was always positive, and his purpose was practical: to guide her towards the possibility of a reconciliation with her husband. In one letter, he even drew up a numbered list of things – activities, interests, people – that the pair of them had in common. I doubt that the trained counsellors from Relate could have done very much more.

Ultimately, Philip's mission failed. 'To be fair,' says Paul Burrell, 'Prince Philip did more to save the marriage than Prince Charles.' Burrell was once a personal footman to the Queen and his wife, Maria, was the Duke of Edinburgh's maid. He professes to admire them both, but they are certainly now not at all happy with him. Members of staff who write books about their years in royal service are betraying the trust their former employers once placed in them. Burrell (though not his wife) was dis-invited to the Windsor party marking the Duke of Edinburgh's eightieth birthday in 2001. Diana's friends, Lucia Flecha da Lima and Rosa Monckton, once quite cosy with the Princess's butler, and ready to stand up for him at his trial, now have no time for him. 'He was just a servant,' the ambassador's wife reminded me, skewering a lettuce leaf over our light lunch at Le Caprice. 'He opens doors, he closes door, then he goes. He is the butler, he is the *servant*. We were her friends.' 'It's very sad,' said Rosa, 'he shouldn't have written that book. He shouldn't have sold his story. He is exploiting Diana now – for money. It's bad.'

And it will get worse. When I first recorded a conversation with Paul Burrell, not long after Diana's death, he was quite circumspect. He talked of her with enormous affection, but with a certain reserve. He told me how she loved to watch her favourite weepie, *Brief Encounter*, on the television, feet curled under her on the sofa, box of tissues to hand. She invited him to sit with her to watch, but he wouldn't. He was the butler, after all. He described her at breakfast-time, pressing him to join her at the table to help open the post, but he was reluctant. He knew his place. Now the reserve has gone. When I saw him last (in the summer of 2004: I know him quite well and like him), he talked of Diana with a frankness and familiarity that felt uncomfortable. He said, 'I knew she wasn't pregnant when she died, because of all sorts of things – her menstrual cycle, the pills she was taking . . .' He described 'the privilege of attending to her personally' in the French hospital, after she was dead, in mawkish detail. He is as devoted to Diana's memory as ever, but he no longer guards it with the tenderness and discretion that once he did.

As the years go by, he will have yet more – and more – to say. In 2004, he published the paperback of his book about Diana, with an 'extra chapter' of hotly touted revelations. The new material prompted the headline in the *Daily Mail*: 'Charles "had a deal with Philip to dump Diana in five years".' According to Burrell, Diana suspected that Prince Philip had been 'a collaborating architect in the marriage's downfall', that he had given Charles 'his blessing, with a nudge and a wink, to renew his liaison with Camilla'. Burrell claimed that Diana was told by Charles himself – in the heat of a row – that 'he had always had his father's blessing – from the outset of the marriage – to return to Camilla if the Princess did not make him happy'. Diana was capable of saying many things – and different things on different days – but her friends, Rosa Monckton and Lucia Flecha da Lima, are quite clear on this: Diana had great respect and affection for her father-in-law, she trusted him and knew that he wanted only to help. The idea that Prince Philip would have arranged 'a five-year get-out clause' on his son's marriage is simply laughable. Philip told Diana what he thought of his son's mistress. 'I cannot imagine anyone in their right mind leaving you for Camilla,' he wrote to her, and she believed him.

Paul Burrell still speaks of the Queen with respect and acknowledges that the Duke of Edinburgh's intentions towards Diana were essentially well meant, even if Philip 'wore steelworker's gloves for a situation that required kid mittens'. He no longer much cares what the rest of the royal establishment thinks of him. He has some cause, of course. In the aftermath of Diana's death, he was arrested, charged and eventually put on trial at the Old Bailey, accused of stealing 310 personal items belonging to Diana, Prince Charles and their children. The case came to trial because, as Paul put it to me, 'Charles and the boys had been told by the police that I'd dressed up in Diana's clothes and already sold some of her stuff in America.' The case collapsed because, as the trial was reaching its climax, on 25 October 2002, the Queen and Prince Charles and Prince Philip – travelling by car to St Paul's Cathedral to attend a memorial service for the victims of the Bali bombings – had a brief conversation in which the Queen, prompted by her husband, told her son that she recalled having had a meeting with Paul Burrell, shortly after Diana's death, at which Burrell confided to her that he had taken some of Diana's possessions from Kensington Palace to his home where he was storing them for safe-keeping.

This revelation – relayed by the Prince to his private secretary who confirmed it with the Queen and then transmitted it to the proper authorities – established that Burrell had had no intention to deceive. The prosecution case crumbled, no further evidence was offered, he was found not guilty and released from the dock with words from the judge that must have sounded sweet indeed: 'Mr Burrell, you are free to go.'

It was a good day for the butler, but an uncomfortable one for the Queen. For a start, the case that collapsed was 'Regina v Burrell' and what brought it to its knees was an intervention from Regina herself. Had Her Majesty really only just recalled her meeting with her former footman? Or had she chosen this moment to mention the matter because she was fearful of what damage might be done if the trial continued and the defence offered evidence about her son and his marriage that might be better left unheard? If her intent was not Machiavellian (and I am happy to accept that it was not), then, at best, the eleventh-hour timing of the Queen's contribution illustrated all too clearly how little and how poorly mother and son communicated.

In his book Paul Burrell recalled, in vivid detail, his celebrated meeting with the Queen. It took place in the Queen's private apartments at Buckingham Palace on Thursday 19 December 1997, not quite four months after Diana's death. According to Burrell's book, the encounter lasted almost three hours and culminated with Her Majesty looking at her former footman over her half-rimmed spectacles, and uttering an eerie warning. 'Be careful, Paul,' she said, fixing him with a penetrating stare. 'There are powers at work in this country about which we have no knowledge.'

When, recently, I challenged Paul to tell me what he thought Her Majesty meant by this, he wouldn't or couldn't tell me. I told him that it didn't, to me, sound very much like the Queen's way of speaking. I told him, too, that the idea of the Queen granting anyone a three-hour audience seemed a bit improbable. He conceded that, perhaps, three hours had been a bit of an exaggeration. 'It was about 2.30 when the meeting began. She had just finished coffee – her dining room is next to her sitting room. Her personal page said, "Paul, Her Majesty will see you now." We stood throughout, of course. I can see Her Majesty lifting her feet as we chatted. She does that. She's used to standing, but she lifts her feet. We talked about much more than Diana. We talked about family problems. Then she said, "I must take the corgis for a walk." They normally go at 3.30 and she has her tea at five, so it was after 3.30. We must have been talking for at least an hour. She's a lovely Christian lady. You know, she gets up at six in the morning to go into her private chapel to pray at Christmas and Easter.'

Paul Burrell's respect for the Queen and devotion to Diana are not in doubt. He fell completely in love with Diana and, after her death, hoarded her possessions because he could not bear to be parted from her. He said as much in a letter to the Prince of Wales: 'All I ever wanted to do was "take care" of what I considered to be "my world".' I said to Paul recently, 'Your trouble was that you fell in love with Diana because Judy Garland was dead.' He laughed, but I think he understood what I meant. Diana was a star and she was dazzling.

Diana was a star and that was her strength. She began her life in the public eye, aged nineteen, as a shy, blushing nursery assistant, sharing a mansion flat in Earl's Court with a bunch of other upper-class Sloane Rangers. She died, sixteen years later, world-famous, iconic: tall, strong, beautiful, compelling. At the start of her last summer, she travelled to Washington DC and helped raise millions for the Red Cross; she called on Hillary Clinton at the White House; she went to New York where Christie's auctioned seventy-nine of her dresses in aid of five AIDS and cancer charities in Britain and the USA. She did great good works, with style and with feeling. On the world stage, she had presence. One on one, she was special, too. To see her with the very old, and the frail, and the very young, was something lovely. She had a magic touch.

The 'magic touch', of course, is part of the stock-in-trade of royalty. Once upon a time, the Sovereign's touch was the one certain cure for the scrofula. In 1712, Samuel Johnson, as a sickly child, was taken from Lichfield to London to be 'touched' by Queen Anne. He lived to the age of seventy-five. In the 1920s, Uncle David – Edward, Prince of Wales – recalled 'the touching mania' as 'one of the most remarkable phenomena connected with my travels': 'Whenever I entered a crowd, it closed around me like an octopus. I can still hear the shrill, excited cry, "I touched him!" If I were out of reach, then a blow on my head with a folded newspaper appeared to satisfy the impulse.'

If being a star was Diana's strength, from the perspective of the Royal Family that was her weakness, too. The Queen and Prince Philip were not, for a moment, envious of Diana's phenomenal popularity with the public (as Charles may well have been), but they were troubled by it. For them, royalty is not about 'celebrity' or 'star quality', hysterical crowds or newspaper column inches. It is about duty and service, and providing a thread of continuity that links the past with the future and helps bind communities together, whether it is a local community or the country or the Commonwealth. In one of his letters to Diana, Philip praised her for her good works, but reminded her that being consort to the Prince of Wales 'involved much more than being a hero with the British people'. More than once, the Duke of Edinburgh has reminded me that, in the 1950s, he and the Queen were objects of 'adulation – such adulation – you wouldn't believe it, you really wouldn't.' The Queen was 'the world's sweetheart':[171] hundreds of thousands – no,

[171] At the time of the Coronation the phrase was used on radio and television, in newspapers and magazines, all over the world. In January 1953, Jock Colville recorded the American financier Bernard Baruch saying to him that 'England now had three assests: her Queen, "the world's sweetheart", Winston Churchill, and her glorious historical past'.

millions – filled the streets to cheer her. But the Queen did not take it personally. Diana believed in her own publicity. The press used her and she used the press. Diana played to the gallery. It was a dangerous game.

Diana did much that was wonderful, but what she did was not unique. For example, early in 1956, in Nigeria, the Queen and Prince Philip, aged twenty-nine and thirty-four, young and oh-so-glamorous, visited a leper colony. They did so, not simply to visit Commonwealth citizens suffering from leprosy, but, more significantly, to allay the widespread, irrational fear that was attached then to any physical contact with the disease. This was a lifetime before Diana – with the same good intentions – got stuck into AIDS. Diana did much that was wonderful, but the way in which she did it was not necessarily the only way in which it might be done. Princess Anne, a loving mother and pro-active President of the Save the Children Fund since 1970, says pointedly: 'The very idea that all children want to be cuddled by a complete stranger I find utterly amazing.'

The Queen and Prince Philip did not find Diana easy, because she was not easy. They found some of her behaviour frustrating, bewildering and troublesome, because that is what it was. In his book about the Queen, Graham Turner quoted an unnamed courtier who recalled hearing Her Majesty refer to Diana as 'that impossible girl' and 'quite mad'. Those are phrases the Queen could well have used, and with some justification. The 'war of the Waleses' was an unhappy time for all concerned.

On 9 December 1993, Buckingham Palace announced the formal separation of the Prince and Princess of Wales. If the Sovereign and her consort hoped for a cessation of hostilities, they were soon disappointed. In the autumn of 1994, Jonathan Dimbleby published his authorised biography of the Prince of Wales. In print, and on television, Charles confessed to his own adultery. In the autumn of 1995, Diana sought her right of reply and gave an interview to Martin Bashir for *Panorama*. It was the most watched television programme in the history of British broadcasting. Twenty-three million viewers tuned in and saw Diana, dewy-eyed, pouring scorn on her husband, confessing to her own adultery, but blaming Charles – and Camilla. She expressed her opinion that Charles would never become King and defined the role she sought for herself. 'I would like to be queen of people's hearts,' she said. Nicholas Soames, a close friend of Prince Charles (and a government minister at the time), said Diana 'seemed on the edge of paranoia'. The Queen said, 'Enough is enough.'

The Queen and the Duke talked it through. Her Majesty consulted the Prime Minister (John Major), the Archbishop of Canterbury (George Carey), her private secretary (Robert Fellowes). She then wrote concisely, but unequivocally, to both the Prince and the Princess giving it as her decided opinion, supported by her husband, that an early divorce was now desirable. 'If it were done when 'tis done, then 'twere well it were done quickly', as Shakespeare has it in *Macbeth* – the play that once made the Duke of Edinburgh laugh. In fact, the Wales' divorce settlement took many months to negotiate and the Duke was said to be far from amused by reports that his daughter-in-law's demands included the suggestion that any future children she might have by another husband should bear hereditary titles. The Duke was reported to have proposed that, as well as losing her rank as a Royal Highness, Diana should be downgraded from Princess of Wales to Duchess of Cornwall – on the basis that 'when it's over it's over'. 'I am not vindictive,' the Duke of Edinburgh said to me, emphatically, 'I am not vindictive.' In the event, Diana surrendered her royal status,[172] and agreed to be known as 'Diana, Princess of Wales', in return for a lump-sum sweetener of £17 million and an annual staff and office allowance of £400,000. And that was that.

Except, of course, it wasn't. When it was over, it wasn't over. The worst was yet to be. In the early hours of Sunday 31 August 1997, the chauffeur-driven Mercedes in which Diana and her current lover, Dodi Fayed, were travelling across Paris at speed, pursued by paparazzi on motorbikes, entered the tunnel at the Place de l'Alma and crashed into a concrete pillar. Diana and Dodi and the driver were all killed. The Queen was at Balmoral, on holiday with her family. At 2 a.m. she was woken with news of the accident. At 3.30 a.m., the British Embassy in Paris confirmed that Diana, Princess of Wales, was dead.

---

[172] As well as losing the letters HRH before her name (the letters Uncle David had so wanted for his wife all his life), Diana's departure from the Royal Family also meant that her name was no longer included in the prayers said for the Royal Family in churches throughout the Church of England. I was an MP at the time and, at the House of Commons, at the start of every day's business, led by the Speaker's Chaplain, we would pray for the Queen and her family, including, by name, the Princess of Wales. One day she was there, the next she was not. Anthony Holden, in his most recent biography of Prince Charles, says the 'letters patent', detailing all this, 'were rather brutally published, on the Queen's personal instructions, in "the noticeboard of the Establishment", the *London Gazette*.' This is unfair. The Queen had no desire to be vindictive. This is how such royal announcements are always published.

That day the Queen and Prince Philip did exactly what anyone who knows them would have expected them to do. They comforted their grandsons in private and, in public, went about their business as usual. They took William and Harry to church with them on that fateful Sunday morning because William and Harry wanted to go, and because the Queen believes that, at times of tribulation, there is no better place to be. Her faith is her rock and doing things much as they have always been done is a practice that, on the whole, has served her well. There is comfort to be had from familiar hymns and prayers. There is solace to be found in form and custom long-established, and in doing what you have to do in the way that you normally do it.

While Prince Charles flew to Paris to accompany Diana's body home, the Queen and Prince Philip kept William and Harry at Balmoral, out of harm's way, out of the public eye. The Queen viewed Diana's death as a private tragedy for William and Harry. The public displays of grief – worldwide and extraordinary – caught her by surprise. Her instinct and upbringing had taught her – and her generation – that you kept your tears for the pillow. Crying in public was not something the Queen would allow of herself, or expect of her children and grand-children. It is not the royal way. It is neither dignified nor necessary – nor helpful. But, on television, in the first week of September 1997, it seemed the whole world was openly weeping and wailing – and baying for Her Majesty to shed some tears, too.

'Show Us You Care' chorused the headline writers. The Queen was at Balmoral, invisible, unhappy and confused. Above Buckingham Palace, the flagpole, traditionally empty except when the Sovereign is in residence, remained bare. The people – or, at least, the tabloids on their behalf – demanded a sign from the Sovereign: a flag above her principal residence flying at half-mast. By tradition, the only flag to fly above the palace was the Royal Standard and, famously, even at the death of his own father Edward VII, his son George V would not countenance the Royal Standard flying at half-mast. But that was then and this was now. 'Your Majesty, Please Look and Learn' read a hand-written notice left, amid the field of flowers, outside Buckingham Palace. Her Majesty – pressed from all sides: from family, friends and Tony Blair – took notice and, biting the inside of her bottom lip, did as she was counselled. She broke with all precedent and commanded that the Union flag be flown above her palace at half-mast. She returned to London. With Philip at her side, she got out of her car and inspected the tributes – the single flowers, the bouquets, the poems, the teddy bears – left, in their thousands, in remembrance of her ex-daughter-in-law. On Friday night, 5 September, on the eve of the funeral, the Queen gave a live broadcast that changed the national mood. She said no more than she meant, that Diana was 'an exceptional and gifted human being' whom she admired 'for her energy and commitment to others, and especially for her commitment to her two boys'. She spoke of the 'extraordinary and moving reaction to her death' and the 'lessons to be learnt' from it. She spoke as a Queen and 'as a grandmother' – and what she said and how she said it, simply and directly, with sincerity but without false sentiment, reminded the people who watched that she wasn't such a bad old stick after all. With dignity, and retaining her integrity, she showed us she cared. (Is it any wonder the Queen and Prince Philip despise the tabloid press?[173])

On Saturday morning, before the funeral, the Queen, with her family, stood at the gates of Buckingham Palace, and Her Majesty led by example, bowing her head slowly as Diana's coffin was driven past. In the funeral procession, Diana's former husband and younger brother, Prince Charles and Charles Spencer, were due to walk behind the gun carriage bearing her coffin along the route to Westminster Abbey. Prince Harry and, in particular, Prince William were uncertain as to whether or not they wanted to walk behind the coffin, too. Prince Philip, who had not planned to walk, said to William, 'If you don't walk, I think you'll regret it later. If I walk, will you walk with me?' As grandparents, Philip and Elizabeth did their best by their grandsons that week.

The funeral itself was not a comfortable experience. Elton John is not their favourite artiste. Tony Blair's overemotional reading of the Lesson was embarrassing. And Charles Spencer's address, while perhaps forgivable under the circumstances, was, from the point of view of the Queen and the Duke, both illogical and insulting. In the course of it, referring to William and Harry, Earl Spencer spoke directly to Diana's spirit and, on behalf of his mother and his sisters, with a catch in his throat, solemnly vowed 'that we, your blood family, will do all we can to continue the imaginative way in which you were steering these

---

[173] The Queen understands and accepts that a modern monarchy requires sensitive and effective press and public relations, but having to dance to the tabloid tune sticks in the royal craw. Her Majesty did not like having to break all precedent in the matter of the flagpole. She was initially uncertain about the broadcast, but, once she had agreed to it, did it with a will and in a way that rang true. Her script was drafted by Robert Fellowes, with input from 10 Downing Street. Tony Blair and Alastair Campbell claim credit for 'as a grandmother': it was, indeed, a brilliant touch.

two exceptional young men so that their souls are not simply immersed by duty and tradition, but can sing openly as you planned'. Outside the Abbey, the listening crowd applauded the earl's oration. The noise of applause spilt into the Abbey. The congregation began to clap. The applause rumbled down the nave. William and Harry, a little uncertainly, clapped, too. The Queen and the Duke of Edinburgh did not join in.

Quite recently, when I talked to Charles Spencer about his sister's funeral, he told me he had had no intention of upsetting the Royal Family with his remarks. He had simply spoken as he had felt at the time, from the heart. I asked him how much hands-on involvement the 'blood family' now had with the boys and their upbringing, and he admitted, 'Not a lot', because it was not necessary. He said, 'Prince Charles is obviously a good father and the boys are doing really well. I think Diana would be very happy about the way they have grown up. She'd be very proud of them.' I asked him how he felt about Camilla. He said, 'It's none of my business. I wish Charles every happiness. He should do whatever he wants to do.'

Diana despised Camilla. She had good cause. She thought about her rival a great deal, but tended to avoid mentioning her by name, referring to her simply as 'you-know-who' or 'her' or 'that woman' or 'the third party'. What Diana would have felt about Charles and Camilla marrying is anybody's guess. She changed her opinion with her mood – and with the company she kept. On one occasion, she said, 'Marry her? Over my dead body.' On another, 'Oh, what the hell, let him marry her. Why not? I'm past caring.'

She was never past caring what those in the Royal Family whom she respected thought about her – though, in the view of the Queen and Prince Philip, especially post the *Panorama* interview, she had a funny way of showing it. She spoke well of Princess Anne and of Princess Margaret, each of whom, of course, had had matrimonial difficulties of their own. She said that Anne 'could be surprisingly supportive at times' and that Margaret 'even defended me against the occasional tirades of my father-in-law'. Often, she said, she wanted 'to give my mother-in-law a great big hug', but she knew that was not exactly her mother-in-law's style. She conceded that the Queen, who felt sorely tested at times, 'behaved pretty impeccably throughout'. She reckoned that the Queen would never approve of Charles marrying Camilla, 'And he wouldn't without her blessing.'

Well, now he has. On 8 April 2005, in the Guildhall, in Windsor

High Street, His Royal Highness Prince Charles Philip Arthur George, The Prince of Wales, aged 56, married Camilla Rosemary Parker Bowles, aged 57. Publicly, the Queen and the Duke of Edinburgh put on a happy face and offered the bride and groom their 'warmest wishes'. Privately, I doubt that they welcomed the news with unalloyed pleasure – but the Duke is a pragmatist, self-confessed, and, increasingly, "Go with the flow' is the Queen's order of the day, so together, with a good grace, they have bowed to the almost-inevitable and accepted their son's decision to marry the love of his life. There are advantages, of course: the relationship between Charles and Camilla is now 'regularised'. There are disadvantages, too. Charles may one day be King: will not Camilla then inevitably be Queen?

Who knows what may happen down the road? Prince Philip, I reckon, thinks that, whatever it is, he won't be around to see it. Talking to him at the time of Queen Elizabeth the Queen Mother's centenary, he said to me, laughing, "God, I don't want to live to be a hundred, I can't imagine anything worse.' When I asked him what the future held for the monarchy, he said, 'I'm not going to be drawn into speculating on that. All I'll say is that I've tried to help keep it going while I've been here." He added, 'I'm not sure how useful it is to speculate about the future. Making the most of the present is quite important.' And, right now, in 2005, the daughter-in-law situation is, in many ways, a good deal more straightforward than it has been. Diana is dead and buried. Camilla is now legitimately in place. Sophie is sweet, and settling in well, and – *pace* the 'sheikh' episode – fundamentally sound. Philip and Elizabeth are losing very little sleep over Charles' and Edward's wives, past or present, and, these days, the thought of Sarah Ferguson does not trouble them at all. Mind you, as Prince Philip put it to me, 'Her behaviour was a bit odd.'

When Sarah Ferguson joined the Royal Family, in the summer of 1986, hopes were high. She was twenty-six and full of fun. I recall being told at the time by Philip's cousin, King Constantine, that 'Everybody agrees that Sarah is the best thing to have happened to the Royal Family in years. She's a breath of fresh air.' She was certainly as lively as they come. She had a past (a live-in relationship with the racing driver, Paddy McNally, twenty-two years her senior), but she also had a pedigree (her maternal grandmother was a first cousin of Princess Alice, Duchess of Gloucester, and, on her father's side, she was a second cousin to Robert Fellowes) and Prince Andrew was head-over-heels in love with her. On their wedding day, he was created Duke of York (the Queen's father's old title), and the wedding itself, at Westminster

Abbey on 23 July 1986, was as glamorous and optimistic an occasion as, once upon a time, royal weddings used to be. Sadly, the Yorks' honeymoon with the press and public was not prolonged. As the United Kingdom moved into one of its most punishing economic recessions since the war, Andrew and Sarah were building for themselves a £3.5 million mansion on the Sunninghill Estate. Sarah, initially acclaimed by the press as fun and feisty, was soon depicted as free-loading, grasping and ridiculous. She was mocked for her fashion sense, berated for charging *Hello!* magazine £200,000 for a family photo-shoot, and accused of bringing out the worst in her sister-in-law and fellow Sloane, Diana. 'Vulgar! Vulgar! Vulgar!' is how the senior courtier, Lord Charteris, described her.

At first, the Queen and Prince Philip thought she was rather jolly. Philip had known her father, Ronald Ferguson, 'Major Ron', when he had played on Prince Philip's polo team in the 1960s. Philip had been friendly, too, with the major's first wife, Susie, Sarah's mother, who ran off to Argentina with her lover, Hector Barrantes, when Sarah was twelve – much as Diana's mother had run off with Peter Shand Kydd when Diana was a little girl. The Queen liked Sarah because she was 'outgoing and outdoorsy' and because her son evidently adored her and their two daughters (Beatrice and Eugenie, born 1988 and 1990 respectively) were very sweet indeed. When the marriage went wrong, Andrew's parents were disappointed and saddened, but understanding. Through their divorce, Andrew and Sarah remained friends, continuing even to live under the same roof, and Sarah hoped that she would be able to remain on intimate terms with the rest of the Royal Family, too. She might have managed it, had it not been for press reports of her extra-marital behaviour.

On 20 August 1992, while Sarah and Andrew, with their children, were holidaying at Balmoral with the Queen and her family, the *Daily Mirror* published photographs, taken earlier in the month, of the Duchess of York enjoying a rather different kind of summer break. At the beginning of August, Sarah had rented a villa in the South of France and gone there, with her daughters, to soak up some Mediterranean sun. John Bryan, her American 'financial adviser', had come along for the holiday, too. Unhappily for Sarah, across the valley from the villa, lurking up in the hillside, was an eagle-eyed jumbo-lensed freelance photographer who managed to take a series of gobsmackingly lurid holiday snaps of Sarah, topless, cavorting with her financial adviser at the poolside, clearly tickling his fancy as – wait for it – he sucked her toes.

The Queen and Prince Philip were, understandably, unamused. Andrew stood by his errant wife, completely and without hesitation, and Sarah, for the sake of form and the children, stayed on at Balmoral for a further three days. The atmosphere was distinctly frosty. At mealtimes, Sarah, as usual, sat next to her husband, but she spent most of the time staring at her plate. She told me later that the Queen had been 'furious, really cross'. She had 'a session with her' after breakfast on the morning that the photographs appeared and the Queen kept repeating to her 'how dreadfully let down she felt'. Prince Philip's actions spoke louder than words. He decided to steer clear of Sarah altogether. 'It was ridiculous,' she told me, 'as soon as I came in through one door he'd be falling over the corgis to get out of the other. It was very funny. Except, of course, it wasn't.'

After their separations from her sons, the Queen continued to see Sarah and Diana from time to time, to have tea with them and find out how they were. Prince Philip has no plans to meet Sarah again. This she knows and it pains her. 'Of course, I want to see him,' she said to me. 'I am the mother of his granddaughters, after all.' When I raised this with Prince Philip, he shrugged and said, 'But the children come and stay.' When I asked him why he would not see Sarah any longer, he said simply, 'I don't see her because I don't see much point.'

Sarah, for her part, is determined to keep on trying. For Philip's eightieth birthday, she sent him a handsome dinner service. (It was supposed to have twelve settings, but it arrived with thirteen . . . the 'sample' had been included with the set . . . with Sarah, somehow, something always goes wrong.) He sent her a nice thank you note and signed it, 'With love' from 'Pa'.

Sarah cannot speak too highly of the Queen. 'She's my icon,' she told me, her eyes glistening. 'I look up to her. I think she's the finest woman I know. HM has got a wonderful sense of humour. She loves to sing. She is the widest-read woman in the world and yet she has this wonderful compassion and total and utter understanding. She is very forgiving. She doesn't poke her nose in. She lets you have free rein, but she doesn't miss a trick.'

Sarah makes sure that her daughters are on their best behaviour when they go to see the Queen. 'We have three sets of table manners,' Sarah explained to me. 'This is very important. Table Manners C is for at home, when it's just Andrew and me. Anything goes. Table Manners B is for in a restaurant. You can have fun, but always remember people are looking at you. I tell the girls always to smile – because it costs so little and it means so much. Table Manners A is for Granny – their granny – the Boss.'

'And what does that involve?' I asked.

'If we go to tea at Windsor or Balmoral, we do it properly,' Sarah explained to me, acting it out as she described the correct royal teatime etiquette. 'We have our little napkin. We offer Granny the sandwiches first, before we take the whole lot onto our plate. We don't take the raisins out of the scones half-way through a conversation – or flick them across the table. We don't ask for ketchup when the Duke of Edinburgh is sitting there. We don't say, "Oh, the Ribena tastes old", which it probably is. We don't say, "We don't eat paté sandwiches". We just shut up and eat what we're given. We can have fish fingers when we get home.'

I suggested 'Speak when you're spoken to' was the order of the day.

'No,' said Sarah, 'I encourage them to speak up actually – even on Table Manners A. It keeps the conversation going, and saves me having to do it.'

Sarah Ferguson is a huge admirer of the Queen – 'If we're voting for the best granny in the world,' she says, 'I have to tell you the Boss is the best granny' – but she no longer has any time for the 'repressed emotions' that she found were part and parcel of life at the heart of the House of Windsor. She sees it as a generational thing. 'They believe in the virtues of the stiff upper lip. I don't any more.' Sarah reckons that bottling up your feelings is positively harmful. 'My mother's generation said, "Don't speak. Don't say you're unhappy. Don't say you're angry." I think that's all wrong. I say to my girls, "Go on, tell me. Are you angry with me? Have I annoyed you?" We sit down and talk. "Was that a grubby day? Why was it a grubby day?" Or I'll make them stand in the middle of Sunninghill Park and scream – which is what I do.' Sarah suddenly goes 'Aargh!' for me. 'I make them scream. They say, "Mummy, we can't." I say, "Why not? Who's going to hear? Scream."'

The prospect of encountering his former daughter-in-law screaming in the middle of Sunninghill Park could be one of the reasons the Duke of Edinburgh is giving her a wide berth these days. He is not a screamer. He still believes in the virtues of the stiff upper lip. So does the Queen. Philip and Elizabeth see reticence as a virtue and self-control as a quality to be admired. Also, they are not entirely sure that endless introspection is a good thing. They go along with Iris Murdoch, a writer and philosopher very much of their generation (born two years before Prince Philip): 'Happiness is a matter of one's most ordinary everyday mode of consciousness being busy and lively and unconcerned with self.' Philip and Elizabeth are clearly devoted and doting grandparents, loving and much loved. As parents, they have done their best by their children. They have acted, always with one accord and always with the best intentions. As parents, they do not feel guilty. They are not brooding. They are busy people with lives of their own to lead.

PHILIP & ELIZABETH

Conclusion

'A happy marriage perhaps represents the ideal of human relationships – a setting in which each partner, while acknowledging the
need of the other, feels free to be what he or she by nature is: a
relationship in which instinct as well as intellect can find
expression, in which giving and taking are equal; in which each
accepts the other, and I confronts Thou.'

Anthony Storr (1920–2001), *The Integrity of the Personality*

I happen to be writing this in March 2004, on the day of the funeral of
the late Queen Juliana of the Netherlands. Tonight, Queen Elizabeth
II is hosting a private party in London to celebrate the fiftieth
anniversary of her Coronation. The party is taking place a year later
than planned. It was postponed from 2003 because of the war on Iraq.
These things happen. The Duke of Edinburgh will be at tonight's
celebration, of course, but he may arrive late. He has had to fly to The
Hague for the day to represent the United Kingdom at Queen Juliana's
funeral. These things happen.

Queen Juliana was an interesting woman. In her day – she reigned
from 1948 until 1980, when she abdicated in favour of her eldest
daughter, Crown Princess Beatrix – she was Europe's richest reigning
monarch, but she eschewed pomp and ceremony, and abolished the
curtsy among other court formalities. She was kindly, deeply religious,
devoted to her four daughters and her people (in that order), and
married, for sixty-seven years, to Prince Bernhard, a German princeling
whose way with women and money did him little credit and, on more
than one occasion, came close to toppling the Orange throne. Bernhard
and Juliana each had their foibles. In 1956, for example, it came to light
that, for the previous eight years, the Dutch Queen had been relying
heavily on the spiritual services of a faith healer named Greet Hofmans.

Hofmans, apparently, used her position to obtain posts at the palace for her friends and tried to influence government policy. She also persuaded the Queen to move from her quarters 'because the earth waves were not right'. In 1959, the Queen and the Prince invited a self-styled American 'professor' (and former hamburger vendor) named George Adamski to visit them privately to report on what he described as his flight around the moon in a spaceship from Venus. More seriously, in 1976, Prince Bernhard was accused of soliciting money from the Lockheed Corporation of America and found – by the official enquiry into the case – to be a man 'open to dishonourable requests and offers'.

We have had none of these embarrassments with Queen Elizabeth II and the Duke of Edinburgh. I wonder if we appreciate how fortunate we are? Elizabeth II is neither eccentric nor quixotic, and she and her husband are both as honest as the day is long.

If there is just one word that sums up Elizabeth II, it is 'dutiful'. Her life has been driven by duty. She was a dutiful daughter. She has been a dutiful Queen. Because I have met her – because, at close quarters, I have observed her as she has carried out a range of her official duties – people sometimes ask me, leaning forward, narrowing their eyes, 'What's the Queen really like?' My answer disappoints them. 'She seems very nice,' I say, 'rather normal, actually; quite straightforward; much as you'd expect, in fact.'

The truth is, the Queen is wholly predictable. On 30 April 2002, in Westminster Hall, I watched her as she addressed the joint Houses of Parliament on the occasion of her golden jubilee. In the outfit you would expect (peacock blue, matching hat, smashing pearls, lovely brooch, black gloves, spectacles firmly in place), in the voice you recognise (Gainsborough Studios, c. 1947), she said all the things you knew that she would say. The speech – brief, balanced, well-phrased – reflected both the moderate and modest nature of the monarch, and the decent, enduring values she holds dear. As she concluded with her pledge to continue to serve her country in the years to come, the journalists sitting around me twitched with excitement. 'She's staying,' hissed one. 'That's our story,' whispered another. In the following morning's newspapers it was, indeed, everybody's lead story, but it was hardly news. Anyone who has had five minutes – let alone fifty years – to consider the Queen knows that when, as Princess Elizabeth, aged twenty-one, she said, 'I declare before you all that my whole life, whether it be long or short, shall be devoted to your service', she meant it. The Queen, once crowned, was never going to abdicate. At her Coronation she made a commitment to God as well as to her people, and her faith sustains her in all she does. She is God's anointed Queen.[174] 'It's a job for life,' she says. 'It's a question of maturing into something that one's got used to doing and accepting the fact that it's your fate, because I think continuity is very important.'

The Queen's has been a life of duty, but also one of immense privilege. She has met everyone and been everywhere. She has never wanted for anything. Wherever she goes she is cosseted. And the corgis come, too – flown, if need be, in an Andover of the Queen's Flight. Her days are sometimes long (and often arduous: she is seventy-eight years old), but she has staff ever in attendance and the comfort of a routine that rarely varies. At 8.00 a.m. Her Majesty's dresser enters the royal bedroom with the 'calling tray' and a pot of Earl Grey tea. The curtains are drawn, the bath is run (to a depth of seven inches and a temperature of 72° Fahrenheit – tested by thermometer), the Palace begins to stir. (No vacuuming is permitted before 8 a.m.) Her clothes are laid out for her, her hairdresser is at hand. At 9 a.m., as her personal piper plays beneath her windows, the Queen walks from her bedroom, through her sitting room to her dining room, holding her Roberts radio, listening to the news of the day. Breakfast is modest: cereal (from those Tupperware containers), a slice of granary toast, a layer of Oxford marmalade. At ten o'clock the business of the day begins: Sir Robin Janvrin, her private secretary, appears; correspondence is considered, state papers scanned; if it is the morning for receiving ambassadors or

---

[174] '. . . so be thou anointed, blessed and consecrated Queen over the Peoples, whom the Lord thy God hath given thee to rule and govern . . .' were the words said to her by the Archbishop of Canterbury at the most solemn moment of her Coronation – and she has not forgotten them. Queen Juliana of the Netherlands abdicated in favour of her daughter, Queen Beatrix, just as *her* mother, Queen Wilhelmina had abdicated in her favour, but the Dutch way is not the British way. The Queen will never abdicate, not – as some commentators suggest – because she does not want to see her son become King, but because her faith, her commitment and her heritage mean that abdication is simply not a possibility. A commitment made before God is an absolute commitment as far as Her Majesty is concerned. Religion matters to the Queen. I noticed, during her New Year holiday at Sandringham, there was just one official duty listed in the Court Circular for 11 January 2004: 'Mr Roger Harman (Headteacher of Fitcham Voluntary Aided Primary School) was received by The Queen when Her Majesty presented a Bible to Joshua York for proficiency in Religious Instruction.'

the day of an investiture, Her Majesty studies her briefing material. At one o'clock, before a light lunch (she is not fussy about her food), she might treat herself to a gin and Dubonnet: equal measures, two lumps of ice and a slice of lemon. (The lemon is sliced for her.) After lunch (if Paul Burrell has not come to call) she will walk the corgis. At five she will take tea. At six o'clock the drinks tray reappears and Her Majesty might allow herself a moderate gin and tonic. At 8.15 p.m. it is dinner time.

On some days the Queen and Prince Philip share breakfast, lunch and dinner. On other days, they don't. For example, yesterday as I write, Philip and Elizabeth had breakfast alone together. At one o'clock, together, they hosted one of their regular, informal Buckingham Palace luncheons for the great, the interesting and the good – an idea instituted by the Duke in 1956. Yesterday, the party of eight included representatives of the worlds of business, music and sport, the director of the National Maritime Museum and the chairman of the Woking Shah Jahan Mosque. In the evening, the Duke of Edinburgh, without the Queen, attended a dinner at Drapers' Hall in the City of London on behalf of the Royal Academy of Engineering. The Queen is accustomed to evenings on her own. She watches television, she completes the *Daily Telegraph* crosswords, she gives the corgis their late supper. She telephones friends. She chats with her personal page.[175]

In fact, I can tell you exactly what the Queen is like. She has the interests, attributes and tastes of an English (or Scottish) country-woman of her class and generation. Dogs and horses, courtesy, kindliness and community service, count with her. Essentially conservative (with radical flourishes), intelligent (not intellectual), pragmatic (not introspective), utterly reliable (she will not let you down), she is what she is and makes no pretence to be what she is not. She may be formally apolitical, but she is definitely not politically correct. If she chooses, she will wear fur, she won't wear a seat belt, she will go out riding without a hard hat and, in her assorted residences, cigarettes are freely available to her guests. (I am told she even smokes one herself from time to time. Can that be true?)

---

[175] She chats with her staff, but she does not share confidences with them. For the Queen, one of the sadnesses of a book like Paul Burrell's is that it is a reminder of how few people she can trust. Even George Carey, the Archbishop of Canterbury, included accounts of confidential royal conversations in his memoirs.

She is a skilful mimic – not so much of individuals, but of accents, be it Cockney or Norfolk – and she has a lively, even impish, sense of humour. When Lech Walesa was Polish President and came to stay, she told an aide, 'He only knows two English words,' then paused, before adding, '. . . They are quite interesting words.' More recently, at an art gallery, she was confronted by a series of Lucian Freud nudes: heavy, spreading bosoms, weighty blue-veined thighs. Sensing that the photographers present were frantic to get a shot of her gazing up at one of them, Her Majesty moved herself adroitly out of range. When her host enquired, 'Haven't you been painted by Lucian Freud, Ma'am?', she grinned and said, *sotto voce*, 'Yes, but not like that.'

Given the weirdness of her life (imprisoned by her fate: destined to be Queen from the age of ten), she seems to me to be quite remarkably well balanced, rounded, grounded and at ease with herself, the world and her place in it. This is, of course, a problem for the media – where's the story? – and for her biographers, too. At the heart of the biographies (and autobiographies) that become best-sellers these days is trauma – true 'trauma' from the Greek for 'wound'. The Queen's story has known moments of high drama, but her own life, her personal life – in my view, at least – has not been traumatised.

Others disagree. At the time of her golden jubilee, my psychologist friend, Brett Kahr (the disciple of Lucian Freud's grandfather, Sigmund), told me he was quite concerned for the Queen. 'She has lost her only sister and her mother at the anniversary of her father's death,' he said solemnly. 'She is vulnerable.' (He also told me that, in psychiatric circles, a rumour has circulated for years that the Queen once had ECT treatment for depression.) As a psychologist I am unqualified, of course, but I told Brett, 'For what it's worth, my hunch is that Her Majesty has not had and will not be having a breakdown in this or any other year.' There was a streak of hysteria in Diana: you sensed it even with a brief acquaintance. There is none in the Queen. She is sane. She is sensible. She has her feet on the ground. She is not self-conscious: she will apply her lipstick whoever is watching. She is not easily flustered: however hectic the schedule, however many stops on the tour, her own steady pace never varies. She has a good team around her: senior courtiers who know what they are doing (unstuffy, for the most part; unfussy, with a couple of exceptions), loyal ladies-in-waiting who are real friends, and a husband who is an ally. She is not complaining.

Inevitably, she has had her ups and downs. In 1957, a thirty-three-year-old peer, writer and historian, the 2nd Lord Altrincham,[176] became internationally notorious overnight for publishing what many regarded as an unforgivable personal attack on the Queen. Altrincham accused the thirty-one-year-old Queen of being out of touch, living entirely within the confines of her own class, surrounded by courtiers of 'the "tweedy sort"', making speeches that amounted to 'prim little sermons' in the manner of 'a priggish schoolgirl' and speaking with a voice that was 'a pain in the neck'. 'Like her mother,' wrote Altrincham, the young Queen 'appears to be unable to string even a few sentences together without a written text.' He went on:

> When she has lost the bloom of youth, the Queen's reputation will depend, far more than it does now, upon her personality. It will not then be enough for her to go through the motions; she will have to say things which people can remember and do things on her own initiative which will make people sit up and take notice. As yet there is little sign that such a personality is emerging.

Fifty years on, the Queen's reputation does indeed rest upon her personality. With a handful of exceptions, she has not said things which people can remember, or done things which have made people sit up and take notice, but her personality has emerged, nonetheless. We know what the Queen stands for and cares about. Take, for example, her dogged commitment to the Commonwealth. When her reign began, the British Empire was already set on its inevitable decline and the Commonwealth, as we know it, still in its infancy. In 1952, there were eight members of the Commonwealth. Today, there are fifty-four, of which sixteen are still constitutional monarchies with the Queen as Head of State. Whitehall and Westminster may be more preoccupied with the United Kingdom's relations with Europe and the United States, but the Queen's interest in the Commonwealth has never

---

[176] John Grigg, as he became when he was able to renounce his title in 1963. In the 1950s, others attacked the monarchy – John Osborne spoke of it as 'a gold filling in a mouth full of decay', Malcolm Muggeridge called it 'soap opera . . . ersatz religion' – but Altrincham's strictures caused the real scandal because they were so personal. Grigg (1924–2001) was denounced as a republican and attacked in the street by outraged royalists. By the time I met him, the young firebrand had become a cosy old buffer. He told me he thought the Queen was 'charming' and chuckled at the recollection of the furore he caused all those years ago.

wavered. Indeed, her knowledgeable enthusiasm for what she describes as a 'free and voluntary association of equal partners' that 'in all history has no precedent' is a wonder to behold.

When her husband Boy Browning was still Comptroller of the Duke of Edinburgh's household,[177] the novelist Daphne du Maurier stayed at Balmoral and was struck by the way Prince Philip could talk about anything – literature, art, murder, military manoeuvres – while the Queen's range of interests – and conversation – was much more limited. Her Majesty's face only really 'lit up' when the talk was of horses – and world affairs.

The Queen is exceptionally well-informed. This is because she is conscientious. She does her 'boxes' week in, week out, throughout the year. She says she is a quick reader, 'though I do rather begrudge some of the hours that I have to do instead of being outdoors'. She knows the presidents and prime ministers of the Commonwealth personally. The way they speak of her – invariably with respect, often with affection, occasionally with awe – suggests their admiration is genuine, not simply a matter of form. In the United Kingdom she has had ten prime ministers, each one of whom has liked to give the impression that he has known her even better than the last. She has maintained a cordial relationship with them all. Margaret Thatcher told me that the talk of her having a strained relationship with the Queen was 'a lot of nonsense'. 'The Queen,' said Lady Thatcher, 'is simply marvellous. And her commitment to the Commonwealth and to our armed services have been especially important.' When parliament is sitting, Queen and prime minister meet once a week, and, in September, prime minister and consort are briefly guests of Her Majesty at Balmoral. (It is possible that the Blairs' baby Leo, born, a tad prematurely, on 20 May 2000, was conceived under the royal roof.) The Queen sees herself as a 'sounding board' for her prime ministers. She says, 'They unburden themselves, or tell me what's going on. If they've got any problems, sometimes one can help in that way, too. I think it's rather nice to feel that one's a sort of sponge. Some things stay there and some things go out the other ear and some things never come out at all. Occasionally you can put one's point of view when perhaps they hadn't seen it from that angle.'

---

[177] Browning left the Duke's service in 1959. In 1957 he had suffered a nervous breakdown. His marriage was under pressure and he drank too much. He died in 1965, aged sixty-nine.

On the whole, the Queen has accepted what the politicians have thrown at her across the years. In 1964, Sir Anthony Blunt, Surveyor of the Royal Pictures, confessed to an MI5 interrogator that he had been a Soviet spy since before the Second World War. In return for his confession, he was offered legal immunity, and, to avoid alerting the KGB, Her Majesty was asked to keep him in royal service until the due date of his retirement. She acquiesced. She does. She has little choice, in the end. That is why the Civil List has gradually been curtailed and, since 1993, the Queen and the Prince of Wales have been paying tax on their private income. There was negotiation – a bit of give and take on either side – but, ultimately, the government of the day calls the shots. The Queen successfully resisted an attempt by Tony Benn (when Postmaster-General in the mid-1960s) to have the Sovereign's profile removed from British postage stamps, but, in the 1990s, failed to secure a successor to the Royal Yacht *Britannia*.[178]

The Queen is still charged by some with being out of touch and slow to react (for example, in the case of Paul Burrell's trial and at the outset of the week of Diana's death) and even her keenest admirers, who regard her as a force for good, would not describe her as a force for change. The world changes. The Queen does not. In some ways, that is the essence of her. She is reassuringly familiar. She keeps the show on the road. She keeps her profile on the postage stamps, not for reasons of vanity, but because that is where it belongs, that is where you expect it to be.

On 24 November 1992, I attended the lunch at Guildhall at which the Queen gave probably the most memorable speech of her reign. She had a cold and a sore throat, but she had some things she wanted to say and she hoped to be heard and wasn't sure how long her voice would last, so she decided to speak before we all tucked into the turbot, partridge and Ruby soufflé, rather than after. The speech – wry, reflective, personal – was made all the more moving by being spoken in

[178] In his diaries, Tony Benn gives an hilarious account of his attempt to reform the design of the postage stamp. He was comprehensively outmanoeuvred by the Queen, who listened to his proposals with interest but without comment, and then, once Benn had left the Palace, had a quiet word with her private secretary who had a quiet word with No 10 (Harold Wilson was Prime Minister) who saw to it that the *status quo* was left undisturbed.

The Royal Yacht *Britannia*, successor to the Royal Yacht *Victoria and Albert*, was launched by the Queen on 16 April 1953 and commissioned on 7 January 1954. During forty-four years of active service, *Britannia* steamed a total of 1,087,623 nautical miles,

a husky voice. The Queen talked of her *annus horribilis*,[179] 'not a year I shall look back on with undiluted pleasure'. She did not mention Anne's divorce, Andrew's separation or Charles's marriage on the rocks, but they were in her mind – and ours. She talked, poignantly, about the fire that had done so much damage to Windsor Castle the weekend before and – because the lunch was to mark the fortieth anniversary of her accession – reflected on lessons learnt over four decades. She said, rather wistfully, that, of course, any institution – monarchy included – must accept scrutiny and criticism, but asked, 'Couldn't it be done with a touch of humour, gentleness and understanding?' She commended loyalty and 'moderation in all things'.

conducting 696 royal visits overseas and 272 in home waters. Among her deployments, she sailed to the Antarctic in 1956/57, was used to open the St Lawrence Seaway in 1959 and, in January 1986, while on passage for the Queen's state visit to New Zealand and Australia, was diverted to assist in the evacuation of refugees from Aden. She was decommissioned on 11 December 1997 when, famously, the Queen and the Princess Royal were photographed with tears in their eyes – ready, apparently, to weep publicly for the passing of a boat in a show of emotion that they rarely displayed when faced with human tragedy. In fact, the tears were prompted as much by the bitterly cold weather as by fond recollections of good times had on board a vessel that had served Queen and country well. At the beginning of the 1990s, the Queen would have liked to see a successor to *Britannia*, but the political will was not there. Prince Philip was closely involved in the design and kitting out of *Britannia*. He told me, in May 2003, that the Labour government of the late 1940s handled the issue of financing the new Royal Yacht so much more effectively than the Conservative government of the early 1990s. 'Attlee [the Prime Minister] did it properly. He got the Opposition on board. Major [as Prime Minister] was blocked by Lamont [Chancellor of the Exchequer]. And didn't get the Opposition on board. And then Portillo [as Defence Secretary] got involved and made a complete bollocks of it. Absolutely idiotic.' The Duke was of the view that a new Royal Yacht might have been a viable proposition – properly thought through and correctly 'sold'. 'Yes, it would need to have a dual role, as a training ship or a command ship. We used *Britannia* to help trade, for exhibitions and so on. It'd be fine for 'invisibles', but you couldn't go down a completely commercial route. I don't think we'd want Mr Fayed hiring the royal yacht to promote Harrods, do you?'

When he read the above paragraph in the hardback edition of this book, Norman Lamont wrote to me to set the record straight: 'The decision about *Britannia* was made after I was Chancellor and I distinctly remember being shocked and annoyed by Michael Portillo's uncharacteristic prevarication and his eventual very disappointing decision. My view was we should simply have replaced *Britannia*.' Lord Lamont of Lerwick (as he now is) had something else he thought I might be interested to know (I was): 'I was opposed to John Major's successful persuasion of HM The Queen to pay income tax. I regarded that as a slippery slope, and I am not convinced yet that I was wrong on that.'

[179] A phrase suggested by her former assistant private secretary, Sir Edward Ford, and brilliantly translated by the *Sun* newspaper's headline writer as 'One's Bum Year'.

'*Annus horribilis*' is one of just a few of the Queen's turns of phrase that will not be forgotten. 'My husband and I . . .' is another. It was a phrase that the Queen used in almost every public utterance in the early years of her reign. She used it to such an extent that it became a joke and she was forced to drop it. She used it because, it seemed, wherever she went, he came, too. They were a double act. They still are. At every key moment in the Queen's reign – at every significant event – every one – the Duke of Edinburgh has been there.

I once asked him what he considered to be his lifetime's prime achievements. We were sitting in his library at Buckingham Palace. It is a large room, with a workmanlike feel, airy, ordered, user-friendly, serviceable rather than cosy. I put my question and a silence fell. He snorted. He spread his hands across the sofa and sighed. Stupid question. Where do you begin? Beyond his multiple service appointments, the man is founder, fellow, patron, president, chairman, member of at least 837 organisations. The first achievement is simply to have endured, to have survived – to have put up with – nearly sixty years of royal flummery, official mumbo-jumbo, parades, processions, receiving lines, receptions, lunches, dinners, upwards of twenty thousand official engagements. He has measured out his life in handshakes and small talk. They have their value, of course. According to William Blake, 'He who would do good must do it by minute particulars.' Most of the contact that the Queen and her husband have with the people they meet is fleeting – 'hello, well done, goodbye' is about as much as most of it ever amounts to.

But to keep his sanity, alongside all the surface stuff (necessary, unavoidable, worthwhile in its way), the Duke of Edinburgh has got stuck in to a range of particular projects where in-depth involvement has (I hope) given him the satisfaction of a worthwhile job well done.

The Duke of Edinburgh's Award Scheme is clearly a considerable 'achievement', though, as we talked of it, his one anxiety seemed to be to give credit to John Hunt as its first director. The creation of the Commonwealth Study Conferences is clearly another 'achievement'. His impact on the World Wide Fund for Nature is certainly a third.[180]

---

[180] Ornithology has been a life-long enthusiasm for Prince Philip (there are 781 books on birds on his shelves), but his involvement with WWF (UK president since 1961, international president from 1981, president emeritus since 1996) has seen his interest in wildlife broaden from a commitment to the conservation of natural habitats to a passionate and tireless championing of global environmental issues. He credits the late

But all these fine endeavours – and do please check out the list on page 402 – are almost incidental. The essence of his role in life has been to support the Queen. He does not talk openly about his feelings for the Queen, because that is not his style,[181] but he is fiercely loyal. On walkabout, if a photographer or cameraman is encroaching on Her Majesty, he barks at them to get out of the way. When, once, a journalist asked him about the overseas tour on which he was reported to have fallen asleep during the Queen's speech, he retorted sharply, 'Not at all, it wasn't during the Queen's speech, it was during the president's!'

There is no question: the Queen and Prince Philip have enjoyed an outstanding working partnership. But are they happy – whatever happiness means?

I once asked Dr Anthony Clare to define happiness for me. He laughed, but, obligingly, had a go. 'I would say happiness is a cognitive state, an intellectual perception or understanding of you, the person, and your relationship with your environment. It does have pleasurable components, but that's not the essence of happiness. The essence of happiness is a conscious appreciation of the rightness of being. And it's a state. It's not a permanent trait. People aren't "happy" – they have experiences of happiness. Most people's customary state is one of balance between conflicting needs and desires and emotions, and happiness comes into play as one of those experiences which people from time to time describe and clearly aim for.' I can buy into that. I imagine the Queen and Prince Philip could, too.

Prince Bernhard of the Netherlands with getting him involved in WWF. The Duke's personal list of 'achievements' would certainly include his involvement with the International Equestrian Federation. Philip was the active (some felt hyperactive) IEF president for twenty-two years. He introduced international rules for carriage-driving, long-distance riding and vaulting; he added international competitions for pony, juniors and young riders; he steered the veterinary committee; he ran the show.

[181] Perhaps we should be grateful. Here is Crown Prince Haakon of Norway addressing his bride, Crown Princess Mette-Marit, at their wedding banquet in August 2001: 'Your soul sparkles with light. Everything we do with love comes alight. Mette-Marit, you are sensitive, easy to please, obsessed with detail, sometimes a bit apathetic, intensely committed, highly strung, courageous, inscrutable. You can be defensive or resolute. You have a good sense of humour and a big warm heart. In other words you are an absolutely fantastic, complex person. I don't think I have ever been so angry, adrenaline angry, with anyone as with you. I don't think I have ever been so weak or so strong as when I've been together with you . . . Thank you for your love and for everything you've done. Mette-Marit, I am proud to call myself your husband. For now we are here. Now we are together. Mette-Marit, I love you!'

I then asked Professor Clare to go further, to forget his caveats, throw caution to the wind and give me a prescription for happiness – tell me what it takes, in his experience, to be 'happy' in the way most of us understand the word. He laughed again, but, again, sitting in his consulting room at St Patrick's Hospital in Dublin, he did his best to oblige. 'Okay,' he said. 'Here goes. Number one: cultivate a passion. How important it seems to me in my model of happiness is having something that you enjoy doing. Next, be a leaf on a tree. You have to be both an individual – you have to have a sense that you are unique and you matter – and at the same time you need to be connected to a bigger organism, a family, a community. Some very interesting stuff has been done over the years on the issue of networks. The people who are best protected against certain physical diseases – cancer and heart disease, for example – in addition to doing all the other things they should do, seem to be much more likely to be part of a community, socially involved. If you ask them to enumerate the people that they feel close to and would connect and communicate with, those who name most seem to be happiest and those with least unhappiest. Of course, there may be a circular argument here. If you are a rather complicated person, people may avoid you. If, on the other hand, you are a centre of good feeling people will come to you. I see the tragedy here in this room where some people may sit in that chair and say they don't think they've got very many friends and they're quite isolated and unhappy, and the truth is they are so introspective they've become difficult to make friends with. So that's my third rule: avoid introspection. Next, don't resist change. Change is important. People who are fearful of change are rarely happy. I don't mean massive change, but enough to keep your life stimulated. And finally, live in the moment. Live now.'

On the basis of Professor Clare's 'happiness index', I reckon the Queen and Prince Philip are happy individuals. The Queen is much more resistant to change than her husband, but a score of four out of five isn't bad. Both of them live in the moment, neither is introspective, each could be described as 'a leaf on a tree', both are undoubtedly community-orientated and socially involved. Each has a consuming passion: the Duke has his carriage-driving, the Queen has her horses and her dogs. Philip and Elizabeth are happy individuals.

But are they happy together? They seem to spend quite a lot of time apart. And if they do, is that a crime? Or simply a reflection of the bizarre lives they lead and of how well they understand one another? The Queen is frequently on her own, walking the dogs, riding her horses, playing Patience, completing a jigsaw, sorting her photograph albums, watching television, phoning friends. Is she neglected? Is she suffering? Or does she simply understand her man?

Robin Dalton, his cousin David Milford Haven's girlfriend, said to me, 'Philip's a cold fish.' Reginald Bennett, once an MP, a member of the Thursday Club, and a sailing companion of the Duke's said, 'Philip is the coolest man I know.' Talk with Lord Buxton or Lord Brabourne and the impression you get is a different one. They have stories to tell of Philip holding his wife's hand, gently stroking her hair, coming into the room at the end of the day and saying simply 'Lovely to see you' and watching her face light up with happiness. 'Philip is not sentimental,' Lord Brabourne said to me, 'but he is sensitive, profoundly so. When our son was killed [by the IRA bomb that killed Lord Mountbatten] the first letter that arrived was from Philip. It was wonderful. You can talk to him about matters of the heart.'

Countess Mountbatten said to me, 'The Queen and Prince Philip have a mutual understanding that's profound. And they get on. They are good together – anyone who knows them well will tell you that.' But what about Philip's testiness, his grumbling and his grouches? Lord Charteris said to me, 'Prince Philip is the only man in the world who treats the Queen simply as another human being. He's the only man who can. Strange as it may seem, I believe she values that. And, of course, it's not unknown for the Queen to tell Prince Philip to shut up. Because she's Queen, that's not something she can easily say to anybody else.'

Lord Charteris also pointed me in the direction of this line from *The Unquiet Grave* by Cyril Connolly: 'The true index of a man's character is the health of his wife.' This was ten years ago and, by implication, the Queen's longest-serving courtier was inviting me to compare and contrast Her Majesty's robust and life-long good health with the frailty of the then Princess of Wales.

Countess Mountbatten said to me, 'They're good together. They're good for one another. They always have been. Make no mistake.' 'Oh, yes,' said Gina Kennard, who has known them, individually and as a couple, for something like seventy years, 'They own each other. Nothing could come between them. What they have for one another is the greatest respect – which counts for so much – and deep love. Deep love that goes back a long, long way.'

'After all,' as Lord Mountbatten reminded Prince Charles, 'Mummy never seriously thought of anyone else after the Dartmouth encounter when she was thirteen!' Mountbatten's son-in-law, John Brabourne, said to me, 'Philip learnt singularity of purpose from Mountbatten. The course that's set is the course that's followed. Philip is not a man to be deflected. When he gave Elizabeth his love and his loyalty, he gave them to her for life. He has not deviated from that.'

Philip and Elizabeth are two very different human beings. Their childhoods were so different. Each is royal, they have shared values, a joint heritage and a common purpose, but as characters, as personalities, they are not at all alike. They have different attributes and different interests. Philip is more adventurous, more physical, more intellectual than his wife. She is more placid, more cautious, more conventional, less changeable in mood. They are different people. Yet they understand one another. Completely. And they are allies. I saw that, one November night, three years ago, in the interval at the Royal Variety Performance, as they looked at one another across a crowded room, and smiled. I caught then a glimpse of the conspiracy – the shared secret – that has sustained them over what will soon be sixty years. It was seeing them in that brief moment, apart yet together, that made me want to write this book.

Life is complicated. Marriage is not easy. But, somehow, these two distinct, unusual, profoundly impressive people have made it work. They have given one another respect and freedom. They have accepted one another for what they are. He is active. She is passive. But both are strong. As I heard a Jungian say once, 'The passive are not necessarily weak or put-upon. Passivity is a kind of control: control by what one doesn't do.' The Queen is in command of her ship – and she knows all about the movement of the tides. Her father explained that to her many moons ago.

In 1930, when Philip was nine and Elizabeth was four, Philip's middle sister, Cécile – the one who died in the aeroplane crash in 1937 – was engaged to be married. From her sanatorium, near Lake Tegel, Philip's mother, Princess Alice, sent her daughter a letter of congratulation and advice. 'For you know, dear child,' she wrote, 'each woman manages & directs her married life herself, just as she would control herself in a profession if she had one & so you see when a girl marries a decent boy, she makes her *own* happiness with her *own* judgement and self-control. No marriage entered into, in that spirit, with the most dissimilar characters even, ought to be a failure. A little patience in the first years & one has an enduring happy love & friendship for life & which unlike ordinary friendships will be just as fresh when you are old.'

Philip and Elizabeth are old now. The tide is in, and they are friends.

APPENDICES

State & Commonwealth Visits

The Queen acts as host to Heads of State when they pay formal visits to Britain. There are usually two incoming state visits each year. Invitations are sent on the advice of the Foreign and Commonwealth Office. Each visit lasts from a Tuesday to a Friday, and the visiting Head of State stays either at Buckingham Palace, Windsor Castle or, occasionally, the Palace of Holyroodhouse in Edinburgh. The Head of State will attend a state banquet in his or her honour, and host a banquet in turn. One day is spent by the visiting Head of State outside London or Edinburgh.

Incoming state visits to the United Kingdom since 1952:

1954
28 June–1 July	King Gustaf VI Adolf and Queen Louise of Sweden
14–16 October	Emperor Haile Selassie of Ethiopia

1955
25–28 October	President and Madame Craveiro Lopes of Portugal

1956
16–19 July	King Faisal of Iraq

1958
13–16 May	President and Signora Gronchi of Italy
21–23 October	President Heuss of Germany

1959
5–8 May	The Shahanshah of Iran

1960
5–8 April	President and Madame de Gaulle of France
19–21 July	King Bhumibol and Queen Sirikit of Thailand
17–20 October	King Mahendra and Queen Ratna of Nepal

1962
10–13 July   President and Mrs Tubman of Liberia
16–19 October   King Olav V of Norway

1963
14–17 May   King Baudouin and Queen Fabiola of Belgium
12–23 June   President Radhakrishnan of India (a Commonwealth visit)
9–12 July   King Paul I and Queen Frederika of Greece

1964
26 May–4 June   President Ferik Ibrahim Abbood of Sudan

1965
13–17 July   President and Señora de Frei of Chile

1966
17–21 May   President and Frau Jonas of Austria
19–28 July   King Hussein and Princess Muna al Hussein of Jordan
17–25 November   President Ayub Khan of Pakistan (a Commonwealth visit)

1967
9–17 May   King Faisal of Saudi Arabia
1–8 November   President and Madame Cevdet Sunay of Turkey

1969
22–30 April   President Saragat and Signora Santacatterina of Italy
15–20 July   President and Madame Kekkonen of Finland

1971
5–8 October   Emperor Hirohito and Empress Nagako of Japan
7–10 December   King Zahir Shah of Afghanistan

1972
11–15 April   Queen Juliana and Prince Bernhard of the Netherlands
13–16 June   The Grand Duke and Grand Duchess of Luxembourg
24–27 October   President and Frau Heinemann of Germany

1973
3–6 April   President and Señora de Echeverria of Mexico
12–15 June   General and Mrs Gowon of Nigeria
11–14 December   President and Madame Mobutu of Zaire

1974
30 April–3 May   Queen Margrethe and Prince Henrik of Denmark

| 9–12 July | The Yang di-Pertuan Agong and the Raja Permaisuri of Malaysia |

1975
| 8–11 July | King Carl XVI Gustaf of Sweden |
| 18–12 November | President Nyerere of Tanzania |

1976
| 4–7 May | President and Senhora Geisel of Brazil |
| 22–25 June | President and Madame Valéry Giscard d'Estaing of France |

1978
| 13–16 June | President and Madame Ceauşescu of Romania |
| 14–17 November | President and Senhora Eanes of Portugal |

1979
| 12–15 June | President Arap Moi of Kenya |
| 13–16 November | President and Madame Soeharto of Indonesia |

1980
| 18–21 November | King Birendra and Queen Aishwarya of Nepal |

1981
| 17–20 March | President Shagari of Nigeria |
| 9–12 June | King Khaled of Saudi Arabia |

1982
| 16–19 March | HM Qaboos Bin Al Said, Sultan of Oman |
| 16–19 November | Queen Beatrix and Prince Claus of the Netherlands |

1983
| 22–25 March | President and Mrs Kaunda of Zambia |

1984
| 10–13 April | His Highness Shaikh Isa bin Sulman Al Khalifa of Bahrain |
| 23–26 October | President and Madame François Mitterrand of France |

1985
16–19 April	President Banda of Malawi
11–14 June	President and Señora de la Madrid of Mexico
12–15 November	His Highness Sheikh Khalifa bin Hamad Al-Thani of Qatar

1986

22–25 April   King Juan Carlos and Queen Sofia of Spain
1–4 July   President and Freifrau von Weizsacker of Germany

1987

24–27 March   King Fahd of Saudi Arabia
14–17 July   King Hassan II of Morocco

1988

12–15 April   King Olav V of Norway
12–15 July   President Evren of Turkey
8–11 November   President and Madame Diouf of Senegal

1989

9–12 May   President and Mrs Babangida of Nigeria
18–21 July   Sheikh Zayed bin Sultan Al Nahyan of United Arab
                              Emirates

1990

3–6 April   President and Shrimali Venkataraman of India
23–26 October   President Cossiga of Italy

1991

23–26 April   President and Mrs Walesa of Poland
23–26 July   President and Mrs Mubarak of Egypt

1992

3–6 November   The Sultan of Brunei and the Raja Isteri

1993

27–30 April   President and Senhora Soares of Portugal
9–12 November   The Yang di-Pertuan Agong and the Raja Permaisuri
                              Agong of Malaysia

1994

17–20 May   President Mugabe of Zimbabwe
5–8 July   King Harald V and Queen Sonja of Norway

1995

23–26 May   Shaikh Jabir al Ahmed Jabir al Sabah (the Amir) of
                              Kuwait
17–20 October   President and Madame Ahtisaari of Finland

1996

14–17 May   President and Madame Chirac of France
9–12 July   President Mandela of South Africa

1997
25–28 February   President and Mrs Weizman of Israel
2–5 December   President and Senhora Cardoso of Brazil

1998
26–29 May   Emperor Akihito and Empress Michiko of Japan
1–4 December   President and Frau Herzog of Germany

1999
22–25 June   President and Mrs Goncz of Hungary
19–22 October   President and Madame Wang Yeping of China

2000
16–18 February   Queen Margrethe II and Prince Henrik of Denmark

2001
12–15 June   President and Mrs Mbeki of South Africa
6–9 November   King Abdullah II and Queen Rania of Jordan

2003
24–27 June   President Putin and Mrs Putina of the Russian Federation
18–21 November   President and Mrs Bush of the United States of America

2004
5–7 May   President and Mrs Kwasniewska of Poland

State visits undertaken by the Queen, accompanied by the Duke of Edinburgh, since 1952:

1955
24–26 June   Norway, visiting King Haakon VII

1956
8–10 June   Sweden, visiting King Gustaf VI Adolf

1957
18–21 February   Portugal, visiting President Craveiro Lopes
8–11 April   France, visiting President René Coty
21–23 May   Denmark, visiting King Frederick IX
17–21 October   USA, visiting President Eisenhower

1958
25–27 March   The Netherlands, visiting Queen Juliana

1961

26 February–1 March	Nepal, visiting King Mahendra
2–6 March	Iran, visiting Shahanshah Mohammad Reza
2–5 May	Italy, visiting President Gronchi
5 May	Vatican City, visiting Pope John XXIII
23 November	Liberia, visiting President Tubman

1965

1–8 February	Ethiopia, visiting Emperor Haile Selassie
8–12 February	Sudan, visiting President Dr El Tigani El Mahi
18–28 May	Germany, visiting President Lübke

1966

9–13 May	Belgium, visiting King Baudouin and Queen Fabiola

1968

5–11 November	Brazil, visiting President da Costa e Silva
11–18 November	Chile, visiting President Frei

1969

5–10 May	Austria, visiting President Jonas

1971

18–25 October	Turkey, visiting President Sunay

1972

10–15 February	Thailand, visiting King Bhumibol and Queen Sirikit
13–14 March	Maldives, visiting President Nasir
15–19 May	France, visiting President Pompidou
17–21 October	Yugoslavia, visiting President Tito

1974

15–22 March	Indonesia, visiting President Soeharto

1975

24 February–1 March	Mexico, visiting President Echeverria
7–12 May	Japan, visiting Emperor Hirohito

1976

25–28 May	Finland, visiting President Kekkonen
6–11 July	USA, visiting President Ford
8–12 November	Luxembourg, visiting the Grand Duke and Grand Duchess

1978

22–26 May	Germany, visiting President Scheel

1979

16–19 May	Denmark, visiting Queen Margrethe
19–22 July	Tanzania, visiting President Nyerere
22–25 July	Malawi, visiting President Banda
25–27 July	Botswana, visiting President Seretse Khama
27 July–4 August	Zambia, visiting President Kaunda

1980

29 April–2 May	Switzerland, visiting President Chevallaz
14–17 October	Italy, visiting President Pertini
17 October	Vatican City, visiting Pope John Paul II
21–23 October	Tunisia, visiting President Bourguiba
25–27 October	Algeria, visiting President Chadli
27–30 October	Morocco, visiting King Hassan II

1981

5–8 May	Norway, visiting King Olav V
21–25 October	Sri Lanka, visiting President Jayewardene

1983

25–28 May	Sweden, visiting King Carl Gustaf XVI and Queen Silvia
10–14 November	Kenya, visiting President Arap Moi
14–17 November	Bangladesh, visiting President Chowdhury
17–26 November	India, visiting President Zail Singh

1984

26–30 March	Jordan, visiting King Hussein and Queen Noor

1985

25–29 March	Portugal, visiting President and Senhora Eanes

1986

17–21 February	Nepal, visiting King Birendra and Queen Aishwarya
12–18 October	China, visiting President Li Xiannian

1988

17–21 October	Spain, visiting King Juan Carlos and Queen Sofia

1989

9–11 October	Singapore, visiting President Wee Kim Wee
14–17 October	Malaysia, visiting the Yang di-Pertuan Agong

1990

25–27 June	Iceland, visiting President Vigdis Finnbogadottir

1991
14–17 May USA, visiting President Bush
8–10 October Namibia, visiting President Nujoma
10–15 October Zimbabwe, visiting President Mugabe

1992
28–30 May Malta, visiting President Tabone
9–12 June France, visiting President Mitterand
19–23 October Germany, visiting President von Weizsacker

1993
4–7 May Hungary, visiting President Goncz

1994
17–20 October Russia, visiting President Yeltsin

1995
19–25 March South Africa, visiting President Mandela

1996
25–27 March Poland, visiting President Kwasniewska
27–29 March Czech Republic, visiting President Havel
28 October–1 November Thailand, visiting King Bhumibol

1997
6–12 October Pakistan, visiting President Sharma
12–18 October India, visiting President Narayanan

1998
17–20 September Brunei, visiting the Sultan of Brunei
20–23 September Malaysia, visiting the Yang di Pertuan-Agong

1999
19–22 April South Korea, visiting President Kim Dae-jung

2000
16–19 October Italy, visiting President Ciampi

2001
30 May–1 June Norway, visiting King Harald V and Queen Sonja

2004
5–7 April France, visiting President and Madame Chirac

The Queen's commitment to the Commonwealth is famous. Since 1952 she has visited Canada twenty times, Australia fourteen times, New Zealand ten times and Jamaica six times. Visits undertaken by the Queen and the Duke of Edinburgh to Commonwealth countries since 1952:

1952

6 February	Kenya (visiting Sagana Lodge, Kiganjo, where the Queen learnt of her Accession)

1953

24 November	Canada (refuelling in Newfoundland)
24–25 November	Bermuda
25–27 November	Jamaica
17–19 December	Fiji
19–20 December	Tonga

1953–4

23 December 1953– 30 January 1954	New Zealand

1954

3 February–1 April	Australia (New South Wales [NSW], Australian Capital Territory [ACT], Tasmania, Victoria, South Australia, Queensland, Western Australia)
5 April	Cocos Islands
10–21 April	Ceylon
27 April	Aden
28–30 April	Uganda
3–7 May	Malta
10 May	Gibraltar

1956

28 January–16 February	Nigeria

1957

12–16 October	Canada (Ontario)

1959

18 June–1 August	Canada (opening of St Lawrence Seaway, Newfoundland, Quebec, Ontario, Alberta, British Columbia, Yukon, Northwest Territories, Saskatchewan, Manitoba, New Brunswick, Prince Edward Island, Nova Scotia)

1961

20 January	Cyprus (refuelling)
21 January–1 February	India
1–16 February	Pakistan
16–26 February	India
1–2 March	India
9–20 November	Ghana
25 November– 1 December	Sierra Leone
3–5 December	Gambia

1963

30 January–1 February	Canada (refuelling in Edmonton and overnight stop in Vancouver)
2–3 February	Fiji
6–18 February	New Zealand
18 February–27 March	Australia (ACT, South Australia, Victoria, Tasmania, NSW, Queensland, Northern Territory, Western Australia)
28 March	Fiji (refuelling)
29 March	Canada (refuelling in Vancouver)

1964

5–13 October	Canada (Prince Edward Island, Quebec, Ottawa)

1966

1 February	Canada (refuelling in Newfoundland)
1 February	Barbados
2 February	Mustique (private)
4–5 February	British Guiana
7–9 February	Trinidad
10 February	Tobago
11 February	Grenada
13 February	St Vincent
14–15 February	Barbados
16 February	St Lucia
17 February	Antigua (private visit)
18 February	Dominica
19 February	Montserrat
20 February	Antigua
21 February	Antigua (private visit)
22 February	St Kitts
22 February	Nevis
23 February	British Virgin Islands (Tortola, Beef Island, Virgin Gorda)
25 February	Turks and Caicos Islands (Grand Turk, South Caicos)

26 February	Conception Island (private visit)
27–28 February	The Bahamas (Nassau)
1 March	Conception Island (private visit)
3–6 March	Jamaica

1967

29 June–5 July	Canada (Centennial celebrations and EXPO at Montreal)
14–17 November	Malta

1970

2–3 March	Canada (Ottawa for refuelling and Vancouver for overnight stop)
4–5 March	Fiji
7 March	Tonga
12–30 March	New Zealand
30 March–3 May	Australia (NSW, Tasmania, Victoria, Queensland)
3 May	Fiji (refuelling)
3–4 May	Canada (Vancouver and Gander for refuelling)
5–15 July	Canada (Northwest Territories and Manitoba)

1971

3–12 May	Canada (British Columbia)

1972

18–20 February	Singapore
22–26, 28 February	Malaysia
29 February	Brunei
2 March	Malaysia
5 March	Singapore
6, 8 March	Malaysia
19–20 March	Seychelles
24–26 March	Mauritius
26 March	Kenya (Nairobi)

1973

25 June–5 July	Canada (Ontario, Prince Edward Island, Regina, Calgary)
31 July–4 August	Canada (Ottawa – Commonwealth Conference)
15 October	Canada (Vancouver for refuelling)
16–17 October	Fiji
17–22 October	Australia (ACT and Sydney for the opening of the opera house)
23 October	Singapore (refuelling)

1974

27 January	Canada (Ottawa and Vancouver for refuelling)

28–29 January	Cook Islands (opening of Rarotonga International Airport)
30 January–8 February	New Zealand (visit to Commonwealth Games)
11 February	Norfolk Island
15–16 February	New Hebrides
18–21 February	British Solomon Islands (San Cristobal Honiara, Gizo)
22–27 February	Papua New Guinea
27–28 February	Australia (ACT; the Queen returned to London on 28 February for a general election in the UK, cutting short the tour, which the Duke of Edinburgh completed)
28 February	Singapore (refuelling)
14 March	Singapore (refuelling)
22 March	Singapore (refuelling)

1975

16–18 February	Bermuda
18–20 February	Barbados
20–21 February	Bahamas
1 March	Bermuda (refuelling)
26–30 April	Jamaica (Commonwealth Conference)
4–7 May	Hong Kong

1976

13–25 July	Canada (Nova Scotia, New Brunswick and Montreal for Olympic Games)

1977

10–11 February	Western Samoa (Apia, Tiafau)
14 February	Tonga
16–17 February	Fiji
22 February–7 March	New Zealand
7–23 March	Australia (ACT, NSW, Queensland, Tasmania, Victoria, South Australia)
23–26 March	Papua New Guinea
26–30 March	Australia (Northern Territory, Western Australia)
14–19 October	Canada (Ontario)
19–20 October	Bahamas
22 October	West Plana Cay (private)
23 October	Little Inagua Island (private)
26 October	British Virgin Islands (Tortola, Virgin Gorda)
27 October	Antigua (private)
28 October	Antigua
30 October	Mustique (private)
31 October–2 November	Barbados

1978

26 July–6 August | Canada (Newfoundland, Saskatchewan, Alberta for Commonwealth Games, Edmonton, accompanied by Prince Andrew and Prince Edward)

1979

19–22 July | Tanzania (Arusha, Dar es Salaam, Zanzibar, Kilimanjaro)
22–25 July | Malawi (Blantyre, Lilongwe, Zomba Plateau)
25–27 July | Botswana (Gaborone)
27 July–4 August | Zambia (Lusaka for Commonwealth Conference, Kitwe, Ndola)

1980

24 May | Singapore (refuelling)
24–28 May | Australia (Canberra, Sydney, Melbourne)
29 May | Singapore (refuelling)

1981

26 September | Singapore (refuelling)
26 September–
12 October | Australia (Commonwealth Heads of Government Meeting [CHOGM] in Melbourne, Tasmania, Western Australia, South Australia)
12–20 October | New Zealand
20–21 October | Australia (overnight stop in Perth)
21–25 October | Sri Lanka (Colombo, Anuradhapura, Kandy, Victoria Dam)

1982

15–18 April | Canada (Ottawa, Patriation)
5 October | Singapore (refuelling)
5–13 October | Australia (NWT, Queensland for Commonwealth Games, Brisbane, ACT, NSW)
13–14 October | Papua New Guinea
18 October | Solomon Islands
21 October | Nauru
23 October | Kiribati
26–27 October | Tuvalu
30 October–1 November | Fiji

1983

13 February | Bermuda (refuelling)
13–16 February | Jamaica
16–17 February | Cayman Islands
8–11 March | Canada (British Columbia)

9–10 November	Cyprus (overnight stop)
10–14 November	Kenya (state visit – Nairobi, Sagana)
14–17 November	Bangladesh (state visit – Dhaka)
17–26 November	India (state visit – New Delhi, Hyderabad and Pune, CHOGM in New Delhi)

1984

25–26 March	Cyprus (overnight stop)
24 September–7 October	Canada (New Brunswick, Ontario and Manitoba)

1985

9–11 October	Belize
11–18 October	Bahamas (CHOGM)
20 October	Little Inagua Island (private)
23 October	St Kitts-Nevis
24 October	Antigua
25 October	Dominica
26 October	St Lucia
27 October	St Vincent and the Grenadines
28–29 October	Barbados
30 October	Mustique (private)
31 October	Grenada
1–3 November	Trinidad and Tobago

1986

22 February–2 March	New Zealand
2–13 March	Australia (ACT, NSW, Victoria, South Australia)
21–23 October	Hong Kong

1987

9–24 October	Canada (CHOGM, British Columbia, Saskatchewan and Quebec)

1988

19 April–10 May	Australia (Western Australia, Tasmania, Queensland, NSW and ACT)

1989

8–11 March	Barbados (350th anniversary of Barbados Parliament)
9–11 October	Singapore (state visit)
14–21 October	Malaysia (state visit 14–17, CHOGM 17–21)

1990

31 January	Singapore (refuelling)
1 February	Australia (refuelling in Brisbane)

1–16 February	New Zealand (Commonwealth Games, Auckland, 150th anniversary of Treaty of Waitangi, Wellington, Christchurch)
17 February	Australia (refuelling in Brisbane)
17 February	Singapore (refuelling)
27 June–1 July	Canada (Alberta, Ontario, Quebec)

1991

7 October	Kenya (overnight stop)
8–10 October	Namibia (state visit)
10–19 October	Zimbabwe (state visit 10–15, CHOGM 15–19)

1992

18–25 February	Australia (Sesqui-centenary of founding of city of Sydney, ACT and Southern Australia)
28–30 May	Malta (state visit)
30 June–2 July	Canada (celebration of 125th anniversary of Confederation)

1993

18–24 October	Cyprus (CHOGM)

1994

18 February	Puerto Rico (transfer flight)
18 February	Anguilla
19 February	Dominica
19–22 February	Guyana
22–24 February	Belize
26–27 February	Cayman Islands
1–3 March	Jamaica
6–8 March	Bahamas
8–10 March	Bermuda
13–22 August	Canada (Nova Scotia, British Columbia, Northwest Territories)

1995

19–25 March	South Africa
30 October–11 November	New Zealand (visit and CHOGM in Auckland)

1997

23 June–2 July	Canada (Newfoundland, Ontario, National Capital Region)
6–12 October	Pakistan
12–18 October	India

1998

17–20 September	Brunei Darussalam
20–23 September	Malaysia (closing of Commonwealth Games)

1999

7–9 November	Ghana
9–15 November	South Africa (including CHOGM in Durban)
15 November	Mozambique

2000

17 March–1 April	Australia (ACT, NSW, Victoria, Tasmania, Northern Territory (Alice Springs), Western Australia

2002

18–20 February	Jamaica (Kingston and Montego Bay)
22–27 February	New Zealand (Wellington, Christchurch and Auckland)
27 February–3 March	Australia (South Australia and Queensland, including CHOGM in Maroochydore, Queensland)
4–15 October	Canada (Nunavut, British Columbia, Manitoba, Ontario, New Brunswick and the National Capital Region)

2003

3–6 December	Abuja, Nigeria (CHOGM)

Prince Philip's Achievements

I first read a draft obituary of the Duke of Edinburgh in 1991. It did not do him justice. The article, destined for eventual publication in a national newspaper, paid proper tribute to the support Prince Philip has given the Queen throughout her reign, but barely touched on the range of his own achievements. It mentioned his many overseas visits, but did so only to highlight his reputation for 'gaffes'.

When, recently, I interviewed him and told him I had made a list of the popular myths that exist about him, he asked at once, 'Tactless overseas? Is that on your list?' He glanced at my notebook, saw the words 'Slitty eyes', and sighed.

On 16 October 1986, in Beijing, when the Queen and the Duke were on a state visit to China, Prince Philip met a group of British students studying at the North West University in Xian. The Duke was particularly interested in the students because they came from Edinburgh University (he has been Chancellor of four universities: Edinburgh since 1952) and chatting to them informally (with neither Chinese nor press present) he expressed surprise when he discovered that they were spending a whole year in China – long enough 'to go native and come home slit-eyed'. It was a joke, a bit of badinage, but, because one of the students later gave a friendly account of the conversation to a journalist, an inconsequential private aside was turned into banner headlines around the world. 'The great wally of China' said the *Mirror*; 'The Duke gets it wong' said the *Sun*. As well as depicting the Duke as accident-prone, there was the unpleasant implication that he was some kind of closet racist. (He may not be a disciple of all that is politically correct, but I have never detected a hint of racism in him. That said, he is not inclined to apologise when what he says is misinterpreted. When questioned about his comment about a fuse box with so many wires hanging out that it looked as if it had been put together 'by an Indian', he said, 'Have you ever been to India and looked at a fuse box there?')

Since 1991, I have read other draft obituaries and the 'gaffes' feature in all of them. 'How do you keep the natives off the booze long enough to get them through the test?' he asked a driving instructor in Oban, Scotland, in 1995. 'You managed not to get eaten, then?' he said, in 1998, to a student who had been trekking in Papua New Guinea. To a Briton he met in Budapest, Hungary, in 1993, he remarked: 'You can't have been here that long – you haven't got a pot belly.' In Australia in 2002, at an Aboriginal cultural display, he enquired of his host, 'Do you still throw spears at each other?'

As a reminder that there is more to the Duke of Edinburgh than these off-the-cuff remarks that now dominate the press cutting files about him, here is a list of his 'involvements and offices' since 1947. It has been prepared by Anne Griffiths, the Duke's archivist at Buckingham Palace, and, though it is not exhaustive, it gives a flavour of the Prince's range of interests and achievements.

1947–	Patron, London Federation of Boys' Clubs (later London Federation of Clubs for Young People, then Federation of London Youth Clubs and now London Youth)
1948–	President, National Playing Fields Association
1948–2000	Trustee, National Maritime Museum Patron from 2000
1948–	Hon. Member, Royal Yachting Association Hon. Member of Council from 1980 President, 1956–70 and 1975–80
1948	Member, Royal Yacht Squadron Admiral from 1953 1962–8 Commodore and rewrote Statutes
1948–	Hon. Life Member, Marylebone Cricket Club (MCC) President, 1949–50 and 1974–5
1948–76	Chancellor, University of Wales
1949–	Life Member, Variety Club of Great Britain
1950	Patron and Twelfth Man, Lords Taverners President 1960–61
1951–61	President, Automobile Association Hon. Life Member from 1947 Ex-officio Member of the Committee from 1961
1951–	President, Central Council of Physical Recreation and saved it from extinction
1951	Co-founder, with Frank Carr, the Cutty Sark Preservation Society (now Cutty Sark Trust), Patron 1952–2000 President from 2000
1951–	President, City and Guilds of London Institute

	1962 initiated Prince Philip Medal
1951–2	President, British Association for the Advancement of Science
1951–4	HM Yacht *Britannia* – involved in design until commissioned
1952–99	President, Royal Mint Advisory Committee on the design of coins, seals and medals
1952–	President, English-speaking Union of the Commonwealth
	Chairman, English Language Committee from 1977
1952–	Chancellor, University of Edinburgh
1952–2002	Grand Master, Guild of Air Pilots and Air Navigators
	1979 Prince Philip Prize for Helicopter Rescue
	Patron from 2002
1952–	Elder Brother, Trinity House
	Master from 1969
1952–	Patron, Air League
	President in 1969
1952–2000	President, British Amateur Athletic Board (later British Athletic Federation and now UK Athletics)
	Patron from 2000
1952	First flight on 12 November – Chipmunk from White Waltham
1952–	President and Hon. Life Fellow, Royal Society for the Encouragement of Arts, Manufactures and Commerce
1953–	Patron, Outward Bound Trust
	1995–2000, Chairman of Trustees
1956–92	Patron, Sail Training Association
1955–90	President, Commonwealth Games Federation
1955	Founder and President, Guards Polo Club (originally Household Brigade Polo Club)
1956	Founder, Commonwealth Study Conferences, held every six years – 1956, 1962, 1968, 1974, 1980, 1986, 1992, 1998, 2003
1956	Co-founder with Kurt Hahn and Chairman of Trustees, the Duke of Edinburgh Award Scheme
	Patron and Trustee 1961–2001
	Patron from 2001
1956	Initiator, Lunches at Buckingham Palace
1957	Co-founder with Sam Hordern, Royal Agricultural Society of the Commonwealth, President from 1958
1957	Patron and co-founder with Michael Ansell, Pony Club Mounted Games Championship – Prince Philip Cup
	President, the Pony Club 1997–2002
1957	Initiator, Commonwealth Technical Training Week, held in 1961
1959	Initiated Designer's Prize with the Design Council (formerly the Duke of Edinburgh's Prize for Elegant Design (1959), the Duke of Edinburgh's Design Prize (1971) and the Duke of Edinburgh's Prize for Industrial Design (1976–89). Since 1990 the Prince Philip Designer's Prize for the Designer of the Year)

1960–77	President, Zoological Society of London
	Life Fellow 1959–77
	Hon. Fellow from 1977
1960	Founder with Lord Buxton of Alsa, 'Countryside in 1970'
	Conferences, 1963, 1965 and 1970
1961–	Patron, Voluntary Service Overseas
1961–81	UK President and International Trustee, World Wildlife Fund
	(now World Wide Fund for Nature)
	1981–96 International President
	1996– President Emeritus
1964–70	President, Game Research Association
	1970–73 President, the Game Conservancy
	1973– Patron and Life Member
1964–86	President, International Equestrian Federation (FEI)
	Introduced International Rules for Carriage-Driving, Long-Distance Riding, Vaulting and initiated Veterinary Committee and Veterinary Regulations
	Added International Competitions for Pony Riders, Juniors and Young Riders
1965–	President, Royal Commission for the Exhibition of 1851
1965–	Co-founder with Robin Woods, Dean of Windsor, and Trustee of the Council, St George's House, Windsor Castle
1965	Chairman, Originating Committee, Queen's Award for Industry, now the Queen's Awards for Export & Technology
1965–75	President, Council of Engineering Institutions
	1976 Initiator, Fellowship of Engineering
	1976– Senior Fellow
	From 1992 Royal Academy of Engineering
1966–	Chairman and President Panel of Judges, Tiger Club 'Dawn to Dusk' (flying) Competition for the Duke of Edinburgh Trophy
1967–	Patron, British Association for Shooting & Conservation (formerly WAGBI)
1967–91	First Chancellor, University of Salford
1968	Initiator, Standing Conference on Schools Science and Technology (SCSSI), subsequently Patron, Association for Schools' Science Engineering and Technology
	From 1961 Patron, Association for Science Education
1969–	Co-founder with Frank Carr and President, the Maritime Trust
1970	Patron, British Trust for Conservation Volunteers
1971	Initiator, International Carriage-driving Grand Prix, Royal Windsor Horse Show
1971	Founder and Life Member, Windsor Park Equestrian Club, Patron 1971–84
	President from 1984
1972	Initiator, Private Dinners at Buckingham Palace

1973–97	Chairman, Westminster Abbey Trust
1974–	Grand President, British Commonwealth Ex-Services League and known from 2003 as the Royal Commonwealth Ex-Services League
1975–80	President, National Federation of Housing Associations Patron from 1981
1976–	Chancellor of the University of Cambridge
1976–	Co-founder with Sir Kit Aston, then Mayor of Windsor, and Chairman of Trustees, Prince Philip Trust for the Royal Borough of Windsor and Maidenhead
1977–8	Promoter, Degrees in Military Studies for Service Officers
1978	Co-founder with Colonel Anderton of Standing Conference on Countryside Sports
1978	Member of the British Team at the Four-in-Hand World Driving Championships which won the Team Bronze Medal at Kecskemet, Hungary
1980	Member of the British Team at the Four-in-Hand World Driving Championships which won the Team Gold Medal at Windsor
1981	Member of the British Team at the Four-in-Hand European Driving Championships which won the Team Bronze Medal at Zug, Switzerland
1982	Member of the British Team at the Four-in-Hand World Driving Championships which won the Team Bronze Medal at Apeldoorn, Netherlands
1984	Member of the British Team at the Four-in-Hand World Driving Championships which won the Team Bronze Medal at Szilvasvarad, Hungary
1984–91	Chairman of Inquiry into British Housing as Patron of the National Federation of Housing Associations (1st Report 1985, 2nd Report 1991)
1987	Patron, British Trust for Ornithology
1989	President, British Sports Trust
1991	President, Royal Windsor Horse Show
1992–7	Chairman, Restoration Committee following Windsor Castle Fire
1997	Last flight on 11 August – Carlisle to Islay in BAe 146 after 5,986 hours in fifty-nine types including nine helicopters

Prizes and Medals Donated by the Duke of Edinburgh

1949–	Edinburgh Cup for Yachts of the International Dragon Class
1955–	'Royal Windsor Cup' for Ascot Week Polo Tournament
1957–	Prince Philip Cup for Isle of Wight inter-club racing
1957–	Prince Philip Cup for Pony Club Mounted Games
1959–	Prince Philip Designer's Prize for the Designer of the Year
1961–	Silver Wink for Inter-University Tiddlywinks Championships
1962	Coweslip Trophy for Championships held by the Australian Flying

	Fifteen Association
1962–	Prince Philip Medal for outstanding achievement in work with Science or Technology, City and Guilds of London Institute
1962–	Silver collar for Greyhound Racing
1962–	Grand Master's Medal, Guild of Air Pilots and Air Navigators
1963–	Bagpiping trophy for the Pakistan Army
1963–	President's Prize for Design Management, Royal Society of Arts
1964–	Prince Philip Challenge Cup for coxed fours, Henley Regatta
1972–	Trophy for World Individual Team Driving Champion
1991–	Duke of Edinburgh's Trophy for the Royal Windsor Horse Show
1993–	Prince Philip Cup for Modern Horse-drawn Machinery
1997–	Duke of Edinburgh Conservation Medal, World Wide Fund for Nature

Houses and Gardens

Buckingham Palace

1962   Conversion of chapel to the Queen's Gallery

Windsor

South slopes, moved road and laid out border and beds
East terrace beds and fountain
'Coronation' Oak Avenue from Golf Course Cottage
'Hurricane' Lime Avenue
'Grenadier' Avenue
Budgerigars and pigeons
Queen Anne's Ride – replanting

Balmoral

North side, fountain court, kitchen garden, water garden, 'heath' beds
Oak bank
Log cabin, conversation of Gelder Shiel and Inchnabobart
Demolition of dry-rotten Victorian addition to Abergeldie Castle

Birkhall

Replacement of the 'tin wing'

Sandringham

Wood Farm – conversion
Coronation Lime Avenue from Appleton to Gatton Water
Copper Beach Avenue – Norwich Gates, Dersingham Hill
Game coverts, marsh 'sanctuary', new hedgerows
Construction of the two log cabins
Conversion of new lunch room

Appendices

Collections

Books on carriage-driving
Bird books
Pictures of birds and animals
Coach and carriage driving books
Contemporary Scottish pictures (mostly at Holyrood)
Contemporary watercolours
Sixty oil paintings by Edward Seago from World Tour 1956–7
Competition carriage-driving scrapbooks and videos
Photographs – 150 albums of Minox from foreign visits
100 albums of conventional photographs

Books

1957	*Selected Speeches – 1948–55*
1960	*Selected Speeches – 1956–59*
1962	*Birds from Britannia*; American edition, *Seabirds from Southern Waters*
1970	*Wildlife Crisis* (with James Fisher)
1978	*The Environmental Revolution – Speeches on Conservation 1962–1977*
1982	*Competition Carriage Driving*, French edition 1984, second edition 1984
1982	*A Question of Balance*
1984	*Men, Machines and Sacred Cows*
1984	*A Windsor Correspondence* (with Michael Mann)
1988	*Down to Earth – Collected Writings and Speeches on Man and the Natural World*, 1961–87, paperback edition 1989, Japanese edition 1992
1989	*Survival or Extinction: A Christian Attitude to the Environment* (with Michael Mann)
1994	*Competition Carriage Driving*, revised edition
1996	*Driving and Judging Dressage*
2004	*Thirty Years On, and Off, the Box Seat*

Service Appointments Held by the Duke of Edinburgh

1952–92	Admiral, Sea Cadet Corps
1953	Admiral of the Fleet (15/1/53)
	Field Marshal (15/1/53)
	Marshal of the Royal Air Force (15/1/53)
	Captain-General, Royal Marines (1/6/53)
	Colonel-in-Chief
	The Queen's Own Cameron Highlanders until February 1961
	The Queen's Own Highlanders (Seaforths and Camerons) until September 1994

The Highlanders (Seaforth, Gordons and Camerons) from
September 1994
Colonel-in-Chief
The Wiltshire Regiment until June 1959
The Duke of Edinburgh's Royal Regiment (Berkshire and
Wiltshire) until 1994
The Royal Gloucestershire, Berkshire and Wiltshire Regiment
from April 1994
Colonel-in-Chief
The 8th King's Royal Irish Hussars until October 1958
The Queen's Royal Irish Hussars until September 1993
Deputy Colonel-in-Chief from September, 1993 and Colonel-in-
Chief from 2002
The Queen's Royal Hussars (The Queen's Own and Royal Irish)
Colonel-in-Chief, Royal Canadian Regiment
Air Commodore-in-Chief, Air Training Corps (15/1/53)
Colonel-in-Chief, Army Cadet Force (15/1/53)
Air Commodore-in-Chief, Royal Canadian Air Cadets
Colonel-in-Chief, Royal Canadian Army Cadets
Admiral, Royal Canadian Sea Cadets (15/1/53)
Royal Hon. Colonel, University of Edinburgh and Heriot Watt
Officer Training Corps and from 1994 City of Edinburgh
Universities Officers' Training Corps

1953–75	Colonel, Welsh Guards
1954	Field Marshal, Australian Military Forces (1/4/54)
	Marshal, Royal Australian Air Force (1/4/54)
	Admiral of the Fleet, Royal Australian Navy (1/4/54)
	Extra Master, Merchant Navy
1957	Member, Honourable Artillery Company
1958	Admiral of the Fleet, Royal New Zealand Navy (21/4)
	(seniority backdated to 15/1/53)
	Colonel-in-Chief, the Queen's Royal Irish Hussars (see above)
1959	Colonel-in-Chief, The Duke of Edinburgh's Royal Regiment
	(Berkshire and Wiltshire) (see above)
	Colonel-in-Chief, Royal Australian Corps of Electrical and
	Mechanical Engineers
1961	Colonel-in-Chief, The Queen's Own Highlanders (Seaforth and
	Camerons) (see above)
1963	Colonel-in-Chief, Australian Cadet Corps

FAMILY TREES

The British Royal Family: A select family tree (I)

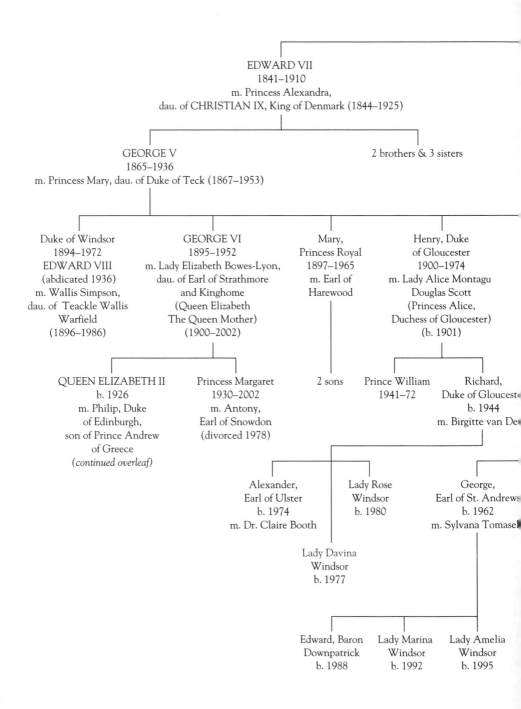

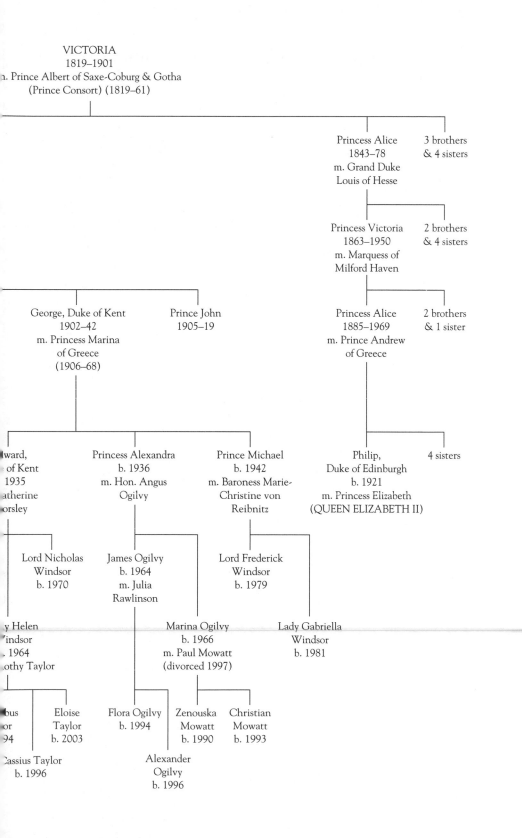

The British Royal Family: A select family tree (II)

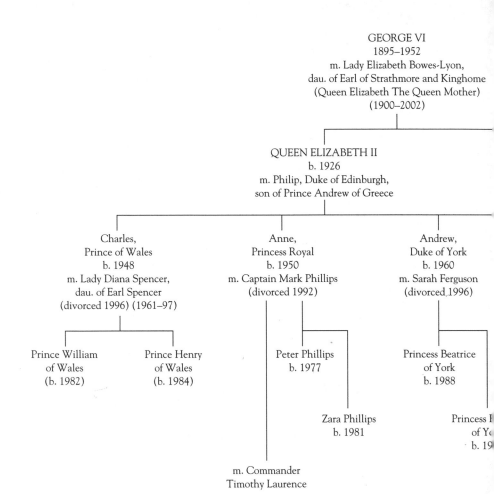

GEORGE VI
1895–1952
m. Lady Elizabeth Bowes-Lyon,
dau. of Earl of Strathmore and Kinghome
(Queen Elizabeth The Queen Mother)
(1900–2002)

QUEEN ELIZABETH II
b. 1926
m. Philip, Duke of Edinburgh,
son of Prince Andrew of Greece

Charles,
Prince of Wales
b. 1948
m. Lady Diana Spencer,
dau. of Earl Spencer
(divorced 1996) (1961–97)

Anne,
Princess Royal
b. 1950
m. Captain Mark Phillips
(divorced 1992)

Andrew,
Duke of York
b. 1960
m. Sarah Ferguson
(divorced 1996)

Prince William
of Wales
(b. 1982)

Prince Henry
of Wales
(b. 1984)

Peter Phillips
b. 1977

Princess Beatrice
of York
b. 1988

Zara Phillips
b. 1981

Princess E
of Yc
b. 19

m. Commander
Timothy Laurence

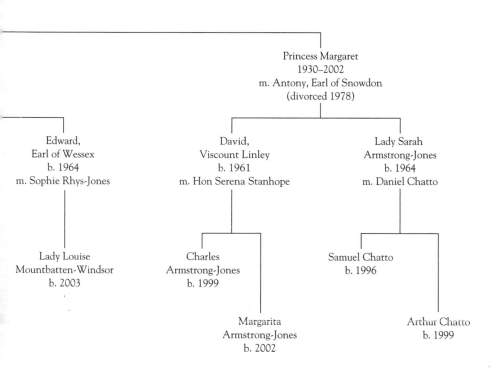

Princess Margaret
1930–2002
m. Antony, Earl of Snowdon
(divorced 1978)

Edward,
Earl of Wessex
b. 1964
m. Sophie Rhys-Jones

David,
Viscount Linley
b. 1961
m. Hon Serena Stanhope

Lady Sarah
Armstrong-Jones
b. 1964
m. Daniel Chatto

Lady Louise
Mountbatten-Windsor
b. 2003

Charles
Armstrong-Jones
b. 1999

Samuel Chatto
b. 1996

Margarita
Armstrong-Jones
b. 2002

Arthur Chatto
b. 1999

The Greek Royal Family: A select family tree

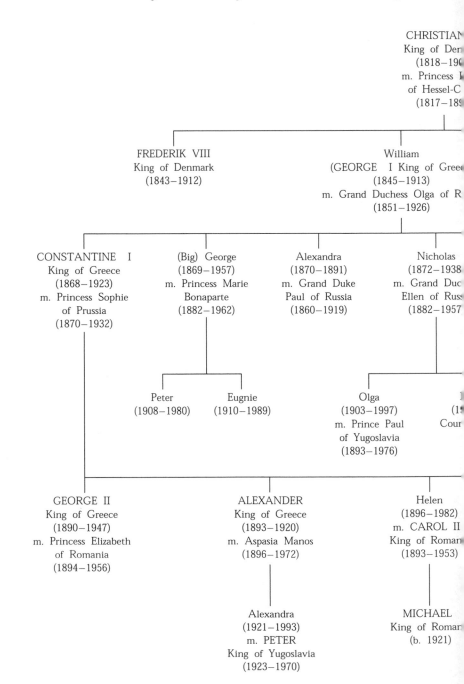

CHRISTIAN
King of Den
(1818–19(
m. Princess I
of Hessel-C
(1817–18!

FREDERIK VIII
King of Denmark
(1843–1912)

William
(GEORGE I King of Gree
(1845–1913)
m. Grand Duchess Olga of R
(1851–1926)

CONSTANTINE I
King of Greece
(1868–1923)
m. Princess Sophie
of Prussia
(1870–1932)

(Big) George
(1869–1957)
m. Princess Marie
Bonaparte
(1882–1962)

Alexandra
(1870–1891)
m. Grand Duke
Paul of Russia
(1860–1919)

Nicholas
(1872–1938
m. Grand Duc
Ellen of Russ
(1882–1957

Peter
(1908–1980)

Eugnie
(1910–1989)

Olga
(1903–1997)
m. Prince Paul
of Yugoslavia
(1893–1976)

!
(1!
Cour

GEORGE II
King of Greece
(1890–1947)
m. Princess Elizabeth
of Romania
(1894–1956)

ALEXANDER
King of Greece
(1893–1920)
m. Aspasia Manos
(1896–1972)

Helen
(1896–1982)
m. CAROL II
King of Roman
(1893–1953)

Alexandra
(1921–1993)
m. PETER
King of Yugoslavia
(1923–1970)

MICHAEL
King of Roman
(b. 1921)

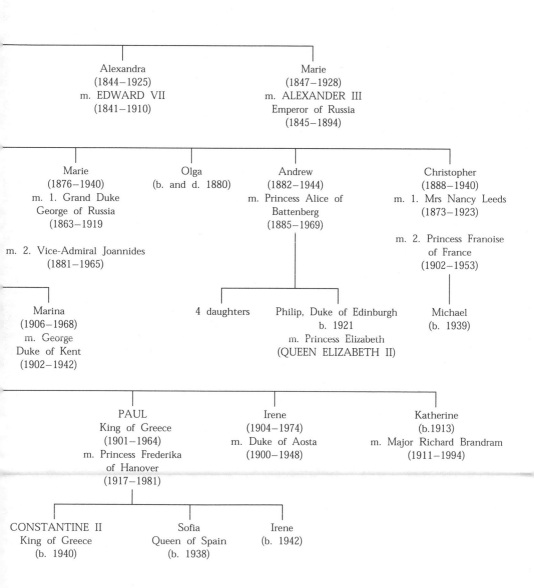

Alexandra
(1844–1925)
m. EDWARD VII
(1841–1910)

Marie
(1847–1928)
m. ALEXANDER III
Emperor of Russia
(1845–1894)

Marie
(1876–1940)
m. 1. Grand Duke
George of Russia
(1863–1919

m. 2. Vice-Admiral Joannides
(1881–1965)

Olga
(b. and d. 1880)

Andrew
(1882–1944)
m. Princess Alice of
Battenberg
(1885–1969)

Christopher
(1888–1940)
m. 1. Mrs Nancy Leeds
(1873–1923)

m. 2. Princess Franoise
of France
(1902–1953)

Marina
(1906–1968)
m. George
Duke of Kent
(1902–1942)

4 daughters

Philip, Duke of Edinburgh
b. 1921
m. Princess Elizabeth
(QUEEN ELIZABETH II)

Michael
(b. 1939)

PAUL
King of Greece
(1901–1964)
m. Princess Frederika
of Hanover
(1917–1981)

Irene
(1904–1974)
m. Duke of Aosta
(1900–1948)

Katherine
(b.1913)
m. Major Richard Brandram
(1911–1994)

CONSTANTINE II
King of Greece
(b. 1940)

Sofia
Queen of Spain
(b. 1938)

Irene
(b. 1942)

The Battenbergs: A select family tree

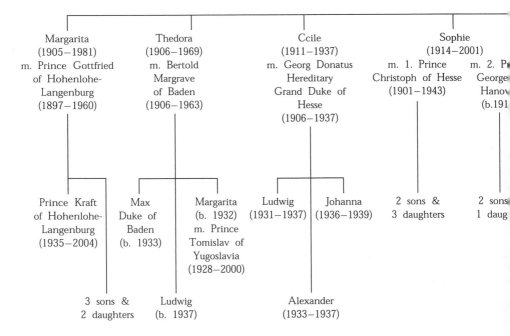

Margarita (1905–1981) m. Prince Gottfried of Hohenlohe-Langenburg (1897–1960)

Thedora (1906–1969) m. Bertold Margrave of Baden (1906–1963)

Ccile (1911–1937) m. Georg Donatus Hereditary Grand Duke of Hesse (1906–1937)

Sophie (1914–2001) m. 1. Prince Christoph of Hesse (1901–1943) m. 2. P George Hanov (b.191

Prince Kraft of Hohenlohe-Langenburg (1935–2004)

Max Duke of Baden (b. 1933)

Margarita (b. 1932) m. Prince Tomislav of Yugoslavia (1928–2000)

Ludwig (1931–1937)

Johanna (1936–1939)

2 sons & 3 daughters

2 sons 1 daug

3 sons & 2 daughters

Ludwig (b. 1937)

Alexander (1933–1937)

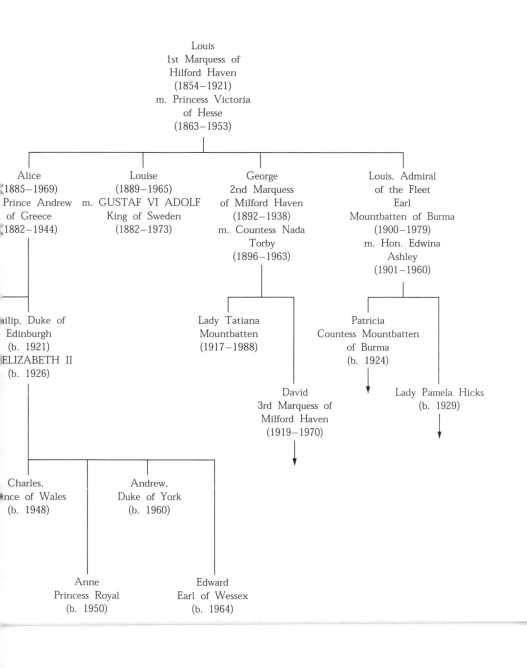

Louis
1st Marquess of
Hilford Haven
(1854–1921)
m. Princess Victoria
of Hesse
(1863–1953)

Alice
(1885–1969)
Prince Andrew
of Greece
(1882–1944)

Louise
(1889–1965)
m. GUSTAF VI ADOLF
King of Sweden
(1882–1973)

George
2nd Marquess
of Milford Haven
(1892–1938)
m. Countess Nada
Torby
(1896–1963)

Louis, Admiral
of the Fleet
Earl
Mountbatten of Burma
(1900–1979)
m. Hon. Edwina
Ashley
(1901–1960)

ilip, Duke of
Edinburgh
(b. 1921)
ELIZABETH II
(b. 1926)

Lady Tatiana
Mountbatten
(1917–1988)

Patricia
Countess Mountbatten
of Burma
(b. 1924)

David
3rd Marquess of
Milford Haven
(1919–1970)

Lady Pamela Hicks
(b. 1929)

Charles,
ince of Wales
(b. 1948)

Andrew,
Duke of York
(b. 1960)

Anne
Princess Royal
(b. 1950)

Edward
Earl of Wessex
(b. 1964)

Sources & Acknowledgements

I hope this book is accurate. If, on reading it, you find errors of fact, please let me know so that I can make corrections for subsequent editions. If you disagree with my interpretation of the facts, please let me know as well. I would like this 'portrait' to be as true as possible. It has been informed by my encounters – some brief, some extended – with the principal characters in the story. It has also been informed by my reading of the work of a range of royal biographers and historians to whom I am much indebted, most notably Hugo Vickers, whose meticulously researched (and beautifully written) authorised biography of Prince Philip's mother, *Alice: Princess Andrew of Greece* (2000), I have drawn on extensively. The family trees of the Greek royal family and of the Battenbergs that I have used are based on those in Hugo Vickers' book.

Many people have been involved in the creation of this book. I want to thank my literary agent, Ed Victor, for making it happen; my editor at the *Sunday Telegraph*, Dominic Lawson, for his unfailing support; my friends Martin Jarvis and Rosalind Ayres for their encouragement; and my wife, Michèle Brown, for both enduring the process with her customary grace, and assisting it professionally. Her research has been invaluable, as has access to her comprehensive library of royal books and papers.

I have had a wonderful friend (and mentor) in my publisher, Mark Booth, and I am greatly indebted to him and all the members of the Century team, including Kate Watkins, Charlotte Bush and Rina Gill. Very considerable thanks are due, too, to my copy editor, Richard Collins; indexer, Douglas Matthews; and picture researcher, Amanda Russell.

I am grateful to the Queen's private secretary, Sir Robin Janvrin, and Her Majesty's press officer, Penny Russell-Smith, for their kindness and for enabling me to spend time with the Queen as she went about her royal duties. I am grateful to the Duke of Edinburgh's private secretary,

Sir Miles Hunt-Davis, and His Royal Highness's archivist, Anne Griffiths, for their kindness and practical assistance. I am especially grateful to Prince Philip for the use of his family photographs and to the Queen for the use of photographs from the Royal Collection, notably pictures from her grandmother Queen Mary's photograph albums.

Below I have listed the principal conversations and books I have relied on for each chapter. Of course, the blame for any errors of commission or omission should be laid at my door and no one else's.

Chapters 1 and 2

Conversations with Prince Philip, the Queen of Denmark, Brett Kahr, Lady Kennard, Countess Mountbatten of Burma, Hugo Vickers.

Alice: Princess Andrew of Greece by Hugo Vickers, 2000
An Appreciation of Kurt Hahn, with a foreword by HRH The Duke of Edinburgh, 1975
The Duke: A Portrait of Prince Philip by Tim Heald, 1991
Elizabeth, Grand Duchess of Russia by Hugo Mager, 1998
Hessian Tapestry by David Duff, 1967
Ionian Vision by Michael Llewellyn Smith, 1973
Lillie Langtry: Manners, Masks and Morals by Laura Beatty, 1999
Marie Bonaparte by Celia Bertin, 1982
Memoirs 1849–1897 by Prince von Bülow, 1931
Mountbatten by Philip Ziegler, 1985
Queen Victoria's Relations by Meriel Buchanan, 1954
The Royal House of Windsor by Elizabeth Longford, 1974
Towards Disaster by Prince Andrew of Greece, 1930

Chapters 3 and 4

Conversations with Prince Philip, Lord David Cecil, the Countess of Longford, Countess Mountbatten of Burma, Nigel Nicolson, Graham Payn, the Hon. Margaret Rhodes, the Earl of Snowdon, Lord Wyatt of Weeford.

Among the Bohemians by Virginia Nicholson, 2002
The Asquiths by Colin Clifford, 2002
Chips: The Diaries of Sir Henry Channon, edited by Robert Rhodes James, 1967

Dearest Child: Private Correspondence of Queen Victoria and the Crown Princess of Prussia, 1858–61 edited by Roger Fulford, 1964

Edward VII by Christopher Hibbert, 1976

Elizabeth by Sarah Bradford, 1996

Elizabeth The Queen Mother by Grania Forbes, 2002

George VI by Sarah Bradford, 1989

Harold Nicolson Diaries and Letters 1930–39 edited by Nigel Nicolson, 1966

A King's Story by the Duke of Windsor, 1951

King Edward the Seventh by Philip Magnus, 1964

Kings, Queens and Courtiers by Kenneth Rose, 1986

Letters from a Prince: Edward Prince of Wales to Mrs Freda Dudley Ward, March 1918–January 1921 edited by Rupert Godfrey, 1999

The Little Princesses by Marion Crawford, 1950

The Lyttelton Hart-Davis Letters, Correspondence of George Lyttelton and Rupert Hart-Davis, 1979

A Moment's Liberty: The Shorter Diary by Virginia Woolf, abridged and edited by Anne Olivier Bell, 1990

Queen Mary and Others by Osbert Sitwell, 1974

Recollections of Three Reigns by Frederick Ponsonby, 1951

Thatched with Gold by Mabell, Countess of Airlie, 1962

The Tongs and the Bones by the Earl of Harewood, 1981

The Wheel of Life, The Diary of Beatrice Webb, Vol. 4, 1924–43, edited by B. and J. Mackenzie, 1985

Victoria R.I. by Elizabeth Longford, 1964

Chapters 5 and 6

Conversations with Prince Philip, Professor Anthony Clare, Tim Heald, Elizabeth Longford, Countess Mountbatten of Burma, the Hon. Margaret Rhodes.

Alice: Princess Andrew of Greece by Hugo Vickers, 2000

Cabbages to Kings by Lisa Sheridan, 1955

The Duke: A Portrait of Prince Philip by Tim Heald, 1991

Elizabeth by Sarah Bradford, 1996

Elizabeth R by Elizabeth Longford, 1983

The Fringes of Power: Downing Street Diaries 1939–1955 by John Colville, 1985

George VI by Sarah Bradford, 1989

George VI: His Life and Reign by John Wheeler-Bennett, 1958

Harold Nicolson Diaries and Letters 1930–39 edited by Nigel Nicolson, 1966

A Horseman through Six Reigns: Reminiscences of a Royal Riding Master by Horace Smith, 1955

It Wasn't All Mayhem by Harry Hargreaves, 2004

John Buchan by Andrew Lownie, 1995

The Killearn Diaries edited by Trefor Evans, 1972

The Little Princesses by Marion Crawford, 1950

Mountbatten by Philip Ziegler, 1985

The Noël Coward Diaries edited by Graham Payn and Sheridan Morley, 1982

Prince Philip: A Family Portrait by Alexandra of Yugoslavia, 1959

The Queen by Ben Pimlott, 1996

Royal: Her Majesty Queen Elizabeth II by Robert Lacey, 2002

To Be a King: A Biography of HRH Prince Charles by Dermot Morrah, 1989

Wallis & Edward, Letters 1931–37 edited by Michael Bloch, 1986

Chapters 7 and 8

Conversations with Prince Philip, Larry Adler, Henry, 7th Earl of Carnarvon, Geordie, 8th Earl of Carnarvon, Robin Dalton, the Rt Hon. Michael Foot, Tim Heald, Lady Kennard, Countess Mountbatten of Burma and Lord Brabourne, Commander Mike Parker, the Hon. Margaret Rhodes, Tom Utley.

Alice: Princess Andrew of Greece by Hugo Vickers, 2000

Chips: The Diaries of Sir Henry Channon edited by Robert Rhodes James, 1967

The Daily Telegraph Book of Military Obituaries by David Twiston Davies, 2003

The Duke: A Portrait of Prince Philip by Tim Heald, 1991

Elizabeth by Sarah Bradford, 1996

Elizabeth R by Elizabeth Longford, 1983

Footprints in Time by John Colville, 1976

Friends, Enemies and Sovereigns by Sir John Wheeler-Bennett, 1976

The Fringes of Power: Downing Street Diaries 1939–1955 by John Colville, 1985

Harold Nicolson Diaries and Letters 1930–39 edited by Nigel Nicolson, 1966

A Horseman through Six Reigns: Reminiscences of a Royal Riding Master by Horace Smith, 1955

An Incidental Memoir by Robin Dalton, 1998

King George VI by Sir John Wheeler-Bennett, 1958

The Little Princesses by Marion Crawford, 1950

Long Walk to Freedom by Nelson Mandela, 1994

Mountbatten by Philip Ziegler, 1985

The Noël Coward Diaries edited by Graham Payn and Sheridan Morley, 1982

Philip: An Informal Biography by Basil Boothroyd, 1971

Prince Philip: A Family Portrait by Alexandra of Yugoslavia, 1959

The Queen by Ann Morrow, 1983

The Queen by Ben Pimlott, 1996

Royal: Her Majesty Queen Elizabeth II by Robert Lacey, 2002

Step Aside for Royalty by Eileen Parker, 1982

Time and Chance by Peter Townsend, 1978

To Be a King: A Biography of HRH Prince Charles by Dermot Morrah, 1989

Wallis & Edward, Letters 1931–37 edited by Michael Bloch, 1986

Chapters 9 and 10

Conversations with Prince Philip, Sarah Bradford, Lord Charteris of Amisfield, Sir Robin Janvrin, Commander Mike Parker, the Hon. Margaret Rhodes.

Alice: Princess Andrew of Greece by Hugo Vickers, 2000

Charles by Anthony Holden, 1998

Chips: The Diaries of Sir Henry Channon edited by Robert Rhodes James, 1967

Daily Telegraph interview with Sonia Berry by Cassandra Jardine, 2002

The Duke: A Portrait of Prince Philip by Tim Heald, 1991

Elizabeth by Sarah Bradford, 1996

Elizabeth R by Elizabeth Longford, 1983

Footprints in Time by John Colville, 1976

The Fringes of Power: Downing Street Diaries 1939–1955 by John Colville, 1985

Harold Nicolson Diaries and Letters 1930–39 edited by Nigel Nicolson, 1966

HRH Prince Philip, Duke of Edinburgh: A Portrait by John Dean, 1954

King George VI by Sir John Wheeler-Bennett, 1958

Kings, Queens and Courtiers by Kenneth Rose, 1986

The Little Princesses by Marion Crawford, 1950

The Macmillan Diaries edited by Peter Catterall, 1950–57

Mountbatten by Philip Ziegler, 1985

The Noël Coward Diaries edited by Graham Payn and Sheridan Morley, 1982

Philip: An Informal Biography by Basil Boothroyd, 1971

Prince Philip: A Family Portrait by Alexandra of Yugoslavia, 1959

The Queen by Ann Morrow, 1983

The Queen by Ben Pimlott, 1996

Royal: Her Majesty Queen Elizabeth II by Robert Lacey, 2002

Royal Secrets by Stephen Barry, 1985

Time and Chance by Peter Townsend, 1978

To Be a King: A Biography of HRH Prince Charles by Dermot Morrah, 1989

Chapters 11 and 12

Conversations with Prince Philip, the Duchess of Abercorn, Katie Boyle, Lord Brabourne, Sarah Bradford, Paul Burrell, Geordie, 8th Earl of Carnarvon, Lord Charteris of Amisfield, Robin Dalton, Andrew, 11th Duke of Devonshire, Sir Miles Hunt-Davis, Lord Jenkins of Hillhead, Lady Kennard, Pat Kirkwood, Lucia Flecha da Lima, Countess Mountbatten of Burma, the Hon. Rosa Monckton, Commander Mike Parker, the Hon. Margaret Rhodes, Baroness Thatcher, Sarah, Duchess of York.

Alice: Princess Andrew of Greece by Hugo Vickers, 2000

Baron by Baron with a foreword by Peter Ustinov, 1957

Born Bewildered by Hélène Cordet, 1961

Charles, A Biography by Anthony Holden, 1998

Charles, Prince of Wales by Anthony Holden, 1979

Daily Mirror interview with Norman Barson, 1996

Daily Telegraph interview with Sonia Berry by Cassandra Jardine, 2002

The Diaries of Kenneth Tynan edited by John Lahr, 2001

The Duke: A Portrait of Prince Philip by Tim Heald, 1991

Elizabeth by Sarah Bradford, 1996

Elizabeth, The Woman and The Queen by Graham Turner, 2002

Feather from the Firebird by Sacha Abercorn, 2003

George V by Kenneth Rose, 1984

George VI by Sarah Bradford, 1989

The Heart Has Its Reasons by the Duchess of Windsor, 1956

An Incidental Memoir by Robin Dalton, 1998

Kings, Queens and Courtiers by Kenneth Rose, 1986

Khrushchev Remembers edited by Edward Crankshaw, 1971

Mountbatten by Philip Ziegler, 1985

Niv: The Authorised Biography of David Niven by Graham Lord, 2003

Philip: The Man Behind the Monarchy by Unity Hall, 1987

The Prince of Wales by Jonathan Dimbleby, 1995

Queen and Country: interview with The Princess Royal for the BBC TV series presented by William Shawcross, produced and directed by John Bridcut (a Mentorn production), 2002

The Queen by Ben Pimlott, 1996

The Queen 50 Years – A Celebration by Ronald Allison, 2001

Reagan, A Life in Letters by Ronald Reagan, edited by Kiron K. Skinner, Annelise Anderson and Martin Anderson, 2003

A Royal Duty by Paul Burrell, 2003

Royal: Her Majesty Queen Elizabeth II by Robert Lacey, 2002

Royal Orders: The Honours and the Honoured by Hugo Vickers, 1994

Royal Yacht Britannia: The Official History by Richard Johnstone-Bryden, 2003

Step Aside for Royalty by Eileen Parker, 1982

Picture Credits

Section One

ILN/Camera Press London, Photography by Spice/Camera Press London, Private Collection, Private Collection, Getty Images-Hulton, Private Collection, Private Collection, Private Collection, Getty Images-Hulton, Private Collection, Getty Images-Hulton, Private Collection, Private Collectioin, ILN/Camera Press London, Private Collection, Getty Images-Hulton, Getty Images-Hulton, Private Collection.

Section Two

Sir William Peek, Topham Picturepoint, ILN/Camera Press London, Getty Images-Hulton, Getty Images-Hulton, © Bettmann/CORBIS, Private Collection, Topham Picturepoint, Topham Picturepoint, Getty Images-Hulton, Private Collection, Private Collection, The Royal Archives © 2004 HM Queen Elizabeth II, Getty Images-Hulton, Getty Images-Hulton, Photograph by Bassano/Camera Press London, Getty Images-Hulton, Topham Picturepoint.

Section Three

Private Collection, Photograph by Baron/Camera Press London, Private Collection, Private Collection, The Royal Archives © 2004 HM Queen Elizabeth II, Getty Images-Hulton, Getty Images-Hulton, B/S/Camera Press London, B/S/Camera Press London, Getty Images-Hulton, © Bettmann/CORBIS, *The Times*/Camera Press London, Getty Images-Hulton, *The Times*/Camera Press London, *The Times*/Camera Press London, Getty Images-Hulton, Getty Images-Hulton, Getty Images-Hulton.

Section Four

Photograph by James Reid/Camera Press London, Topham Picture-point, Topham Picturepoint, Camera Press, Private Collection, Photograph by Snowdon/Camera Press London, Topham Picturepoint, Private Collection, Private Collection, Private Collection, Private Collection, Private Collection, Private Collection, Getty Images-Hulton, Getty Images-Hulton, Topham Picturepoint, Getty Images-Hulton, Rex Features.

Section Five

Photograph by Lichfield/Camera Press London, Getty Images-Hulton, Photograph by Lichfield/Camera Press London, Photograph by Djukanovich/Camera Press London, Photograph by Lichfield/Camera Press London, © Tim Graham, The Sun/John Frost Historical Newspaper Archive, Getty Images-Hulton, Reuters, Topham Picturepoint/©UPPA LTD, Reuters/Toby Melville, Rota/Camera Press London, Photograph by The Duke of York/Camera Press London, © Tim Graham, Wiltshire Herald and Gazette, Topham Picturepoint/© UPPA Ltd.

Index

Abdication crisis (1936), 77–9, 83

Abdul Karim ('the Munshi'), 49

Abercorn, Alexandra Anastasia, Duchess of (née Phillips; 'Sacha'), 278–81, 283–4

Abercorn, James, 5th Duke of, 278

Acheson, Dean, 217

Adamski, George, 336

Adeane, Sir Michael, 245

Adler, Larry, 162, 268–9

Aga Khan, 171

Airlie, David Ogilvy, 7th and 11th Earl of, 97

Airlie, Mabell, Countess of, 63

Aisher, Sir Owen, 280n

Aitken, Jonathan, 216n

Alah see Knight, Clara Cooper

Albemarle, Joost van Keppel, 1st Earl of, 51n

Albert, Prince Consort, 17, 47n, 48–50, 191, 215

Alexander, King of Greece, 21

Alexandra, Princess, 257, 285

Alexandra, Queen of Edward VII, 49, 51–2, 57, 69

Alexandra, Queen of Yugoslavia, 130, 166; *Prince Philip: A Family Portrait*, 104n

Alexandra, Tsarina, 21

Alice, Princess, Grand Duchess of Hesse-Darmstadt, 10–11, 17–18, 49

Alice, Princess (Philip's mother; Princess Andrew of Greece): birth and childhood, 11–12; deafness, 12; meets and marries Andrew, 14–15; children, 16; annuity, 17; spends time abroad, 17; community and medical work, 18–19; mental instability, 18n, 31–2, 44, 294; in First World War, 21; and Philip's birth, 23; standing, 23–4; and Andrea's trial, 27; in exile, 28–9; finances, 29, 103; religious and occult interests, 30–1, 186, 202; unfulfilled love affair, 31; confined in asylum, 32, 34; freed under surveillance, 34–6; relations with Philip, 42–3, 94; photographed with Queen Victoria, 50; and death of granddaughter Johanna, 94; returns to Greece (1938), 116, 122–3; Philip visits in Greece, 123, 294; stays in Athens throughout war, 123–5; meets Philip in London after war, 143; chooses Elizabeth's engagement ring, 156; and Philip's engagement, 159–60; and Philip-Elizabeth wedding, 166, 168; moves to Tinos, 186; told of birth of Prince Charles, 186–7; absent from Charles's christening, 191; friendship with Lady Alice Egerton, 200n; and birth of Princess Anne, 202; at Elizabeth's Coronation, 231; on Dolla, 293; qualities, 293–4; moves to Buckingham Palace, 294; smoking, 294–5; death, 295; letter to Cécile on married life, 348

Anatolia: Greek-Turkish war in (1921), 25–7

Anderson, Mabel, 192, 195, 298n, 301n

Andrea, Prince of Greece (Andrew; Philip's father): meets and marries Alice, 14–15; birth, 15; children, 16; annuity, 17; attends Edward VII's funeral, 17; military career, 18, 21–2, 24–5; in exile, 21; financial circumstances, 23–4, 103, 143n; in war in Asia Minor, 25–7; arrested, tried and exiled, 27–9, 43; moves to Monte Carlo, 33–6, 94; death, 35, 122, 126; romances, 35, 261; at Wolfsgarten, 40; relations with Philip, 41, 94; depressions, 43–4; as ADC to English monarchs, 104–5; burial, 143; *Towards Disaster*, 15, 26, 27n

Anne, Princess Royal: discretion, 85; dancing lessons, 110n; on Porchey's friendship with Elizabeth, 138; disapproves of Caroline Brown's behaviour, 154n; birth, 194, 202–3; marriage to Mark Phillips, 222, 307; rebuffs author, 234n; and parents' absences abroad, 244; at Cowes Week, 280; sees grandmother Alice at death, 295; sailing with father, 299; character, 301; relations with father, 301, 309; equestrianism, 307; schooling, 307–8; attempted abduction, 308; divorce and remarriage, 309; honours and titles, 309n; charitable activities, 322

Ardent (production company), 305–6

Armstrong-Jones, Lady Sarah (Lady Sarah Chatto), 290

Ashley, Wilfrid and Maud (*née* Cassel), 103n

Asquith, Margot (Countess of Oxford and Asquith), 59

Assisi: Conference (1986), 282–3

Astor, Nancy, Viscountess, 155

Athlone, Alexander Cambridge, Earl of, 176–7

Athlone, Princess Alice, Countess of, 176–7

Atkins, Dame Eileen, 69n

Atkinson, Rowan, 304

Attenborough, Richard, Baron, 262n

Attlee, Clement (*later* 1st Earl): premiership, 140–1; and royal tour of South Africa (1947), 150; and birth of Prince Charles, 185; loses 1951 Election, 205; and *Britannia*, 343n

Australia: Philip in as naval officer, 130–1; Elizabeth and Philip set out to visit (1952), 210; royal visits to (1953–4), 244; (1956–7), 251–4

Avon, Clarissa, Countess of (*née* Churchill), 253n

Bacall, Lauren, 272–3

Baden-Powell, Lieut.-General Robert, 1st Baron, 92n

Bagehot, Walter, 189

Baker, James, 306

Baldwin, Stanley (*later* 1st Earl), 76, 86

Balkan wars, 18–19

Balmoral, Scotland: Elizabeth's childhood at, 71; as honeymoon centre, 172 & n

Baltimore Sun, 254, 265

Bangor, William Ward, 8th Viscount, 276n, 277

Baron (photographer; i.e. Baron Henry Sterling Nahum): meets Philip at Broadlands, 162, 267; photographs Elizabeth-Philip wedding, 167; on 'Boy' Browning, 177; and Philip at Thursday Club, 221, 267–70; not asked to photograph Coronation, 230–2; operation and death, 265–6; social life, 266–7, 275, 278

Baronscourt, Co. Tyrone, 278

Barrantes, Hector, 328

Barry, Stephen, 294

Barson, Norman, 285

Bartok, Eva, 171n

Baruch, Bernard, 321n

Bashir, Martin, 322

Bean, Deborah, 136n
Beaton, Cecil, 113, 165, 188n, 230–2
Beatrice, Princess, 123n, 261
Beatrice of York, Princess, 328, 330
Beatrix, Queen of the Netherlands, 335, 337n
Beaverbrook, William Maxwell Aitken, 1st Baron, 155, 220–1
Beckham, David, 3
Bellaigue, Antoinette, Vicomtesse de ('Toinon'), 90, 115, 139, 181
Benenden school, Kent, 307–8
Benn, Tony, 342
Bennett, Reginald, 347
Benning, Osla, 132
Bernhard, Prince of the Netherlands, 335–6, 344n
Berry, Sonia (née Graham-Hodgson), 72, 87, 244
Berthold, Margrave of Baden, 38, 125, 292–3
Bevan, Aneurin, 140n
Bigne, Comtesse Andrée de la, 35, 122, 143, 159
Binswanger, Dr Ludwig, 32
Birds from Britannia (Philip), 282n
Black, Conrad, Baron, 285
Blair, Leo, 192, 341
Blair, Tony, 192, 305, 324, 325 & n
Blake, Pat, 114
Blake, William, 344
Bluebottle (yacht), 280n
Blunt, Anthony, 267n, 342
Bobo *see* MacDonald, Margaret
Boisot, Marcel, 271–2
Boisot, Max and Louise, 271–2
Bonaparte, Princess Marie (wife of 'Big George'), 29, 32, 41–2, 44, 166, 286, 295
Bond, Jennie, 190
Booth, Cherie, 192
Boothroyd, Basil, 132, 245n
Borge, Victor, 281
Bowes-Lyon, David (Queen Mother's brother), 147–8, 232
Boyle, Katie, 270

Brabourne, John Knatchbull, 7th Baron: marriage, 141; Philip visits, 142; on royals' rejection of Philip, 159; on Philip's love for Elizabeth, 160, 347; on David Milford Haven, 171n; on Philip's difficult life at court, 175, 246; on Philip's temper, 176; on complaints about Philip, 218; on Lascelles's obstructiveness, 219, 224; and Mountbatten-Windsor name, 220
Bradford, Sarah (Viscountess Bangor): on Princess Margaret's naughtiness, 112; on Elizabeth's passionate nature, 169; on Elizabeth as mother, 195, 302n; on Lady Alice Egerton, 200n; on Charles's childhood, 202; on Philip as naval commander, 203; on Elizabeth's reaction to father's death, 216; on Margaret's renouncing Townsend, 238; on Philip's rumoured infidelities, 276–8; on Elizabeth's attitude to Margaret's life-style, 292
Briand, Aristide, 41
Britannia (Royal Yacht), 244, 251–4, 265, 342 & n
Broadlands (house), Hampshire, 103n, 142, 167–70, 172
Broome, John, 304
Brown, Caroline, 154n
Brown, John, 49
Browning, Lieut.-General Sir Frederick ('Boy'), 177–8, 191, 207, 219, 223, 244, 341
Browning, Robert, 287
Bryan, John, 329
Bryant, Mrs Warwick, 193
Buckingham Palace: 'themed days', 25; flag, 56n, 324; Elizabeth moves to on father's accession, 87, 89; Girl Guide Company, 91; bombed in war, 107; Elizabeth and Philip in, 177, 179; intruder disturbs Queen in, 179–80; as official royal residence, 219; household, 223; Philip reviews organisation, 225; luncheons, 338

Bulganin, Nikolai, 250
Bülow, Prince von, 16
Burrell, Maria, 317–18
Burrell, Paul, 172, 193n, 294n, 317–20, 338, 342
Bush, George W., 208–9
Bush, Laura, 208–9
Buthlay, Major George, 154
Buxton of Alsa, Aubrey, Baron, and Katherine, Lady (Kay), 283, 347

Callaghan, James (Baron), 274
Campbell, Alastair, 325n
Campbell, Patrick (3rd Baron Glenavon), 268, 269n
Canada: George VI and Elizabeth visit, 95; Elizabeth II and Philip visit (1951), 205–9
Carey, George, Archbishop of Canterbury, 323, 338n
Carnarvon, George Herbert Porchester, 8th Earl of ('Geordie'), 138, 258
Carnarvon, Henry Molyneux Herbert, 7th Earl of (earlier Lord Porchester; 'Porchey'), 137–9, 258
Carroll, Lewis (Charles Lutwidge Dodgson), 287
Carter, Angela, 2
Cartland, Dame Barbara, 313n
Cassel, Sir Ernest, 103n
Cecil, Lord David, 62
Cécile, Grand Duchess of Hesse (Philip's sister), 16, 43; killed, 35, 37, 94, 103, 125, 292; engagement, 348
Chamberlain, Neville, 94, 105, 107–8, 288
Channon, Sir Henry ('Chips'), 2, 58n, 133–4, 166, 197
Charcot, Jean-Martin, 41
Charles, Prince of Wales: and grandmother's death, 298; father's attitude to, 233, 240, 296–7, 299–300, 303–4, 313; spiritual interests, 18n; sulks, 51; dancing lessons, 110n; hunting, 158n; engagement, 159; birth, 185–8; christened, 190; upbringing, 192, 194–6, 201–2; temper, 193n; Dimbleby biography of, 195, 296, 299, 301, 322; and parents' absences abroad, 201–2, 209, 244, 254; and birth of Princess Anne, 202–3; portraits and photographs, 209; third birthday, 209; lives at Clarence House, 219; at mother's Coronation, 231; on grandmother Elizabeth, 231; parents' relations with, 239–40, 243, 296–7, 313; education, 248, 296–8; at Berthold's funeral, 293; unhappy childhood, 296–7; extravagance, 298–9; and press, 299; sailing with father, 299; shyness and sensitivity, 300–1; naval career, 303–4; courtship and marriage, 310–12; attachment to Camilla Parker Bowles, 311, 312, 316–17, 326–7; marriage breakdown and divorce, 312–16, 318, 322–3; and Diana's death and funeral, 324; relations with children, 326
Charlotte, Queen of George III, 47
Charteris, Martin, Baron: on North American tour with Elizabeth and Philip (1951), 206–8; serves Elizabeth, 206–7; on Philip's manner, 209; on Elizabeth's ignoring unpleasant things, 210; in Kenya with Elizabeth, 212–13; on Elizabeth's accession, 216; on Clarence House, 219; and Philip's reaction to family name, 220; role, 223; on Philip's role, 224; on Elizabeth's Coronation, 227; believes Queen Mother jealous of Elizabeth, 231; on Peter Townsend, 235–6; on Elizabeth's relations with children, 243; on Elizabeth's formal life as monarch, 246; on Elizabeth's marriage relations, 249, 347; on Patrick Plunket's death, 259; and rumours of Philip's infidelities, 265; on birth of Prince Andrew, 302; on Duchess of York, 328

Chatto, Lady Sarah *see* Armstrong-Jones, Lady Sarah

Cheam school: Philip attends, 33, 38; Charles attends, 248, 297

Chequers, HMS, 198, 233

Christiansen, Arthur, 221, 268

Christoph, Prince of Hesse, 125, 142

Christopher, Prince of Greece (Philip's uncle), 29, 122n

Churchill, Sir Winston: and Battenberg's resignation, 20; on Elizabeth as child, 68; and Edward VIII's abdication, 84, 108; relations with George VI, 108, 140–1; wartime premiership, 108; opposes wartime evacuation of princesses, 109; loses office (1945), 139, 141; on VE Day, 139; welcomes Elizabeth's wedding, 163; on birth of Prince Charles, 186; resumes premiership (1951), 205; and George VI's death, 212, 217; relations with Elizabeth, 217, 224; insists on Buckingham Palace as royal residence, 219; and royal family surname, 220–1; retires (1955), 221; and Margaret-Townsend romance, 236; proposes making Philip prince, 255

Clare, Anthony, 115, 139, 345–6

Clarence House, London, 176 & n, 192–4, 219, 223–4

Clarence, Prince Albert Victor, Duke of (Eddy), 52–3, 84

Clifton, Nellie, 50–1

Clinton, Bill, 263

Cohen family (Athens), 124

Colthurst, James, 314

Colville, Lady Cynthia, 177

Colville, Sir John ('Jock'): on Elizabeth's first broadcast, 111; as Elizabeth's private secretary, 164, 177; rescues pearls at Elizabeth's wedding, 164; on Elizabeth and Philip's return from honeymoon, 174, 176; background and career, 177; marriage, 177, 200, 206; on Elizabeth's public impression,

181; and Elizabeth's reading of official papers, 198; returns to Foreign Office, 206; and Churchill's reaction to George VI's death, 212; and Mountbatten's family boast, 220; on Churchill's conversations with Elizabeth, 224; *Footprints in Time*, 206n

Colville, Margaret, Lady (*née* Lady Margaret Egerton; 'Meg'), 177, 200 & n

Colville, Commander Richard, 185, 189, 253–4, 265

Commonwealth: Elizabeth's commitment to, 16, 340–1; tour (1953–4), 243–4

Commonwealth Study Conferences, 344

Competition Carriage Driving (Philip), 282n

Connaught, Prince Arthur, Duke of, 113, 123n

Connolly, Cyril: *The Unquiet Grave*, 347

Constantine I, King of Greece: attends Edward VII's funeral, 14; marriage relations, 16, 260; accession, 17; neutrality in First World War, 19–20; deposed and restored, 21–2; overthrown and exiled, 27; romantic liaisons, 261

Constantine II, King of Greece, 328

Cook, Peter, 275

Cooke, Alistair, 254

Corbett, Jim, 212

Cordet, Hélène (*née* Foufounis; *later* Boisot), 270–2

Corfu, 17, 23

Coronation (1953), 225–30

Coronation Commission: Philip chairs, 225–6, 232

Coward, Sir Noël, 60, 120n, 135, 148n, 166, 227n, 262n

Cowes, Isle of Wight, 280

Crawford, Marion ('Crawfie'): as governess to Elizabeth and Margaret, 73, 75, 89–90, 110; and Abdication crisis, 78–9; and George VI's

Crawford, Marion (*continued*)
accession, 79–80; and George VI's
Coronation, 87; on move to
Buckingham Palace, 89; on Palace
Guide Company, 91; meets George VI
and Queen on return from America,
96–7; visits Royal Yacht, 98; on visit
to Dartmouth, 100–2; on Philip, 101,
134–6; on outbreak of war, 106;
relations with Elizabeth, 109; on
wartime stay at Windsor Castle, 109;
on Elizabeth's first broadcast, 111; on
Elizabeth's serious-mindedness, 112;
on Elizabeth's private apartment, 135;
chaperones Elizabeth on VE Day, 139;
and Elizabeth's attachment to Philip,
145, 156; and royal tour of southern
Africa (1947), 149–50; marriage and
retirement, 154–6; on Elizabeth's
wedding, 163–4, 167; writes on royal
family, 172; on birth of Prince Charles,
187–8; *The Little Princesses*, 73–5, 155,
294n
Crete, battle of (1941), 119
Cunard, Maud Alice (Emerald), Lady, 86n
Cunningham, Admiral Sir Andrew, 118
Curzon, George Nathaniel, Marquess, 27
Cutsem, Hugh and Emilie van, 327
Cyril (footman), 169–70

Daily Mail, 286
Daily Telegraph, 207n
Dalton, Hugh, 188, 216
Dalton, Robin, 131, 160, 162, 170–1,
266–8, 347
Danischewsky, Monja, 268, 269n
Dartmouth *see* Royal Naval College
Davies, Nicholas, 257, 270
Dawson, Les, 304
Dean, John: on Philip's popularity with
servants, 142; on Philip's devotion to
Elizabeth, 145; on Philip's bachelor
quarters, 162; accompanies Elizabeth
and Philip on honeymoon, 169–70;
writes book on royal service, 172,

294n; on Bobo MacDonald, 173; on
Charles as baby, 187; on Philip in
Clarence House, 193; on Danny Kaye
at Windlesham Moor, 197; on Philip
and Elizabeth in Malta, 199–200; in
Canada, 208–9; in Kenya, 212–13
Derby, Edward George Villiers Stanley,
17th Earl of, 275n
Devonshire, Andrew Cavendish, 11th
Duke of, 263–4
Devonshire, Deborah, Duchess of (*née*
Mitford), 263
Diana, Princess of Wales: public celebrity,
51–2, 181, 316n, 321; death and
funeral, 56n, 188, 321, 324–6, 342;
Betty Vacani's view of, 110n; courtship
and marriage, 310–12; character and
behaviour, 312–13, 322, 339, 347;
marriage breakdown and divorce,
312–16, 318, 322–4; letters from Philip,
315–17; *Panorama* TV broadcast, 322,
326; loses status, 324 & n
Dimbleby, Jonathan, 195, 296, 299, 301,
322
Disraeli, Benjamin (Earl of
Beaconsfield), 49
Doyle, Sir Arthur Conan, 30
Driberg, Tom, (Baron Bradwell), 148, 160
Dudley Ward, Freda, 60–1
Duff, Sir Michael, 165
Duke of Edinburgh's Award Scheme, 39,
247, 257, 344
du Maurier, Daphne (Lady Browning),
341

Ede, James Chuter, 147
Eden, Anthony (*later* 1st Earl of Avon),
237, 253
Edward VII, King: coronation, 14–15;
death and funeral, 17, 56; birth, 49;
behaviour, 50–1, 54–5; marriage and
children, 51; accession, 54; reign, 54;
horse-breeding, 138
Edward VIII, King *see* Windsor, Edward,
Duke of

Egerton, Lady Alice, 199, 200n
Eisenhower, Dwight D., 210
Elizabeth II, Queen: as embodiment of
history, 2; reserve, 76, 92–3, 112, 240,
290, 331; appearance and dress, 92,
108; sense of humour, 231, 339; and
father's death, 211–13; spoken French,
180–1; keeps corgis, 75, 89 & n, 93,
110, 243, 337–8, 346; religious
devotion, 110, 290, 320;
speechmaking, 198, 342; devotion to
Philip, 134, 156; relations with
children, 192, 194–6, 201–3, 239, 243,
279, 296, 301–2, 306; commitment to
Commonwealth, 16, 340–1; reign, 54;
birth, 69; childhood homes, 70;
behaviour as child, 71–2, 112; as
prospective Queen, 71; upbringing as
child, 72–5; concern for order, 75;
swimming lessons, 78–9; and father's
accession, 79, 86–7, 90; discretion, 85;
on father's Coronation, 87–9; moves
to Buckingham Palace, 87, 89;
education, 90–1, 110, 113; in line for
throne, 90; in adolescence, 91–2, 110,
115; as Girl Guide, 91, 110; as public
figure, 93; and parents' absences
abroad, 94, 96–7; first meetings with
Philip, 98, 99–102, 104–5; on
Chamberlain's resignation, 108; at
Windsor Castle during war, 109, 111;
interest in horses and riding, 109–10,
138, 201, 250n, 346; confirmed, 110,
115; performs in Christmas
pantomimes, 110, 134; broadcasts,
111–12, 115; serious-mindedness,
112–13; as Colonel of Grenadier
Guards, 113; portraits and
photographs, 113–14; joins ATS,
114–15; wartime public duties, 115;
and Philip as prospective husband,
132–4, 143–5; wartime
correspondence with Philip, 132, 135;
courtship, 135–7, 141; male
friendships, 137–8; on VE Day,
139–40; engagement, 149, 156–60;
tour of southern Africa (1947),
149–53; twenty-first birthday
declaration, 152–3, 156, 336–7; and
Crawfie's retirement and death, 156;
wedding, 160–1, 163–7, 171–2;
honours, 161; honeymoon, 168–70,
172, 174; marriage relations, 169–70,
175, 179–80, 239, 248–9, 258, 265,
287, 345–6; married homes, 176,
193–4; household, 177–8, 223;
overseas tours and state visits, 180–1,
205–11, 243, 250–2, 322, 351–66;
pregnancy and birth of Charles, 181,
185–8; desire for privacy, 188–9;
attitude to press, 189–90, 325n; and
birth of Princess Anne, 194, 202–3;
entertainments and relaxation, 196–7;
increasing public duties, 196; reads
official papers, 198, 207, 224, 246,
341; in Malta with Philip, 199–203;
newspaper reading, 207 & n; ignores
unpleasant things, 210; returns from
Kenya on accession, 212–13, 215–16;
and family name, 220–2; confidence as
Queen, 224; Coronation, 225–32; and
Margaret's attachment to Townsend,
236, 238; formal life as Queen, 244–6;
and rumours of Philip's romances,
254–5, 277, 285–6, 287; appoints
Philip prince of United Kingdom, 255;
rumoured infidelities, 258–60; visits
'Porchey' Carnarvon, 258; shooting,
286; family background and relations,
288–90; relations with mother, 289;
relations with Princess Margaret,
289–91; praises Charles, 298;
assassination attempt on, 303n; and
Falklands War, 303; and Charles-
Diana marriage breakdown and
divorce, 313–15, 322–3; remembers
conversation with Burrell, 319–20;
public celebrity, 321–2; relations with
Diana, 322, 329; visits leper colony in
Nigeria, 322; and Diana's death and

Elizabeth II, Queen (*continued*)
funeral, 324–6, 342; and Charles's
relations with Camilla Parker Bowles,
326–7; and Duchess of York, 329–30;
declines to abdicate, 336–7; integrity,
336, 342; daily routine, 337–8;
interests and activities, 338, 341;
mimicry, 339; Altrincham criticises,
340; speech on *annus horribilis* (1992),
342–3
Elizabeth the Queen Mother (*née* Bowes-
Lyon): and Abdication crisis, 79;
death and funeral, 139; George
(Bertie) meets, 61; popularity and
charm, 62–5, 96–8; background and
family, 63–4; courtship and marriage,
65–7; relations with press, 66;
marriage relations, 67–8, 85; children,
69; and children's upbringing, 72–3,
240; attitude to Windsors, 85; life at
Buckingham Palace, 89; official visits
abroad, 94–6; on bombing of
Buckingham Palace, 107; writes to
Chamberlain on resignation, 108;
wartime activities, 111; portraits of,
113; entertaining, 136; supposed
betting, 139n; attitude to Philip, 147,
158, 231–2; tour of South Africa
(1947), 149–50; opposes Crawfie's
wish to leave service, 154;
unselfishness, 154; and George VI's
death, 211; entertains Duke of
Windsor, 218; Beaton favours as sitter,
230, 392; and Princess Margaret's
break with Townsend, 238; fidelity to
husband, 260; and mother's death,
288; extravagance, 289; relations with
Elizabeth, 289; relations with Charles,
297, 300
Ella, Grand Duchess, 18, 21, 30
Ellen (Princess Nicholas of Greece;
Philip's aunt), 133
Ernst August von Hanover, Prince, 220
Eugénie, Princess of Greece, 29, 41n, 166
Eugenie of York, Princess, 328, 330

'Everage, Dame Edna' *see* Humphries,
Barry

Fagan, Michael, 179, 180n
Fairbanks, Douglas, Jr, 273
Faisal, King of Iraq, 250
Falklands War (1982), 302–3
Farish, William, 250n
Farouk, King of Egypt, 251
Fayed, Dodi, 324
Fellowes, Robert, Baron, 314 & n, 323,
325
Ferguson, Major Ronald, 328
Fermoy, Ruth, Lady, 313
Festival of Britain (1951), 204
Fisher, Geoffrey, Archbishop of
Canterbury, 165, 227–8
Flecha da Lima, Lucia, 316–19
Fleming, Launcelot, Bishop of Norwich,
282
Foot, Michael, 141
Ford, Sir Edward, 212, 343n
Formby, George, 136n
Forster, E.M., 58n
France: Elizabeth and Philip visit, 180–1
Franks, Sir Oliver, 209
Frederick VIII, King of Denmark, 15
Frederika of Hanover, Queen of Greece,
94, 133, 166, 203, 204n
Freud, Anna, 42
Freud, Lucian, 314n, 339
Freud, Martin, 41
Freud, Sigmund, 29, 32, 41
Frobisher, HMS, 100
Furness, Thelma, Viscountess, 77

Gage, Henry, 6th Viscount, 64
Gandhi, Mohandas Karamchand
(Mahatma), 171
Garbett, Cyril, Archbishop of York, 165
Garter, Order of the, 264
General Elections: (1945), 139, 141;
(1951), 205
Genet, Jean: *Chant d'Amour* (film), 275
George I, King of Greece, 15–17, 260

George II, King of Greece, 21, 116, 123, 143, 146

George III, King, 47

George V, King: statue unveiled, 2; decorates Princess Alice, 19; changes family name, 20, 220–1; and fate of Tsar and family, 21; and Philip's family in exile, 28–9; and Alice's manic behaviour, 31; marriage and children, 53, 57; accession, 56, 84; manner, 56, 58, 77; and children's upbringing, 58–9; Elizabeth the Queen Mother's attitude to, 68; on Bognor, 70n; death, 76–7, 288; wilfulness, 153; rumoured liaisons, 260 & n; watches films, 275n

George VI, King (Bertie): death and funeral, 211–14, 215, 217–18, 289; manner, 59, 67; stammer, 59, 67–8, 84, 106; upbringing, 59; appearance and character, 60, 84; early romances, 60–1; meets and courts Elizabeth Bowes-Lyon, 61, 65–6; communal and welfare work, 66–7; marriage, 66–7; 'gnashes' (temper outbursts), 67, 196, 233; marriage relations, 67–8, 85; and children's upbringing, 72–3, 288; and Edward VIII's abdication, 78; accession, 79–80, 83–4; constitutional status, 86; Coronation, 86–8; official visits abroad, 94–6; qualities, 95–6; sporting interests, 105 & n; and war threat, 105; broadcasts, 106–7, 210; wartime role and activities, 107; on 'family firm', 142; relations with Churchill, 108, 140–1; view of daughters, 112; and death of brother Duke of Kent, 114; visits Eighth Army in Italy, 115; on VE Day, 139; and Attlee's premiership, 140–1; and Philip's naturalisation, 146; liking for Philip, 149; tour of South Africa (1947), 149–50; and Elizabeth's engagement, 157–8; and Philip's titles, 161, 255; smoking, 163; at Elizabeth's wedding, 165, 167; letter to Elizabeth

after wedding, 168; health decline, 196, 204–6, 210; lung removed, 205; appoints Townsend as equerry, 233

George Donatus, Hereditary Grand Duke of Hesse, 35, 40, 43

George, Prince of Greece (Philip's uncle; 'Big George'), 29, 41, 166, 295

George Wilhelm, Prince of Hanover, 142, 292

Germany: and outbreak of World War II, 106; Elizabeth and Philip visit, 293

Ghana, 302

Gibraltar, 253 & n

Girl Guides, 91, 110

Giscard d'Estaing, Valéry, 256

Gladstone, Margaret, 62

Gladstone, William Ewart, 49

Glamis Castle, Scotland, 63–4, 67, 71

Glenconner, Christopher Tennant, 2nd Baron, 65

Gloucester, Prince Henry, Duke of, 59, 140, 178, 196, 204, 222

Gloucester, Prince William of, 165, 167

Goering, Hermann, 35n, 125

Gordon, John, 155, 221

Gordonstoun school, Scotland, 38–9, 104, 142, 248, 272, 296–8, 302, 307

Gorell, Ronald Barnes, 3rd Baron, 64

Gottfried, Prince of Hohenlohe-Langenburg ('Friedel'), 125, 293

Grafton, Fortune, Duchess of (Mistress of the Robes), 137, 194–5, 208

Grafton, Hugh Denis Charles FitzRoy, 11th Duke of, 137

Grancy, Baron Augustus Senarclens von, 10

Greece: monarchy, 14–16; political unrest in, 17–18; neutrality in First World War, 20; war with Turks in Anatolia, 25–7; Germans invade and occupy, 123, 125–6

Greenacre, Phyllis, 42

Greene, Graham, 83, 105

Greville, Mrs Ronald (*née* Margaret McEwan), 67n

Grigg, John *see* Altrincham, 2nd Baron
Gustaf VI Adolf, King of Sweden, 13n, 94, 166, 250

Haakon VII, King of Norway, 52, 164
Haakon, Crown Prince of Norway, 345n
Hague, William, 305
Hahn, Kurt, 37–40, 142, 293n, 298
Haley, Bill, 255n
Halifax, Edward Frederick Lindley Wood, 1st Earl of, 108
Hardinge, Sir Alexander, 85, 113
Harewood, George Lascelles, 7th Earl of, 58, 78, 290–1
Hargreaves, Harry, 121–2
Harman, Roger, 337n
Harry, Prince *see* Henry, Prince
Hart-Davis, Sir Rupert, 77n
Hartnell, Norman, 163, 167, 173, 250
Hattersley, Roy, Baron, 13n
Hay, Jessica, 286–7
Heald, Tim, 28n, 130, 203
Hearst, William Randolph, 259
Helen, Queen of Romania, 166
Hélène d'Orléans, Princess, 53
Henneker, Helen, 55n
Henry ('Harry'), Prince, 313, 324, 326
Hewitt, James, 316n
Himmler, Heinrich, 148n
Hitler, Adolf: rise to power, 38; and outbreak of war, 105–6
Hofmans, Greet, 335–6
Holden, Anthony, 195, 201, 323n
Hordern, Sam, 247
Houdini, Harry, 29
Hoyle, Fred, 282
Hunt, John, Baron, 344
Hunt-Davis, Sir Miles, 3, 247, 251–2
Huth, Angela, 291n

Illustrious, HMS, 120
In Which We Serve (film), 120n
International Equestrian Federation, 344n
It's A Knockout! (TV show), 304

Jacques, Sandra, 131
Jamagne, Marie-Luce, 239
Janvrin, Sir Robin: author consults, 3; on Philip, 208; duties, 337
Jenkins, Roy, Baron, 263
Johanna, Princess of Hesse, 94
John Paul II, Pope, 283
Johnson, Samuel, 285, 288, 321
Jones, Arthur, 10n
Jonsson, Ulrika, 306
Joyce, William ('Lord Haw-Haw'), 106
Juliana, Queen of the Netherlands, 335–6, 337n
Jung, Carl Gustav, 281, 283

Kahr, Brett, 42–4, 286, 339
Kaye, Danny, 197
Keeler, Christine, 267
Kelly, HMS, 119–20
Kennard, Sir George ('Loopy'), 37n
Kennard, Georgina, Lady (*née* Wernher): on Nada Milford Haven, 31n; birth, 37; on Bath Club, 79; praises George Milford Haven, 102; on youthful behaviour, 131; Philip's liking for, 132; criticises David Bowes-Lyon, 147; on Philip's temper, 176; on Fagan's intrusion at Buckingham Palace, 180n; on Philip and Elizabeth as parents, 191–2, 243; on Elizabeth and Philip's social life, 197; and birth of daughter Sacha (Abercorn), 278; on Philip's sharp remarks, 300; on Elizabeth-Philip relationship, 347
Kenneally, John, VC, 161n
Kent, HMS, 117
Kent, Prince Edward, Duke of (Queen Victoria's father), 47
Kent, Prince Edward George Nicholas Patrick, Duke of, 235n
Kent, Prince George, Duke of, 59–60, 105; killed, 114–15, 122n
Kent, Prince Michael of, 165, 167
Kent, Princess Marina, Duchess of: marriage, 60, 105; widowed, 114,

122n; entertains Channon, 134; Philip stays with, 142, 145; absent from Elizabeth's wedding party, 166; on Prince Charles's appearance, 191

Kent, Victoria, Duchess of (Queen Victoria's mother), 47–8, 50n

Kenya, 211–13

Keppel, Alice, 51, 311

Keppel, George, 51n

Khrushchev, Nikita S., 250

Kipling, Rudyard, 92 & n, 104

Kirby, William, 271, 272

Kirkwood, Pat, 269–70, 277

Klass, Mylene, 102n

Knatchbull, Amanda, 311

Knatchbull, Nicholas, 286

Knight, Clara Cooper ('Alah'): as nanny to Elizabeth and Margaret, 70, 75, 173; Crawfie on, 74–5; and Abdication, 78; and princesses' swimming lessons, 79; moves to Buckingham Palace, 89; accompanies princesses to meet parents on return from North America, 96–7; visits Dartmouth, 98; at outbreak of war, 106; Elizabeth's closeness to, 109; death, 135

Ladies' Home Journal, 155

Lamont, Norman, Baron, 343n

Lang, Cosmo, Archbishop of Canterbury, 112

Langtry, Lillie, 10n, 17, 51

Lascelles, Sir Alan ('Tommy'): and Philip's naturalisation, 146; attitude to Philip, 149, 158, 171n, 175, 224; background and character, 149; writes Elizabeth's twenty-first birthday speech, 153; recommends Colville as Elizabeth's private secretary, 177; and Elizabeth's reading official papers, 178; and Charteris, 206; informs Churchill of George VI's death, 212; and Elizabeth's accession, 215; refuses Philip's request to remain in Clarence

House, 219; retires, 221, 245; and Margaret's attachment to Townsend, 235; view of Mike Parker, 269

László, John de, 234

László, Philip de, 295

Laurence, Rear Admiral Timothy: marriage to Princess Anne, 309

Lazzolo, Vasco, 267–8

Leeds, Nancy (Prince Christopher's first wife), 29

Letellier, Yola, 266

Leveson-Gower, Lady Rose, 73

Lewin, Admiral of the Fleet Terence, Baron, 118, 121, 199

Lightbody, Helen, 192, 195, 298n

Lillie, Beatrice, 166

Linley, David Armstrong-Jones, Viscount, 290

Llewellyn, Roddy, 291

Llewellyn Smith, Michael: *Ionian Vision*, 27n

Lloyd George, David, 1st Earl, 86

Locock, Dr Sir Charles, 48, 49n

Locock, Henry, 49n

Locock, Victoria, 48n

Logue, Lionel, 67

Longford, Elizabeth, Countess of, 49n, 50n, 77, 224

Longford, Francis Aungier Pakenham, 7th Earl of, 169

Lopes, Craveiro, President of Portugal, 254

Lopez, Jennifer, 276

Lord, Graham, 272–3

Lorne, John Douglas Sutherland Campbell, Marquess of (*later* 9th Duke of Argyll), 49n

Lorne, Marchioness of *see* Louise, Princess

Loughborough, Sheila Chisholm, Lady, 61

Louis IV, Grand Duke of Hesse-Darmstadt, 10

Louise, Princess (Marchioness of Lorne; *later* Duchess of Argyll), 49n, 123n

Louise, Princess Royal, Duchess of Fife, 52
Louise, Queen of Sweden (Philip's aunt), 12, 94, 166, 191, 250
Lyttelton, George, 77n

MacDonald, Margaret ('Bobo'): as assistant nanny, 70; Crawfie on, 74; and Elizabeth's description of parents' Coronation, 87; moves to Buckingham Palace, 89; at outbreak of war, 106; Elizabeth's closeness to, 109; at Windsor, 135; accompanies Elizabeth on honeymoon, 169–70; role, 173–4, 179, 223; Elizabeth confides in, 194; in Malta with Elizabeth and Philip, 199, 202; in Canada with Elizabeth, 208; in Kenya with Elizabeth, 212–13
MacDonald, Ruby, 74
McGrath, Sir Brian, 274
MacJannet, Mr & Mrs (US schoolteachers in Paris), 33
Macmillan, Harold (1st Earl of Stockton), 218, 222, 255
McNally, Paddy, 328
Magpie, HMS, 203–4
Major, John, 263, 323, 343n
Malta, 199–200, 202–4
Mandela, Nelson, 151n
Mandelson, Peter, 204n
Mann, Michael, Dean of Windsor, 282–3
Margaret, Princess: marriage to Snowdon, 239, 260, 290; death and funeral, 138; bequest from Mrs Ronald Greville, 67n; birth, 71, 173; behaviour and character, 72, 75–6, 235, 240, 291n; swimming lessons, 78–9; and father's Coronation, 88; life at Buckingham Palace, 89; education, 90; in line for throne, 90; as Brownie, 91; dress, 92, 108; and parents' absence abroad, 96–7; visits Dartmouth, 101; on Hitler, 106; at Windsor Castle throughout war, 109, 111; performs in Christmas pantomimes, 110, 134; joins in Elizabeth's first broadcast, 112; portraits and photographs, 113; and Philip's courtship of Elizabeth, 135–6; on parents' marriage, 137; on VE Day, 139–40; on tour of South Africa (1947), 150; breaks with Peter Townsend, 153, 237–8; and Crawfie's retirement and death, 156; at Elizabeth's wedding, 165; and naming of Prince Charles, 191; on father's death, 211, 235; attachment to Peter Townsend, 233–7, 290; love life, 260; sees Tynan's blue films, 275; relations with Elizabeth, 289–91; divorce from Snowdon, 291–2
Margarita, Princess of Hohenlohe-Langenburg (Philip's sister), 125, 293
Margrethe II, Queen of Denmark, 13n, 14n, 228–9
Marie, Princess of Greece (later Joannides), 123n
Marten, Sir Henry, 90–1, 96, 110, 113, 152
Mary, Princess Royal (Countess of Harewood), 58
Mary, Queen of George V (May): betrothed to Eddy, 53; style, 56–7; relations with children, 57–9; welcomes Elizabeth as wife of son George, 66, 68; and Abdication crisis, 79, 86n; discretion, 85; attends George VI's Coronation, 88; on granddaughters' upbringing, 90; on Philip as boy, 104; on Elizabeth's devotion to Philip, 134; selfishness, 153–4; reservations over Philip's engagement, 158; disparages Gandhi's wedding gift to Elizabeth and Philip, 171; and infant Prince Charles, 191; visits Elizabeth on accession, 215–16; and royal family name, 220–1; death, 221, 289; Duke of Windsor attends funeral, 226n; marriage, 259
Massey, Anna, 276n
Massey, Vincent, 276n

Massigli, René, 84

Matapan (Cape), battle of (1941), 118–19, 123

Maud, Queen of Haakon VII of Norway, 52

Max, Prince of Baden, 38, 293n

Melbourne: 1956 Olympic Games, 251–2

Menzies, Sir Robert, 276n

Mercer, Mr and Mrs (of Cheltenham), 104

Mette-Marit, Crown Princess of Norway, 345n

Milford Haven, David Mountbatten, 3rd Marquess of: friendship with Philip, 33, 145; as Philip's best man, 33, 162, 171; naval service, 120; Robin Dalton and, 131, 170, 266–8; on Philip's plans to marry Elizabeth, 160; at Philip's stag night, 161–2; and Elizabeth-Philip's marriage relations, 170; marriage, 171; and Baron, 266; in Thursday Club, 268, 274–5

Milford Haven, George Mountbatten, 2nd Marquess of: and Edward VII's Coronation, 14; naval service, 20; and Greek throne, 21; marriage, 31, 36, 261; schooling, 33; influence on Philip, 40, 102, 223, 261; death, 43, 102–3, 122n

Milford Haven, Janet, Marchioness of (*née* Bryce), 171n

Milford Haven, Admiral of the Fleet Louis, Marquess of (*earlier* Battenberg): marries Victoria, 10–11, 261, 307; resigns as First Sea Lord, 20; titles and rank, 20; death, 24; love life, 261

Milford Haven, Nadejda, Marchioness of (*née* Countess Nada Torby), 31n, 36, 261

Milford Haven, Victoria, Marchioness of: marriage, 10–11, 20, 307; home in Kensington Palace, 24–5; and Philip's birth, 24; and Alice's mental instability, 32; with Philip at Wolfsgarten, 40; Philip stays with, 103; and Alice's life in Athens, 123; and Philip's naturalisation, 146; at Philip-Elizabeth wedding, 166; on infant Prince Charles, 191; influence on Philip, 310n

Mills, Sir John, 62

Milne, A.A., 69, 93

Milne, Christopher, 93

Mon Repos *see* Corfu

monarchy: Philip's view of, 16, 215; remoteness, 55, 189; and press publicity, 188–90; criticisms of, 343

Monckton, Rosa, 316–19

Monkman, Phyllis, 60

Monroe, Marilyn, 3

Montaudon-Smith, Mrs ('Monty'), 90

Monte Carlo: Andrea in, 33–6, 94; Philip visits, 143

Moran, Charles McMoran Wilson, 1st Baron, 205, 217

Morrah, Dermot, 153

Morrison, Herbert, Baron, 140, 204n

Morrison, Sir Peter, 207n

Morton, Andrew: *Diana: Her True Story*, 314–15

Mountbatten, Edwina, Countess (*née* Ashley): courtship, 24; generosity to exiled Alice, 29, 103; romances, 132, 261–2; financial help for Prince Andrea, 143n; on Elizabeth's return from Malta, 204; and Charles and Anne's childhood visit to Malta, 244; marriage relations, 261; liking for Yola Letellier, 266n

Mountbatten, Admiral of the Fleet Louis, 1st Earl ('Dickie'): love of uniforms, 11; birth and career, 14; appointed First Sea Lord, 20n; murdered, 21, 273, 303n, 310; courtship, 24; supports Andrea during trial, 27; attends funeral of Cécile, Georg and family, 35n; and George VI's accession, 83–4; relations with

Mountbatten (*continued*)
Duke of Windsor, 83n; on royal visit
to Dartmouth, 100–2; as Philip's
guardian, 103; and Philip's wartime
naval service, 117; war service, 117,
119–20, 122; and Philip's prospective
marriage to Elizabeth, 144–5, 148; and
Philip's naturalisation, 146; hostility
to, 148; and Philip-Elizabeth wedding,
160–1, 166; recommends Browning to
Philip, 177; post-war naval command
in Malta, 199–200, 202, 244; and
Philip's naval promotion, 203;
practical joking, 204n; family
ambitions, 220–3; Philip's attitude to,
223, 310n; promoted Admiral, 228n;
energy, 246; on Philip's relations with
Elizabeth, 249, 347; love life, 261–2,
266; marriage relations, 261; advice to
Charles on marriage, 310; Charles's
attachment to, 310–11
Mountbatten, Lady Pamela (Lady
Pamela Hicks), 212–13
Mountbatten, Patricia, Countess of: on
Philip's stubbornness, 36; in
Buckingham Palace Girl Guides, 91;
on Elizabeth in adolescence, 92; and
sinking of HMS *Kelly*, 120; marriage,
141; Philip visits, 142; on father's
progressive views, 148; on Philip's
apprehensions over marriage, 163; on
Elizabeth-Philip's marriage relations,
169, 175, 347; on David Milford
Haven, 171n; on Bobo MacDonald,
174; as godmother to Charles, 190,
195, 300; on Philip's dynamism, 198,
246; on Philip's anger over family
surname, 219–20; on father's relations
with women, 261–2; and Philip's
reaction to infidelity rumours, 265; on
Philip's relations with women, 286; on
relations between Philip and Charles,
300
Mountbatten-Windsor: adopted as
surname for Queen's descendants, 221

Mountbatten-Windsor, Lady Louise
Alice Elizabeth Mary (Wessexes'
daughter), 222n, 304
Muggeridge, Malcolm, 320n
Muir, Frank, 269n
Murdoch, Dame Iris, 331
Murdoch, Rupert, 207n, 305
Mylius, E.F., 260n

Nahum, Jack, 266, 268
Nasser, Gamal Abdel, 251
National Playing Fields Association, 175,
198, 247–8, 276
Nazi-Soviet Pact (1939), 105
New Zealand: Elizabeth and Philip set
out for (1952), 210; Elizabeth and
Philip visit (1953–4), 244
News of the World, 305
Nicholas II, Tsar, 21
Nicholas, Prince of Greece, 122n
Nicholson, Mrs (Philip's nanny), 23
Nicolson, Sir Harold, 2, 67n, 85–6, 97,
149, 196, 205, 211
Nicolson, Nigel, 2
Nigeria, 250, 322
Niven, David, 268, 272–4
Nkrumah, Kwame, 302
Norfolk, Bernard Fitzalan-Howard, 16th
Duke of, 226
Norfolk, Lavinia Mary, Duchess of (*née*
Strutt), 226
North, Sir Dudley, 102
Nottingham Cottage, Kensington Palace,
155

Oberon, Merle, 257, 277
Ogilvy, Sir Angus, 285
Ogilvy, Bruce, 65
Olga, Queen of George I of Greece, 15,
18, 58n
Osborne, John, 320n
Other-Gee, Sue, 131
Otto (of Bavaria), King of Greece, 14 & n
Outward Bound Trust, 39, 247n, 257,
300

Owen, Frank, 268
Owen (groom), 75

Panorama (TV programme), 322, 326
Papoulas, General, 25–7
Paris: Philip's family's exile in, 29;
    Elizabeth and Philip visit, 180–1
Parker, Eileen (Michael's wife), 131,
    177, 252
Parker, Michael: meeting and friendship
    with Philip, 126, 129–30, 133, 274;
    background and career, 129–30;
    marriage, 131; accompanies Philip to
    Monte Carlo, 143; and Philip's
    courtship, 145–6; on Philip's love for
    Elizabeth, 160; organises stag night for
    Philip, 161; on Bobo MacDonald, 174;
    divorce, 177, 252–4; as Philip's
    equerry, 177; plays squash with Philip,
    186; on Philip's energy, 198; on Philip
    and Elizabeth in Malta, 199; and
    Philip's promotion to Lieutenant-
    Commander, 203; and Philip's return
    from Malta, 204; in Kenya with Philip
    and Elizabeth, 212–13; on Clarence
    House organisation, 219; on Philip's
    frustrations over role, 223–4;
    accompanies Philip by helicopter, 225;
    and review of Palace organisation,
    225; on courtiers, 248n; on Philip's
    dutiful attitude to Queen, 249; on tour
    to Australia (1956), 251–3, 265;
    leaves royal service, 253–4; testifies to
    Philip's fidelity, 265; in Thursday
    Club, 268–9; old courtiers' view of,
    269
Parker Bowles, Andrew, 311, 314n
Parker Bowles, Camilla: relations with
    Charles, 51, 257, 311–12, 316–17,
    326–7; Sophie Wessex disparages,
    305; marriages, 311, 326–7
Paul, King of Greece, 94, 133, 143, 203
Paul, Prince of Yugoslavia, 64
Payn, Graham, 60
Peebles, Catherine ('Mispy'), 298n

Peter, King of Yugoslavia, 104n
Peter, Prince of Greece, 29, 41n
Philby, Kim, 269
Philip, Prince, Duke of Edinburgh:
    attitude to press, 2, 161, 189–90,
    207n, 299, 305; diet, 3 & n; reputation
    for outspokenness and rudeness, 176,
    347; exile in Paris, 30; rumoured
    extramarital romances, 254–8,
    264–73, 276–8, 284, 287; marriage
    relations, 134, 169–70, 175, 179, 180,
    239, 248–9, 265, 287, 345–8; attitude
    to Charles, 233, 240, 296–7, 299–300,
    303–4, 313; carriage driving, 284–5,
    344n, 346; reading and books, 116,
    247n, 281, 344 & n; background and
    family, 9–10, 32–5, 41–3, 93–4, 146,
    240; childhood and upbringing, 12, 24;
    denies rudeness to deaf children,
    12–13; view of monarchy, 16;
    intellectual and spiritual interests, 18n,
    281–4, 341; birth, 22, 23; appearance,
    24, 26, 101, 130, 271; lifestyle, 24;
    view of Greece and Greeks, 27–8; and
    father's banishment, 28; schooling, 33,
    38–9, 104; characteristics in boyhood,
    36–7; attends Royal Naval College,
    Dartmouth, 40, 98, 100, 104; interest
    in flying, 40; first meetings with
    Elizabeth, 98, 99–102, 104–5; financial
    position, 103, 171; under
    Mountbatten's guardianship, 103;
    lacks permanent home as young man,
    104, 142; leadership qualities, 104;
    disapproves of image-making, 113;
    given Freedom of City of London, 116;
    war service, 116–22, 129–30; and
    father's death, 122, 126; visits mother
    in Greece, 123; attitude to mother,
    124–5; privacy, 124, 274; romances
    and girl friends, 130–2; prospective
    marriage to Elizabeth, 132–4, 143–5;
    wartime correspondence with
    Elizabeth, 132, 135; attends Windsor
    Castle pantomime, 134; courtship,

Philip, Prince (*continued*)
135–7, 141; post-war naval postings
and career, 141–2, 198–200, 203;
meets mother in London after war,
143; acquires British nationality,
146–7; takes surname Battenberg, 147;
objectors to marriage, 148, 158–9;
engagement, 149, 156–60; never
hunts, 158n, 197; wedding, 160–1,
163, 166–7, 171–2; honours, ranks
and titles, 161, 228n, 255, 258, 264;
stag party, 161–2; apprehensions over
marriage, 162–3; gives up smoking,
163; honeymoon, 168–70, 172, 174;
querulousness, 174–5; married homes,
176–7, 193–4, 219; temper, 176;
household, 177–8; life and work as
royal, 178–9; French speaking, 180–1;
overseas tours and state visits, 180–1,
205–11, 243, 250–4, 322, 351–66; and
birth of Charles, 186; relations with
children, 191–2, 194–6, 201–3, 239,
243, 279, 303, 306; relations with
personal staff, 193; entertainments and
relaxation, 196–8; shooting, 197, 258;
charitable good works, 198; polo-
playing, 200–1; leaves Malta, 204;
establishes role, 208; manner, 209,
249; sense of humour, 209; and
George VI's death, 212–15; and
Elizabeth's accession, 216; as Privy
Councillor, 216; Establishment
complains about behaviour, 217–18;
and family name, 219–23; attitude to
Mountbatten, 223, 310n; frustrations
over position, 223–4; limited access to
official business, 224; reforms at
Palace, 224–5; chairs Coronation
Commission, 225–6, 232; uses
helicopter, 225; at Elizabeth's
Coronation, 228–30; role as Queen's
consort, 228–9, 246, 248; relations
with Queen Mother, 232;
flirtatiousness, 234n; on Princess
Margaret's romance with Townsend,
236; activities and duties, 247–50; TV
programme on, 251; role models and
influences, 260–1; friendships, 273–4;
letter-writing, 274, 309, 315;
discretion and restraint, 275–6, 331;
sailing, 280n, 299; fondness for sisters
and families, 292–3; and Margaret-
Snowdon divorce, 292; on media
representation of royal family, 295–6;
and Princess Anne, 301, 309; and
Charles-Diana marriage breakdown
and divorce, 313–16, 318–19, 324;
writes to Diana, 315–17; visits leper
colony in Nigeria, 322; and Diana's
death and funeral, 324–6; and
Charles's relations with Camilla Parker
Bowles, 326–7; and Duchess of York,
329–31; integrity, 336; on non-
successor for *Britannia*, 343n;
achievements, 344, 367–74;
ornithology, 344n; support for Queen,
345; qualities, 347
Phillips, Lieut.-Colonel Harold Pedro
Joseph ('Bunnie'), 278
Phillips, Captain Mark: marriage to
Princess Anne, 222, 307–9; divorce,
309
Phillips, Nicholas, 278n, 281
Phillips, Peter, 308
Phillips, Zara, 308
Pinter, Harold, 275
Plunket, Patrick, 7th Baron, 259
Plunket, Terence, 6th Baron ('Teddy'),
and Dorothé, Lady, 259n
Poe, Edgar Allen, 41
Ponsonby, Sir Frederick ('Fritz'), 55, 58n
Porchester, Henry, Baron ('Porchey') *see*
Carnarvon, 7th Earl of
Portillo, Michael, 343n
Portugal, 254–5
Powell, Colin, 209
Powell, Enoch, 218
Presley, Elvis, 3
Press Council, 189
Prince's Trust, 298, 300

Index

Privy Council: at Elizabeth's accession, 216 & n

Profumo, John, 267 & n

Question of Balance, A (Philip and Michael Mann), 282

Raine, Kathleen, 300

Ramillies, HMS, 116–17

Reagan, Ronald and Nancy, 261

Real Prince Philip, The (TV programme), 251

Really Useful Group (theatre company), 305

republicanism, 258

Rhodes, Margaret (*née* Elphinstone): qualities, 62; on Queen Mother, 62; on Strathmores, 63–4; on George VI's sense of humour, 67; plays with Elizabeth as child, 71; on Crawfie, 73; on Queen Mother's attitude to Windsors, 85; and George VI's accession, 86; and Elizabeth in line of succession, 87; on Elizabeth in adolescence, 92–3; at Windsor in war, 111; on Princess Margaret, 112; on Elizabeth's devotion to Philip, 134, 145; on Elizabeth's serious temperament, 135; denies Queen Mother's betting and heavy drinking, 139n; on Elizabeth's wedding, 163, 170; on Philip, 174–5; on Elizabeth's relations with Princess Margaret, 236; on Elizabeth-Philip marriage and family relations, 239–40; and Philip's supposed infidelities, 265; on Elizabeth's relations with mother, 289

Robertson-Justice, James, 268, 269n

Romsey Abbey, 169

Romsey, Penelope, Lady, 284–6, 313

Roose, Emily, 271

Roosevelt, Eleanor, 112

Roosevelt, Franklin Delano, 95–6

Rose, Kenneth, 189, 275n

Royal Agricultural Society of the Commonwealth, 247

Royal Arthur, HMS (training establishment), 142

Royal Lodge, Windsor Great Park, 72, 90

Royal Marriages Act (1772), 236n, 291

Royal Naval College, Dartmouth, 40, 98, 100–2, 104

Royal Oak, HMS: sunk, 106

Royal Variety Performance, 225n

Royal Victorian Order, 308n

Royle, Betty, 114

Rutland, Charles John Robert Manners, 10th Duke of, 137

Sackville-West, Vita (Lady Nicolson), 2, 97

St George's House, Windsor, 281, 283

Saint-Exupéry, Antoine de, 185

Salem (school), 142, 292–3

Salisbury, James Edward Hubert Gascoyne-Cecil, 4th Marquess of, 148

Salisbury, Robert Arthur James Gascoyne-Cecil, 5th Marquess of, 236n, 237

Salote, Queen of Tonga, 227

Save the Children Fund, 322

Saxe-Coburg-Gotha family, 221

Selden, John, 215

Sellar, W.C. and R.J. Yeatman, 68

Shakespeare, William: *Henry IV Part II*, 9; *Twelfth Night*, 2

Sheridan, Lisa, 113

Sheridan, Richard Brinsley, 47

Shropshire, HMS, 117

Sicily: invasion of (1943), 121

Simmel, Dr Ernst, 32

Simpson, Ernest, 77

Simpson, Romaine (David Milford-Haven's first wife), 171n

Sitwell, Sir Osbert, 64, 67n, 71, 107, 211

Smith, Horace, 109, 134

Smuts, Field Marshal Jan Christian, 151–2

Snowdon, Antony Amstrong-Jones, 1st Earl of: marriage to Princess Margaret, 239, 260, 290; on Elizabeth the Queen Mother, 63; courtship, 222; Mike Parker meets, 266n; sees Tynan's blue films, 275; divorce, 291–2; Elizabeth's fondness for, 291

Snowman, Dr Jacob, 188

Soames, Nicholas, 313, 322, 327

Somerville, Admiral Sir James, 129

Sophie, Princess of Hesse (Philip's sister; 'Tiny'), 16, 28, 124–5, 142, 166, 292, 294

Sophie, Queen of Constantine of Greece, 16

South Africa: royal tour (1947), 149–53

Spencer, Charles, 9th Earl (Diana's brother), 325–6

Spencer, John, 8th Earl (Diana's father), 313n, 316n

Stamfordham, Arthur Bigge, Baron, 70n

Stevens, Anthony: Archetypes, 283

Stewart, Don, 268

Storr, Anthony, 335

Strathmore, Claude George Bowes-Lyon, 17th Earl of, 63, 288; death, 92

Strathmore, Nina-Cecilia, Countess of (née Cavendish-Bentinck), 63–5, 288

Stuart, James, 65, 67

Suez crisis (1956), 251–2, 253n

Sunday Pictorial, 254

Sunninghill Estate, Windsor Great Park, 176, 328

Survival or Extinction: A Christian Attitude to the Environment (Philip with Michael Mann), 282–3

Sykes, Sir Christopher, 55n

Talbot, Gerald, 27

Tennant, Colin, 65

Thatcher, Margaret, Baroness: on Reagans' marriage, 262; on Elizabeth, 341

Theodora, Margravine of Baden (Philip's sister; 'Dolla'), 16, 38, 292–3

Thorpe, Marion, 291n

Thursday Club, 267–9, 274

Times, The, 207n

Tinos (island), 186, 202n

Townsend, Captain Michael, 233

Townsend, Group Capain Peter: Princess Margaret breaks with, 147, 237–8; on tour of southern Africa (1947), 151–2; accompanies royal family to theatre, 211; appointed equerry, 233–4; Princess Margaret's romance with, 233–7, 290

Townsend, Rosemary, 234

Truman, Harry S., 206, 209–10

Turkey: war with Greece (1921), 25–7

Turner, Graham: Elizabeth: The Woman and the Queen, 290n, 301, 322

Tweedsmuir, John Buchan, 1st Baron, 95–6

Tynan, Kenneth, 269, 275

United States of America: George VI and Queen Elizabeth visit, 94–6; Elizabeth II and Philip visit (1951), 205–7

Ustinov, Sir Peter, 269

Vacani, Betty (dancing-mistress), 110 & n

Valiant, HMS, 118, 133

Vanderbilt, Gloria, 31n

Vanguard, HMS, 149, 156

VE Day (8 May 1945), 139–40

Venizelos, Eleutherios, 21

Vickers, Hugo, 19n, 27n, 31, 123–4, 264n, 292n, 295

Victoria and Albert (Royal Yacht), 98, 100–2

Victoria, Princess (Edward VII's daughter), 52, 77

Victoria, Princess (later Empress Frederick of Germany), 49

Victoria, Queen: family, 10–11, 47, 49–51; death, 14, 54; birth and reign, 48–9, 54; as executive monarch, 48, 86, 215

VJ Day (15 August 1945), 140

Wallace, HMS, 121–2
Walsh, Bernard, 268
Ward, Stephen, 267
Webb, Beatrice, 77
Wernher family, 36
Wernher, Sir Harold, 37 & n, 40, 143n, 280n
Wernher, Julius, 280n
Wernher, Zia, Lady, 37
Wessex, HMS, 129
Wessex, Prince Edward, Earl of: paternity questioned, 259; at Gordonstoun, 298, 302; birth, 302; career, 303–5; father's relations with, 303–4; as prospective Duke of Edinburgh, 304; marriage, 305; sexuality questioned, 305–6; resigns from production company, 306
Wessex, Sophie, Countess of (née Rhys-Jones): indiscretion to press, 305–6; marriage, 305; resigns from business, 306; relations with royal family, 327
Westminster, Natalya Ayesha, Duchess of (née Phillips; 'Tally'), 279
Wheeler-Bennett, Sir John: *Friends, Enemies and Sovereigns*, 149n
Wheeler's Restaurant, Soho, 268
Whelp, HMS, 122, 129–30, 139, 141
White Lodge, Richmond Park, 70
Whitelaw, William, Viscount, 180n
Wilde, Oscar, 288
Wilhelm II, Kaiser, 20, 52n
William, Prince, 313, 324–6
Williams, Hwfa, 55n
Williams, Kenneth, 291n
Wilson, Harold, Baron, 216, 342n
Windlesham Moor, Berkshire, 3, 176, 192–4, 285
Windsor, House of: name adopted, 20, 220
Windsor, Barbara, 304
Windsor Castle: Elizabeth and

Margaret's wartime stay at, 109, 111; fire (1992), 343
Windsor Correspondence (Philip with Michael Mann), 282
Windsor, Edward, Duke of: and nature of monarchy, 55–6; upbringing, 57–9; appearance and behaviour, 60–1; unmarried state, 71; meets Wallis Simpson, 77–8; Abdication, 78–9, 83–6; relations with Mountbatten, 83n; wedding, 83n; Mountbatten attempts matchmaking for, 144; at Elizabeth's wedding, 165; and public discretion, 188–9; at father's lying-in-state and funeral, 218–19; on Mountbatten, 220; absence from Elizabeth's Coronation, 225n; love life, 260; marriage, 290; Mountbatten warns Charles about, 311; and royal touching, 321; *A King's Story*, 55
Windsor, Wallis, Duchess of (earlier Simpson), 60n, 77–9, 83n, 165, 218, 246
Woman's Day (Australian magazine), 257
Woman's Own (magazine), 155
Wood, Robert, 210
Woods, Robin, Bishop of Worcester, 281–2
Woolf, Virginia, 76
World Wide Fund for Nature, 282, 344
Wyatt, Woodrow, Baron, 62

York, Joshua, 337n
York, Prince Andrew, Duke of: flirting, 234n; parentage rumour, 258–9; at Gordonstoun, 302; birth, 302; naval career, 302–4; marriage to and divorce from Sarah Ferguson, 328–9
York, Sarah, Duchess of (née Ferguson), 189, 304, 327–31

Ziegler, Philip, 144, 148n, 223, 261, 262n, 266n